D0042521

THE REGULATION OF INTERNATIONAL FINANCIAL MARKETS

International financial relations have become increasingly important for the development of global and national economies. At present these relations are primarily governed by market forces, with little regulatory interference at the international level. In the light of numerous finanical crises, this abstinence must be seriously questioned. Starting with an analysis of the regulatory problems at the international level, with only minimal powers entrusted to international organisations, this book develops various possibilites for reform. On the basis of an historical analysis, the book first adopts a comparative approach to national attempts to regulate international financial markets, then outlines the potential of relevant institutions (such as the European Central Bank, Basle Committee, IMF and World Bank) and finally develops a policy perspective. It seeks to provide a framework for analysing options for the regulation of international financial markets from a public international law and comparative law perspective.

RAINER GROTE is Senior Research Fellow at the Max-Planck Institute for Comparative Public Law and International Law, Heidelberg, Germany.

THILO MARAUHN is Professor of Public Law, International Law and European Law at the Justus Liebig University, Giessen, Germany.

THE REGULATION OF INTERNATIONAL FINANCIAL MARKETS

Perspectives for Reform

Edited by

RAINER GROTE AND THILO MARAUHN

CAMBRIDGE UNIVERSITY PRESS

CAMBRIDGE UNIVERSITY PRESS
Cambridge, New York, Melbourne, Madrid, Cape Town, Singapore, São Paulo

CAMBRIDGE UNIVERSITY PRESS
The Edinburgh Building, Cambridge CB2 2RU, UK

Published in the United States of America by Cambridge University Press, New York

www.cambridge.org
Information on this title: www.cambridge.org/9780521831444

First published 2006

Printed in the United Kingdom at the University Press, Cambridge

A catalogue record for this book is available from the British Library

ISBN-13 978-0-521-83144-4 hardback
ISBN-10 0-521-83144-X hardback

CONTENTS

NOTES ON CONTRIBUTORS

Benjamin J. Cohen is Louis G. Lancaster Professor of International Political Economy at the University of California, Santa Barbara. Educated at Columbia University, he previously taught at Princeton University and the Fletcher School of Law and Diplomacy, Tufts University. He is the author of nine books, including most recently *The Geography of Money* (1998) and *The Future of Money* (2003).

Susan Emmenegger is Professor of Law, University of Fribourg, Switzerland, and holds a Law degree from Fribourg University and an LLM from Cornell Law School. She worked as an associate for a New York law firm and clerked for the Zurich District Court before joining the Swiss Banking Supervisory Authority in Berne. In 2002, she joined the Fribourg Faculty where she teaches contracts and financial market law.

Eilís Ferran, MA, PhD, is a Reader in Corporate Law and Financial Regulation and the Director of the Centre for Corporate and Commercial Law ('3CL') at the University of Cambridge. She is an Editor of the *Journal of Corporate Law Studies*. Her published works include *Company Law and Corporate Finance* (1999) and *Regulating Financial Services and Markets in the 21st Century* (2001, co-edited with C. A. E. Goodhart).

Rainer Grote is a Senior Reasearcher at the Max Planck Institute for Public Comparative Law and Public International Law. He has served as a legal adviser in the Department of Legal Affairs of the German Ministry of Foreign Relations in Berlin and taught international economic law and environmental law as a Visiting Professor at the University Panthéon-Assas (Paris II). His recent research has focused on the impact of globalisation on the constitutional and legal transformation processes in developing countries. He has also been closely involved with several major administrative law reform projects. Recent publications cover a wide range of topics, including international human rights law, the law of regional integration, and comparative constitutional and administrative law.

Till Hafner, LLM (Duke) is an associate in the Corporate and Finance Group at the Frankfurt office of Wall Street firm Kaye Scholer LLP. He studied law at the Universities of Mannheim, Heidelberg, Cambridge and Duke. He is also a PhD candidate at the University of Heidelberg.

He is admitted to practise law in Frankfurt (Rechtsanwalt) and in the State of New York (attorney-at-law). Having worked in both jurisdictions, he focuses primarily on cross border mergers and acquisitions and corporate finance transactions as well as corporate restructuring.

Michael J. Hahn is a Senior Researcher at the Europa-Institut of the Universität des Saarlandes, Saarbrücken, Germany. He holds a Doctor iuris from the University of Heidelberg and a Master's degree from the University of Michigan Law School. His fields of interest include German constitutional law, law of the European Communities, and Public International Law, in particular International Economic Law; he has taught these subjects both in Germany and in the United States. His latest pertinent publication is an extensive analysis of the European Community's Common Commercial Policy after the entry into force of the Treaty of Nice (Art. 131 to Art. 134 EC) in C. Callies and M. Ruffert (eds.), *Kommentar zu EU-Vertrag und EG-Vertrag* (2nd edn, 2002).

Qingjiang Kong obtained his PhD from Wuhan University, China. He currently holds a full professorship at the Hangzhou University of Commerce, China. He has authored numerous articles in international journals such as the *Journal of International Economic Law, International and Comparative Law Quarterly, Heidelberg Journal of International Law,* and *Journal of World Trade, Issues and Studies.* His most recent publication is *China and the World Trade Organization: A Legal Perspective* (2002).

Thilo Marauhn is Professor for Public Law, International Law and European Law at the Justus-Liebig-University Giessen and permanent Visiting Professor for Constitutional Theory at the University of Lucerne, Switzerland. He holds a doctor iuris from the University of Heidelberg and a Master of Philosophy from the University of Aberystwyth. He was Research Fellow at the Max Planck Institute for Comparative Public Law and International Law from 1991 to 2001. Among other official positions, Thilo Marauhn is a member of the National Committee on International Humanitarian Law of the German Red Cross and of the Scientific Advisory Board of the Federal Ministry for Economic Co-operation and Development.

Peter Nunnenkamp is a senior research fellow at the Kiel Institute for World Economics in Kiel, Germany, where he is head of the 'International Capital Flows' research division. His recent research has focused on: the globalisation of production and markets; the experience of developing and newly industrialising countries in the process of globalisation; international capital transfers, especially the determinants and effects of foreign direct investment; causes and consequences of financial crises; and the reform of the international financial framework.

John Ohnesorge is Assistant Professor at the University of Wisconsin Law School, where he teaches in the areas of administrative law, business organisation law, and comparative law focusing on East Asia. He received his JD from the University of Minnesota Law School, and his SJD from the Harvard Law School. He has been a visiting scholar at the Max Planck Institute for Comparative Public Law and International Law. His recent publications focus on law and economic development in East Asia, and on legal reforms in East Asia since the Asian financial crisis of 1997.

Axel Peuker is Manager of the World Bank Group, contributing to the institution's work on the investment climate. In his previous assignment as Economic Advisor, he helped co-ordinate the Bank Group's activities on the international financial framework. He is the author of *The Theories of Nicholas Kaldor*, and has published on debt and fiscal issues.

Kunibert Raffer is Associate Professor at the Department of Economics of the University of Vienna and Senior Associate of the New Economics Foundation (London). In 1979–80 and 1983–4 he was a consultant to UNIDO, and in 1989 was Visiting Fellow of the Institute of Development Studies at the University of Sussex. From 1990 to 1993 he was Honorary Research Fellow in the Department of Commerce at the University of Birmingham. He is joint author (with Hans W. Singer) of *The Economic North-South Divide: Six Decades of Unequal Development* (2002).

Volker Röben, LLM (College of Europe, Bruges), LLM (UC Berkeley) is Research Fellow at the Max Planck Institute for Public Comparative Law and Public International Law. He clerked for Judge Udo Di Fabio of the Federal Constitutional Court of Germany. His publications include *The Impact of the ECJ's jurisprudence on Member State procedural law* (1999).

Stefan Voigt is Professor of Economic Policy at the University of Kassel. He is author of *Explaining Constitutional Change – A Positive Economics Approach*, Cheltenham: Edward Elgar, 1999, and editor of *Constitutional Political Economy*, Cheltenham: Edward Elgar, 2003. He has published in numerous journals (including *Kyklos*, *Public Choice*, the *International Review of Law and Economics*, and the *European Journal of Political Economy*) and is on the editorial board of *Constitutional Political Economy*, the *Review of Austrian Economics*, the *Journal des Economistes et des Etudes Humaines*, and *Schmollers Jahrbuch*.

Michael Weiss is research assistant to Professor Dr Thilo Marauhn, and is a doctoral candidate at the Justus-Liebig-University of Giessen. He studied at both the Justus-Liebig-University of Giessen and Warwick University Law School. His fields of interest are German and International Economic Law, European Law and Public International Law.

PREFACE

Most of the contributions included in this volume were originally presented during a workshop held at the 'Evangelische Akademie Loccum' in 2001. The editors wish to explicitly acknowledge the financial and logistical support provided by the 'Evangelische Akademie Loccum'. In particular, we appreciate the contribution of Dr Christoph Hüttig to the conceptual framework of the workshop and the establishment of contacts with Benjamin J. Cohen and Axel Peuker through him. Further papers were added and existing papers were revised subsequently, with final editing being done in 2004. The editors are grateful to the VolkswagenStiftung for its financial support in respect of both the workshop and the preparation of the publication. We also appreciate the editorial assistance provided by Michael Weiss. Due to the long editing process which is the sole responsibility of the editors the final versions of the various contributions differ in respect of timing. Authors have, however, successfully contributed to a meaningful interdisciplinary volume which the editors have sought to draw conclusions upon in their final chapter. This chapter also outlines perspective for further research. Finally, the editors wish to express their gratitude to the publisher and all the assistance provided by Cambridge University Press.

ABBREVIATIONS

ADB	Asian Development Bank
AFTA	ASEAN Free Trade Area
AICPA	American Institute of Certified Public Accountants
AMF	Asian Monetary Fund
APA	Administrative Procedure Act
APEC	Asia-Pacific Economic Co-operation forum
ASEAN	Association of South-East Asian Nations
ASEAN + 3	ASEAN + Japan, China and South Korea
ASEM	Asia-Europe Meeting 2000
ATS	Alternative Trading System
ATTAC	Action pour la Taxation des Transactions Financières pour l'Aide aux Citoyens (Association for the Taxation of Financial Transactions for the Benefit of Citizens)
BCBS	Basle Committee on Banking Supervision
BGBl.	Bundesgesetzblatt
BIS	Bank for International Settlements

BVerfGE	Sammlung der Entscheidungen des Bundesverfassungsgerichts (Collection of the Decisions of the German Federal Constitutional Court)
CCL	Contingent Credit Line
CEO	Chief Executive Officer
CESR	Committee of European Securities Regulators
CFA	Commodities Futures Act
CFMA	Commodities Futures Modernization Act
CFO	Chief Financial Officer
CFTC	Commodities Futures Trading Commission
CGFS	Committee on the Global Financial System
CIA	Central Intelligence Agency
CMCG	Capital Market Consultative Group
CO	Colorado
CPSIPS	Core Principles for Systemically Important Payment Systems
CPSS	Committee on Payment and Settlement Systems
CTT	Currency Transaction Tax
DC	District of Columbia
DSU	Dispute Settlement Understanding
DTEFs	derivatives transaction execution facilities
EAEC	East Asia Economic Caucus
EAEG	East Asian Economic Group
EASDAQ	European Association of Securities Dealers Automatic Quotation System

EC	European Community
ECB	European Central Bank
ECJ	European Court of Justice
ECOFIN	A configuration of the Council of Ministers of the European Union concerned with economic and financial affairs
ECOSOC	Economic and Social Council
EEA	European Economic Area
EEC	European Economic Community
EMI	European Monetary Institute
EMU	Economic and Monetary Union
ERM	Exchange Rate Mechanism
ESC	European Securities Committee
ESCB	European System of Central Banks
EU	European Union
FASB	Financial Standards Supervisory Board
FATF	Financial Action Task Force on Money Laundering
FBI	Federal Bureau of Investigation
FDI	Foreign Direct Investment
FDIC	Federal Deposit Insurance Corporation
FESCO	Forum of European Securities Commissions
FFIEC	Federal Financial Institutions Examination Council
FFSA	Federal Financial Supervisory Authority (Bundesanstalt für Finanzdienstleistungsaufsicht)

FIRREA	1989 Financial Institutions Reform, Recovery, and Enforcement Act
FSA	Financial Services Authority
FSAP	European Commission's Financial Services Action Plan
FSAP	Financial Sector Assessment Program
FSF	Financial Stability Forum
FSLC	Financial Sector Liaison Committee
FSLIC	Federal Savings and Loan Insurance Corporation
FSMA	Financial Services and Markets Act 2000
GAB	General Agreement to Borrow
GATS	General Agreement on Trade in Services
GATT	General Agreement on Tariffs and Trade
GDDS	General Data Dissemination System
GDP	gross domestic product
HM	Her Majesty
IAIS	International Association of Insurance Supervision
IAPC	International Accounting Practices
IASB	International Accounting Standards Board
IASC	International Accounting Standards Committee
IBRD	International Bank for Reconstruction and Development
ICC	Interstate Commerce Commission

IFAC	International Federation of Accountants
IFIs	International Financial Institutions
IMF	International Monetary Fund
IMFC	International Monetary and Financial Committee of the Board of Governors of the IMF
INSOL	International Federation of Insolvency Professionals
INTOSAI	International Organisation of Supreme Audit Institutions
IOSCO	International Organisation of Securities Commissions
IPO	initial public offer
IRS	Internal Revenue Service
ISA	International Standards on Auditing
ISD	Investment Services Directive 93/22/EEC
LDC	less developed country
MAI	Multilateral Agreement on Investment
MFN rule	most-favoured-nation-rule
MoU	memorandum of understanding
MPIFG	Max-Planck-Institut für Gesellschaftsforschung' (Max Planck Institute for the Study of Societies)
NAB	new arrangements to borrow
NAFTA	North American Free Trade Agreement
NAIC	National Association of Insurance Commissioners

NAMU	North American Monetary Union
NASD	National Association of Securities Dealers
NASDAQ	National Association of Securities Dealers Automated Quotation (system)
NCOIL	National Conference of Insurance Legislators
NCUA	National Credit Union Administration
NEWEX	New Europe Exchange
NFA	National Futures Association
NGO	Non-Governmental Organisation
NJ	New Jersey
NY	New York
NYSE	New York Stock Exchange
OCC	Office of the Comptroller of the Currency
OECD	Organisation for Economic Co-operation and Development
OEEC	Organisation for European Economic Co-operation
OJ	Official Journal of the European Union
OTC	over-the-counter
OTS	Office of Thrift Supervision
RCH	Recognised Clearing Houses
RIE	Recognised Investment Exchanges
ROSC	Reports on the Observance of Standards and Codes
RTC	Resolution Trust Corporation
S&Ls	savings and loan associations

SAIF	Savings Association Insurance Fund
SDDS	Special Data Dissemination Standard
SDRM	Sovereign Debt Restructuring Mechanism
SEC	US Securities and Exchange Commission
SRF	Supplemental Reserve Facility
SROs	self-regulatory organisations
TRIPS Agreement	Agreement on Trade Related Aspects of Intellectual Property Rights
UCITS	Directive 85/611/EEC on Undertakings for Collective Investment in Transferable Securities
UK	United Kingdom
UN	United Nations
UNCTAD	United Nations Conference on Trade and Development
UNICEF	United Nations Children's Fund
US	United States of America
USD	US dollar
WTO	World Trade Organisation
WTO Agreement	Marrakesh Agreement establishing the World Trade Organisation
XBOTs	exempt boards of trade

Introduction: the regulatory dilemma in international financial relations

THILO MARAUHN

I. The globalisation of capital markets: benefits and risks

The globalisation of capital markets has become the subject of a broad public debate.[1] It is no longer perceived as a purely technical topic. Its benefits and risks are part of a truly political discourse that has long left the secluded environment of the financial and academic elite. Benefits and risks of such globalisation are thus not only discussed from the perspective of economic rationality but are assessed against a whole set of heterogeneous values, such as democracy,[2] human rights,[3] and many more. While the debate has thus become much more vivid it is increasingly at risk to be governed by ideological motivations rather than rational arguments. Pleading for rationality does not mean to return to purely technical or even elitist considerations. Rather it aims at establishing a procedural framework to accommodate all the relevant aspects that should be taken into account by political, economic, and other decision-makers. Such procedural framework can effectively be provided by public international law arrangements. While this has been realised in other sectors of an increasingly global

---

[1] See, *inter alia*, Richard A. Grasso, 'Globalization of Capital Markets', (1997) 21(2) *Fordham International Law Journal* 390–6; Dragana M. Đurić, 'Globalization of Financial Markets', (1999) 50(1082/83) *Review of International Affairs* 15–21; Sol Picciotto and Jason Haines, 'Regulating Global Financial Markets', (1999) 26(3) *Journal of Law and Society* 351–68; Eilís Ferran and C. A. E. Goodhart (eds.), *Regulating Financial Services and Markets in the Twenty First Century* (Oxford, 2001); Joseph E. Stiglitz, 'Principles of Financial Regulation – A Dynamic Portfolio Approach', (2001) 16(1) *World Bank Research Observer* 1–18.

[2] Chantal Thomas, 'Does the "Good Governance Policy" of the International Financial Institutions Privilege Markets at the Expense of Democracy?' (1999) 14(2) *Connecticut Journal of International Law* 551–62.

[3] Cf. Ross P. Buckley, 'The Essential Flaw in the Globalisation of Capital Markets – Its Impact on Human Rights in Developing Countries', (2001) 32(1) *California Western International Law Journal* 119–31.

economy,[4] capital markets have for one and another reason largely escaped the regulatory power of public international law. Even the academic discourse has long been led by economists and experts in private law with a significant silence on the side of political scientists as well as experts in public law.[5] The situation seems about to change, most probably due to the topic moving into the wider political arena.

It is against this background that the research for this publication was undertaken. The basic question to be addressed from a variety of angles is whether there is a meaningful potential in the regulation of international financial relations at the level of public international law. In spite of grand rhetoric such as 'international financial architecture'[6] the present contribution of public international law to a regulatory framework for global capital markets is rather limited. Neither does the reference to an 'international financial architecture' describe an existing regime nor does it provide a blueprint for governance in international financial relations. Rather it covers a great variety of institutions and numerous forms of co-operation among actors on the international financial markets. Whether or not there is a need for and a potential impact of public international law in international financial relations can only be assessed against the background of a much broader analysis.

A first part of this analysis must be a historical one,[7] considering the factual dimension of the problem and the ups and downs of capital

---

[4] Bilateral as well as multilateral agreements related to foreign direct investment rather provide a framework for the settlement of disputes than a set of substantive standards; cf. Christian Tietje, 'Die Beilegung internationaler Investitionsstreitigkeiten', in Thilo Marauhn (ed.), *Streitbeilegung in den internationalen Wirtschaftsbeziehungen. Völkerrechtliche Einhegung ökonomischer Globalisierungsprozesse* (Tübingen, 2005), pp. 47–62 at 49–51. Similarly, the World Trade Organisation (WTO) does not integrate national economies into the global economy but only tears down barriers to economic transactions in between these economies; see Hans van Houtte, *The Law of International Trade* (2nd ed. 2002), at p. 128: 'A free market requires . . . liberalisation of the movement of goods and services as well as the prohibition of restrictions on competition by the market participants.'

[5] Rochael M. Soper, 'Promoting Confidence and Stability in Financial Markets – Capitalizing on the Downfall of Barings', (1997) 7(2) *Duke Journal of Comparative and International Law* 651–70; Herbert Kronke, 'Capital Markets and Conflict of Laws', (2001) 286 *Recueil des Cours/Académie de Droit International de La Haye* 245–385; Douglas W. Arner, 'Globalisation of Financial Markets – An International Passport for Securities Offerings?' (2001) 35(4) *International Lawyer* 1543–88.

[6] Cf. Peter Behrens, 'The International Architecture of Global Financial Markets' (1999) 6(3) *Maastricht Journal of European and Comparative Law* 271–98.

[7] Such analysis is provided in this book by Benjamin J. Cohen (chapter 1). See also William F. Shepherd, *International Financial Integration – History, Theory and Applications in OECD Countries* (Aldershot, 1994).

internationalisation. In this regard it must be noted that, in contrast to what is sometimes argued, the internationalisation of capital is not a totally new phenomenon.[8] At the beginning of the twentieth century national capital markets were much more interpenetrated than during the inter-War and the Cold War periods; they were not as segmented and compartmentalised as until some twenty years ago. Nevertheless, developments over the last two decades demonstrate some unique characteristics.[9] Thus, the cross-border flow of financial assets has exponentially grown, and there is a dramatic increase in the number of foreign listed companies at the major stock exchanges. Also, cross-border mergers, increasingly international portfolio investment strategies, a rapidly growing share of foreign investors in the bond market, and even alliances between stock exchanges have by now become commonplace. The fact that a period of internationalisation a century ago was followed by fragmentation of financial markets can be considered a warning that – at least in theory – regulatory change can reverse the interpenetration of national financial markets.[10]

Another part of a kind of preliminary inquiry must be into existing regulations at the national level. A comparative analysis[11] of the national regulation of international financial markets can provide insights into perceptions, motivations and reactions of a broad variety of actors towards a regulatory framework. Findings may extend from a more or less positive assessment of national regulation with a beneficial impact on regional and global markets to the identification of a particular need for co-ordinated, if not partially harmonised approaches towards regulatory issues at the international level. If such a need is identified then the question arises what should actually be covered by an international

---

[8] Cf. Harald Baum, 'Globalizing Capital Markets and Possible Regulatory Responses', in Jürgen Basedow and Toshiyuki Kono (eds.), *Legal Aspects of Globalization – Conflict of Laws, Internet, Capital Markets and Insolvency in a Global Economy* (The Hague, 2000), pp. 77–132 at 81.

[9] Such characteristics have been aptly analysed by Richard Dale, 'Regulating the New Financial Markets', in Malcolm Edey (ed.) *The Future of the Financial System* (proceedings of a conference held at the H.C. Coombs Centre for Financial Studies, Kirribilli on 8/9 July 1996) (Sydney, 1996), pp. 215–45 at 220–2, available at http://www.rba.gov.au/PublicationsAndResearch/Conferences/1996/Dale.pdf.

[10] Baum, 'Globalizing Capital Markets', above note 8, at p. 81.

[11] Cf. the various contributions in this volume by Eilís Ferran (chapter 2), Rainer Grote (chapter 3) and John K. M. Ohnesorge (chapter 4). For a comprehensive comparative approach see, *inter alia*, Jean-Baptiste Zufferey, *Regulation of Trading Systems on Financial Markets* (London, 1997).

instrument. This depends on the existing normative[12] and institutional[13] framework but must take into account a policy perspective.[14] This, in particular, necessitates an economic and a political analysis of international markets and interventions into such markets. A policy perspective must also address the interfaces between economic, political and legal considerations which are part and parcel of today's debate on the globalisation of financial markets.

Addressing the benefits and risks of global capital markets by way of introduction can only set the scene. To this end, a more or less 'neutral' perspective on historical developments at the outset of a discussion of whether or not – and if so, how – to regulate international financial markets cannot be sufficient. Before developing a regulatory strategy – and there may be at least agreement on 'prudential regulation'[15] (whatever this means) – some benefits and risks of capital internationalisation must be highlighted. While a detailed assessment would go beyond the scope of this introduction, only a brief overview will be given. As a whole the analysis – and this is also the thrust of the present volume as such – takes a fairly general view without putting too much weight on details of specific regulatory issues. This may be the subject of a follow-up project.[16]

As far as benefits are concerned, integrated markets are economically advantageous in allowing world savings to be allocated effectively, thus favouring their most productive uses across the globe.[17] Also, a political advantage can be seen in improved possibilities for the management of systemic risks, inherent in financial markets, be they local, regional or global. In a more or less perfect economic and political environment this offers countries in recession options for the external financing of investment and thus for the promotion of economic growth while, on the

---

[12] See the contributions by Volker Röben (chapter 5), Till Hafner (chapter 6), Qingjiang Kong (chapter 7) and Michael J. Hahn (chapter 8), in this volume.

[13] Cf. Thilo Marauhn and Michael Weiss (chapter 9), Susan Emmenegger (chapter 10) and Axel Peuker (chapter 11), in this volume.

[14] See Peter Nunnenkamp (chapter 12), Stefan Voigt (chapter 13) Kunibert Raffer (chapter 14), in this volume.

[15] While the concept of prudential regulation is very popular its precise substance and contents are far from clear. Nevertheless, it can be applied in a meaningful way, cf. Sydney J. Key, 'Trade Liberalization and Prudential Regulation – The International Framework for Financial Services', (1999) 75(1) International Affairs 61–75.

[16] For some first thoughts consider Rainer Grote and Thilo Marauhn (Conclusions and agenda for further research), in this volume.

[17] Baum, 'Globalizing Capital Markets', above note 8, at p. 79.

other hand, national policy failures will be punished by low rates of foreign investment.[18] It must be borne in mind that policy failures can be both, excessive regulation imposing non-competitive costs on transactions, or underregulation burdening potential investors with non-manageable risks. Global financial markets thus offer positive incentives. However, such incentives are not without negative counterparts. Some of them are related only tentatively to the internationalisation of capital as such but rather to interrelated developments. This is, among others, true for the innovation in information and communication technologies and the consequential speed of change. But it also applies to other forces of change, such as deregulatory policies which may be perceived as a weakening of democratic control, in particular if paralleled by a tremendous degree of institutionalisation and professionalisation of market participants. Finally, regulatory powers are generally lagging behind when new financial products join the market. The strongest criticism vis-à-vis global capital markets builds upon their inherent risks and the way such risks have been handled until now. The essence of such risks can be easily explained in referring to the operation of the banking system. Success and potential weaknesses build upon the same sources: intermediation and leverage.[19] Intermediation is a process whereby banks collect deposits and lend them on, with deposits being highly liquid and loans less so. The involved maturity transformation leads to an increased amount of money available for income-earning loans. Leverage means this ability of banks to develop an initial cash deposit into loans that are a substantial multiple of that amount. While intermediation and leverage can be the source of economic growth, their downside is the financial risk they create. Such risks have been considered manageable as long as national capital markets and their risks were contained by national borders and the management of such risks remained the responsibility of the national regulator. With the internationalisation of financial markets numerous crises have given rise to the question of whether and how far such risks can be contained or whether these risks are as infectious as to cause world economic crises. Examples that can be given are manifold, with the

---

[18] *Ibid.*, at 80.
[19] Cf. Gary Gorton and Andrew Winton, *Financial Intermediation*, National Bureau of Economic Research (NBER) Working Paper 8928, 2002; Felicia Marston and Susan Perry, 'Implied Penalties for Financial Leverage: Theory versus Empirical Evidence' (1996) 35 *Quarterly Journal of Business and Economics* 77–97.

Mexican,[20] the Asian,[21] the Russian,[22] and eventually the Argentine[23] crises being the most recent (and perhaps the most dramatic).

Referring only to the process of globalisation as the cause of such risks would fall short of proper analysis. What has to be borne in mind additionally is that the public–private dichotomy has seriously changed. The decisive step promoting the development towards globalised capital markets was to remove state controls on external financial relations and to privatise the risk involved. Such privatisation of risks[24] – which occurred in the 1970s with the breakdown of the Bretton Woods system[25] – stimulated a development that first proved beneficial for most actors in international financial relations. Only when governments failed to introduce alternative risk management strategies such privatisation of risks brought about negative consequences, finally leading to a socialisation of such risks with bail-out strategies. When assessing the benefits and risks of capital market liberalisation, there must also be reference to the object and purpose of financial markets, as well as to their functioning. In a liberal (national) market economy such markets provide the financial means for investment and development. However, the liberalisation of international financial markets, their privatisation, and the parallel process of deregulation have not necessarily led to an

---

[20] Cf. Maxwell A. Cameron and Vinod K. Aggarwal, 'Mexican Meltdown – States, Markets and post-NAFTA Financial Turmoil' (1996) 17(5) *Third World Quarterly* 975–87.

[21] Drawing consequences out of the Asian crisis see Desh Gupta, 'Lessons from South Asian Currency, Stock Market and Economic Crises – Opportunities for Business', (1998) 7(Special Edition) *Canterbury Law Review* 88–101. See also Ian F. Fletcher, 'An Analysis of International Support Packages in the Mexican and Asian Financial Crises', (1998) *Journal of Business Law* 380–96, with some critical remarks on the handling of the two crises by international institutions.

[22] Martin Feldstein, *Economic and Financial Crises in Emerging Market Economies: Overview of Prevention and Management*, NBER WP 8837 (2002); Homi J. Kharas, Brian Pinto and Sergei Ulatov, 'An Analysis of Russia's 1998 Meltdown Fundamentals and Market Signals', (2001) (1) *Brookings Papers on Economic Activity*.

[23] Cf. John V. Paddock, 'IMF Policy and the Argentine Crisis', (2002) 34(1) *University of Miami Inter-American Law Review* 155–87.

[24] The privatisation of risks is only part of what has been described as the privatisation of world politics; cf. Tanja Brühl (ed.), *Die Privatisierung der Weltpolitik. Entstaatlichung und Kommerzialisierung im Globalisierungsprozess* (Bonn, 2001); see also Keith E. Maskus and Jerome H. Reichman, 'The Globalization of Private Knowledge Goods and the Privatization of Global Public Goods', (2004) 7(2) *Journal of International Economic Law* 279–320.

[25] Cf. Richard Sylla, 'The Breakdown of Bretton Woods and the Revival of Global Finance', (2002) 1 *Jahrbuch für Wirtschaftsgeschichte* 81–8. See also H. S. Houthakker, 'The Breakdown of Bretton Woods', (1977) *Harvard Institute of Economic Research. Discussion Paper* no. 543.

optimal allocation of financial resources. Over the past two decades, financial transactions have not necessarily met the needs of the 'real economy'.[26] What can today be described as 'new financial markets'[27] is characterised by a high degree of volatility, and must be considered a challenge to a global economic framework aiming at stability and sustainable development. While in the long run, liberalisation may end up in a new market equilibrium, the medium and short-term effects have created a culture of speculation with new actors who perceive themselves affiliated to a new powerful economic and political elite. At the same time something close to a regulatory vacuum has emerged.

While the picture that can be drawn of global capital markets is thus ambivalent and complex, it must be recognised that – notwithstanding political preferences of the various actors involved – the internationalisation (and globalisation) of financial markets can be considered much more a *factum* than a *desideratum*. While the interpenetration of markets may be less than complete, it is still as intense as to allow for such a statement. The decisive question from a public international law perspective is whether existing regulatory frameworks at the national, regional and international level are sufficient in order to safeguard the benefits of international financial markets and to reduce the risks. Within this context it is important to recognise that the liberalisation of financial markets was not in the first place the outcome of a deliberate and legally framed political decision of governments and international organisations but was driven primarily by economic actors who won the support of their respective national governments to open up national financial markets. The only – partial – exception to this is the process of European integration. However, as will be demonstrated within this volume,[28] the implementation of the rules on the free movement of capital within the European Union (EU) has only occurred rather late. By way of introduction we will now, nevertheless, first proceed to move forward towards the identification of what may be called the regulatory dilemma in international financial relations.

---

[26] Cf. Piti Disyatat, 'Currency Crises and the Real Economy – The Role of the Banks', (2001) *IMF Working Paper* no. 49.

[27] Stephen Hessler, 'Neue Regulierungsmodi für neue Finanzmärkte – Zur Notwendigkeit einer Tobin-Steuer', (2002) 77(3) *Die Friedens-Warte. Journal of International Peace and Organization* 249–77 at 254–5.

[28] See the contributions of Till Hafner (chapter 6) and Volker Röben (chapter 5), in this volume.

II. International markets – national regulation

Financial markets are thus indeed *de facto* international, if not global. Such internationalisation has been driven by economic, primarily non-state actors. Nevertheless, it is important to recognise that at least some governmental support was necessary in order to move ahead. Economic internationalisation and globalisation do not take place in a vacuum. They take place in a regulatory environment that is – at least in the beginning – predominantly national.[29] This national environment is simply due to the existence of the nation-state as the primary standard-setting and enforcement agency in what has been characterised as the 'Westphalian system'.[30] Regulatory power is first and foremost exercised at the level of the nation-state, economically, politically and legally endowed with sovereignty. Such sovereignty – at least as a matter of principle – is still in existence. However it has been modified to a large extent. Such modification perhaps first took place in the field of economic activities and then extended through to political – and at least to some extent – to legal matters.

In order to identify and understand the role of national regulation in the process of economic internationalisation (and eventually globalisation) one may step back a little and consider a fictitious example. Let us consider the case where two undertakings in two different jurisdictions have become aware of each other and consider it useful to enter into economic transactions – both in goods and in financial services. If such undertakings were both operating within the same jurisdiction their contractual relations would be subject to the laws of the land. However, when involving two jurisdictions they must agree on specific rules which may at least be different from those of one of the two. Even if the two undertakings agree on particular contractual arrangements,

---

[29] For an introductory analysis see Stephen J. Choi and Andrew T. Guzman, 'National Laws, International Money – Regulation in a Global Capital Market', (1997) 65(5) *Fordham Law Review* 1855–908; see also Christopher J. Mailander, 'Financial Innovation, Domestic Regulation and the International Marketplace – Lessons on Meeting Globalization's Challenge drawn from the International Bond Market' (1997/98) 31(3) *George Washington Journal of International Law and Economics* 341–92.

[30] Today, the phrase 'Westphalian system' is used to describe the traditional state-centred system. While there is a tendency to question the predominance of the state, the state enjoys continued relevance in public international law. Cf. Christopher Harding, 'The Significance of Westphalia: An Archaeology of the International Legal Order', in Christopher Harding (ed.), *Renegotiating Westphalia. Essays and Commentary on the European and Conceptual Foundations of Modern International Law* (The Hague, 1999), pp. 1–23.

those arrangements are only enforceable if the two different jurisdictions provide the pertinent rules to this end. This involves two dimensions: a jurisdiction must allow its 'own' undertakings to extend their activities beyond national boundaries and it must allow 'foreign' undertakings into the country. As far as the exchange of goods is concerned governments may reduce their involvement to a more or less permissible approach. However, in the field of financial relations the situation is much more complicated. A first complication is related to national currencies which are not only of practical but very often of symbolic relevance. The law of money,[31] the regulation of a currency, in particular, its exchange,[32] is a much more sensitive issue than the regulation applicable to the exchange of goods because the currency is often linked to the concept of sovereignty. Even if this is overcome, a second complication must be borne in mind: financial markets have with their increasing relevance always been under close scrutiny of governments. Even at the national level (at least since economic growth during the nineteenth century) they have never been an exclusively private matter but have always given rise to public interference – the most prominent obviously being the exercise of supervisory powers in the fields of banking, insurance, and securities. With the existence of such a supervisory system at the national level, states can still preserve a large degree of sovereignty within the process of internationalisation by, first, allowing foreign actors in and, second, supervising home actors also abroad. The notion of extraterritorial jurisdiction thus comes into play.[33] This still keeps regulatory powers at the national level.

An internationally active undertaking with a strong economy and a solid government at home will not perceive too many problems if it can rely on the extraterritorial reach of its home government. This, however, only applies to a very limited number of jurisdictions, in particular countries with an already strong position in foreign trade and – after the end of the gold standard – countries with a strong currency that is in

---

[31] For an impressive and still relevant study of the law of money see Fritz A. Mann, *The Legal Aspect of Money – With Special Reference to Comparative Private and Public International Law* (Oxford, 1992).

[32] Cf. Joseph Gold, *Exchange Rates in International Law and Organization* (New York, 1988).

[33] For a general account of the impact of national regulation on international economic activities see Reuven S. Avi-Yonah, 'National Regulation of Multinational Enterprises – An Essay on Comity, Extraterritoriality, and Harmonization', (2003) 42(1) *Columbia Journal of Transnational Law* 5–34. Focusing on the transboundary administrative activities cf. Christian Tietje, *Internationalisiertes Verwaltungshandeln* (Berlin, 2001).

law (but above all in practice) widely spread and has largely acquired the status of a reserve currency.[34] Not only undertakings from other countries but also undertakings originating in such jurisdictions, however, will be confronted with transaction costs when moving beyond national financial markets. Such transaction costs, *inter alia*, are due to the different legal environments and to different supervisory mechanisms. It goes without saying that those costs will be comparatively higher in the case of undertakings originating in economically less strong jurisdictions. It would thus seem fairly natural that an economically active or at least supportive government will support the interests of private actors in reducing such transaction costs – in other words: it will have an interest to reduce the burden of heterogeneous national regulatory environments.

From the perspective of public international law an international agreement dealing with conflict of laws and perhaps even aiming at some approximation or even harmonisation of normative standards comes to mind. However, this has not been the approach that has been adopted in international financial relations. Private actors, regulatory bodies, and governments have chosen a much more pragmatic but at the same time much less transparent, less democratic and – in the long run – perhaps even less sustainable approach: they opted for international co-operation *below* the level of formal juridification. In other words: they have preferred loose co-operation within the framework of international regulatory financial organisations to international treaty-based regimes. This can be proved by numerous examples: the so-called Basle Concordat of 1983,[35] the Basle Core Principles for Effective Banking Supervision of 1997,[36] and the Basle

---

[34] Most interesting in this regard is the development of the European currency, as illustrated by Patrick F. H. J. Peters, 'The Development of the Euro as a Reserve Currency', (1997) 2(4) *European Foreign Affairs Review* 509–33.

[35] The 1983 Concordat is a revision of the 1975 original. For a text of the Basle Concordat of 1983 consult http://www.bis.org/publ/bcbsc312.pdf; an analysis of its substance is provided by Peter Cooke, 'The Basle "Concordat" on the Supervision of Banks' Foreign Establishments', (1984) 39(1/2) *Aussenwirtschaft (Zurich)* 151–65. See also C. J. Thompson, 'The Basle Concordat: International Collaboration in Banking Supervision', in Robert C. Effros (ed.), *Current Legal Issues Affecting Central Banks* (Washington: IMF, 1992), pp. 331–40.

[36] The Basle Core Principles for Effective Banking Supervision of 1997 present a comprehensive set of twenty-five principles that have been developed by the Basle Committee as a basic reference for effective banking supervision. They are available at http://www.bis.org/publ/bcbs30a.pdf; for a discussion cf. William Rutledge, 'Presentation on Basle Core Principles for Effective Banking Supervision', (1999) 2(2) *Review of Pacific Basin Financial Markets and Policies* 161–70.

Capital Accord of 1988,[37] replaced by a revised version,[38] but also the International Monetary Fund (IMF) sponsored Code of Good Practices on Fiscal Transparency[39] as well as the also IMF sponsored Code of Good Practices on Transparency in Monetary and Financial Policies Rules.[40] Reference may further be made to the International Organisation of Securities Commissions' (IOSCOs') Objectives and Principles for Securities Regulation,[41] to the International Accounting Standards of the Basle Committee[42] as well as to the International Standards on Auditing of the International Federation of Accountants.[43] Another document of particular relevance is the set of Forty Recommendations of the Organisation for Economic Co-operation and Development (OECD)-related Financial Action Task Force on Money Laundering (originally drawn up in 1990, revised in 1996[44] and supplemented in 2001[45]). All these documents neither qualify as treaties nor can they be regarded as any other type of traditionally accepted source of public international law *stricto sensu*. We thus find a variety of rules

---

[37] The Basle Capital Accord of 1988 sets down the agreement among the G10 central banks to apply common minimum capital standards to their banking industries. The original version is available at http://www.bis.org/publ/bcbs04A.pdf.

[38] The revision of the Capital Accord was a fairly controversial matter, see Patrik Buchmüller und Christian Macht, 'Basle II und internationaler Bankenwettbewerb', (2003) 58(3) *Aussenwirtschaft (Zurich)* 413–38. On 26 June 2004 central bank governors and the heads of bank supervisory authorities in the G10 countries issued a press release and endorsed the publication of 'International Convergence of Capital Measurement and Capital Standards: a Revised Framework', the new capital adequacy framework commonly known as Basle II (available at http://www.bis.org/publ/bcbs107.htm). Generally on the role of such standards see Susan Emmenegger (chapter 10), in this volume.

[39] The Code was approved by the Executive Board on 23 March 2001. The text is available at http://www.imf.org/external/np/fad/trans/code.htm#code.

[40] The document is available at http://www.imf.org/external/np/mae/mft/code/index.htm (adopted on 26 September 1999).

[41] http://www.iosco.org/pubdocs/pdf/IOSCOPD125.pdf.

[42] http://www.bis.org/publ/bcbs70.pdf.

[43] http://www.ifac.org/Store/Category.tmpl?Category=Auditing%2C%20Assurance%20% 26%20Related%20Services.

[44] Text available at http://www1.oecd.org/fatf/40Recs-1996_en.htm. For further developments visit the website of the FATF at http://www1.oecd.org/fatf/index.htm.

[45] In this regard the interrelationship between organised crime and terrorism has to be borne in mind, as well as the distinctions that have to be drawn between the two; cf., on the one hand, Bruce Zagaris, 'The Merging of the Counter-Terrorism and Anti-Money Laundering Regimes', (2002) 34(1) *Law and Policy in International Business* 45–108 and, on the other hand, Alyssa Phillips, 'Terrorist Financing Laws Won't Wash', (2004) 23(1) *University of Queensland Law Journal* 81–101. The Eight Special Recommendations on Terrorist Financing are available at http://www1.oecd.org/fatf/SRecsTF_en.htm.

in the nature of administrative co-operation and quite often in the form of a code of conduct rather than any type of binding agreement. Nevertheless, these standards are implemented at the national level in an incredibly effective way. Compared to many binding international agreements some of these codes enjoy an impressive implementation record. Most of them, indeed, have become part of regional or national law.[46]

This does not mean that we do not find other types of agreements. Reference may be made, among others, to the General Agreement on Trade in Services (GATS)[47] and to the regional arrangements in Europe[48] and North America.[49] They touch upon financial services – but they are concerned with the liberalisation of such services rather than with their regulation or supervision. The objectives of these (legally binding) agreements are to tear down barriers to trade in (financial) services, neither to uphold them nor to provide a regulatory framework for such services. There are only a very limited number of public international law treaties that follow a regulatory approach. Typically those treaties aim at fighting organised crime, in particular, the financial resources of such crime. They include the OECD Convention on Combating Bribery of Foreign Public Officials in International Business Transactions of 1997,[50] the Council of Europe Criminal Convention on Corruption of 1999,[51] the Inter-American Convention

---

[46] Mario Giovanoli, 'A New Architecture for the Global Financial Market: Legal Aspects of International Financial Standard Setting', in Mario Giovanoli, *International Monetary Law. Issues for the New Millennium* (Oxford, 2000), pp. 3–59 at 45–50.

[47] See the contribution by Michael J. Hahn (chapter 8), in this volume. Bringing the regulatory approach into the liberalisation provided for by GATS cf. Mahmood Bagheri and Chizu Nakajima, 'Optimal Level of Financial Regulation under the GATS – A Regulatory Competition and Cooperation Framework for Capital Adequacy and Disclosure of Information', (2002) 5(2) *Journal of International Economic Law* 507–30.

[48] See the contribution by Volker Röben (chapter 5), in this volume.

[49] See Valerie J. MacNevin, 'Policy Implications of the NAFTA for the Financial Services Industry', (1994) 5(2) *Colorado Journal of International Environmental Law and Policy* 369–99.

[50] (1998) XXXVII(1) *International Legal Materials* 1; available also at http://www.oecd.org/document/21/0,2340,en_2649_34859_2017813_1_1_1_1,00.html; the Convention entered into force on 15 February 1999. For a brief analysis of the Convention see Otto Dietrich, 'OECD Convention on Combating Bribery of Foreign Officials in International Business Transactions', (1998) 3(1) *Austrian Review of International and European Law* 159–69.

[51] European Treaty Series no. 173; text available at http://conventions.coe.int/treaty/en/Treaties/Html/173.htm.

against Corruption of 1996[52] and the recent UN Convention Against Transnational Organised Crime of 2000.[53] It may thus be argued that the focus of legally binding international regulation so far is limited to fighting criminal activities, including corruption, bribery, and money laundering. It has to be noted that the implementation record of these agreements is mixed.

In spite of all these efforts and political developments two aspects are striking: (1) Up until now, the regulatory framework for international financial markets is provided by a set of institutions rather than by standards. Such interlocking – perhaps sometimes inter-blocking – institutions are not empowered to establish a substantive system of international financial governance but they only serve to co-ordinate the activities of national regulatory bodies and authorities – and this largely limited to economically powerful states. (2) Although there is thus some form of international co-operation it is highly questionable whether the institutions are really international (in the sense that they enjoy a certain degree of autonomy), rather national actors – at least from the perspective of law – seem to be the decisive ones. In other words, there seem to be numerous international activities, but as soon as it comes to regulation in the narrow sense, we must admit that this is national regulation.

Bringing together the findings of the first part of this introduction and the second one, there can be no doubt that there is a globalised capital market as of today. Financial relations are not limited to national or regional markets. Financial transactions are performed within truly international markets. This finding is in sharp contrast with the regulation of such markets. It would not be true to argue that international financial markets are not at all regulated. They are indeed regulated – but rather by national (or in the case of the EU, by regional supranational) law than by public international law. As a commentator, one may perceive this as a kind of misinterpretation of the motto 'Think globally, act locally'.

We may perceive this as a regulatory dilemma in international financial relations: international markets are regulated in the first place at the

---

[52] (1996) XXXV(3) *International Legal Materials* 724. Cf. Robert H. Sutton, 'Controlling Corruption through Collective Means: Advocating the Inter-American Convention Against Corruption' (1997) 20(4) *Fordham International Law Journal* 1427–78.

[53] UN Doc A/55/383, Annex. For a broad introduction into the Convention cf. Hans-Jörg Albrecht et al. (eds.), *The Containment of Transnational Organized Crime. Comments on the UN Convention of December 2000* (Freiburg i.Br., 2002).

national level and such national legislation is only co-ordinated to a limited extent. There is a certain risk – at least from the perspective of public international law – that regulatory efforts are deprived of their 'governance potential' or that a specifically (either politically or economically) powerful national regulator determines the regulatory framework for international financial relations on his own.

III. The public–private dilemma: hybrid regulation

While considerations of effective national implementation may provide arguments in favour of such loose co-operation between regulatory authorities, the problem is much more essential when it comes to the question of who actually is the most powerful player on stage. A large number of institutions, initiatives and *fora*, dealing with risk management in international financial relations, are neither participatory nor democratically controlled. We often identify hybrid forms of regulation where the beneficiaries of the regulatory environment themselves establish the regulatory framework which does not include sanctions or regulations that effectively protect the weaker participants of such markets. Rather we experience some kind of discriminatory regulatory framework, and the failure to agree upon a Multilateral Agreement on Investment (MAI),[54] the confined club of the G20, and the development of the Basle II Agreement reflect such discriminatory approaches. While it has already been demonstrated that there is little regulation of international financial markets at the level of public international law it must further be stated that the institutions co-ordinating the activities of national regulatory bodies are hardly ever international organisations in the traditional sense. Thus we talk of institutions or international regulatory arrangements rather than of international organisations *stricto sensu*. The following specific characteristics of international institutions that contribute to the regulation of international financial markets have been identified: such institutions largely consist of sub-state actors, they have been informally established, their internal organisation is rather flexible, their 'arrangements' are

---

[54] On the substance of the envisaged MAI see Rainer Geiger, 'Towards a Multilateral Agreement on Investment', (1998) 31(3) *Cornell International Law Journal* 467–75. On its failure see Jürgen Kurtz, 'NGOs, the Internet and International Economic Policy Making. The Failure of the OECD Multilateral Agreement on Investment' (2002) 3(2) *Melbourne Journal of International Law* 213–46.

implemented in a decentralised way, there is a lack of transparency (the institutions largely act in secrecy – as far as the general public is concerned), and their 'outcome' is of an ambiguous legal quality.[55]

Looking more closely at the actors involved it is noteworthy that the range of institutions is fairly broad – IOSCO is a private organisation that developed out of the Interamerican Association of Securities Commissions and Similar Agencies in 1984, originally incorporated by a private bill of the Quebec National Assembly;[56] the International Association of Insurance Supervisors (IAIS) is a non-profit corporation incorporated in Illinois;[57] the Basle Committee is hosted[58] by the Bank for International Settlements (BIS) which itself has a unique legal basis.[59] In spite of this multitude of institutional arrangements, two problems can be identified which at the same time must be separated from each other: (1) the involvement of regulatory authorities and civil servants (rather than political agents); and (2) the participation of private actors that are at the same time drafters and addressees of regulatory standards.

As far as the involvement of private actors in regulatory financial institutions is concerned we may not only point towards the difficulty of determining precisely the public–private divide but the advantages of self-regulation come into play.[60] Many areas of economic activities which are in the interest not only of the individual economic actor but also of the economic community – whether at the local, national, regional or global level – are today being promoted by governments while public authorities at the same time recognise the need to establish a regulatory framework for such activities. This concerns, among others,

---

[55] David Zaring, 'International Law by Other Means: The Twilight Existence of International Financial Regulatory Organizations', (1998) 33(2) *Texas International Law Journal* 281–330.

[56] Zaring, 'International Law by Other Means', above note 55, at 292, referring to An Act Respecting the International Organization of Securities Commissions, ch. 143, 1987 S.Q. 2437 (Can.).

[57] See Zaring, 'International Law by Other Means', above note 55, at 295.

[58] The Committee's mandate can be taken from a press communiqué from the central bank governors, issued through the Bank for International Settlements on 12 February 1975; cf. Zaring, 'International Law by Other Means', above note 55, at 287.

[59] Helmut Coing, 'Bank for International Settlements', in: Rudolf Bernhardt (ed.), *Encyclopedia of Public International Law*, vol. I (Amsterdam, 1992), pp. 342–3, with Addendum 1990 by Gunnar Schuster (at 343–4).

[60] A good example can be taken from James Fisher, 'Privatizing Regulation – Whistleblowing and Bounty Hunting in the Financial Services Industries', (2000) 19(1) *Dickinson Journal of International Law* 117–43.

telecommunications, in particular the internet; it applies to the mass media, the approach is used in the field of energy, and a number of other activities which come close to public services (*état providence/ Daseinsvorsorge*). Due to the fact that governments are no longer (economically) capable of providing such services they encourage non-state actors, in particular private undertakings, to develop economic activities in the field. In order not to curb such activities in their embryonic stages and in order to reduce transaction costs, governments increasingly rely upon self-regulation or partial self-regulation. Such an approach seems to be workable and provides both sides with some legitimacy while it cannot be easily accommodated with the traditional approach towards democratic legitimacy (which is input-oriented). If following an output-oriented model of democratic legitimacy[61] the participation of non-state (i.e. primarily private) actors in the regulation of financial markets becomes much more acceptable. Whether or not it is even necessary to develop a public–private partnership[62] in order to develop a regulatory framework for more or less global financial markets is a question that deserves further research. For the time being it may be argued that the involvement of banks, insurance companies, and other financial service providers in the activities of international and regional regulatory institutions has the twofold advantage of bringing expert knowledge into the process of regulation while at the same time facilitating the implementation of any co-ordinated approach since the acceptability of standards that have been developed in a participatory process is much higher than pure governmental regulation.

It must be pointed out that all this is not really new – although it is not a common feature of international regulation. As a rule, states still develop a public international law framework. However, at the regional level – in particular within European integration, including the committee procedures which are commonly referred to as 'comitology'[63] – hybrid regulatory techniques are well known. Such techniques build

---

[61] On the two models cf. Christian Tietje, 'Die Staatsrechtslehre und die Veränderung ihre Gegenstandes. Konsequenzen von Europäisierung und Internationalisierung', (2003) 118(17) *Deutsches Verwaltungsblatt* 1081–96, at 1094 et seq.

[62] Instructive within the context of the internet Wolfgang Kleinwaechter, 'Form Self-Governance to Public–Private Partnership. The Changing Role of Governments in the Management of the Internet's Core Resources', (2003) 36(3) *Loyola of Los Angeles Law Review* 1103–26.

[63] A conceptual approach to comitology is provided by Christian Joerges and Jürgen Neyer, 'From Intergovernmental Bargaining to Deliberative Political Processes: The Constitutionalisation of Comitology', (1997) 3(3) *European Law Journal* 273–99.

upon epistemic communities the members of which are part of governmental as well as private entities but are linked to each other by virtue of their expertise and their complementary interests. Such communities and their activities can best be understood by applying the so-called network model.[64] This was indeed originally developed to analyse forms of negotiated policy,[65] with much of the work being empirical and explanatory. In international relations theory the network model has primarily been used to conceptualise a system of exchanges or negotiations which are controlled by the subjects involved.[66] Focus has always been on the relationship between state and non-state actors. Applying network analysis to the study of European integration has become popular because it does not focus on the state(s) as such, but on governance.[67] This means that it is not necessary to qualify actors in a certain way (above all, as to their legal personality) before analysing their activities. Also, it broadens the number of actors included in the analytical framework. Network analysis does not confine itself to describing a varying grouping of negotiated relationships among stable subjects. It provides an insight into the complementarity and interdependence of the components, considering also 'new options which are accessible through the network as such, and are not the mere products of actors bargaining with each other'.[68] Network analysis thus helps to overcome various unfruitful normative and analytical polarisations. In order to avoid a more or less ideological debate on democratic legitimacy *in abstracto*, the network concept can be applied as an analytical tool.

This would then necessitate certain clarifications. With its focus on the relationships between various persons and organisations within

---

[64] The model is also applied in economics, cf. Christian Jochum, 'Network Economics and the Financial Markets – The Future of Europe's Stock Exchanges', (1999) 54(1) *Aussenwirtschaft* (Zurich) 49–74.

[65] Early contributions focus on federalist structures; see Fitz W. Scharpf, Bernd Reissert and Fritz Schnabel, *Politikverflechtung. Theorie und Empirie des kooperativen Föderalismus* (Kronberg/Ts., 1976).

[66] See Bernd Marin and Renate Mayntz (eds.), *Political Networks. Empirical Evidence and Theoretical Considerations* (Frankfurt/Main, 1991).

[67] For examples see Fritz W. Scharpf and Matthias Mohr, *Efficient Self-Coordination in Policy Networks. A Simulation Study* (MPIFG Discussion Paper 94/1, Cologne, 1994). The focus on governance facilitates a study of government-like activities; see Knud Erik Jørgensen, 'Introduction', in Knud Erik Jørgensen (ed.), *Reflective Approaches to European Governance* (New York, 1997), p. 2 et seq.

[68] Karl-Heinz Ladeur, 'Towards a Legal Theory of Supranationality – The Viability of the Network Concept' (1997) 3 *European Law Journal* 48.

international regulatory financial institutions the concept assumes that the properties of the network that is established on the basis of these relationships have an impact on the activities of the participating subjects and on the outcome of their activities. In order to establish a pertinent framework of analysis it is necessary to first identify the actors within the network. Second, the relationships between these actors have to be considered. Third, the analysis can extend to qualitative elements, *inter alia*, the importance of certain actors, the number of actual compared to the number of potential relations, and the difference between direct and indirect contacts. While such analysis can not be provided in an introductory chapter of a book that strives to develop first steps towards a public international law contribution in the field of financial regulation, it is important to point out that hybrid regulation as such can form an important part of the prospective 'international financial architecture'. It is neither *per se* negative nor *per se* positive, but the various regulatory elements must be analysed carefully and their impact assessed critically. While a debate about democratic legitimacy is indispensable – as has become clear in the context of the so-called 'Lamfallusy' procedure in the European context[69] – new problems may require new approaches. If it is admitted that the involvement of public and private actors in international regulatory financial institutions creates a regulatory dilemma, this introduction seeks to point out that such a dilemma can be effectively addressed, both from an empirical and from a normative perspective. This, however, will be done on the basis of individual chapters within this book and, hopefully, by future research in this field.

IV. Institutionalisation and juridification

While standards have only been agreed upon to a limited extent, there is an increasing tendency towards institution-building in international financial relations. For the purposes of this introduction an international institution is not merely an international organisation but it is understood as a common set of values and rules of behaviour established for a group of actors.[70] Only if – as is quite often the case – international

---

[69] Cf. Niamh Moloney, 'The Lamfalussy Legislative Model: A New Era for the EC Securities and Investment Services Regime', (2003) 52(2) *International and Comparative Law Quarterly* 509–20.

[70] This concept is widely used in political science. Cf., among others, Peter M. Haas, Robert O. Keohane, Marc Levy (eds.), *Institutions for the Earth. Sources of Effective International Environmental Protection* (Cambridge, Mass., 1993), at pp. 4–5.

institutions are supported by specialised personnel, organs, a budget, and other related characteristics, they are at the same time international organisations. Under public international law the criteria for such organisations to acquire legal personality are more or less generally recognised. To a certain extent 'international regimes'[71] as employed by political science are similar to 'international organisations' as defined by international law doctrine, but the term is both wider and narrower: while regimes do neither require international legal personality nor a treaty basis, they must have some real world effectiveness. An informal arrangement between supervisory authorities in international financial relations managing some agreed tasks can be a regime, but not an international organisation. It is thus possible to describe international regimes as organised institutions which enjoy a degree of effectiveness in a double sense: they effectively contribute to solve a real world problem, and they live up to their own agenda.

If institutions are thus understood, they can be a framework for self-regulation by the actors involved. Their role can further be active in the sense of steering the behaviour of their clientele, thus amounting to what is called governance. Such a term, however, is not appropriate if institutions only react. The term institution is therefore broader than the term governance. This is one of the reasons why there is a certain reluctance to apply the concept of 'governance' or even 'multilevel governance' to the existing regulatory environment in international financial relations because such concept assumes that there is a consciously steering actor. Such an actor, however, for the time being, is not in sight. There is not yet a design for an international financial architecture but developments are largely an unintended – or only partially intended – result of common arrangements.[72] As already indicated, the institutional response to global capital markets is not in the first instance global institutions. Many levels of institutions are involved, with still a primary regulatory impact at the level of national institutions. Nevertheless,

---

[71] Cf. Robert M. A. Crawford, *Regime Theory in the Post-Cold War World. Rethinking Neoliberal Approaches to International Relations* (Aldershot, 1996).

[72] Legal scholars adopt a broad variety of approaches. Cf. Ludwig Gramlich, 'Eine neue internationale "Finanzarchitektur" oder: Der IMF in der Krise?', (2000) 38(4) *Archiv des Völkerrechts* 399–454; Betsy Baker Röben and Volker Röben, 'Institutional Aspects of Financing Sustainable Development After the Johannesburg Summit of 2002', (2003) 63(2) *Zeitschrift für ausländisches öffentliches Recht und Völkerrecht* 517–30. A fairly innovative approach on global economic governance is outlined by Christian Tietje, 'Global Governance and Inter-Agency Co-operation in International Economic Law', (2002) 36(3) *Journal of World Trade* 501–15.

there is an increasing need to discuss global institutions or at least institutions that have a worldwide impact.

Neither traditional public international law nor regime theory provides convincing explanatory approaches. It is even doubtful whether they provide an analytical framework in order to follow recent developments. The reason for their failure to do so is rooted in the state-centred approach of both public international law and regime theory. Neo-functionalism[73] at least offers an alternative explanatory model since it recognises what recent developments demonstrate: that domestic actors matter in international relations and international law. Thus, neo-functionalism predicts that international co-operation is likely to develop along task specific lines. Such co-operation can attain momentum leading to an increasing complexity of co-operation and its expansion towards other issues.

Apart from institutionalisation, the second tendency in international financial relations is towards juridification[74] – though not in the traditional sense. International relations theory has opened up for and included normative elements, sometimes even based on conceptions of law. However, it remains difficult to include particular sets of rules adopted by sub-state actors into the framework of traditional public international law. This can only be done if public international law is no longer perceived as a hierarchical concept of law. Recently, constructivist theories of public international law have been developed as an alternative.[75] Their roots can be traced back to the 'security communities' of Karl Deutsch[76] and they focus on identities of and communication between various actors, thus on inter-subjectivity. Some

---

[73] Functionalism has been particularly popular in the context of European integration; cf. Philippe C. Schmitter, 'Second Thoughts on Neo-Functionalism and European Integration', in Victor Yves Ghebali and Dietrich Kappeler (eds.), *Les multiples aspects des relation internationals – études à la mémoire du Jean Siotis* (Brussels, 1995), pp. 265–83.

[74] The contribution of law towards the stability of financial markets is obviously a very strong aspect with regard to the juridification of international financial markets; cf. Mamiko Yokoi-Arai, 'Regional Financial Institutionalization and the Creation of a Zone of Law – The Context of Financial Stability/Regulation in East Asia', (2001) 35(4) *International Lawyer* 1627–69.

[75] Cf. David J. Bederman, 'Constructivism, Positivism, and Empiricism in International Law', (2001) 89(2) *Georgetown Law Journal* 469–99.

[76] The term was coined in his much quoted standard reference work *Political Community and the North Atlantic Area. International Organization in the Light of Historical Experience* (New York, 1957).

authors[77] consider the priority of identity over interest, the relevance of non-material explanations of actor behaviour, the possibility of collective intentions or shared understandings and the mutual construction of agent and structure as the essential commitments of this approach. Law then develops within networks. It is not static but considered as a process ('the enterprise of subjecting human conduct to the governance of rules'[78]). The binding force of such rules is then based on their self-binding effect.

Constructivist approaches, however, remain closely related to traditional concepts of sources. Another alternative, linking institutionalisation and juridification, may be to come back to the concept of governance, in particular, good governance. The adoption of such a concept of good governance and its focus on the proper exercise of political power to manage a nation's affairs, including principles of democracy, human rights, and a certain degree of procedural transparency to some extent is due to the criticism of the new institutional economics vis-à-vis neo-liberal approaches. The new approach of institutional economics considers the state an important actor providing for a regulatory framework. On the basis of 'property rights', transaction costs are considered. In order to reduce these costs, institutions ('rules, enforcement characteristics of rules, and norms of behaviour that structure repeated human interaction'[79]) are developed. These institutions combine horizontal and vertical integration, an approach that may be considered an adapted concept of governance. Regulation is one of the most important fields of governance so defined.

Thus understood, the concept of governance brings together institutionalisation and juridification, however, in different terms than traditional approaches do. If law is considered a process, then juridification may be considered a proper means to reform the international financial architecture.

V. Prospective elements of a global regulatory strategy

The regulatory dilemma in international financial relations is rooted in the problem of international markets and (primarily) national regulation

---

[77] Jutta Brunnée and Stephen Toope, 'International Law and Constructivism: Elements of an International Theory of International Law', (2000) 39(1) *Columbia Journal of Transnational Law* 19–74.

[78] Lon L. Fuller, *The Morality of Law* (New Haven, 1964), at 106.

[79] Douglass C. North, 'Institutions and Economic Growth. An Historical Introduction', (1989) 17(9) *World Development* 1319–32 at 1321.

which is complicated by the fact that hybrid forms of regulation involving private actors are not the only, but the still predominant, regulatory techniques. As has been explained in this introductory chapter, this dilemma can best be addressed by applying the concept of network analysis and focusing on institutions. Thereby the process of institutionalisation and juridification can be accommodated and made use of in order to develop an – at least tentative – global regulatory strategy.

It will be an essential question to be addressed, not only in this volume but generally, what elements should form part of such a global regulatory strategy. While regulation at the global level and by means of public international law is not the only feasible approach to frame international financial relations, it has its proper place. This place must be identified. Thereby use can be made of the fact that public international law in many instances has been able to provide a procedural framework for regulatory strategies. This can be done by various regulatory techniques, ranging from piecemeal strategies to the framework convention and protocol approach. In particular, in the field of more or less technical standards, ways of distinguishing political from technical decisions have been followed in many areas.

A global regulatory strategy should not totally replace existing approaches to establish a normative framework for international financial relations but it should accommodate such approaches. What seems to be essential – above all – is to establish a forum which brings together the various regulatory institutions and bodies, national, regional and global, in order to co-ordinate their approaches and strategies. Merely factual co-ordination will neither provide the necessary legal certainty for a further growth in a global financial market nor will it handle pertinent risks effectively. Whether, for this purpose, use is made of an existing forum is of secondary importance.

In order to set the frame for a global regulatory strategy with regard to international financial relations the following elements must be taken into account: Who are the actors in international financial relations and what is their respective role and interest? Have such actors been involved in pertinent regulatory activities in the past, and what place should they take in global financial governance? Which level of regulation (local, national, regional or universal) is best suited to establish a framework for international financial relations? How far is hybrid regulation suitable in order to establish an international financial architecture and how can hybrid regulation be accommodated within more traditional forms of public international law-making? The answers to all these questions very much depend on the substance of any regulatory instrument. This gives rise to the rather political and less legal question of what policies should be pursued at the international level and what should be left to the market, in particular, what areas are suitable for a kind of regulatory competition. The present volume seeks to develop first steps towards a public international approach on international financial relations. Historical, political and economic analysis have been combined with a discussion of existing national, regional and international regulatory approaches. The object and purpose of this book is to explore the regulatory potential of public international law with regard to global financial markets and to develop questions – perhaps even an agenda – for further research.

PART I

An historical perspective

1

Monetary governance and capital mobility in historical perspective

BENJAMIN J. COHEN

Of all the challenges facing economic policymakers at the dawn of the new millennium, few are as daunting as the problem of governance of international financial markets and the free movement of capital. Half a century ago, after the ravages of the Great Depression and World War II, financial markets everywhere – with the notable exception of the United States – were generally weak, insular, and strictly controlled, reduced from their previously central role in global economic relations to offer little more than a negligible amount of trade financing. But then, in the 1950s, deregulation and liberalisation began to combine with technological and institutional innovation to breach many of the barriers separating national currencies and monetary systems. In a cumulative process driven by the pressures of domestic and international competition, the range of market opportunities has gradually widened for borrowers and investors alike. The result has been a remarkable growth of capital mobility across political frontiers, reflected in a scale of financial flows unequalled since the glory days of the nineteenth century gold standard. Elsewhere I have likened these dramatic developments to a phoenix risen from the ashes. The key issue, I wrote, is what the resurrection of international financial markets means for monetary governance and the authority of the contemporary sovereign state. 'The phoenix has risen. Does it also rule the roost?'.[1]

The search for effective responses to this daunting challenge must begin with a proper understanding of political and historical context. What do we understand by monetary governance, and what are its motivations and origins? These questions are taken up in the first

---

[1] Benjamin J. Cohen, 'Phoenix Risen: the Resurrection of Global Finance' (1996) 48(2) *World Politics* 268–96 at 270.

section of this chapter. Monetary governance today is formally centred in the state. The state's embrace of that responsibility, however, is not a categorical imperative but a strategic choice – a choice driven by far more than just a selfless concern to provide an essential public good. At issue, most fundamentally, is political economy, not disinterested statesmanship.

In the second section I consider the relationship between contemporary monetary governance and capital mobility. That relationship, I submit, can only be comprehended in the context of the longer-term development of money itself. Free movement of capital is a challenge only when governments are resolved to protect their traditional monopoly of monetary governance. Regulation of capital mobility, in turn, must be viewed as a legitimate policy option when a government's monetary monopoly appears to come under threat. In this chapter, I will use the term capital controls to refer to any form of public intervention intended to limit or regulate the flow of funds across national borders. Capital controls are best understood as part of a state's overall strategy to preserve or promote an exclusive national currency.

The pros and cons of capital controls are briefly explored in the third section. Though the subject remains controversial, analysis suggests that the case for selective limitations on financial flows is, in principle, actually a good deal stronger than conventionally supposed. Yet in practice most governments in the industrial world and newly emergent economies remain hesitant to impede the free movement of capital. The fourth section of the chapter considers why that is so. The reason, I argue, has much to do with politics at both the domestic and international levels.

Finally, in a concluding section, I outline a list of critical research questions suggested by the preceding discussion.

I. Monetary governance[2]

Money is a public good that serves three essential functions: medium of exchange, unit of account, and store of value. As a medium of exchange, money is synonymous with the circulating means of payment. In this role, its key attribute is its general acceptability to satisfy contractual

---

[2] The discussion in this section, which is necessarily condensed, is based on arguments presented at greater length in Benjamin J. Cohen, The Geography of Money (Ithaca, NY, 1998).

obligations. As a unit of account, money provides a common denominator, or numéraire, for the valuation of diverse goods, services, and assets. Here, its key attribute is its ability to convey pricing information both reliably and expeditiously. As a store of value, money offers a convenient means for holding wealth. In this role, its key attribute is its ability to preserve purchasing power, bridging the interval, however transitory, between receipts from sales and payments for purchases.

Monetary governance involves control over the issue and circulation of money. In the modern world, nation-states are conventionally accepted as the legitimate agents of monetary governance, each within the confines of its own sovereign territory. With relatively few exceptions, governments sanction the creation and use of an exclusive national currency – a geography of One Nation/One Money, as I have described it.[3] Money is intended to be strictly *territorial*, a monopoly of the state. Currency territorialisation is a strategic choice, reflecting the full breadth of a government's political priorities.

1. Motivations

Why would a state seek a monetary monopoly? Motivation plainly involves more than just a disinterested willingness to take responsibility for providing an essential public good. Governments are far more calculating than that. In fact, genuine power resides in the privilege that money represents. Four main benefits are derived from a strictly territorial currency: first, a potent political symbol to promote a sense of national identity; second, a potentially powerful source of revenue to underwrite public expenditures; third, a possible instrument to manage the macroeconomic performance of the economy; and finally, a practical means to insulate the nation from foreign influence or constraint. Within each state, all four advantages privilege the interests of the government in relation to societal actors.

At the symbolic level, a territorial currency is particularly useful to rulers wary of internal division or dissent. Centralisation of political

---

[3] See Cohen, *The Geography of Money*, above note 2. The biggest exception is of course Europe's new monetary union, which came into being in January 1999. Monetary unions also exist in the Caribbean (Eastern Caribbean Currency Area) and the Commodities Futures Act (CFA) Franc Zone in francophone Africa. Yet other exceptions can be found in the variety of smaller states that legally employ another country's money in lieu of or alongside a currency of their own – a relationship generically labelled full or formal dollarisation. I will have more to say about both types of exception below.

authority is facilitated insofar as citizens all feel themselves bound together as members of a single social unit – all part of the same 'imagined community,' in the apt phrase of cultural anthropologist Benedict Anderson.[4] Anderson stresses that states are made not just through force but through loyalty, a voluntary commitment to a joint identity. The critical distinction between 'us' and 'them' can be heightened by all manner of tangible symbols: flags, anthems, postage stamps, public architecture, even national sports teams. Among the most potent of these tokens is money, as central banker Tommaso Padoa-Schioppa has noted: 'John Stuart Mill once referred to the existence of a multiplicity of national moneys as a "barbarism" . . . One could perhaps talk of a tribal system, with each tribe being attached to its own money and attributing it magical virtues . . . which no other tribe recognises.'[5]

Money's 'magical virtues' serve to enhance a sense of national identity in two ways. First, because it is issued by the government or its central bank, a state-sanctioned currency acts as a daily reminder to citizens of their connection to the 'imagined community' and oneness with it. Second, by virtue of its universal use on a daily basis, the currency underscores the fact that everyone is part of the same social entity – a role not unlike that of a single national language, which many governments also actively promote for nationalistic reasons. A common money helps to homogenise diverse and often antagonistic social groups.

A second benefit of a territorial currency is seigniorage – the capacity a monetary monopoly gives national governments to augment public spending at will. Technically defined as the excess of the nominal value of a currency over its cost of production, seigniorage can be understood as an alternative source of revenue for the state beyond what can be raised via taxation or by borrowing from financial markets. Public spending financed by money creation appropriates real resources at the expense of the private sector, whose purchasing power is correspondingly reduced by the ensuing increase of inflation – a privilege for government if there ever was one. Because of the inflationary implications involved, the process is also known popularly as the 'inflation tax.'

Despite the economic disadvantages associated with inflation, the privilege of seigniorage makes sense from a political perspective as a

[4] Benedict Anderson, *Imagined Communities: Reflections on the Origins and Spread of Nationalism* (revised edition, London, 1991).
[5] Tommaso Padoa-Schioppa, 'Tripolarism: Regional and Global Economic Cooperation' *Occasional Paper no. 42* (Washington, 1993), p. 16.

kind of insurance policy against risk – an emergency source of revenue to cope with unexpected contingencies, up to and including war. Decades ago John Maynard Keynes wrote: 'A government can live by this means when it can live by no other.'[6] Generations later another British economist, Charles Goodhart, has described seigniorage as the 'revenue of last resort'[7] – the single most flexible instrument of taxation available to mobilise resources in the event of a sudden crisis or threat to national security. It would be the exceptional government that would *not* wish to retain something like the option of an inflation tax.

A third benefit derives from money's potential impact on real economic performance – aggregate output and employment – as well as prices. So long as governments can maintain control of currency supply within their own territory, they have the capacity, in principle at least, to influence and perhaps even manage the overall pace of market activity. Money may be used to promote the broad prosperity and strength of the state as well as the government's own narrowly drawn fiscal requirements.

Currency territorialisation equips government with two potent policy instruments. First is the money supply itself, which can be manipulated to increase or decrease levels of expenditure by domestic residents. The second is the exchange rate – the price of home currency in terms of foreign currency – which can be manipulated to increase or decrease spending in the national economy through induced shifts between home and foreign goods. Neither instrument is infallible, of course; nor is either likely to attain a truly sustained impact on economic activity over the proverbial long term, if recent theoretical developments are to be believed. But over the shorter time horizons that are of most interest to public officials, monetary and exchange rate policies do manifest substantial influence as tools for macroeconomic management. It would be an exceptional government that would not wish to retain these weapons in its arsenal as well.

Finally, an important benefit is derived in a negative sense – from the enhanced ability a territorial money gives government to avoid dependence on some other provenance for this critical economic resource.

---

[6] John Maynard Keynes, 'Tract on Monetary Reform', reprinted in *The Collected Writings of John Maynard Keynes*, vol. 4 (London, 1924).

[7] Charles A. E. Goodhart, 'The Political Economy of Monetary Union,' in Peter B. Kenen (ed.), *Understanding Interdependence: The Macroeconomics of the Open Economy* (Princeton, NJ, 1995), ch. 12, p. 452.

Currency territoriality draws a clear economic boundary between the state and the rest of the world, promoting political authority. The closer government is able to come to achieving national monetary autarky, the better it will be able to insulate itself from outside influence or constraint in formulating and implementing policy.

That sovereign states might use monetary relations coercively, given the opportunity, should come as no surprise. As political scientist Jonathan Kirshner recently reminded us: 'Monetary power is a remarkably efficient component of state power . . . the most potent instrument of economic coercion available to states in a position to exercise it.'[8] Money, after all, is simply command over real resources. If a nation can be denied access to the means needed to purchase vital goods and services, it is clearly vulnerable in political terms. The lesson is simple: if you want political autonomy, don't rely on someone else's money.

2. Origins

Given the multiple advantages of a monetary monopoly, we should hardly be surprised that most governments might prefer an exclusive money of their own. But it is important to note that the monopoly so many states seek is by no means a natural one. Indeed, quite the contrary. The strategy of creating One Money for One Nation was never a categorical imperative. Rather, it was a deliberate, calculated choice – one choice among many – and best understood as a unique product of a particular stage of history.

The origins of currency territorialisation go back to the emergence of the modern nation-state in the nineteenth century, with all the state's claims to a consolidation of formal powers within a sovereign territory. Throughout most of recorded history, there was never any such thing as an exclusive national money. Coins of diverse heritage circulated freely across political frontiers, and choice among rival monies was virtually unlimited. Competition among currencies, not monopoly, was the norm. It was only during the nineteenth century, an era of rising nationalism, that governments began to claim a right to control the issue and circulation of money, abolishing currency competition. Over the course of the 1800s, throughout the Western world, the principles embodied in the Peace of Westphalia of 1648 – above all, the concept of

---

[8] Jonathan Kirshner, *Currency and Coercion: The Political Economy of International Monetary Power* (Princeton, NJ, 1995), pp. 29, 31.

absolute sovereignty based on exclusive territoriality – achieved a new level of tangible expression. Governments undertook to suppress all threats to their rule, whether from counterparts abroad or rivals at home. Their goal was to build up the nation, as far as possible, as a unified community led by a strong central authority. Control of money was simply a logical part of the process. As one source has commented: 'Just as all rival centers of power were absorbed into one monopoly of power so too all rival sources of money were absorbed into one monopoly of money creation.'[9]

The task was not easy. In fact, an enormous and sustained effort was required to overcome centuries of monetary tradition. Control was asserted in two principal ways – first, by promoting the development of a robust national money; and second, by seeking to limit the role of rival foreign currencies. The former was targeted by consolidating and unifying the domestic monetary order, standardising banknotes and coins and firmly lodging ultimate authority over money supply in a government-sponsored central bank. The latter was sought by means of new laws restricting or abolishing the legal-tender status of foreign monies, as well as by so-called public-receivability provisions specifying what currency might be used to pay taxes or satisfy other contractual obligations to the state.

Yet however difficult, the effort ultimately proved successful. Territorial currencies became the new norm. The process began in Britain, with coinage reforms enacted after the Napoleonic Wars and later with the Bank Charter Act of 1844, which finally consolidated the central position of the Bank of England in the national financial system. Fully fledged territorial currencies also began to emerge elsewhere in Europe, along with the United States and Japan, during the second half of the century; and then later, in the early 1900s, in the British Empire and throughout Latin America. By the middle of the twentieth century, the geography of One Nation/One Money had become universally recognised and enshrined in international practice. When the great wave of decolonisation got under way after World War II, ultimately bringing scores of new states into existence, few questioned the now conventional assumption that each nation might legitimately aspire to create its own central bank and exclusive national money.

---

[9] David O'Mahony, 'Past Justifications for Public Interventions', in Pascal Salin (ed.), *Currency Competition and Monetary Union* (The Hague, 1984), pp. 127–30 at 127.

II. Capital mobility

But then came the resurrection of international financial markets, with the attendant growth of capital mobility. Free movement of capital poses a direct challenge to a national monetary monopoly, forcing governments to consider anew the merits of a territorial currency. In effect, we have arrived at yet another stage in the longer-term development of money, where once again states must make a calculated strategic choice. Should they still aspire to an exclusive national money, as most governments have done since the nineteenth century? And if so, should they reconsider the merits of capital controls as one way to help cope with today's increasing volume of financial flows?

1. The economic dimension

For specialists in open-economy macroeconomics, the significance of growing capital mobility lies mainly in implications for the choice of an exchange rate regime. The critical issue, going back to the familiar Mundell-Fleming model, is best summarised by the so-called 'Unholy Trinity'[10] – the intrinsic incompatibility of capital mobility, currency stability, and autonomy of national monetary policy. The dilemma, assuming free movement of capital, is to fashion a regime that will neither encourage adverse exchange rate speculation nor compromise management of the domestic economy.

Traditionally, the choice was cast in simple binary terms: fixed versus flexible exchange rates. A country could adopt some form of peg for its currency or it could float. Pegs might be anchored on a single currency or to a basket of currencies; they might be formally irrevocable (as in a currency board) or based on a more contingent rule; they might crawl or even take the form of a target zone. Floating rates, conversely, might be managed (a 'dirty' float) or else left to the interplay of market supply and demand (a 'clean' float). For any level of capital mobility, governments were assumed to tailor their choices to attain some desired, or at least acceptable, trade-off between the objectives of currency stability and policy autonomy.

---

[10] Benjamin J. Cohen, 'The Triad and the Unholy Trinity: Lessons for the Pacific Region', in Richard Higgott, Richard Leaver and John Ravenhill (eds.), *Pacific Economic Relations in the 1990s: Cooperation or Conflict?* (Boulder, CO, 1993), pp. 133–58.

More recently, as capital mobility has grown, the issue has been recast – from fixed versus flexible exchange rates to a choice between, on the one hand, contingent rules of any kind and, on the other hand, the so-called 'corner solutions' of either free floating or some form of monetary union. According to some economists, neither free floating nor irrevocably fixed rates can be regarded today as truly viable options. Fixed rates, we are told, are too rigid, risking prolonged misalignments and payments disequilibria, while floating rates are too volatile and prone to speculative pressures. The only real choices are intermediate regimes that promise a degree of adaptability without generating undue uncertainty – 'stable but adjustable rates', to borrow a phrase from an earlier era. Quite the contrary, retort others, who insist that in fact it is the intermediate choices that are discredited, not the corner solutions, owing to the huge masses of mobile wealth now capable of switching between currencies at a moment's notice. Governments, according to this increasingly fashionable view, can no longer hope to defend policy rules designed to hit explicit exchange rate targets. The middle ground of contingent rules has in effect been 'hollowed out', as economist Barry Eichengreen[11] memorably put it.[12]

In practice, of course, neither corner solutions nor contingent rules are truly discredited, for the simple reason that in an imperfect world there is no perfect solution. The views of both sides rest on implicit – and questionable – political judgments about what trade-offs may or may not be tolerable to policymakers. Eichengreen's hollowing-out hypothesis, for example, obviously assumes that governments will be unwilling to pay the price of coping with occasional speculative crises. Defenders of contingent rules, conversely, assume that governments will naturally prefer to avoid absolute commitments of any kind – whether to monetary union or to market determination of currency prices – whatever the cost. The reality is that such trade-offs are made all the time when exchange rate regimes are decided. No option is ruled out *a priori*.

The political dimension of such decisions tends to be discounted in conventional economic discourse, where governments are assumed to be concerned more or less exclusively with maximising output and

---

[11] Barry Eichengreen, *International Monetary Arrangements for the 21st Century* (Washington, DC, 1994).

[12] For a useful survey of this recent debate, see Jeffrey A. Frankel, *No Single Currency Regime is Right for All Countries or at All Times*, Essays in International Finance 215 (Princeton, NJ: Princeton University, International Finance Section, 1999).

minimising inflation in the context of an open economy subject to potentially adverse shocks. In fact, political factors enter in two ways. First, as political scientist Jeffry Frieden has reminded us, 'domestic distributional considerations are also central to the choice of exchange rate regimes'.[13] The calculus is obviously affected by domestic politics: the tug and pull of organised interest groups of every kind. The critical issue is familiar: Who wins and who loses? The material interests of specific constituencies are systematically influenced by what a state decides to do with its money. Policy strategies are bound to be sensitive to the interplay among domestic political forces as well as to the institutional structures through which interest-group preferences are mediated.

Second, the utility function of governments obviously includes more than just macroeconomic performance. As a practical matter, sovereign states also worry about other things – not least, about their own policy autonomy; that is, their scope for discretion to pursue diverse objectives in the event of unforeseen developments, up to and including war. Key here is seigniorage – the 'revenue of last resort'. The more tightly a currency is pegged, the less room governments have to resort at will to money creation to augment public expenditures when deemed necessary. Monetary firmness is gained, but at a loss of fiscal flexibility. Certainly it is not wrong to attach importance to a reduction of exchange rate uncertainty, which can promote trade and investment and perhaps lower interest rates. But in an insecure world, governments may be forgiven for attaching importance to currency flexibility too, as a defence against *political* uncertainty. Policy strategies are bound to be sensitive to the interplay among such considerations as well.

The political dimension, therefore, is central. Much more is involved here than a simple choice of exchange rate regime.

2. The political dimension

In fact, as I have argued elsewhere,[14] what is really involved is nothing less than a fundamental transformation of monetary governance based

---

[13] Jeffry A. Frieden, 'The Dynamics of International Monetary Systems: International and Domestic Factors in the Rise, Reign, and Demise of the Classical Gold Standard,' in Jack Snyder and Robert Jervis (eds.), *Coping with Complexity in the International System* (Boulder, CO, 1993), pp. 137–62 at 140.

[14] Cohen, *The Geography of Money*, above note 2.

on the conventional geography of One Nation/One Money. What could be more political?

Conventional economic discourse tends to focus on capital mobility alone, thus highlighting only one of the standard functions of money: its use as a store of value. In fact, though, as financial market opportunities have gradually widened, the interpenetration of national monetary systems has come to be far more extensive, involving *all* the standard functions of currency – not just money's role as a private investment medium but also its use as a medium of exchange and unit of account for transactions of every kind, domestic as well as international. Traditional dividing lines between separate national monies, as a result, are becoming less and less distinct. No longer are economic actors restricted to a single currency – their own home money – as they go about their business. Competition among currencies, long common prior the emergence of the modern nation-state, has dramatically re-emerged, resulting in a new configuration of monetary spaces. The functional domains of most monies no longer correspond precisely with the formal jurisdiction of their issuing authority. Currencies instead are becoming increasingly *deterritorialised*, their circulation determined not by law or politics but rather by the dynamics of market forces.

The result is unmistakable. States are no longer able to exert the same degree of control as previously over the creation and use of their monies, whether by their own citizens or others. Instead governments are driven to compete, within and across borders, for the allegiance of market agents – in effect, to sustain or cultivate market share for their own brand of currency. Monopoly, in short, has yielded to something more like oligopoly; and, as the competition among currencies intensifies, monetary governance is rapidly being reduced to little more than a choice among marketing strategies designed to shape and manage demand.

What might those strategies be? Broadly speaking, four options are possible, depending on two key considerations – first, whether policy is defensive or aggressive, aiming either to preserve or promote market share; and second, whether policy is unilateral or collective. The four options are:

(1) *Market leadership*: an aggressive unilateralist policy intended to maximise use of the national money, analogous to predatory price leadership in an oligopoly.
(2) *Market preservation*: a status quo policy intended to defend, rather than augment, a previously acquired market position for the home currency.

(3) *Market alliance*: a collusive policy of sharing monetary authority in a monetary union of some kind, analogous to a tacit or explicit cartel.

(4) *Market followership*: an acquiescent policy of subordinating monetary authority to a stronger foreign currency via a firm peg or currency board, analogous to passive price followership in an oligopoly.

Of these four, the option of market leadership is generally available only to governments with the most widely circulated monies, such as the US dollar, euro, and yen.[15] The vast majority of states, with less competitive currencies, must select from among the remaining three. The basic question is plain. Should governments still seek to protect their monetary monopolies (market preservation)? Or, alternatively, should they consider sharing some of their traditional authority in a monetary union (market alliance) or surrendering it altogether to a dominant foreign power (market followership)? In simplest terms: Where should monetary governance now reside?

For a limited number of states, frustrated by the growing difficulties of coping with capital mobility, the options of sharing or outright surrender – despite considerable political disadvantages[16] – are becoming increasingly appealing. Already some governments have adopted a strategy of market followership in the form of a currency board. These include, most notably, Argentina, Bulgaria, Estonia, and Lithuania. Others have gone even further, abandoning their own money altogether in favour of a more popular foreign currency – a process known, generically, as 'dollarisation'. Ecuador formally adopted the US dollar in January 2000, and more recently El Salvador decided to go the same route. And of course yet others have gone the alternate route of monetary union, as in Europe, or are thinking about it.[17]

---

[15] For more on prospects for the leading currencies, see Benjamin J. Cohen, *Life at the Top: International Currencies in the Twenty-First Century*, Essays in International Economics 221 (Princeton, NJ: Princeton University, International Economics Section, 2000).

[16] Benjamin J. Cohen, 'Monetary Union: The Political Dimension', in Dominick Salvatore, James W. Dean and Thomas D. Willett (eds.), *The Dollarization Debate* (Oxford, 2003).

[17] In fact, prospects for monetary union have been discussed in virtually every region in the world, e.g. in Asia: Barry Eichengreen and Tamim Bayoumi, 'Is Asia an Optimum Currency Area? Can It Become One? Regional, Global, and Historical Perspectives on Asian Monetary Relations,' in Stefan Collignon, Jean Pisani-Ferry, and Yung Chul Park,

Most states, however, appear resolved to stick to the option of market preservation, at least for the present – to keep their own money alive no matter how uncompetitive it may be. Life support may be difficult, given the persistent intensification of currency competition in today's world. But such a policy preference is certainly understandable given the importance most states still attach to the idea of a monetary monopoly. A sovereign money is still seen in most parts of the world as a natural extension of the principle of political sovereignty.

How can a money be kept alive? Market share can be defended by tactics of either persuasion and coercion. Persuasion entails trying to sustain demand by buttressing a currency's reputation, above all by a public commitment to credible policies of 'sound' monetary management. The idea is to preserve market confidence in the value and usability of the nation's brand of money – the 'confidence game,' as Paul Krugman has ironically dubbed it.[18] Alternatively, a government may rely more on coercion, applying the formal regulatory powers of the state to avert any significant shift by users from local currency to a more popular foreign money. That of course is what governments have long done, starting in the nineteenth century, with the implementation of legal-tender laws and public-receivability provisions that limit the role of rival currencies. And it is what governments learned to do in the twentieth century, starting during the Great Depression and World War II, when capital controls were invented to restrain the movement of funds into or out of an economy. Regulation of capital mobility must be regarded as a logical corollary of any strategy of market preservation.

In practice, of course, the trend in recent decades has been all the other way, not toward but rather away from regulation of capital mobility, reflecting what has come to be known as the 'Washington consensus' – a triumphant 'neo-liberal' economics emphasising the virtues of liberalisation wherever possible. The Washington consensus

eds., *Exchange Rate Policies in Emerging Asian Countries* (London, 1999), ch. 21; Africa: Patrick Honohan, Patrick and Philip Lane, 'Will the Euro Trigger More Monetary Unions in Africa?' in Charles Wyplosz (ed.), *The Impact of EMU on Europe and the Developing Countries* (Oxford, 2001), ch. 12; Latin America: Eduardo Levy Yeyati and Federico Sturzenegger, 'Is EMU a Blueprint for Mercosur?' (2000) 110 (April) *Latin American Journal of Economics* 63–99; Australia–New Zealand: Arthur Grimes and Frank Holmes, *An ANZAC Dollar? Currency Union and Business Development* (Wellington, NZ, 2000); and even between the United States and Canada: Willem H. Buiter, 'The EMU and the NAMU: What is the Case for North American Monetary Union?' (1999) 25(3) *Canadian Public Policy/Analyse de Politiques* 285–305.

[18] Paul Krugman, 'The Confidence Game', *New Republic*, 5 October 1998, 23–5.

has been widely promoted by the US government, which eliminated its own controls in 1974, together with the Washington-based IMF and World Bank. First the more advanced economies of Europe, led by Britain in 1979 and Germany in 1984, and then Japan and many emerging-market economies undertook to dismantle as many of their existing restraints as possible.[19] Except in the smallest and poorest developing countries, where inconvertible currencies are still the rule rather than the exception, capital controls came to be frowned upon as a relic of an older, more *dirigiste* mentality – wrongheaded if not downright anachronistic. By the 1980s, financial liberalisation had become the goal of almost every self-respecting rich or middle-income nation. By the 1990s, the tide was clearly moving toward the consecration of free capital mobility as a universal norm. Perhaps the high-water mark was reached in early 1997 when the Interim Committee of the IMF approved a plan to start preparing a new amendment to the Fund's charter to make the promotion of capital account liberalisation a specific IMF objective and responsibility.[20]

But then came the great Asian financial crisis of 1997–98, which forced a fundamental reconsideration of the wisdom of financial liberalisation. Governments in East Asia, which previously had taken pride in the competitiveness of their currencies, suddenly found themselves unable to retain user loyalty. Strategies that once seemed adequate to sustain market share now had to be re-evaluated in the light of a massive 'flight to quality' by mobile capital. Inevitably, policymakers were drawn to take a new look at the old case for controls. Observers could hardly fail to note that China, which had never abandoned its vast panoply of financial restraints, was able to avoid much of the distress afflicting its more liberalised neighbours. Nor could the actions of Malaysia be

---

[19] For a brief review of the liberalisation process in these countries, see Beth A. Simmons, 'The Internationalization of Capital,' in Herbert Kitschelt, Peter Lange, Gary Marks, and John D. Stephens (eds.), *Continuity and Change in Contemporary Capitalism* (New York, 1999), ch. 2, pp. 37–43. The category of emerging-market economy is somewhat ambiguous but is generally assumed to include some thirty or so newly industrialising countries, mostly located in East Asia and Latin America.

[20] Interim Committee Communiqué, 28 April 1997, para. 7. Under the plan, two Articles were to be amended – Article I, where 'orderly liberalization of capital' would have been added to the list of the Fund's formal purposes; and Article VIII, which would have given the Fund the same jurisdiction over the capital account of its members as it already enjoys over the current account. The language would also have *required* countries to commit themselves to capital liberalisation as a goal.

ignored, once its comprehensive control programme was announced in September 1998. As one source commented at the time, 'capital curbs are an idea whose time, in the minds of many Asian government officials, has come back'.[21] Like it or not, an approach once dismissed as obsolete – a leftover of a more interventionist era – was now back on the policy agenda. As an instrument of monetary governance, regulation of capital mobility cannot be dismissed so long as governments prefer to preserve their own national monies.

III. The case for controls

Capital controls are controversial. Critics oppose them as inefficient and unworkable. Advocates justify them as a tonic for stricken economies. For decades the burden of proof was on those who would foolhardedly try to block the seemingly irresistible tide of financial liberalisation. With the crisis in Asia, however, came a new intellectual respectability for limits of some kind on the free movement of capital. Both theory and history suggest that the burden of proof has now shifted to those who would defend the conventional wisdom rather than those who attack it.

1. Pros and cons

The traditional case against capital controls is simple. It is the case for free markets, based on an analogy with standard theoretical arguments for free trade in goods and services. Commercial liberalisation is assumed to be a mutual-gain phenomenon, so why not financial liberalisation too? Like trade based on comparative advantage, capital mobility is assumed to lead to more productive employment of investment resources, as well as to increased opportunities for effective risk management and welfare-improving intertemporal consumption smoothing. We are all presumably better off as a result. In the words of Federal Reserve Chairman Alan Greenspan, an authoritative representative of the conventional wisdom: 'The accelerating expansion of global finance . . . enhances cross-border trade in goods and services, facilitates cross-border portfolio investment strategies, enhances the lower-cost financing of real capital formation on a worldwide basis, and, hence,

---

[21] Robert Wade and Frank Veneroso, 'The Gathering Support for Capital Controls,' (1998) 41(6) *Challenge* 14–26 at 23.

leads to an expansion of international trade and rising standards of living.'[22] All these gains, conversely, would be threatened by controls, which it is assumed would almost certainly create economic distortions and inhibit socially desirable risk-taking. Worse, given the inexorable advance of financial technology across the globe, regulation in the end might not even prove to be effective. Again in Greenspan's words: 'We cannot turn back the clock on technology – and we should not try to do so.'[23] Any government that still preferred controls was, in effect, simply living in the past.

Against these arguments, which have long dominated thinking in policy circles, two broad lines of dissent may be found in the economics literature. One approach focuses on the assumptions necessary to support the conventional wisdom, which are as demanding for trade in financial assets as they are for trade in goods and services. Strictly speaking, as a matter of theoretical reasoning, we can be certain that free capital flows will optimise welfare only in an idealised world of pure competition and perfect foresight. In reality, economies are rife with distortions (such as asymmetries in the availability of information) that prevent attainment of 'first-best' equilibrium. As Richard Cooper, a leading specialist in international monetary economics, has written: 'It has long been established that capital mobility in the presence of significant distortions ... will result in a misallocation of the world's capital and, indeed can even worsen the economic well-being of the capital-importing country.'[24]

A plausible case for regulation, therefore, may be made on standard 'second-best' grounds. Judicious introduction of another distortion in the form of capital controls could actually turn out to raise rather than lower economic welfare on a net basis. For every possible form of market failure, there is in principle a corresponding form of optimal intervention.

The logic of this kind of argument is not disputed. An omniscient government dealing with one clear distortion could undoubtedly improve welfare with some form of capital-market restriction. What is disputed is the value of such logic in the real world of multiple distortions and imperfect policymaking. As Michael Dooley has noted in an

---

[22] Alan Greenspan, 'The Globalization of Finance', (1998) 17(3) *Cato Journal* 243–50 at 246.

[23] Greenspan, 'Globlization of Finance', above note 22, at 249.

[24] Richard N. Cooper, 'Should Capital Controls be Banished?', (1999) 1 *Brookings Papers on Economic Activity* 89–141 at 105.

oft-cited survey of the relevant literature,[25] the issue is not theoretical but empirical. The assumptions necessary to support an argument based on second-best considerations are no less 'heroic' than those underlying the more conventional *laissez-faire* view.

The second line of dissent, much more relevant to today's circumstances, looks not to marginal economic distortions but rather to the very nature of financial markets. Even in the absence of other considerations, financial markets tend to be especially prone to frequent crisis and flux. At issue here are the interdependencies of expectations inherent in the buying and selling of claims, which unavoidably lead to both herd behaviour and multiple equilibria. Financial markets are notoriously vulnerable to self-fulfilling speculative 'bubbles' and attacks. They also have a disturbing tendency to react with unpredictable lags to changing fundamentals – and then to overreact, rapidly and often arbitrarily. The resulting flows of funds, which can be massive, may be highly disruptive to national economies owing to their amplified impact on real economic variables. Hence here too a logical case may be made for judicious intervention by state authorities, in this case to limit the excessive instabilities and contagion effects endemic to the everyday operation of financial markets. Representative are the words of a former governor of the Bank of Mexico:

> 'Recent experiences of market instability in the new global, electronically linked markets ... have made the potential costs of massive speculative flows difficult to ignore or underestimate ... The assumed gains from free capital mobility will have to be balanced against the very real risks such mobility poses. Some form of regulation or control ... seems necessary to protect emerging-market economies from the devastating financial crises caused by massive capital movements.'[26]

Admittedly the value of this sort of argument too may be open to challenge on empirical grounds. Recent research, however, demonstrates that financial liberalisation is almost always associated, sooner or later, with serious and costly systemic crisis.[27] It is precisely the

---

[25] Michael P. Dooley 'A Survey of Literature on Controls over International Capital Transactions', 1996 43(3) *International Monetary Fund Staff Papers* 639–87.

[26] Ariel Buira, *An Alternative Approach to Financial Crises* (Princeton, NJ: International Finance Section, 1999).

[27] John Williamson and Molly Mahar, *A Survey of Financial Liberalization*, Essays in International Finance 211 (Princeton, NJ: Princeton University, International Finance Section, 1998).

explosion of such crises that has been decisive in shifting the terms of discourse. Increasingly the question is posed: why should freedom of capital movement be given absolute priority over all other considerations of policy? Why, in effect, should governments tie one hand behind their back as they seek to shape and manage demand for their currency?

Perhaps most influential in shifting the discourse was a widely quoted article by the prominent trade economist Jagdish Bhagwati, which first appeared in the midst of East Asia's crisis.[28] Although other economists, such as Ilene Grabel,[29] had been making a case for controls for some time, Bhagwati's celebrity succeeded in bringing the issue to a new level of public awareness. After Asia's painful experience, Bhagwati asked, could anyone remain persuaded by the 'myth' of capital mobility's benign beneficence? In his words:

> 'It has become apparent that crises attendant on capital mobility cannot be ignored ... When a crisis hits, the downside of free capital mobility arises ... Thus, any nation contemplating the embrace of free capital mobility must reckon with these costs and also consider the probability of running into a crisis. The gains from economic efficiency that would flow from free capital mobility, in a hypothetical crisis-free world, must be set against this loss if a wise decision is to be made.'[30]

In a similar vein, shortly afterward, Krugman decried the failure of more conventional strategies of market preservation, which he labelled Plan A. 'It is time to think seriously about Plan B', he contended, meaning controls. 'There is a virtual consensus among economists that exchange controls work badly. But when you face the kind of disaster now occurring in Asia, the question has to be: badly compared to what?'[31] Similarly, the financier George Soros wrote that 'some form of capital controls may ... be preferable to instability even if it would not constitute good policy in an ideal world'.[32] Within a short time, the intellectual momentum had clearly shifted toward some manner of reappraisal of the conventional wisdom. As Bhagwati concluded:

---

[28] Jagdish Bhagwati, 'The Capital Myth', (1998) 77(3) *Foreign Affairs* 7–12.
[29] Ilene Grabel 'Marketing the Third World: The Contradictions of Portfolio Investment in the Global Economy', (1996) 24 *World Development* 1761–76.
[30] Bhagwati, 'The Capital Myth', above note 28, at 8–9.
[31] Paul Krugman, 'Saving Asia: It's Time to Get Radical', (1998) 138(5) *Fortune Magazine* 74–80.
[32] George Soros, *The Crisis of Global Capitalism* (New York, 1998), pp. 192–3.

'Despite the ... assumption that the ideal world is indeed one of free capital flows ... the weight of evidence and the force of logic point in the opposite direction, toward restraints on capital flows. It is time to shift the burden of proof from those who oppose to those who favor liberated capital.'[33]

2. Back to the future?

Reappraisal of the conventional wisdom could also be justified on historical grounds. Many people fail to remember that the original design of the IMF did not actually call for free capital mobility. Quite the contrary, in fact. Reflecting an abhorrence for the sort of 'hot-money' flows that had so destabilised monetary relations in the 1920s and 1930s, the charter drafted at Bretton Woods made explicit allowance for the preservation of capital controls as an instrument of monetary governance. Virtually everyone involved in the negotiations agreed with the influential League of Nations study, *International Currency Experience*, that some form of protection was needed against the risk of 'mass movements of nervous flight capital'.[34] The option of controls, therefore, was explicitly reserved to the discretion of individual states, provided only that such restraints might not be intended to restrict international commerce.[35] The idea was to afford governments sufficient policy autonomy to promote stability and prosperity at home without endangering the broader structure of multilateral trade and payments that was being laboriously constructed abroad. It was a deliberate compromise between the imperatives of domestic interventionism and international liberalism – the compromise of 'embedded liberalism,' as political scientist John Ruggie[36] later called it.

Pivotal in promoting that compromise was none other than John Maynard Keynes, universally respected as the greatest economist of his day and intellectual leader of the British delegation at Bretton Woods. For Keynes, nothing was more damaging than the free movement of capital, which he viewed as 'the major cause of instability ... [Without]

---

[33] Bhagwati, 'The Capital Myth', above note 28, at 12.

[34] Ragnar Nurkse, *International Currency Experience: Lessons from the Inter-War Period* (Geneva: League of Nations, 1944), p. 188.

[35] Article VI, sections 1 and 3 of the Articles of Agreement of the IMF.

[36] John G. Ruggie, 'International Regimes, Transactions, and Change: Embedded Liberalism in the Postwar Economic Order' in Stephen D. Krasner (ed.), *International Regimes* (Ithaca, NY, 1983), 195–231.

security against a repetition of this ... the whereabouts of "the better 'ole" will shift with the speed of the magic carpet. Loose funds may sweep round the world disorganising all steady business. Nothing is more certain than that the movement of capital funds must be regulated.'[37] Keynes carefully distinguished between genuinely productive investment flows and footloose 'floating funds'. The former, he concurred, were vital to 'developing the world's resources' and should be encouraged. It was only the latter that should be controlled, preferably as a 'permanent feature of the post-war system'.[38] Following Bretton Woods, Keynes expressed satisfaction that his objectives in this regard had been achieved: 'Not merely as a feature of the transition, but as a permanent arrangement, the plan accords to every member Government the explicit right to control all capital movements. What used to be heresy is now endorsed as orthodox.'[39] As we know, though, that achievement did not last. Over the course of the next half century, as the phoenix of global finance rose from the ashes, Keynes' strictures were largely forgotten. With the Washington consensus increasingly dominant, what had been endorsed as orthodox once again became heresy – until the Asian crisis. Despite determined resistance from neo-liberal economists,[40] the burden of proof now has once more decisively shifted. Even the IMF has changed its tune, dropping active discussion of a new amendment to promote financial liberalisation and talking instead of the possible efficacy of financial restraints[41] – a tentative step back to the future envisaged by Keynes and others when

---

[37] 'Post-War Currency Policy,' a British Treasury memorandum dated September 1941, reprinted in Donald Moggridge (ed.), *The Collected Writings of John Maynard Keynes*, vol. XXV (Cambridge, 1980), p. 31. For 'ole, read hole – a handy place to hide one's money.

[38] 'Plan for an International Currency (or Clearing) Union,' January 1942, reprinted in Moggridge, *The Collected Writings of John Maynard Keynes*, above note 37, at 129–30.

[39] As quoted in Louis W. Pauly, *Who Elected the Bankers? Surveillance and Control in the World Economy* (Ithaca, NY, 1997), p. 94. For more on Keynes' views and how they relate to the contemporary scene, see John Cassidy, 'The New World Disorder', *The New Yorker*, 26 October 1998, pp. 198–207; Jonathan Kirshner, 'Keynes, Capital Mobility and the Crisis of Embedded Liberalism', (1999) 6(3) *Review of International Political Economy* 313–37.

[40] See, e.g., Sebastian Edwards, 'How Effective are Capital Controls?' (1999) 13(4) *Journal of Economic Perspectives* 65–84; Günther G. Schulze, *The Political Economy of Capital Controls* (New York, 2000).

[41] Akira Ariyoshi, Karl Habermeier, Bernard Laurens, Inci Otker-Robe, Jorge Iván Canales-Kriljenko and Andrei Kirilenko, *Country Experiences with the Use and Liberalization of Capital Controls* (Washington, DC: IMF, 2000).

the Fund was first created. Plainly, the pressure of events has conspired with a reawakened sense of history to cast the case for controls in a new light. At the level of intellectual discourse, regulation of capital mobility has gained new legitimacy as an instrument of monetary governance.

IV. Why hesitate?

But this leaves us with a conspicuous puzzle. For all their new-found legitimacy in principle, capital controls have not regained much favour in practice – at least, not yet. Not long after the Asian crisis broke, I proposed that when viewed in historical perspective, the decade of the 1990s might eventually be seen as a high-water mark in the empowerment of financial markets. The tide of liberalisation, I suggested, was starting to turn as policymakers, faced with the worst financial calamity since the Great Depression, began to look again at the case for restraints of some kind. 'Once scorned as a relic of the past, limits on capital mobility [could soon] become the wave of the future.'[42] Looking back, that judgment now seems premature. Restraints do, of course, continue to be enforced in most poor countries, which have never fully subscribed to all the tenets of the Washington consensus. But in the industrial world and newly emergent economies, governments still hesitate to restore impediments to the free flow of capital. Given the importance that so many states attach to protecting their traditional monetary monopolies, such a reluctance seems anomalous. Why do governments hesitate?

A number of inferences are possible, which I have explored elsewhere.[43] Most persuasive, in my opinion, is a political explanation stressing the determined opposition of what amounts to a powerful transnational coalition of interests, including the government of the United States – universally acknowledged as the still dominant power in international finance – together with key private-sector actors in both

---

[42] Benjamin J. Cohen, 'Taming the Phoenix? Monetary Governance After the Crisis,' in Greg Noble and John Ravenhill (eds.), *The Asian Financial Crisis and the Structure of Global Finance* (Cambridge, 2000), ch. 9, p. 193. This paper was first prepared for a conference on the Asian financial crisis held in Melbourne, Australia, in December 1998.

[43] Benjamin J. Cohen, 'Capital Controls: The Neglected Option,' in Geoffrey R. D. Underhill and X. Zhang (eds.), *International Financial Governance Under Stress: Global Structures versus National Imperatives* (Cambridge, 2003). Benjamin J. Cohen, 'Capital Controls: Why Do Governments Hesitate?,' in Leslie Elliott Armijo (ed.), *Debating the Global Financial Architecture* (Albany, NY, 2002), ch. 3.

creditor and debtor nations. Such a formidable alliance of forces is undoubtedly difficult to resist.

1. The United States

Consider first the role of the United States, which continues as it has throughout most of the postwar period to dominate management of the international financial architecture. Though somewhat eclipsed in the 1970s and 1980s, America's monetary hegemony was decisively reaffirmed by the long economic expansion of the 1990s – a record of success that stood in sharp contrast to lingering unemployment in Europe, stagnation in Japan, and repeated crises elsewhere. Not for nothing do the French now call the United States the world's only hyperpower (*hyperpuissance*). Few governments today are inclined overtly to defy Washington's wishes on monetary and financial issues – and Washington has made no secret of its firm opposition to any significant reversal of recent financial liberalisation.

Emerging-market economies, in particular, have been openly pressured to keep on playing the confidence game. Influence has been brought to bear both directly and through the policy conditionality imposed on hardest-hit nations by the IMF, which was once described to me by a high US Treasury official as 'a convenient conduit for US influence'.[44] Typical was the advice of the US Council of Economic Advisers following the Asian crisis. For countries facing the prospect of volatile capital flows, the Council suggested, 'the need [is] to strengthen their domestic financial systems and adopt appropriate macroeconomic policies' – not a resort to capital controls.[45] On the contrary, the Council warned, 'many considerations argue against the use of capital controls'.[46] Similarly, Joseph Stiglitz, the World Bank's recently retired chief economist, has vividly described the close collaboration between the Treasury and Fund that was instrumental in enforcing neo-liberal orthodoxy after the crisis broke.[47] We know that countries such as Korea or Argentina

---

[44] As quoted in Benjamin J. Cohen, *In Whose Interest? International Banking and American Foreign Policy* (New Haven, CN, 1986), p. 229.

[45] Council of Economic Advisers, *Annual Report* (Washington: US Government Printing Office, 2000), p. 226.

[46] Council of Economic Advisers, *Annual Report* (Washington: US Government Printing Office, 1999), p. 281.

[47] Joseph Stiglitz, 'The Insider: What I Learned at the World Economic Crisis', *New Republic*, 17 and 24 April 2000, pp. 56–60.

(which was willing to play the game by Washington's rules) were rewarded with generous financial assistance and other forms of support. Conversely, when Indonesia's newly elected president, Abdurrahman Wahid, briefly flirted with the idea of controls during a period of renewed currency pressure in June 2000, he was firmly discouraged by the IMF's managing director, who insisted that Indonesia must adhere strictly to the Fund's policy prescriptions.[48] We also know that Malaysia came in for much opprobrium after its rash break with the Washington consensus in 1998. In such an atmosphere, is it any wonder that most policymakers might hesitate to follow in Kuala Lumpur's footsteps?

Undoubtedly, one reason for Washington's determined opposition lies in intellectual conviction. Most of the officials recently in charge of US policy, including former Treasury Secretary Robert Rubin and his successor Lawrence Summers, were trained in neo-liberal economics and firmly persuaded of its essential merit; and the same can certainly be assumed of their replacements in the new Bush administration as well. But that is hardly the only reason. Ideological bias can explain only a predisposition toward some set of policies. It is unlikely to wholly dominate hard-nosed political calculation. In practice, two other considerations have clearly taken precedence.

First has been a concern for systemic stability, which obviously seemed jeopardised by the Asian crisis and its subsequent spread to Russia, Brazil, Argentina, and elsewhere. Not only have lending markets around the world threatened periodically to seize up, risking a global credit crunch, there is also always the possibility of collapsing stock markets, worldwide recession, or even resurgent protectionism in international trade. Nightmare scenarios were a dime a dozen at the time of East Asia's crash. As the dominant architect of the prevailing monetary structure, the United States is presumably also one of its principal beneficiaries. In that context America's leaders have every reason to seek to suppress any challenge to the status quo.

Second is domestic politics within the United States, which also favour preservation of the status quo. Few Americans would be directly benefited by restraints on capital mobility in emerging markets. Many constituencies, however, could see their material interests hurt, including especially major financial institutions and investors. Such powerful market actors are not the kind to keep their preferences under a bushel; nor are their elected representatives apt to be entirely insensitive to their

---

[48] *New York Times*, 6 June 2000, C4.

pleas for support. This is not to suggest that Washington is merely the tool of an exploitative capitalist class. The world is rarely as simple as that. But it does imply a common interest in opposing controls – a sort of 'Wall Street-Treasury complex', as political scientist Robert Wade has described it.[49] In Wade's words:

> 'The United States has a powerful interest in maintaining and expanding the free worldwide movement of capital . . . Moreover, Wall Street banks and brokerage firms want to expand their sales by doing business in emerging markets . . . [Hence] there is a powerful confluence of interests between Wall Street and multinational corporations in favor of open capital accounts worldwide. In response, the US Treasury has been leading a campaign . . . to promote capital liberalisation.'[50]

2. Domestic politics

Resistance to Washington's pressures, of course, is not impossible – neither in principle nor in practice. Legally, there is nothing to prevent a sovereign government from limiting capital flows if it so chooses; politically, few emerging-market countries are so supine as to knuckle under to the first whiff of opposition from Washington. Regulation of capital mobility, to repeat, is a logical corollary of a currency strategy of market preservation. Hence something else must also be involved to explain why governments continue to hesitate to make more use of controls, effectively tying one hand behind their back even as they strive to sustain market share for their money. Logic, recalling the distributional implications of financial policy, suggests that the 'something else' is most likely to be found at home, in each country's own domestic politics and political institutions.

Domestic actors with a capacity to influence official policy in such matters are of course not hard to find. For instance, numerous studies have analysed the politics of the wave of financial liberalisation that swept emerging-market economies in the 1980s and 1990s.[51] All point

[49] Robert Wade, 'National Power, Coercive Liberalism and "Global" Finance' in Robert Art and Robert Jervis (eds.), *International Politics: Enduring Concepts and Contemporary Issues* (Ithaca, NY, 1999), pp. 482–9.

[50] Robert Wade, 'The Coming Fight Over Capital Controls', (1998–99) 113 (Winter) *Foreign Policy* 41–54 at 45–7.

[51] See especially Louis W. Pauly, *Opening Financial Markets: Banking Politics on the Pacific Rim* (Ithaca, NY, 1988); Sylvia Maxfield, *Governing Capital: International Finance and Mexican Politics* (Ithaca, NY, 1990); Stephan Haggard, Chung H. Lee and Sylvia Maxfield (eds.), *The Politics of Finance in Developing Countries* (Ithaca, NY, 1993);

to the key role played by powerful societal interests in helping to persuade policymakers to reduce or eliminate past restraints on capital mobility. Core constituencies benefited measurably from the opening of a new range of market opportunities. These included, in particular, big tradable-goods producers, banks and other financial-services firms, and large private asset-holders. Exporters and importers, as well as domestic banks, gained improved access to loanable funds and lower borrowing costs; the owners and managers of financial wealth were freed to seek out more profitable investments or to develop new strategies for portfolio diversification. All these benefits, plainly, would be curtailed or lost if controls were now to be reimposed. It stands to reason, therefore, that these same constituencies would now do everything possible to ensure that governments sustain their commitment to the Washington consensus. These too are actors that are unlikely to keep their preferences under a bushel.

Details differ from country to country, of course, depending on the specific characteristics of each state's economic structure and political institutions. In Mexico, for instance, it was the banking industry that was most prominent in lobbying for liberalisation, acting in a *de facto* coalition with like-minded officials in the federal bureaucracy – what Sylvia Maxfield has called Mexico's 'bankers alliance'.[52] According to Maxfield, the bankers' alliance was able to succeed as it did because of several key characteristics of the country's institutional structure. These included a relatively autonomous central bank, a finance ministry able to exercise hegemony over other state economic-policymaking agencies, and a high degree of conglomeration between private industrial and financial enterprises. In countries like Korea and Taiwan, by contrast, it was the industrial sector that was most directly involved – especially big manufacturers who, as they shifted toward more capital-intensive activities, sought to attain easier access to large-scale external financing.[53]

Michael Loriaux, Meredith Woo-Cumings, Kent E. Calder, Sylvia Maxfield and Sofia A. Pérez, *Capital Ungoverned: Liberalizing Finance in Interventionist States* (Ithaca, NY, 1997); Nancy Neiman Auerbach, *States, Banks, and Markets: Mexico's Path to Financial Liberalization in Comparative Perspective* (Boulder, CO, 2001).

[52] Sylvia Maxfield, 'Bankers' Alliances and Economic Policy Patterns: Evidence from Mexico and Brazil', (1991) 23(4) *Comparative Political Studies* 419–58.

[53] Stephan Haggard and Sylvia Maxfield, 'The Political Economy of Capital Account Liberalisation,' in Helmut Reisen and Bernhard Fischer (eds.), *Financial Opening: Policy Issues and Experiences in Developing Countries* (Paris: OECD, 1993), 65–91; Stephan Haggard and Sylvia Maxfield, 'Political Explanations of Financial Policy in Developing Countries,' in Stephan Haggard, Chung H. Lee and Sylvia Maxfield (eds.), *The Politics of Finance in Developing Countries* (Ithaca, NY, 1993), ch. 10; Meredith Woo-Cumings, 'Slouching Toward the Market: The Politics of Liberalization in South

Again institutional factors, including in particular the relative strength of the central bank and allied agencies within the structure of government, were decisive in determining how much influence such sectoral interests could exercise over policy outcomes. And in yet other economies, such as Indonesia, it was large asset holders who were among the most influential, aided no doubt by close political (and even familial) ties to governmental authorities.[54]

Whatever the details, though, the broad implication is clear. Governments have been under pressure from not one but *two* directions. Opposition to controls comes not just from the United States and IMF, on the outside; but also from key elements of the private sector at home, determined to preserve the benefits and privileges derived from liberalised financial markets. Interacting with the 'Wall Street-Treasury complex,' in other words, is a comparably influential bank-industrial-wealth holder complex – combining, in effect, into a powerful transnational coalition that works in a mutually reinforcing fashion to bar any retreat from the Washington consensus. External pressure from the United States is amplified internally by the natural desire of influential societal actors to defend acquired privileges. In turn, the impact of those same domestic actors is strengthened and legitimised by the backing of the world's acknowledged monetary hegemon.

No evidence exists, of course, to suggest that this sort of coalition, which is informal at best, is in any way the result of deliberate design. No conspiracy is needed to explain a pattern of co-operation when there is so evident a confluence of interests. But premeditated or not, the coalition has certainly proved its effectiveness in constraining the actions of governments that might otherwise have been more partial to a revival of controls. Even the rashest of policymakers are bound to hesitate when faced by such formidable opposition.

V. Conclusion

My central message in this chapter is straightforward. Monetary governance is a matter of choice. States may elect not to preserve an exclusive national currency. But for those governments that do prefer to defend

---

Korea' in Loriaux, Woo-Cumings, Calder, Maxfield and Pérez, *Capital Ungoverned*, above note 51, ch. 3.

[54] Stephan Haggard and Sylvia Maxfield, 'The Political Economy of Financial Internationalization in the Developing World,' in Robert O. Keohane and Helen V. Milner (eds.), *Internationalization and Domestic Politics* (New York, 1996), ch. 9.

their traditional monetary monopolies, regulation of the free movement of capital must be regarded as a legitimate policy option. Both theory and history suggest a useful role for capital controls of some kind. The hesitation of governments is best explained in political terms, stressing the opposition of a powerful transnational coalition of interests.

These observations prompt a number of questions for further research. First is the issue of a state's choice of basic currency strategy. Should governments seek to preserve an exclusive national money or not? And if not, what alternative option might best suit a nation's circumstances and needs? At issue here are broad considerations of both material interest and state power – political economy at its most essential. What is needed is a better understanding of the risk and opportunities associated with different policy choices.

Second is the issue of capital controls. What kinds of capital flows, if any, should be subject to formal limitation, and what forms of regulation might be most effective? Should restraints be incentive-based or more purely administrative? Should regulation be unilateral or co-ordinated? And what role might there be for either multilateral agencies (for example, the IMF or BIS) or private-sector actors in the formulation and implementation of policy? At issue here are matters of both technical economics and legal analysis. What is needed is more detailed, nuanced research to help transform principle – the new-found legitimacy of capital controls – into practice.

Finally, there is the issue of hesitation. How can the opposition to controls be overcome? Against the foes of regulation, can a matching coalition of proponents be mobilised to restore the compromise of embedded liberalism written into the Fund charter at Bretton Woods? At issue here is politics at its most fundamental. Monetary governance, in the end, is nothing if not political.

PART II

A comparative perspective

2

The liberalisation of financial markets: the regulatory response in the United Kingdom

EILÍS FERRAN

With the coming into force of the Financial Services and Market Act 2000 (FSMA) in December 2001, the United Kingdom entered upon a new era in financial regulation. In place of a fragmented regulatory structure where responsibilities were divided between a number of agencies, under the new regime the Financial Services Authority (FSA) is the single regulator of the financial sector. In place of self-regulation by the industry or, even, self-regulation within a statutory framework as the previous regulatory regime for the securities industry was conventionally described, financial regulation has been put onto a clear statutory footing. The FSA has an impressive armoury of statutory powers at its disposal.

These dramatic regulatory changes in the United Kingdom were made in response to developments in financial markets and the failure of the previous regime to keep pace.[1] Well-publicised scandals during the 1980s and 1990s such as the mis-selling of pensions and life assurance products and the collapse of individual financial firms like Barings indicated that the old regime was failing to meet the regulatory goals of protecting the interests of consumers, preventing fraud and maintaining public confidence in the financial sector. This in turn triggered political pressure for reform.

When the Financial Services Act 1986 and the Banking Act 1987 were enacted, many of the features that characterise modern financial services business in developed markets such as the United Kingdom were already appearing. Exchange controls had been abolished and capital could

---

[1] The historical background is explored in more detail at: Eilís Ferran, 'Examining the UK Experience in Adopting the Single Financial Regulator Model', (2003) 28 *Brooklyn Journal of International Law* 257–307.

move freely in pursuit of profit opportunities; financial conglomerates, sometimes foreign-owned, had begun to emerge. Restrictive rules concerning ownership of, and combination of functions performed by, member firms of the London Stock Exchange had been abandoned; technological developments had begun to impact on the way business was conducted; and the trend towards globalisation was already well under way. That regulation needed to respond to challenges presented by financial deregulation, technological advances, conglomeration and globalisation was recognised at that time; but that the organisation and ownership of financial firms and markets, the nature and complexity of their business and the way they would conduct their operations would change so profoundly in response to the new challenges was beyond the boundaries of general expectations. A few examples may illustrate this point.

In 1983, the major merchant banks and brokers in the United Kingdom were British-owned but by 2000 none of the leading investment banks in the UK markets was home-owned. Instead the market has become dominated by US and Continental European banks. Whereas in the 1980s the London Stock Exchange was a mutual organisation performing significant supervisory functions in the public interest, by 2000 it had become a commercial company competing for business with other exchanges and alternative trading system. It had relinquished many of the regulatory responsibilities that it had previously performed.[2] As recent events have demonstrated, the inviolable British institution that the London Stock Exchange had once seemed to be is now, like any other company with publicly traded shares, at risk of falling into foreign ownership through the operation of the market for corporate control. Whilst in the 1980s computer-based trading systems were just beginning to take the place of face-to-face trading, senior market regulators acknowledge that growth in online trading in Europe and the United States and the provision of information via the internet in the late 1990s have been extraordinary.[3]

---

[2] The role of the national competent authority for matters relating to listing was transferred from the London Stock Exchange to the FSA by the Official Listing of Securities (Change of Competent Authority) Regulations 2000 (SI 2000 No. 968).

[3] Gay Wisbey, Mary L. Schapiro and David Shrimpton, 'The Challenge of Technology – Regulating Electronic Financial Markets' in Eilís Ferran and Charles A. E. Goodhart (eds.), *Regulating Financial Services and Markets in the Twenty First Century* (Oxford, 2001), p. 323.

With the old City 'club' already disappearing[4] it is not surprising that the system of self-regulation within a statutory framework that was enshrined in the Financial Services Act 1986 as the basis for regulating financial services business[5] did not endure. This was not so much because the changing character of the markets had made ineffective regulatory mechanisms traditionally associated with self-regulation, such as 'naming and shaming' or 'ostracism' of those who fail to meet the standards expected by the market: whether an industry is made up of a small number of individuals who are known to each other and who share common values or is a vast global business with all of the cultural mix and anonymity that this entails, reputation still matters. Rather it was that the new business environment created new complexities and, for those willing to sacrifice their reputation, new opportunities for fraud that required a more powerful system of regulation than self-regulation within a statutory framework was able to provide.

An interesting perspective on the inadequacies of the 1986 regulatory regime is provided by Philip Augar in his book *The Death of Gentlemanly Capitalism*.[6] Augar argues that by retaining self-regulation the opportunity was lost to force UK industry to raise its own standards in order to be able to compete effectively with US financial institutions that operated under much tougher regulatory rules. For Augar:

> 'This was a solution born out of the old City . . . Chaps would be trusted to behave under the watchful eye of benign authorities. This had worked reasonably well in the old world of small, well-defined, inter-connecting circles where everyone knew each other and deals were done face-to-face. But it was not appropriate for the more complex structures which characterised modern investment banks, nor for the imminent growth in diversity of products and risks carried.'

Further:

> 'The failure to set up a tough regulator like the SEC [US Securities and Exchange Commission] allowed the brokers to persist with the informal

---

[4] For a sometimes critical description of the 'club' atmosphere of the London Stock Exchange in the first half of the twentieth century see David Kynaston, *The City of London*, vol. III: 'Illusions of Gold 1914–1945' (London, 2000), ch. 11. At p. 296 Kynaston remarks that: 'In a nutshell, whom one knew still mattered more than what one knew.'

[5] Barry A. K. Rider, Charles Abrams and Michael Ashe, *Guide to Financial Services Regulation* (3rd edn, Bicester, 1997), ch. 1; Alan C. Page and Robert B. Ferguson, *Investor Protection* (London, 1992), ch. 6.

[6] Philip Augar, *The Death of Gentlemanly Capitalism*, (London, 2000), p. 46.

controls and the seat of the pants management that were to prove inappropriate to the more complex world they were about to enter. The requirement to meet the kind of detailed reporting and control criteria that are compulsory in the United States might have forced the British firms to develop the structured management systems and risk monitoring systems that would have increased their chances of success.'[7]

Although Augar is primarily concerned with exploring the reasons for the failure of the British merchant banks and brokers, his thesis is consistent with the wider proposition that tough regulation and supervision are a necessary counterbalance to economic deregulation of capital flows and of the functions that participants in a particular market are allowed to perform.[8] The shift towards statutory regulation with an emphasis on effective enforcement is also consistent with the argument that there can be competitive advantages in tough regulation since this can instil market confidence in the safety and soundness of the firms that are subject to the regime.[9]

A clear failing of the old regime was its institutional complexity. The existence of separate regulatory regimes for banking, financial services and insurance and, within financial services regulation, the existence of a significant number of self-regulating agencies with responsibility for different parts of the industry, created inefficiencies and uncertainties for industry and consumers alike. The growth of financial conglomerates that operate across traditional sectoral boundaries and the blurring of distinctions between financial products through secondary market techniques such as securitisation and derivatives trading meant that there was an increasing mismatch between the functionally-structured regulatory framework and the way in which businesses operated in practice.[10] It resulted in multi-function firms having to be authorised by more than one regulatory agency which, despite 'lead regulator' arrangements, could result in regulatory duplication, overlap and gaps. One particular criticism was that the number of agencies that could be involved in the investigation and prosecution of criminal offences resulted in a lack of co-ordination and adversely affected the

---

[7] *Ibid.*, p. 50.

[8] John Braithwaite and Peter Drahos, *Global Business Regulation* (Cambridge, 2000), pp. 128–30.

[9] *Ibid.*, p. 131.

[10] Christopher Nicholls, 'Financial Institutional Reform: Functional Analysis and an Illustrative Look at Deposit Insurance' (1998) 13 *Banking and Finance Law Review* 235.

ability of the authorities to secure convictions.[11] There were also suggestions that the Balkanised structure of financial regulation in the United Kingdom was a source of confusion at the international level and acted as an impediment to the development of transnational consistency and co-ordination in financial regulation.

I. The new regime: an overview

Soon after it came to power in May 1997, the Labour government announced proposals to sweep away the discredited regulatory regimes that applied to the United Kingdom's financial sector and to replace them with a single unified, statutory regime. After a protracted and, at times, stormy passage through the various stages of the legislative process, the FSMA was finally enacted in June 2000.

When FSMA came into force on 1 December 2001, the FSA formally assumed full responsibility for regulating the financial sector and replaced the range of agencies that previously performed regulatory functions. Prior to December 2001 the FSA had already taken charge of financial regulation on a *de facto* basis. In the areas of banking regulation and listing of securities, responsibility has already been formally vested in the FSA by the Bank of England Act 1998 and the Official Listing of Securities (Change of Competent Authority) Regulations 2000 respectively.

The central tenet of FSMA, which is broadly familiar from the predecessor legislation, is that no person may carry on a regulated activity in the United Kingdom except with FSA authorisation or an exemption.[12] It is for the government rather than the FSA itself to define the concept of 'regulated activities' and thus to set the so-called 'perimeter' of the regulatory regime.[13] The primary route to authorisation is for a person to obtain permission from the FSA to carry on the particular regulated activity or activities; a person who holds a FSA permission to carry on one or more regulated activities is an authorised person for the purposes of the Act.[14]   European Economic Area (EEA) firms with

---

[11] Peter Howells and Keith Bain, *Financial Markets and Institutions* (3rd edn, Harlow, 2000).

[12] FSMA, s. 19.

[13] FSMA, s. 22 and schedule 2. The relevant statutory instrument establishing the 'perimeter' is the Financial Services and Markets Act 2000 (Regulated Activities) Order 2001 (SI 2001 No. 544).

[14] FSMA, Pts. III and IV.

passporting rights under the single market directives for insurance companies, banks and investment firms or with Treaty rights are also authorised persons with permission to carry on regulated activities covered by their home state authorisation so long as certain conditions set out in the Act are satisfied.[15] Whilst the opportunity has been taken in the Act to simplify provisions relating to the various passport rights[16] there are no significant substantive changes.

As in the predecessor regime, recognised investment exchanges (RIEs) and recognised clearing houses (RCHs) are exempt from the need for authorisation in respect of their businesses as investment exchanges or, as the case may be, providers of clearing services.[17] The FSA is the single regulator in respect of RIEs and RCHs.

Under FSMA there is a single compensation scheme[18] and a single ombudsman scheme[19] for the whole of the financial industry. These schemes take the place of numerous different schemes under existing banking, insurance, financial services and building societies legislation.

Acquiring, or increasing, control of a FSMA authorised firm is a step that requires FSA approval and the FSA may impose conditions. There is also a requirement to notify the FSA if control is lost or reduced.[20]

II. Regulatory objectives and principles

A novel feature of FSMA is that it sets out regulatory objectives and principles.[21] The FSA is under a duty to discharge its general functions in a way which is compatible with the regulatory objectives[22] and it must have regard to the regulatory principles in discharging those functions.[23] One of the criticisms of the Financial Services Act 1986 was its lack of clarity about the objectives of regulation.[24] The express statement of regulatory objectives in FSMA is intended to meet this concern. The importance of clarity of objectives is emphasised also in international statements of good regulatory practice such as the Basle Core Principles for Effective Banking Supervision and the IOSCO Objectives and Principles of Securities Regulation. In its code of Good Transparency Practices for Financial Policies by Financial Agencies the IMF notes that:

---

[15] FSMA, s. 31 and schedules 3–4.
[16] In respect of both incoming EEA firms and outgoing passports for UK firms.
[17] FSMA, s. 285.   [18] FSMA, Pt. XV.   [19] FSMA, Pt. XVI and schedule 17.
[20] FSMA, Pt. XII.   [21] FSMA, ss. 2(2) and 3–6 (objectives) and s. 2(3) (principles).
[22] FSMA, s. 2(1).   [23] FSMA, s. 2(3).
[24] Peter Howells and Keith Bain, *Financial Markets and Institutions*, above note 11, at 368.

'... specifying these key elements in authorising legislation or regulations gives them particular prominence, and avoids ad hoc and frequent changes to these important aspects of the operations of an agency. Specifying the objectives in legislation or regulation also ensures that the goals of financial policy are codified in the legal framework to which the authorities and the public can readily refer.'

The stated regulatory objectives in FSMA are concerned with: maintaining confidence in the UK financial system; promoting public understanding of the UK financial system; securing the appropriate degree of protection for consumers; and reducing the scope for financial crime. The omission of any explicit references to systemic issues and to the promotion of competition in the statement of regulatory objectives has generated some controversy.

The task of managing systemic risk – widely considered to be the primary concern of banking regulators[25] – can be seen to be part of the objective of maintaining confidence in the United Kingdom's financial system. That the FSA's role with regard to systemic issues is not more clearly stated probably reflects political sensitivities about the relationship between the FSA and the Bank of England. When regulatory responsibilities for banking were transferred from the Bank of England to the FSA by the Bank of England Act 1998, this was accompanied by a memorandum of understanding (MoU) between the Bank of England, Her Majesty's (HM) Treasury and the FSA in which was set out a framework for co-operation between the three of them in the field of financial stability. According to the MoU responsibility for the overall stability of the financial system lies with the Bank of England rather than the FSA. An examination of the politics surrounding the structure established by the MoU suggests that it was a compromise reached in order to prevent the Governor of the Bank of England from resigning after the transfer of supervisory responsibilities for banks to the FSA.[26]

With regard to competition, the UK government resisted calls for the promotion of competition to be made a regulatory objective. Instead, the desirability of facilitating innovation in financial services, the international character of financial services and markets and the desirability of maintaining the United Kingdom's competitive position, the need to

---

[25] E.g., Charles A. E. Goodhart, Philip Hartmann, David Llewellyn, Liliana Rojas-Suárez and Steven Weisbrod, *Financial Regulation* (London, 1998), p. 189.

[26] Andrew Rawnsley, *Servants of the People: The Inside Story of New Labour* (London, 2000), pp. 41–4.

minimise the adverse effects on competition that may arise from exercise of the FSA's general functions and the desirability of facilitating competition between those who are subject to FSA regulation are included in the list of regulatory principles to which the FSA must 'have regard'. Justifications that were put forward for not including the promotion of competition as a regulatory objective are that it could inappropriately draw the FSA into areas of explicit promotion of the City of London and essentially commercial issues; also, that there could be concern overseas about a regulator with a specific competitiveness objective which could impact adversely on efforts to achieve international co-operation and consistency in financial regulation.[27]

But abstracting from a potentially rather arid debate about the drafting of the legislation and the positioning of competition issues as matters to which the FSA must have regard rather than objectives which it must seek to achieve (in fact, as discussed below, whether the FSA's legal obligations with regard to objectives are significantly greater than those with regard to principles is open to doubt because of the way in which its duty to achieve objectives is qualified) whether FSMA has got the balance right between investor protection and competition remains an important and difficult question. For Colin Mayer, the achievement of an appropriate balance between investor protection and competition is key to the creation of a successful regulatory regime for the financial sector. He suggests that FSMA may not have properly addressed this fundamental question and that in the United Kingdom, and elsewhere in Europe, there may inadequate emphasis on using regulation to promote competition and diversity through disclosure, auditing and enforcement.[28]

Turning to the direct legal significance of the regulatory objectives, the Act gives the FSA considerable discretion as to how best to meet the objectives. Its duty to act in a way which is compatible with the objectives and for the purpose of meeting them extends only 'so far as is reasonably possible'. It is for the FSA itself to decide on the 'most appropriate' way in which to meet the objectives. Further, the FSA's obligations with regard to the objectives only arise in relation to its

[27] Joint Committee on Financial Services and Markets, *Draft Financial Services and Markets Bill* First Report, vol. II (HL Paper 50-II, HC 328-II, 1999) Q34 (reply by Davies, Chairman FSA).

[28] Colin Mayer, 'Regulatory Principles and the Financial Services and Markets Act 2000' in Eilís Ferran and Charles A. E. Goodhart (eds.), *Regulating Financial Services and Markets in the Twenty First Century* (Oxford, 2001), p. 25.

'general functions' – its functions in making rules, issuing codes, giving general guidance *considered as a whole* (emphasis added) and its function of determining general policy and principles. This careful drafting ensures that there is no mechanism for challenging individual rules or decisions on the grounds that they are incompatible with the objectives. Although FSA actions can be challenged before the courts through the process of judicial review, the qualified and self-referential nature of the duty regarding the regulatory objectives is likely to hamper the effectiveness of judicial review in practice.

From an economic perspective, the value of the regulatory objectives as they have been drafted in FSMA is also open to question. For example, Goodhart, although supportive of the idea of a statement of regulatory objectives, has suggested that for all practical purposes the statutory objectives as they have been drafted are non-operational because no measurement of success can be achieved in respect of them.[29] Goodhart's argument develops concerns about the 'woolly' nature of the objectives which surfaced during the passage of the legislation through Parliament.

But, before dismissing the FSMA statutory statement of regulatory objectives as high-sounding sentiment about good regulatory practice with little real impact, it should be noted that in numerous public statements senior FSA officials have spoken of the disciplining effect of the statutory objectives and principles. They could hardly say otherwise, but if the perception were to develop that the FSA was simply paying lip-service to its obligations regarding regulatory objectives this could cause serious damage to industry and consumer confidence in the regulatory structure. Public perception has legal significance in the new structure. The FSA is required to include a statement in its annual report about how far it considers it has met the objectives and principles and to present this report at an annual public meeting.[30] This requirement is intended to give the public an opportunity to express its satisfaction or otherwise with how the FSA is doing its job. In this regard, the statutory statement of regulatory objectives may prove in practice to be a helpful benchmark for public accountability. At the international level, the IMF

---

[29] Charles A. E. Goodhart, 'Regulating the Regulator: An Economist's Perspective on Accountability and Control' in Eilís Ferran and Charles A. E. Goodhart (eds.), *Regulating Financial Services and Markets in the Twenty First Century* (Oxford, 2001), p. 151.
[30] FSMA, schedule. 1, paras. 10–11.

has recognised the importance of a statutory statement of objectives with regard to transparency and public accountability:

> 'Giving the objectives a firm basis in legislation or regulation enhances transparency by ensuring that there is some degree of constancy in the objectives, enabling the public to form expectations about financial policy operations and to assess the performance of the institution in achieving its objectives. Similarly, by defining the institutional framework in legislation or regulation, the financial agency responsible for achieving the objectives can be held accountable, as the public is able to compare outcomes to goals.'[31]

III. The FSA as law-maker

FSMA is essentially a framework document. Although a few matters have been reserved for the government to specify by means of secondary legislation (e.g., the perimeter of the regulatory regime discussed earlier), for the most part it is for the FSA to supply the details of the regulatory regime in the exercise of its statutory powers to make rules, issue codes and publish guidance. This is a broadly positive feature of the FSMA regime since delegating law-making power to a regulatory agency should ensure that the regime is more flexible and adaptable to market developments than one that is set out in primary or secondary legislation. However, the FSA not only makes the rules, it also interprets and enforces them. This concentration of power in the hands of the FSA has attracted attention. A particular focus for concern is the market abuse regime which is another of the novel features of the new legislation.

IV. Market abuse[32]

The new market abuse regime is the UK government's attempt to bolster the criminal law in the fight against insider dealing, market manipulation and other types of misconduct affecting the financial markets. Widespread concern about weaknesses in enforcement and in particular the failure of the relevant authorities to secure many convictions for insider dealing, formed the background to the adoption of these new

---

[31] IMF Code of Good Transparency Practices for Financial Policies by Financial Agencies, para. 5.1.
[32] FSMA, Pt. VIII.

powers. The market abuse regime allows the FSA to impose disciplinary sanctions on those who abuse the market. Although certain safeguards have been built into the market abuse regime with a view to ensuring that it complies with the rights to a fair trial protected by human rights legislation, abusing the market contrary to the FSMA regime is not a criminal offence under English law so the full elements of the criminal justice process do not apply. Those who are found guilty of market abuse do not acquire a criminal record and they cannot be sent to prison though they can be ordered to pay a large fine. The market abuse regime is designed to catch a broader range of misconduct than the existing offences of insider dealing and market manipulation, although these are retained – for example a person can be guilty despite the absence of an intention to abuse the market which should make it easier to prove than the criminal offences. The government can issue guidance to the FSA on whether market abuse or criminal proceedings should be brought in circumstances where there is an overlap.[33]

The market abuse regime applies to all persons, not just those who are authorised by the FSA to carry on relevant activities or exempt from the need for authorisation; so the FSA is empowered to take disciplinary action even against persons who are not part of the regulated community. 'Market abuse' is very widely defined.[34] It means, broadly: (a) the misuse of non-public information; (b) conduct which may mislead the market; or (c) conduct likely to distort the market. In relation to each form of conduct, there is a further requirement that the conduct must be likely to be regarded by a regular user of the market as falling below the standards reasonably expected. The 'regular user' test is meant to inject an element of objectivity into the market abuse regime but despite the statutory explanation that it means a reasonable person who regularly deals in investments of the kind in question on the market in question,[35] there remains uncertainty about its precise effect. It is expressly provided that inaction as well as action may amount to market abuse.[36]

The investments and the markets to which the market abuse regime applies are designated by the government.[37] The regime currently applies to all UK's RIEs but it may, when necessary, be extended to other markets. Conduct affecting commodities, to which investments which have been designated by the government ('qualifying

---

[33] FSMA, s. 130.   [34] FSMA, s. 118.   [35] FSMA, s. 118(10).   [36] *Ibid.*
[37] The Financial Services and Markets Act 2000 (Prescribed Markets and Qualifying Investments) Order 2001 (SI 2001 No. 996).

investments') relate or affecting investments which are derivatives of qualifying investments, is caught. But care has been taken not to extend the regime beyond what would generally be regarded as realistic limits: for example the requirement that the conduct should fall below standards reasonably expected should exclude from its scope a strike by copper miners that otherwise could conceivably have been caught as affecting copper futures contracts.

The FSA is not required to prove intention to abuse the market nor even recklessness or negligence as to the abusive effect of the conduct: the focus is on the *effect* of the conduct not on the *intention* that underlies it. But the accused can escape liability to pay a penalty by showing a reasonable belief that the conduct was not market abuse or by demonstrating reasonable precautions and due diligence to avoid market abuse.[38]

The market abuse regime applies to any conduct which takes place in the United Kingdom and also to any abuse (wherever occurring) in relation to qualifying investments which are traded on designated markets situated in the United Kingdom or which are accessible electronically in the United Kingdom.[39] This gives the regime a very broad territorial scope: for example, a derivatives contract entered into in Hong Kong which relates to shares quoted on the London Stock Exchange is capable of constituting market abuse.

The FSA plays an important legislative role because, within the limits of the somewhat vague definition of market abuse set out in FSMA, it must issue a code containing guidance on what is and is not market abuse.[40] There is an absolute safe harbour for conduct which conforms to a provision of the code where the code says expressly that conforming conduct is not market abuse.[41] Otherwise, the code performs an evidential function and may be relied upon so far as it indicates whether or not behaviour should be taken to amount to market abuse.[42] The FSA has provided a number of safe harbours, including ones for conduct complying with certain other regulatory requirements such as the Listing Rules and, importantly, the City Code on Takeovers and Mergers.[43]

---

[38] FSMA, s. 123(2).   [39] FSMA, s. 118(5).

[40] FSMA, s. 119. The FSA has fulfilled this legislative obligation: *FSA Handbook, Code of Market Conduct, MAR* (Release 003, July 2002).

[41] FSMA, s. 122(1).   [42] FSMA, s. 122(2).

[43] Generally, MAR 1.4.20.C, MAR 1.4.21.C, MAR 1.4.24.C, MAR 1.4.26.C, MAR 1.4.28.C, MAR 1.5.24.C, MAR 1.5.25.C, MAR 1.5.27.C, MAR 1.5.28.C and MAR 1.6.19.C.

The relationship between the market abuse regime and the regulation of takeovers was particularly controversial during the period that led up to the enactment of FSMA and its subsequent implementation. Takeovers remain an area that is subject to self-regulation in the United Kingdom in the sense that the regulatory body, the Takeover Panel, for the moment, is neither a statutory body nor does it derive its powers from statute. Unlike in other areas, self-regulation is deemed to work in relation to takeovers, with the ability of the Takeover Panel to interpret the City Code flexibly, quickly and decisively being seen to be particular advantages. The concern that was voiced by the financial services industry and its professional advisers is that if the FSA intervenes to deal with what it perceives to be market abuse during the course of a bid this could disrupt a process that has, hitherto, been seen to operate efficiently and effectively under the exclusive control of the Panel. However, despite pressure, the government resisted calls for the Takeover Panel to be given power to determine conclusively whether conduct during a bid amounted to market abuse. Instead there is express provision in FSMA for the FSA, with government approval, to provide in its code of market conduct when compliance with the City Code will not amount to market abuse.[44]

To assuage concerns about the possible disruption to the conduct of takeover bids, the FSA has stated that it will not, save in exceptional circumstances, seek to use its powers during the course of a bid and will wait until the bid is complete before taking action.[45] The FSA's intention to confine the use of its powers until after the event, unless the circumstances are exceptional, is in line with the approach of the courts in relation to judicial review of takeovers. Although the decisions of the Takeover Panel are susceptible to judicial review, the courts have made it clear that such reviews will normally only be entertained after a bid is complete and that litigation is not available as a tactic to be employed by the parties during the course of a bid.[46]

V. Control, governance and accountability

The preceding discussion about the FSA's powers in relation to market abuse in takeover situations provides a convenient specific illustration of an issue that has general significance: FSMA vests very wide powers in

---

[44] FSMA, s. 120.   [45] *FSA Handbook ENF*, para. 14.9.2.
[46] *R v. Panel on Take-overs and Mergers, Ex parte Datafin and Another* [1987] QB 815.

the FSA and gives it considerable discretion about how it exercises those powers. There is an obvious correlation between the amount of power vested in an institution and the importance attached to the checks and balances to which that institution is subject in the exercise of its powers. Accordingly it is not surprising that debate about how best to control the FSA in the exercise of its powers has been centre-stage in the discussions about the new structure.

The FSA is subject to a number of essentially procedural controls with regard to the exercise of its powers. It must engage in public consultation exercises before exercising its powers to make rules or codes; when rules and codes are published in draft form they must be accompanied by a cost benefit analysis.[47] The FSA must publish statements of policy regarding the use of its disciplinary powers;[48] and, again, before such policy statements are finalised there must be a public consultation exercise.[49] There is also a general obligation on the FSA to establish and maintain arrangements for consultation with consumers and practitioners.[50] This gives statutory backing to the arrangements which previously operated on a *de facto* basis whereby the FSA consulted with a consumer panel and a practitioner panel.

Certain of the steps that the FSA must follow in exercising its disciplinary powers are spelt out in the legislation.[51]

The FSA is subject to the scrutiny of the competition authorities in the exercise of its rule-making powers.[52]

As between the FSA and government, the relevant department, HM Treasury, exerts control over appointments to its board,[53] can order independent reviews of its financial affairs[54] and can commission independent inquiries into regulatory failures.[55] However, the Treasury cannot intervene directly in the FSA's affairs save in very limited circumstances concerned with competition.[56] The Treasury is the primary

---

[47] FSMA, ss. 65 (statements and codes relating to approved persons), 121 (market abuse), 155 (rules applicable to authorised firms).

[48] FSMA, ss. 69 (approved persons), 93 (listing), 124 (market abuse), 210 (disciplinary powers).

[49] FSMA, ss. 70 (approved persons), 94 (listing), 125 (market abuse), 211 (disciplinary powers).

[50] FSMA, ss. 8–9.

[51] FSMA, ss. 67–8 (approved persons), 92 (listing), 126–7 (market abuse), 207–9 (disciplinary powers).

[52] FSMA, Pt. X, ch. III.   [53] FSMA, s. 1 and schedule. 1.   [54] FSMA, s. 12.

[55] FSMA, s. 14.   [56] FSMA, s. 308.

party to which the FSA must give an account of how it has conducted its affairs (below).

A slightly odd control provision is a requirement for the FSA to have regard to generally accepted principles of good corporate governance.[57] This provision was inserted into the legislation in response to criticism about the absence of divided responsibility at the head of the FSA where, as presently structured, Sir Howard Davies acts as both chairman and chief executive. Although the FSA is technically a company, it is questionable how far principles of corporate governance that were developed in relation to commercial companies should properly be regarded as applicable to it. But, in any case, the controlling effect of this requirement is muted because the FSA is only required to have regard to such principles as it is reasonable to regard as being applicable to it.

The FSA is accountable to a range of interested parties in the sense of having to explain how it has conducted its affairs.[58] It must make an annual report to the Treasury[59] and, as discussed earlier, that annual report must then be presented to the public at a meeting convened for that purpose. The Treasury must put the FSA's report before Parliament and by this indirect route there is parliamentary accountability. FSA officials can also be ordered to appear before a parliamentary select committee in accordance with the usual procedures of the Houses of Parliament. According to the IMF code of Good Transparency Practices for Financial Policies by Financial Agencies appearances by financial agency officials before a designated public authority, such as a parliamentary committee, promote accountability, especially when the agencies are granted a high degree of autonomy. But the IMF's confidence in the effectiveness of the scrutiny provided by parliamentary committees is not universally shared.[60]

Judicial accountability is provided through judicial review (though note earlier comments about how effective this form of control is likely to be), through the ability to refer FSA decisions to an independent

---

[57] FSMA, s. 8.

[58] The importance of regulatory accountability is clearly recognised at the international level. According to the IOSCO Objectives and Principles of Securities Regulation: 'The regulator should be operationally independent and accountable in the exercise of its functions and powers.'

[59] FSMA, s. 1 and schedule 1. The Treasury can direct the FSA with regard to the contents of the report.

[60] A. Page, 'Regulating the Regulator: A Lawyer's Perspective on Accountability and Control' in Eilís Ferran and Charles A. E. Goodhart (eds.), *Regulating Financial Services and Markets in the Twenty First Century* (Oxford, 2001), p. 127.

Financial Services and Markets Tribunal[61] and through the possibility of challenge under the Human Rights Act 1998 whereby the European Convention on Human Rights is given effect in UK law. However, save for a few limited exceptions, the FSA and its officials enjoy statutory immunity from damages claims. This immunity is, to an extent,[62] counterbalanced by an independent complaints scheme for dealing with complaints against the FSA. If a complaint is made out, the investigator can recommend that the FSA make a compensatory payment though he cannot order it to do so.

It has been claimed that the 'prime accountability route' is through Ministers to Parliament[63] but some commentators have doubted how effective this traditional type of accountability will be in relation to the FSA. The central feature of the FSMA structure is that the FSA is an independent body. This carefully-established independence will give Treasury Ministers a shield to stand behind if or when hard questions are asked in Parliament about FSA actions or failures. Whether public accountability will prove to be a more powerful mechanism is for the moment a matter for conjecture though the fact that much of the work done by the FSA is confidential will inevitably limit the role of public disclosure as an accountability mechanism.

VI. Conclusion

As it prepared for the formal assumption of its new powers in the period leading up to the implementation of the new statutory regime under FSMA, the FSA was at pains to strike all the right notes in terms of current thinking about good regulatory practice.[64] Consumers must be protected but they must also take responsibility for their own interests and will be assisted in this by the FSA's efforts in ensuring that information is made available to them and in improving consumer understanding of the risks and opportunities involved in investment markets. Whilst preserving confidence in the markets is vital, this does not imply 'zero failure'. The FSA will operate according to a transparent

---

[61] FSMA, Pt. IX.

[62] See further, Eilís Ferran, 'FSA Accountability and the Role of Statutory Immunity' (2000) 1(3) *Financial Services Bulletin* 9.

[63] Joint Committee on Financial Services and Markets, *Draft Financial Services and Markets Bill* First Report, vol. II (HL Paper 50-II, HC 328-II, 1999) Q2 (reply by Davies, Chairman FSA).

[64] See, e.g., FSA *A New Regulator for the New Millennium* (January 2000).

framework based on risk identification, assessment and prioritisation, make sensitive use of the full regulatory 'tool kit' available to it under the new legislation, devote resources towards proactive intervention to prevent problems causing significant damage rather than to post-event reaction and create incentives for firms to manage their own risks better and thereby reduce the burden of regulation. The FSA intends to play an active role in international regulation which it sees will secure benefits in information sharing, in understanding risks and in promoting best practice. The internet, which both empowers consumers through global competition in the provision of financial information and investment opportunities and at the same time presents them with new risks, is likely to drive the FSA towards ever closer co-operation with equivalent regulatory authorities elsewhere since it is a mechanism that operates without territorial boundaries.[65] Overall, the FSA's projection is that regulated businesses are likely to see a net reduction in overall routine supervisory activity but that supervisory efforts in relation to specific identified risks across categories of firms (thematic regulation) is likely to increase.

One clear challenge facing the FSA is whether it will be able to discharge the huge responsibilities that have been vested in it with a relatively small number of staff and with the pressures for cost efficiencies to which it is subject – the FSA does not receive government financial assistance and is funded entirely by industry levies. The FSA aims to provide a tough but fair regulatory regime but whether it will be able to attract and (given competitive pressures) retain staff with the ability, experience and expertise to deliver the quality of governance and service that it expects of the firms which it regulates is a key and, as yet, uncertain issue. During the 1980s and 1990s there was often critical commentary about the quality of the staff working for regulatory bodies in the United Kingdom and the report of the inspectors appointed by the UK government to investigate the collapse of Robert Maxwell's empire which was published in April 2001 identified staffing of regulatory bodies as an aspect of regulation in the United Kingdom that still caused some concern. The inspectors recommended that: 'City firms and institutions should do as much as possible to see secondment to a regulator

---

[65] *The Transformation of Financial Services Regulation: Facing up to Markets Without Borders* 2000 Global Internet Summit, George Mason University Monday 13 March 2000 (available via FSA website: www.fsa.gov.uk).

as an important step in the career of their most able employees.'[66]
According to the Maxwell report the incentive for City firms to participate in such secondment programmes is that it is in their general
interests for regulatory bodies to obtain staff who have 'relevant experience of current market practices'.[67] However, high-flying, ambitious
individuals will be unwilling to be sent on secondment and so out of
direct contact with clients and the markets unless they can see clear
career advantages. Current UK practice does not, thus far, fit into what is
sometimes described as the 'SEC model' whereby 'bright young lawyers
know that having worked for the SEC on their *curriculum vitae* they have
a good chance of an illustrious career later in life.'[68] How successful the
FSA will be in achieving the cultural shift involved in it 'becom[ing] part
of a successful career in financial services to spend some time within a
regulatory authority'[69] is something that will only emerge over time.

---

[66] *Mirror Group Newspapers plc. Investigations under Sections 432(2) and 442 of the Companies Act 1985* (London, 2001), paras. 23.42–23.43.

[67] *Ibid.*

[68] Joint Committee on Financial Services and Markets, *Draft Financial Services and Markets Bill* First Report, vol. II (HL Paper 50-II, HC 328-II, 1999) Q98 (question by Lord Eatwell).

[69] Joint Committee on Financial Services and Markets, *Draft Financial Services and Markets Bill* First Report, vol. II (HL Paper 50-II, HC 328-II, 1999) Q98 (reply by Patricia Hewitt, Economic Secretary to HM Treasury).

3

The liberalisation of financial markets: the regulatory response in Germany

RAINER GROTE

I. Introduction

Financial market regulation in Germany has been subject to profound changes during the last decade. The far-reaching reform measures, which have resulted so far in the enactment of four Financial Market Promotion Acts,[1] were introduced with the aim of preserving the attractiveness of the domestic capital market in the era of globalisation of investment and finance. Driven by renewed efforts at the European level to create an integrated European capital market, the reforms have sought to bring the German law into line with the relevant EU market directives and to create the institutional framework necessary for an effective market supervision.[2] The recently enacted Law on the establishment of an integrated financial services supervision[3] has created a unified institutional structure in the supervision of the market activities of financial firms by merging the three main regulatory bodies which had previously existed – the Federal Banking Supervisory Office, the Federal

---

[1] Gesetz zur Verbesserung der Rahmenbedingungen der Finanzmärkte (Finanzmarktförderungsgesetz) vom 22 Februar 1990 (First Financial Market Promotion Act of 22 February 1990), BGBl. I, 266; Zweites Finanzmarktförderungsgesetz vom 26 Juli 1994 (Second Financial Market Promotion Act of 26 July 1994), BGBl. I, 1749; Drittes Finanzmarktförderungsgesetz vom 24 März 1998 (Third Financial Market Promotion Act of 24 March 1998), BGBl. I, 529; Gesetz zur weiteren Fortentwicklung des Finanzplatzes Deutschland (Viertes Finanzmarktförderungsgesetz) vom 21 Juni 2002 (Fourth Financial Market Promotion Act of 21 June 2002), BGBl. I, 2010.

[2] On the conservative approach to regulation of the financial service sector which had prevailed in Germany until the end of 1980s see Martin Weber, 'Deutsches Kapitalmarktrecht im Umbruch' (1994) 47 *Neue Juristische Wochenschrift* 2849 at 2850.

[3] Gesetz über die integrierte Finanzdienstleistungsaufsicht vom 22 April 2002 (Law on the establishment of an integrated financial services supervision of 22 April 2002), BGBl. I, 1310.

Insurance Supervisory Office and the Federal Securities Supervisory Office – into a single body, the Federal Financial Supervisory Authority (Bundesanstalt für Finanzdienstleistungsaufsicht – FFSA). It did not create, however, a unified regulatory framework for the financial services industry as a whole.[4] The substantive law of market regulation still consists of several regulatory regimes which reflect the basic distinction between the banking, insurance and securities sectors. The relevant regulatory concepts are laid down in the Banking Act (Gesetz über das Kreditwesen), the Insurance Supervision Law (Gesetz über die Versicherungsaufsicht) and the Securities Trading Act (Wertpapierhandelsgesetz) respectively.

II. Basic structure of financial market regulation in Germany

Insurance products have historically been among the first financial services which were regulated by statute. The (Federal) Law on the Supervision of Insurance Undertakings was first enacted in 1901. The primary goal of the regulation was then, as it is now, the protection of the insured against risks resulting from reckless or fraudulent business practices.[5] For this purpose, the state does not only exercise a general legal supervision, but also a specific financial supervision. Whereas the objective of legal supervision is the proper operation of insurance business, including the observance of the relevant provisions concerning the insurance contracts and the insured, the financial supervision shall ensure that the liabilities under the insurance contracts may be fulfilled at any time and the insurance companies dispose of an adequate solvency.[6] Insurance companies may not carry on business unless they are authorised to do so by the supervisory authority. In order to obtain the authorisation, they have to submit, with their application, the so-called operating plan which discloses the purpose and organisation of their undertaking as well as the area of intended business operations and states the conditions which make sure that the future liabilities of the undertaking can be met permanently.[7] An important feature of insurance supervision under German law is the principle that undertakings

---

[4] Critical in this regard are Julius Reiter and Jörg Geerlings, 'Die Reform der Bankenaufsicht – Eine Chance für den Verbraucherschutz?' (2002) 55 *Die Öffentliche Verwaltung* 562 at 566–7.

[5] Michael Tigges, *Geschichte und Entwicklung der Versicherungsaufsicht* (Karlsruhe, 1985), pp. 81–2.

[6] Insurance Supervision Law, § 81(1).   [7] Insurance Supervision Law, § 5.

which offer life insurance or health insurance are not allowed to carry on other classes of insurance business. In view of the fundamental importance of life and health insurance for the social security of large parts of the population, the principle of separation between different classes of insurance (Spartentrennung) is meant to prevent the funds accumulated for life and health insurance purposes from being used to cover the losses incurred in other parts of the insurance business.[8]

The introduction of a comprehensive system of banking supervision, on the other hand, was a direct reaction to the deep crisis of the banking sector triggered by the Great Depression in the early 1930s. Until then, commercial banking had only been subject to scant regulation.[9] In the wake of the efforts to establish a comprehensive statutory framework for financial market supervision the scope of the Banking Act has been extended to institutions which specialise in certain financial services like investment broking or portfolio management but do not conduct any deposit or lending business.[10] The main goal of the regulatory regime for the banking sector, however, remains essentially the same. Unlike insurance supervision, banking supervision is not so much concerned with the business practice of individual banks than with the stability of the banking system as a whole.[11] According to section 6(3) of the Federal Banking Act, state supervision shall counteract undesirable developments in the banking and financial services sector which may endanger the safety of the assets entrusted to institutions, impair the proper conduct of banking business or provision of financial services or involve serious disadvantages for the national economy. Thus the primary goal of banking supervision is not the protection of individual bank customers but the preservation of the stability of the financial system as a whole. This has important consequences for the way in which banking surveillance is carried out in practice. The Supervisory Authority is under no obligation to inform the public about the results of its control activities or about the doubts which it may harbour with regard to the ability of certain banks to fulfil their obligations.[12]

In order to preserve the stability of the financial system, the law imposes a series of requirements on the banks concerning their funding

---

[8] Reimer Schmidt, in Erich R. Prölss, *Versicherungsaufsichtsgesetz*, (11th edn, Munich, 1997), § 8, para. 27.
[9] Reiter and Geerlings, 'Reform der Bankenaufsicht', above note 4, at 563.
[10] See § 1(a) of the Banking Act.
[11] Schmidt, above note 8, Vorbem. (preliminary remarks) para. 140.
[12] Reiter and Geerlings, 'Reform der Bankenaufsicht', above note 4, at 568.

and liquidity. Anyone wishing to conduct banking business or to provide financial services as defined in the Act must obtain a written licence from the Banking Supervisory Office. The licence will be refused if, among other things, the resources needed for business operations, in particular adequate initial capital, are not available in Germany.[13] In addition, banks and credit institutions must have adequate funds in order to meet their obligations to their creditors and to safeguard the assets entrusted to them.[14] They are obliged to invest their funds in such a way as to ensure that adequate liquidity for payment purposes is available at all times.[15] Moreover, the Banking Act tries to limit the exposure of banks and credit institutions to individual borrowers through elaborate notification and approval requirements.[16]

The most important piece of legislation with regard to the regulation of financial services, however, is the Securities Trading Act. The Act responds to the profound transformation of the financial markets in the last two decades as a result of the deregulation of cross-border capital flows and the introduction of new information and trading systems based on the advances of communications technology. It brings German law, which had previously left the regulation of securities trading largely to the stock exchanges, into line with the prevailing international standards of centralised market regulation. Enacted in 1994, the Act has already been subject to several major reforms over the past few years[17] which highlight the considerable difficulties associated with the creation of a stable yet flexible regulatory framework in rapidly changing and highly dynamic markets. The Act seeks to protect the investors' confidence in the integrity of the financial market by increasing market transparency and eliminating certain harmful practices.[18] Its application is not limited to investment services in relation to securities but extends to the

---

[13] Federal Banking Act, §§ 32, 33. [14] Federal Banking Act, § 10.
[15] Federal Banking Act, § 11. [16] Federal Banking Act, §§ 13–15.
[17] Whereas the first reform in 1997 considerably extended the scope of the Act, the second in 1998 gave the Federal Supervisory Authority additional powers in the surveillance of market operations; the third reform of 2002 tightened the rules on the manipulation of exchange and market prices with regard to statements concerning facts which are relevant for the evaluation of securities. For details of the two initial reforms see Heinz-Dieter Assmann in Heinz-Dieter Assmann and Uwe Schneider, *Wertpapierhandelsgesetz – Kommentar* (2nd edn, Cologne, 1999), Einl. (introduction), paras. 32–43.
[18] Explanatory note of the Federal Government on its draft project for a Second Financial Market Promotion Act, BT-Drucks. 12/6679, 33–4.

trade in money-market instruments and derivatives.[19] A central feature of the Act is the creation of a federal market surveillance authority which acts as the watchdog of the securities trade at the federal level. The federal authority – which has become the FFSA under the new law on the creation of an integrated financial services supervision (see section I. above) – tops a three-tiered surveillance system which includes the stock exchange supervisory authorities at the state level and the disciplinary bodies of the various stock exchanges. At the same time, the Act contains a number of provisions on the co-operation of the FFSA with foreign institutions which respond to the increasing need for cross-border surveillance of securities transactions (see section V. below). The mission of the FFSA under the Act is formulated in fairly broad terms: it shall use its powers 'to counteract undesirable developments in securities trading which my adversely affect the orderly conduct of securities trading or provision of investment services or which may result in serious disadvantages for the securities market'.[20]

To ensure the proper functioning of the market, the Act imposes a number of obligations on the market participants. They consist mainly of reporting and disclosure requirements. In order to enable the FFSA to exercise its supervisory powers, credit and financial services institutions are required to report any transaction in securities or derivatives which are admitted to trading on an organised market in the European Union or are traded on the free market of a German stock exchange.[21] More specific are those disclosure requirements which concern the immediate publication of price-sensitive information by issuers of securities and the notification of changes in the voting rights of listed companies which cross certain thresholds fixed by the law.[22] In addition, the Act prohibits the use of insider information for the acquisition or disposal of insider securities and their unauthorised disclosure to third persons.[23] The rules against the manipulation of exchange and market prices have been further tightened by the Fourth Financial Markets Promotion Act which prohibits the delivery of incorrect statements about facts that are relevant to the evaluation of securities, such as the profits or sales generated by a company. It is also forbidden to spread rumours or to carry out transactions with the aim of exerting illegal influence on the market or exchange price.[24]

---

[19] Securities Trading Act, § 1.   [20] Securities Trading Act, § 4(1).
[21] Securities Trading Act, § 9.   [22] Securities Trading Act, §§ 15, 21 et seq.
[23] Securities Trading Act, §§ 12–14.   [24] Securities Trading Act, § 20a.

The final part of the Act contains a code of conduct for investment services designed to eliminate certain business practices deemed to be harmful to investors' interests.[25] These include a general rule of conduct for investment firms to provide investment services with the requisite degree of expertise, care and conscientiousness and to avoid conflicts of interests or, if that is not possible, to minimise their negative impact on customers' interests. In addition, brokers have to respect a number of special rules of conduct. Among other things, they may not advise customers to purchase or sell securities if such advice is not in conformity with the customers' interest or motivated by the desire to cause prices movements which favour the brokers' own interests.[26]

III. Powers of FFSA

As has already been noted in the introduction, the recent establishment of an integrated financial services supervision authority was not accompanied by the emergence of a single reglatory regime for the financial market as a whole. The basic distinction between the banking, insurance and financial services sectors has been preserved. These sectors continue to be regulated on the basis of the respective statutes enacted for that purpose by the legislature. The powers which had hitherto been assigned to different regulatory bodies under the Banking Act, the Insurance Supervision Law and the Securities Trading Act have been transferred to the new Financial Supervisory Authority. The internal structure of the new authority, however, reflects the traditional distinction, with separate departments being responsible for the regulation of the different market sectors.[27] In exercising their powers, they have to take into account the regulatory goals relevant for their respective field of competence. Although overlapping in some respects, these goals are not identical. While insurance supervision is primarily concerned with the protection of consumers, banking surveillance remains focused on the stability of the financial system as a whole (see section II. above). On

---

[25] The rules of conduct which implement Arts. 10 and 11 of the EC Financial Services Directive 1993 (Council Directive 93/22/EEC of 10 May 1993 on investment services in the securities field, OJ 1993 No. L 141/27, 11 June 1993) had not been part of the government's draft bill. They were only included at the committee stage on recommendation of the finance committee, see Assmann, above note 17, Einl. (introduction), para. 17.

[26] Securities Trading Act, §§ 31, 32.

[27] See § 6(3) of the law on the creation of an integrated financial services supervision.

the other hand, the distinction between banking supervision and market surveillance under the Securities Trading Act has become more difficult since financial services institutions have been made subject to supervision under the Banking Act. The transparency and proper functioning of the securities markets protected by the Securities Trading Act is also an essential condition for the stability of the financial system as a whole, which is at the heart of banking regulation. The distinction between the powers of the FFSA under the Banking Act and those exercised on the basis of the Securities Trading Act is therefore a predominantly practical one: the powers of the FFSA under the Banking Act refer to the licencing of banks and financial services institutions and the continuing control of their general financial situation including their liquidity, whereas the supervision of specific operations of credit and financial services institutions in the markets is subject to the surveillance exercised under the Securities Trading Act.[28]

The powers of the Financial Supervisory Authority can be divided into two main categories. To the first group belong those competences which it exercises with regard to individual persons and firms operating in the market under its surveillance. The second category consists of the rule-making powers of the authority in the wide sense, that is, its power to fix general rules of conduct and business standards which have to be observed by all market participants. The powers of the first category are those which traditionally belong to administrative authorities policing the conduct of individual firms and businesses in the exercise of their trade. They include licensing powers which allow the supervisory authority to exercise some form of preventive control over potential market participants in order to keep unreliable individuals and firms off the market. In this sense, insurance undertakings as well as banks or providers of financial services may not carry on business unless authorised to do so by the supervisory authority.[29] In order to obtain the licence, the applicant must submit all relevant information which the supervisory authority needs in order to assess whether the proposed business will be conducted in accordance with the requirements of the law. If the applicant is not in a position to make the financial and organisational arrangements necessary for the proper operation of the business, the licence will be refused. Otherwise the licence has to be

---

[28] Georg Dreyling in Assmann and Schneider, *Wertpapierhandelsgesetz*, above note 17, at § 6, para. 4.
[29] Banking Act § 32; Insurance Supervision Law, § 5.

granted since the applicant has a constitutional right to exercise his freely chosen trade or profession which may only be limited to the extent necessary for the effective protection of prevailing public interests. However, the FFSA may make the granting of the licence subject to conditions if these are consistent with the purpose of the statutory requirements.[30]

The other administrative powers relate to the continued surveillance of the compliance of firms already operating in the market with the standards set by the law. By section 6(3) of the Federal Banking Act the FFSA is empowered, in general terms, to issue instructions to the bank and its managers 'that are appropriate and necessary to prevent or overcome undesirable developments at the institution which could endanger the safety of the assets entrusted to the institution or could impair the proper conduct of its banking business or provision of financial services.'[31] In similar vein, section 4(1) of the Securities Trading Act authorises the supervisory authority 'to issue orders designed and necessary to eliminate or to prevent such undesirable developments' (i.e. developments that may adversely affect the orderly conduct of securities trading or result in serious disadvantages for the securities market). The relevant powers include the powers needed for the proper investigation of alleged misconduct as well as (limited) powers to sanction actual breaches of the law. In order to investigate claims of business malpractice the FFSA can require the undertaking to furnish the necessary information and to submit the relevant documents;[32] it may also enter during business hours the property and business premises of the enterprise,[33] search the premises and seize items which could be of importance as evidence in its investigations.[34] If a violation of the law is confirmed, the enterprise may be fined.[35] The FFSA cannot impose criminal sanctions, however. The prosecution of business practices which constitute a criminal offence has to be left to the public attorneys and to the courts.[36] If the infringement is of a certain gravity, it may also

---

[30] Banking Act, § 32(2).
[31] See also § 81(2) of the Insurance Supervision Law: 'The supervisory authority may with respect to the undertakings, the members of their board of directors and other managers or directors, or controllers take any orders which are appropriate and necessary to prevent or remedy any irregularities.'
[32] Securities Trading Act, §§ 16(2), 29(1); Insurance Supervision Law, § 83.
[33] Securities Trading Act, § 16(3); Insurance Supervision Law, § 83.
[34] Banking Act, § 44c(3), (4).
[35] Securities Trading Act, § 39; Banking Act, § 56; Insurance Supervision Law, § 93.
[36] See §§ 38, 40a of the Securities Trading Act; § 60a of the Banking Act.

lead to the revocation of the business licence.[37] Both under the Securities Trading Act and the Banking Act the FFSA has the power to prohibit misleading advertising practices.[38] Under the Banking Act and the Insurance Supervision Law the powers of the Authority extend to direct intervention in the management of the bank or insurance company, if such intervention is necessary to avert the danger of an insolvency. In these circumstances, the FFSA may issue instructions to the managers of the institution, prohibit directors and managers from continuing in the exercise of their functions[39] or issue a (temporary) ban on payments by the institution.[40]

The FFSA not only has functions of a purely administrative nature, it has also an important regulatory role to play. Its regulatory functions, however, have to be seen in the general context of the German regulatory culture. This culture is strongly influenced by the requirements of constitutional law. The German constitution, unlike other constitutions, does not only grant Parliament the right to legislate on (almost) any matter it views as suitable for legislative intervention. It has also been interpreted, by the Federal Constitutional Court, as requiring the legislature to determine all 'essential questions' by statute. 'Essential questions' are primarily – but not exclusively – those which concern the implementation of fundamental rights.[41] Since the rules governing the conduct of banks, insurance companies and providers of financial services constitute the legal framework for the exercise of important constitutional rights in the economic sphere like the freedom of profession, the right to property or the freedom of contract, it would seem that statutory rules are bound to play an important role in the regulation of capital markets in Germany. The detailed and often very complex legislation which has been enacted in the fields of banking and insurance regulation, and finally with regard to the surveillance of securities markets, confirms this assumption.

It is a fact, though, that however detailed the statutory rules may be, they can only provide a framework for the exercise of the market supervision which must necessarily retain a certain degree of flexibility in order to be able to adapt to the permanently changing structures and

---

[37] Banking Act, § 35(2); Insurance Supervision Law, § 87.
[38] Securities Trading Act, § 36b(1); Banking Act, § 23(1).
[39] Banking Act, § 46; Insurance Supervision Law, § 87(6).
[40] Banking Act, § 46a; Insurance Supervision Law, § 89.
[41] BVerfGE 47, 46(78); 49, 89(126).

practices of the markets concerned. This flexibility can be achieved in
two different ways: by granting the executive branch of government
broad powers which enable it to regulate the manner in which the
surveillance shall be carried out more closely; or by using widely framed
concepts in the description of the regulatory goals which shall be pursued by the supervisory authority. Both regulatory techniques can be
used alternatively. This is what the German legislature has done with
regard to financial market regulation. The Securities Trading Act and
the Banking Act provide various examples for the transfer of rule-
making powers on the executive. The Securities Trading Act authorises
the Federal Ministry of Finance, among other things, to issue regulations
on the content, nature, scope and form of the reports on transactions in
securities which have to be submitted to the FFSA by the credit and
financial services institutions.[42] Under the Federal Banking Act, the
Ministry of Finance may, in agreement with the Federal Ministry of
Justice and after consultation of the Bundesbank, issue by regulation
detailed provisions on the legally prescribed audit of the accounts of
banks and credit institutions concerning its object, the time at which is
carried out and the contents of the auditor's reports, insofar as this is
necessary for the performance of the functions of the FFSA.[43] The
relevant legislation permits the delegation of these rule-making powers
to the FFSA.[44] To a large extent, the Ministry of Finance has made use of
this possibility.[45] Regulations issued by the FFSA under the Securities
Trading Act include the Ordinance on the Reporting Requirements
Relating to Trades in Securities and Derivatives and the Ordinance on
the Examination of Investment Services Enterprises pursuant to section 36
of the Act.[46] As statutory instruments the regulations have legally binding force; they are published in the Federal Law Gazette.

The regulations have to be distinguished from the 'guidelines' or
'principles' which the FFSA may establish under the relevant statutory
legislation in order to determine how it will apply its supervisory powers
in certain areas. The existence of these guidelines reflects the impos-
sibility for the legislature to determine the criteria which may be relevant

---

[42] Securities Trading Act, § 9(3).   [43] Banking Act, § 29(4).
[44] E.g. Securities Trading Act, §§ 9(4), 36(5); Banking Act, §§ 29(4), 31(1).
[45] See the Regulation of 16 March 1995 on the delegation of the authority to make
regulations under the Securities Trading Act to the Federal Securities Supervisory
Office, BGBl. I, 390.
[46] The Ordinances can be found on the website of the Federal Financial Supervisory
Authority, http://www.bafin.de.

to an effective market surveillance in a rigid and exhaustive way. These criteria must be formulated in such a way as to allow for their flexible application in view of the developing market practices. The principle of legal security, on the other hand, requires that market participants can reasonably foresee how supervisory powers directly affecting the operation of their businesses will be used in practice. In this situation, the formulation of 'guidelines' or 'principles' by the competent supervisory body can be a valuable instrument in reconciling the conflicting goals of flexibility and legal security. In the regulation of financial markets in Germany this device is used notably with regard to the application of the rules of conduct for financial services enterprises contained in the Securities Trading Act. These rules, which require the investment firms to provide their services with the requisite degree of expertise and not to act contrary to the interests of their customers, are based on a number of loosely framed concepts like 'requisite degree of care', 'due regard to customers' interest', 'proper conduct of the investment service' etc. In order to provide at least a minimum degree of legal certainty, section 36(6) of the Securities Trading Act authorises the Finncial Supervisory Authority to establish guidelines which it shall use 'in normal cases' to judge whether the requirements laid down in the statutory rules of conduct have been met. The guidelines shall be published in the Federal Official Gazette.

A similar regulatory technique is used in the Federal Banking Act. As has been explained in the previous section, the core requirements of this legislation concern the own funds of the banks and their liquidity. The law does not define by itself what 'adequate own funds' and 'adequate liquidity' is supposed to mean. The adequacy of a bank's solvency depend on its size, the kind of business operations it is conducting, the structure of the market and a variety of other factors which are changing permanently and do not lend themselves easily to statutory definition. The Banking Act therefore authorises the Financial Supervisory Authority to draw up 'Principles' by which it assesses 'in the normal case' whether an institution's own funds and liquidity are adequate within the meaning of the law. Like the 'guidelines' under the Securities Trading Act, the 'Principles' are published in the Federal Official Gazette.[47]

With the publication of 'guidelines' and 'principles' the FFSA imposes of its own accord limits on the future exercise of its supervisory

---

[47] Banking Act, §§ 10(1), 11.

powers. This does not mean, however, that the rules referred to as 'guidelines' or 'principles' in the empowering provisions of the Securities Trading Act and the Banking Act have legally binding force. On the contrary, it is generally admitted that the courts are not bound by the interpretation given by the Supervisory Authority to the terms of the law in its 'guidelines' when they have to determine whether the relevant statutory requirements have indeed been met by the market participants. Nevertheless they are of legal significance insofar as they contain a statement on the future policy of the supervisory authority with regard to certain of its powers which is likely to influence the business practice of firms operating in that particular area. Their trust in the policies announced by the authority has to be protected in the interest of the proper functioning of the markets. The supervisory authority may therefore only deviate from its declared policy if it can show that the case before it does not fit into the category of 'normal cases' and therefore requires special treatment. Any deviation from the 'guidelines' or 'principles' which cannot be justified in this way will normally constitute a violation of the constitutional principle of equality.[48]

IV. Control of the FFSA

In the exercise of its regulatory and administrative powers, the FFSA is subject to a number of important 'checks and balances'. The first of these checks results from the position of the FFSA within the hierarchical structure of the federal administration. The FFSA is a federal agency with distinct legal personality, but subject to the legal and administrative supervision by the Federal Ministry of Finance.[49] The Ministry thus is entitled to issue instructions to the FFSA with regard to the use of its supervisory powers. At the same time, the FFSA is fully integrated into the system of parliamentary control by way of its subordination to the Ministry.

Moreover, the FFSA is required to co-operate closely with the German Central Bank (Bundesbank) in the exercise of its powers. This is of particular importance with respect to its responsibility for the maintenance of the stability of the financial system, since the stability

---

[48] See Frank Schäfer, in: Frank Schäfer and Stephan Geibel (eds.), *Wertpapierhandelsgesetz, Börsengesetz, Verkaufsprospektgesetz* (Stuttgart, 1999), WpHG, § 31 preliminary remarks, para. 6.

[49] Law on the Integrated Financial Services Supervision, §§ 1, 2.

of the financial system and the stability of the currency, which the Bundesbank has to protect as part of its brief within the European System of Central Banks, are closely interrelated.[50] The information collected by the Bundesbank and its branch offices in the different parts of the country on the financial situation of banks and credit institutions helps the FFSA in the assessment of the solvency of banks and thus facilitates its mission to ensure the stability of the financial system. For this reason section 7 of the Federal Banking Act explicitly obliges both institutions to work together and to communicate to each other any observations and findings which are necessary for the performance of their respective functions. The consent of the Bundesbank is needed when it comes to drawing up the principles which are used by the FFSA to assess whether the own funds and the liquidity of a bank are adequate.[51] The Bundesbank has to be consulted before the FFSA issues guidelines under section 35(6) of the Securities Trading Act (see section III above) although in this case its agreement is not required. Moreover, the Law on the Integrated Financial Services Supervision has created a Forum for Financial Services Supervision in which both the FFSA and the Bundesbank are represented. The Forum has the task of co-ordinating the co-operation between the FFSA and the Bundesbank.

The system of 'checks and balances' in the area of financial market regulation also has a federal dimension. Although the centralisation of regulatory powers at the federal level had been achieved in the banking and insurance sector early on, the same did not apply to the trade in securities. It is only with the enactment of the Securities Trading Act 1994 that a strong federal authority has been established in this area. Its creation left the existing supervisory mechanisms at the state and regional level intact. The stock exchange supervisory authorities of the states and the market supervision units of the stock exchanges continue to exercise their functions under the Stock Exchange Act.[52] Unlike the powers of the FFSA, however, their sphere of competence is strictly limited to the organisation and control of the trade on stock exchanges.[53] In cases where it is necessary to adopt urgent measures in order to implement the ban on insider trading, the regional stock

---

[50] Reiter and Geerlings, 'Reform der Bankenaufsicht', note 4 above, at 564.
[51] Banking Act, §§ 10(1), 11.   [52] See §§ 2, 4 of the Stock Exchange Act.
[53] See Dreyling, in: Assmann/Schneider *Wertpapierhandelsgesetz*, above note 17, § 3, para. 17.

exchange supervisory bodies act on behalf of the FFSA.[54] The states appoint members to the Securities Council which assists the FFSA with the supervision of the market, in particular with regard to the issuing of regulations and the establishment of guidelines, the effects of supervisory issues on market structures and the demarcation of responsibilities between the FFSA and the stock exchange supervisory authorities.[55]

An important question concerns the influence of the market participants on the exercise of the regulatory functions of the FFSA. The providers of financial services and their customers possess firsthand knowledge about the development of market practices and are thus a valuable source of information for the supervisory authority; at the same time they are likely to lobby for a use of its regulatory powers which favours their own special interests. The existing regulatory framework provides only for limited participation of the market players in the formulation of the FFSA's policies. Banks, insurance companies and investment firms are represented on the Administrative Council of the FFSA. The task of the Council, however, is limited to the surveillance of the Board of Directors; it is not directly involved in the formulation of the policies of the FFSA.[56] Representatives of the credit and insurance sectors as well as of consumer protection associations are sitting in the Advisory Committee which supports the FFSA in the discharge of its functions. It may also submit general recommendations on the progressive development of supervisory standards.[57] One of the few instances in which the law explicitly provides for the participation of interest groups in the elaboration of regulatory policies by the FFSA concerns the formulation of the guidelines which set out in detail the rules of conduct for the providers of investment services. According to section 36(5) of the Securities Trading Act, these guidelines may only be issued after the central associations of the economic sectors concerned have been consulted. Another example is the prohibition of misleading advertising in the investment business: before the FFSA may ban certain types of advertising, it shall listen to the opinions of the head associations of the relevant industry.[58]

---

[54] Securities Trading Act, § 6(2).   [55] Securities Trading Act, § 5(2).
[56] Law on the Integrated Financial Services Supervision, § 7(3).
[57] Law on the Integrated Financial Services Supervision, § 8.
[58] Securities Trading Act, § 36b.

A final check on the powers of the FFSA is provided by the courts. The individual decisions taken by the supervisory authority, including its decisions on the imposition of administrative fines, are subject to judicial review. The guidelines drawn up by the FFSA on the rules of conduct which have to be observed by the providers of investment services in accordance with sections 31–33 of the Securities Trading Act, however, cannot be challenged before the courts. Unlike other legal systems, German law provides only for limited control of the exercise of rule-making powers by administrative agencies.[59] But the courts will check implicitly the validity of the interpretation which the FFSA has given to the rules of conduct concerning the provision of investment services when they are confronted with a legal action in which the civil liability of an investment firm for violation of one or more of those rules is claimed. It is widely recognised that the rules serve the purpose of protecting investors' interests. Their violation can therefore be invoked as a valid basis for the establishment of the delictual responsibility of the respondent under German torts law.[60]

V. International context of financial market regulation

One of the key issues which has to be addressed by a national policymaker with regard to the regulation of financial markets concerns the question to what extent any national attempt at regulation can be successful in an increasingly internationalised market. The central problem here is to determine which jurisdiction or jurisdictions are supposed to regulate a given conduct in connection with cross-border financial transactions.[61] It is evident that the growing volume of cross-border trading in securities requires a greater degree of co-operation between the various national supervisory authorities or, even more ambitiously, the creation of appropriate mechanisms for the formulation and implementation of common regulatory policies at the regional and/or at the international level. Until now, efforts to establish a harmonised regime of securities

---

[59] Mahendra Singh, *German Administrative Law in Common Law Perspective* (2nd edn, Berlin/Heidelberg, 2001), p. 52.

[60] Ingo Koller, in: Assmann/Schneider, *Wertpapierhandelsgesetz*, above note 17, vor (preliminary remarks) § 31, para. 17.

[61] On the different strategies available to national regulators with regard to cross-border transactions see the survey of Harald Baum, 'Globalizing Capital Markets and Possible Regulatory Responses' in Jürgen Basedow and Toshiyuki Kono (eds.), *Legal Aspects of Globalization* (The Hague, 2000), p. 77, at 89 et seq.

regulation have mainly been limited to the European Union and its internal capital market. Even in the European Union, however, Member States have abstained from comprehensive legislative harmonisation. The concept of strict harmonisation which had been pursued in the early years has later been rejected because it proved too complicated and too slow to achieve. In its place, a concept of mutual recognition combined with a harmonisation of minimum standards as a precondition for recognition was adopted. This basically means that financial services enterprises can provide their services anywhere in the European Union if they are duly licensed and regulated under one of the Member State systems which has implemented the common minimum standards ('European passport').[62] The supervisory responsibility thus rests primarily with the state where the enterprise is domiciled, i.e. the 'home regulator.'

This basic approach is reflected by the relevant provisions of the German Securities Trading Act. Although the reporting duty on securities transactions under section 9 of the Act applies in principle to all transactions in securities or derivatives which are admitted to trading on an organised market in any of the EU Member States or in one of the Contracting States to the Agreement on the European Economic Area, compliance enforcement measures by the FFSA are limited to those enterprises which either have a branch in Germany or which provide investment services to German customers, that is, customers which have their habitual place of residence or registered office in Germany.[63] The ban on insider trading, on the other hand, covers all securities admitted to trading on an organised market within the European Union or the European Economic Area. The applicability of the relevant provisions of the Securities Trading Act is neither dependent on a German domicile of the firm issuing the security in question nor on any territorial link of the prohibited insider action to Germany. The authority of German prosecutors to start criminal proceedings for insider trading, on the other hand, is limited to those insider dealings which either take place in Germany or are committed by Germans abroad concerning securities admitted to trading in the European Union or the EEA.[64] The

---

[62] See the chapter by *Volker Röben* on European capital market regulation in this volume.

[63] Securities Trading Act, § 36a.

[64] See Securities Trading Act, § 38 (2) and § 7 (2) no. 1 of the German Criminal Code. The whole issue is discussed in detail by Gunnar Schuster, *Die internationale Anwendung des Börsenrechts* (Heidelberg, 1996), pp. 469 et seq.

investigatory powers of the FFSA, on the other hand, are not subject to similar limitations. The FFSA may require the disclosure of information and the submission of documents relating to insider information not just of issuers of insider securities which are domiciled in Germany or whose securities are admitted to trading on a German stock exchange, but of any person who might have knowledge of such information, regardless of that person's domicile or residence. The broad scope of these powers clearly reflects the extended co-operation duties in the internal European capital market since in the latter case the German authorities act solely in support of the prosecution authorities in other Member States with no national interests at stake.[65] In contrast, the obligations to publish price-sensitive information and to disclose shares purchases or sales which entail major changes in the distribution of voting rights serve the protection of the domestic capital market since they are limited to those issuers of securities and companies whose securities and shares are traded on a German stock exchange.[66] The same concern for the protection of the German market is evident in the territorial application of the rules of conduct for the providers of investment services. They apply to enterprises domiciled abroad only in those cases in which the investment services in question are addressed to German customers and are not provided exclusively abroad.[67] The investigatory powers of the FFSA are limited accordingly.[68]

Similar rules apply with regard to banking services. A deposit-taking credit institution or securities trading firm domiciled in another state of the EEA may conduct banking business, except for investment fund business, in Germany either through a branch office or by providing cross-border services without a licence from the FFSA if the enterprise is licensed by the appropriate authority of the home state, the business is covered by the licence and the enterprise is supervised by the appropriate authorities in accordance with the directives issued for this purpose by the European Communities. This does not exclude that certain provisions of German banking law, in particular those relating to adequate liquidity, apply to foreign banks as well. In this case, however, it is primarily up to the authority of the home state to take the necessary measures if the foreign bank does not comply with its relevant obligations under German law. Only if the home state authority has been duly

---

[65] Schuster, *Internationale Anwendung des Börsenrechts*, above note 64, at 467–8.
[66] See §§ 15, 26 of the Securities Trading Act.   [67] Securities Trading Act, §§ 31(3), 32(3).
[68] Securities Trading Act, § 35(2).

notified and has failed to take sufficient action may the FFSA step in and take the necessary measures, including the prohibition to conduct new business in Germany.[69]

An effective supervision of financial transactions in international markets today requires close co-operation between the supervisory authorities in different countries. The recent German legislation on financial market regulation takes into account the increased need for international co-operation and establishes a detailed framework for the exchange of information between the FFSA and the competent authorities in other countries.[70] The relevant rules authorise the FFSA to communicate facts required for the supervision of securities trading and other financial market activities or for administrative or court proceedings connected with such supervision to foreign supervisory authorities. The information exchange is limited, however, by the constitutional requirements on effective protection of individual data.[71] Therefore, the FFSA is under a duty to specify the purposes for which the data it communicates can be used; the recipient must be notified that the transmitted data may be processed or used only for the purpose for which they were communicated. Even in this limited form the exchange of data is prohibited if there is reason to assume that the communication is in contravention of the intent of a German statute or the recipient country does not guarantee an adequate standard of data protection.[72] The FFSA is similarly limited in the use of data it receives from foreign supervisory authorities.[73]

The FFSA has negotiated legally non-binding agreements (so-called memoranda of understanding) with a number of foreign securities exchange commissions, including the American SEC and the Commodities and Futures Trading Commission (CFTC), on the exchange of confidential information in order to facilitate cross-border co-operation.[74]

---

[69] Federal Banking Act, § 53b.

[70] The general principles of co-operation are laid down in § 7 of the Securities Trading Act. The Securities Trading Act, §§ 19, 30, 36c, specify the co-operation requirements with regard to the information needed to monitor the prohibitions on insider dealing, the compliance with the rules on the disclosure of major changes in company voting rights and the compliance with the rules of conduct for the providers of investment services. Section 8(3) of the Federal Banking Act regulates the co-operation with foreign authorities in banking supervision in the context of the European capital market.

[71] The landmark decision in this respect is BVerfGE 65, 1 (46 et seq.).

[72] Securities Trading Act, § 7(2).   [73] Securities Trading Act, § 7(3).

[74] Dreyling, in: Assmann/Schneider, *Wertpapierhandelsgesetz*, above note 17, at § 7, para. 3.

These agreements try to establish uniform standards for information requests and the procedures used for the communication of sensitive data. The FFSA is also a member of IOSCO, which tries to formulate common principles for the policing of international securities transactions, and the Forum of European Securities Commissions (FESCO), IOSCO's counterpart in the EEA.[75]

VI. Conclusion

It is only under the pressure of the internationalisation of financial markets and of the stepped-up efforts to create a European capital market that the German government has abandoned its traditional reservation with regard to certain aspects of financial market regulation. Until the beginning of the 1990s important aspects of securities transactions like the prohibition on insider dealing had only been subject to rules of good practice which were dependent on the voluntary adherence of market participants. Administrative authorities at that time had no role in the enforcement of these rules which were of a purely private law character.[76] With the enactment of the successive Financial Market Promotion Acts since 1990 this regulatory paradigm has undergone a fundamental transformation. As a result, the supervision of financial markets has lost much of its decentralised, self-regulatory character. It has been replaced by a regulatory model based on central market supervision exercised by a federal agency with important public law powers to regulate the behaviour of market participants and to eliminate business practices harmful to the proper functioning of the market. The main reason for this important shift in regulatory strategy has been the necessity to preserve the attractiveness of the German capital market in a fiercely competitive international environment characterised by far-reaching liberalisation of cross-border capital flows and the desire to take full advantage of the potential benefits of the emerging internal European capital market. It is based on the assumption that the effective protection of investors' confidence is an important factor for a market's success in attracting (foreign) capital and that the required degree of legal security is more easily provided within a formalised legal framework with a strong central supervisory authority.

---

[75] Dreyling, in: Assmann/Schneider *Wertpapierhandelsgesetz*, above note 17, at § 7, paras. 6, 7.

[76] Schuster, *Internationale Anwendung des Börsenrechts*, above note 64, at 459.

The background and the purpose of the reform also help to explain its main features. In a comparative perspective, the new statutory framework for financial market supervision contains few innovative or even surprising elements. The reform has left the traditional distinction between banking, insurance and securities trading intact. In contrast to Britain, the merging of the three existing supervisory agencies into a singular authority has not (yet) given rise to a unified statutory framework for the supervision of the financial services market. As to the substance of the reform, its main thrust is to bring German law into line with the evolving international standards in capital market regulation. The changes in the domestic law are mainly those wich are needed to keep up with the regulatory trends in the developed capital markets, and in particular those required by the relevant EU directives on the creation of a single European capital market. As international standards in financial market regulation continue to develop in response to the permanently changing structures of the markets, it is to be expected that capital market reform in Germany will also see further changes, reflecting the highly dynamic character of this field of regulation.

4

Perspectives on US financial regulation

JOHN K. M. OHNESORGE

I. Introduction

The past few years have seen enormous change in US financial market regulation, with the specifics of some of the most radical changes, in the securities area, yet to be decided. This chapter explores US regulation of the insurance, banking, securities and futures trading sectors, and seeks to present this regulation in the broader context of US public law and politics, particularly as these factors affect recent developments.

II. US regulatory style

US financial regulation reflects the more general US political culture within which it is embedded, which with respect to law and regulation is arguably quite unique. Of the major developed economies, the United States probably displays the political culture most hostile to centrally imposed regulatory solutions to governance problems, and this extends to financial regulation. This hostility manifests itself in at least two ways. First, the US version of federalism leaves the individual states largely autonomous with respect to contract, commercial, and business organisation law, allowing the states a great deal of autonomy to regulate banking, securities, insurance, and other commercial activities within their borders. The US commitment to this style of federalism tends to cut against the occurrence of unified and exhaustive regulatory schemes imposed at the national level. States remain important players in financial market regulation, sometimes to the advantage of the regulated sector, sometimes not.

US hostility to centralised, nationally-imposed regulation is also related to the general hostility which US political culture demonstrates toward any type of regulation, whether enacted in Washington, or in the states. Regulatory government and the administrative state came late to the United States,[1] and publicists across the political spectrum have developed highly influential critiques of regulation, critiques which share the basic claim that regulation is not enforced in furtherance of the public interest, but in practice serves the industries it is meant to protect the public interest against. Mainstream warnings against the dangers of agency 'capture,' or 'orientation' have been heard for at least half a century,[2] and such critiques are echoed by critiques from the political Right in the 'public choice' tradition,[3] as well as more traditional arguments against activist government.[4] Influential critiques from the political Left include neo-Marxist accounts of the origins of the regulatory state,[5] as well as public interest critiques in the activist, Ralph Nader-ite tradition. Whether these critiques form the basis of, or simply confirm, our political culture, at the level of popular public philosophy it seems indisputable that we lack a cultural ideal of the respected public official that one finds, for example, in the German or Confucian traditions.

The uneasy fit between US political culture and regulatory government has resulted in federal regulatory bodies being comparatively open to outside checks, forces and controls. In addition to the fact that they generally trace their existence and legal authority directly to Congress, rather than to the US Constitution, federal regulatory bodies in the United States are subject to specific Congressional oversight via Congressional hearings, Congressional control over budget appropriations, Senate approval for certain appointments, and recently enacted Congressional authority to review certain agency regulations before they can become law. Although Congressional influence varies depending upon the agency and the type of regulatory action undertaken, it is a crucial factor of US regulatory culture. Members of Congress spend a substantial amount of their time in Washington intervening with federal regulatory authorities on behalf of their constituents.

Federal regulatory agencies are also subject to White House oversight through the President's appointment and removal power, which varies depending upon the agency, through review of agency regulatory

---

[1] Stephen Skowronek, *Building a New American State: The Expansion of National Administrative Capacities 1877–1920* (Cambridge, Mass., 1982).

[2] Louis L. Jaffe, Judicial Control of Administrative Action (Boston, 1965); Marver H. Bernstein, Regulating Business by Independent Commission (Boston, 1955).

[3] George J. Stigler, 'The Theory of Economic Regulation' (1971) 2(1) *Bell Journal of Economics and Management Science* 3–21.

[4] Friedrich A. Hayek, *The Constitution of Liberty* (Chicago, 1960).

[5] Gabriel Kolko, *Railroads and Regulation: 1877–1916* (Princeton, N.J., 1965).

initiatives by the White House Office of Management and Budget, and through the President's power to control the Justice Department's litigation agenda and strategies. Thus any given President's regulatory philosophy, as well as the political debts he incurred in obtaining office, will be reflected in the performance of the federal regulatory apparatus during the duration of his presidency. While Americans debate the extent to which the performance of the federal regulatory state should be subject to presidential influence, the basic legitimacy of presidential influence is widely accepted.

Finally, US regulatory bodies can also be subject to intrusive judicial scrutiny, whether in enacting regulations, or in taking action with respect to individual firms. Although on its face the 1946 Administrative Procedure Act (APA) envisioned a fairly limited role for the federal courts in reviewing important categories of administrative action, federal courts did not remain unaffected as society's faith in administrative impartiality and expertise continued to decline through the 1960s and 1970s. As a result, key federal courts placed new, extra-statutory demands upon administrative action, and these demands have largely survived even as the members of the Supreme Court have, in principle, become more committed to judicial restraint. This suggests that an active judicial stance toward administrative agencies has become an accepted feature of US regulatory culture, a development that is perhaps best understood as resulting from the fact that all important political constituencies – whether business, labour, or civil society non-governmental organisations (NGOs) – benefit from intrusive judicial review consistently enough so that they do not seek statutory limitations.

Finally, US regulatory authorities often seem hindered in exercising their full authority over regulated interests by virtue of our 'revolving door' approach to staffing the upper levels of the regulatory bureaucracy, particularly with respect to agency lawyers. This is not simply a matter of lawyers generally circulating between private practice and government service, it is a matter of individual lawyers cycling back and forth between representing regulated interests in private practice before particular government agencies, and then staffing those same agencies. In the abstract, the 'revolving door' has advantages in terms of keeping the regulatory agencies up to date with trends and developments in the regulated sectors, but one cannot assume that those advantages always outweigh possible disadvantages.

As a result of the above factors, private interests enjoy a multiplicity of avenues for pursuing their interests, and given the potential scope of federal regulation their incentives to influence regulatory outcomes are extremely high. Further, given the lack of respect in US political culture for regulatory expertise and autonomy, and the corresponding benefits available to politicians for demonising bureaucracy, bizarre outcomes are by no means unknown. In the mid-1990s, for example, Republicans and their supporters charged the Internal Revenue Service (IRS) and its auditors with the improper use of audits to harass innocent taxpayers.[6] Sensational congressional hearings followed, which resulted in the creation of an Inspector General within the IRS to hear taxpayer complaints against auditors. Studies in the late 1990s found almost no such abuse by IRS auditors, however,[7] but instead concerns were voiced that the new measures had intimidated IRS auditors into being too passive, thus adversely affecting revenue collection.[8] Now, four years after the IRS was 'reformed' to protect against abuses that appear to have been largely imagined, and after four years of possibly sub-optimal tax collection, the Senate Finance Committee is demanding a vigorous enforcement agenda by the IRS.[9] The problem, however, is that for political reasons the IRS is being inadequately funded, leaving billions of dollars in legitimate tax revenue uncollected at a time when federal budget deficits are returning with a vengeance.[10]

III. The formal structure of US financial regulation

Financial market regulation consists in large part of regulatory regimes addressing the insurance, banking, securities, and futures trading industries. Without going into great detail, the basic arrangements for regulating each of these sectors are as follows. The insurance industry in the United States is highly regulated, but that regulation has been conducted primarily at the state level, through state commissioners of insurance.

---

[6] Jacob M. Schlesinger, 'IRS Hearings to Focus on Abuse of Taxpayers', *Wall Street Journal*, 22 September 1997, p. A2.

[7] David Cay Johnston, 'Investigations Uncover Little Harassment by I.R.S.', *New York Times*, 15 August 2000, p. A1; Albert B. Crenshaw, 'Probe Finds Little IRS Abuse', *Washington Post*, 16 August 2000, p. E1.

[8] David Cay Johnston, 'Rate of All I.R.S. Audits Falls; Poor Face Particular Scrutiny,' *New York Times*, 16 February 2001, p. A1.

[9] John D. McKinnon, 'IRS Rides the Ups and Downs of Congressional Whim: Onetime Critics of Tax Agency's Zeal Now Clamor for Tougher Enforcement', *Wall Street Journal*, 8 April 2002, p. A28.

[10] David Cay Johnston, 'Departing Chief Says the I.R.S. is Losing its War on Tax Cheats', *New York Times*, 5 November 2002, p. A1.

Until the Supreme Court ruled on the issue in 1944, it was not clear that insurance constituted 'interstate commerce' so as to bring it within the federal government's jurisdiction under the Commerce Clause. The Supreme Court's decision that insurance could be federally regulated forced the issue, resulting in the enactment of the McCarran-Ferguson Act in 1948. That statute reconfirmed that insurance regulation would remain primarily with the states, except that federal antitrust and fair trade law may apply to the extent that state regulation is absent.

The primary thrust of state insurance regulation has been consumer protection, so the states have substantial bodies of statutory law addressing, for example, the terms insurance policies offered for sale, licensing requirements for those who wish to sell and market insurance products, and the financial health of insurers to ensure that they have the means to pay the potential claims of their policy holders. The statutes are administered by state insurance commissioners, such as the State of Wisconsin Commissioner of Insurance.[11]

US banking regulation is noteworthy for its complexity, which arises in part from the fact that layers of federal banking regulation, and federally chartered banks, were over time superimposed upon a pre-existing system of banks chartered and regulated by the individual states. Following earlier failed experiments with national central banks, and with relatively unregulated 'free banking,' the National Currency Act of 1863 and the National Banking Act of 1864 established a national currency and a system of national bank regulation. National regulation did not preempt the field, however, so that from that time US banking regulation has been characterised by dual systems: banks can be chartered by the states, and subject to state regulation, or by the federal Office of the Comptroller of the Currency (OCC), and subject to national banking regulation.

State regulation of state-chartered banks is carried out by bodies that may perform other regulatory duties as well. In Minnesota, for example, banking regulation is administered by the Department of Commerce,[12] which also administers the state's regulation of securities and insurance. State banking supervision is funded in part through assessments on state banks, and in part through earnings on the Bank Insurance Fund, into which national as well as state-chartered banks must contribute. This funding arrangement is criticised for in effect requiring large state banks

---

[11] http://oci.wi.gov/.   [12] http://www.commerce.state.mn.us/.

to subsidise the supervision of smaller state banks, and for forcing national banks to subsidise state bank regulation.

The state-chartered banks do not escape federal regulation, however. The primary authority for federal regulation of state banks is the Federal Reserve, which has supervisory and regulatory authority over state-chartered banks that elect to be members of the Federal Reserve System. The Federal Reserve Act of 1913, which created the Federal Reserve, was enacted in the aftermath of the severe financial panic of 1907, and represented a compromise between proponents of a single national bank with the power to control credit, and those who opposed such a concentration of power in the federal government. Thus instead of a single, national institution, the Federal Reserve System consists of twelve independent Federal Reserve Banks, each given responsibility over a specific region of the country. Institutionally, the Federal Reserve was established as in 'independent agency', rather than being situated within the executive branch.

The Great Depression that began for the United States in 1929 ushered in another important wave of banking regulation. The Banking Act of 1933, better known as the Glass-Steagall Act, enacted three innovations which were to be of lasting significance. First, the Act mandated the separation of commercial and investment banking that was to shape the US financial industry for the next sixty-five years. Second, the Act created a temporary system of federal deposit insurance, later formalised into the Federal Deposit Insurance Corporation (FDIC). Third, the Act formalised the Federal Reserve's Open Markets Committee, the body which sets certain rates at which the Federal Reserve lends to private banks, and thereby influences interests rates in the economy as a whole.

As noted above, since 1863 national banks have been chartered, regulated and supervised by the OCC, established as a bureau of the Department of the Treasury. The Comptroller is appointed by the President, with advice and consent of the Senate, for a five-year term. The Comptroller also serves as one of the directors of the FDIC. The OCC has jurisdiction over more than 2,200 national banks, plus 56 federal branches of foreign banks operating in the United States, which together comprise over 55% of the total assets of all US commercial banks. The OCC is not funded by Congress, but instead relies primarily on assessments it imposes on national banks. National banks are also regulated by the FDIC, which exercises important regulatory functions in connection with its role of providing deposit insurance to commercial banks, functions that increased substantially under a 1991 statute. State-chartered banks that elect not to be members of the Federal Reserve, but which participate in the FDIC insurance system, are regulated at the federal level by the FDIC.

Also acting at the federal level is the Office of Thrift Supervision (OTS), again established as a bureau of the Department of the Treasury. OTS is a recent creation, however, having been created by the 1989 Financial Institutions Reform, Recovery, and Enforcement Act (FIRREA) to serve as the primary regulator of federally chartered 'thrifts', i.e., savings associations and savings banks, as opposed to commercial banks. The assets of the thrift industry are heavily concentrated in home loans, and OTS receives its regulatory authority from the Home Owners' Loan Act, which also authorises OTS to regulate state-chartered thrifts. OTS regulates roughly a thousand thrift institutions, representing a total of nearly one trillion dollars in assets. Deposit insurance for thrifts was provided for many years through the Federal Savings and Loan Insurance Corporation (FSLIC). In the process of cleaning up the savings and loan crisis of the 1980s, however, Congress shifted the functions of the FSLIC to the Resolution Trust Corporation (RTC), created in 1989 to respond to the insolvencies of about 750 savings and loan associations ('S&Ls'). As receiver for the failed S&Ls, the RTC sold assets and paid insured depositors. In 1995 its duties, including insurance of deposits in thrift institutions, were transferred to the Savings Association Insurance Fund (SAIF), administered by the FDIC. Finally, the National Credit Union Administration (NCUA), an independent federal agency, supervises and insures approximately 6,000 federal credit unions, and insures approximately 3,300 state-chartered credit unions.

In order to facilitate co-ordination among all the various federal regulators, Congress in 1979 created the Federal Financial Institutions Examination Council (FFIEC). The FFIEC is a formal interagency body empowered to prescribe uniform principles, standards, and report forms for the federal examination of financial institutions by the Federal Reserve, the FDIC, the OCC, the OTS, and the NCUA, and to make recommendations to promote uniformity in the supervision of financial institutions. The various federal authorities co-ordinate action on issues that are common to the institutions they regulate, so, for example, in August 2001 the Federal Reserve, the OCC, the OTS, and the FDIC jointly released a 'guidance' on measures credit card issuing banks should take in order to properly manage risk and recognise income and losses.

US securities markets are regulated at both the federal and the state levels. At the federal level the regulatory authority is the SEC, a typical example of an independent regulatory commission. The SEC is headed by five commissioners, who are appointed to five-year staggered terms by the President, with the advice and consent of the Senate. The SEC has rule-making and enforcement powers, but is overseen in its activities by committees in each house of Congress. The SEC undertakes administrative enforcement actions and brings civil enforcement actions on its own, but must co-operate with criminal justice authorities to seek criminal sanctions.

The federal regulatory scheme has traditionally delegated a good deal of authority to 'self-regulatory organisations' (SROs), such as the New York Stock Exchange (NYSE), NASDAQ, and the National Association of Securities Dealers (NASD). Stock exchanges, for example, have delegated authority to develop minimum listing standards, which prescribe corporate governance structures and accounting and auditing standards with which companies must comply if they wish to list their shares. To give another example, the NASD has authority to fine securities firms who violate NASD rules, authority which the NASD recently used to fine Salomon Smith Barney $5 million for issuing misleading research reports on Winstar Communications Inc. in 2001.[13] In the accounting field the SEC has traditionally relied upon the American Institute of Certified Public Accountants (AICPA), and the Financial Standards Supervisory Board (FASB) for the development of standards governing auditing practices and financial accounting and reporting. The recent financial scandals have brought about important changes in the SEC's approach, however, which are discussed below. Finally, private parties also play an important part in regulating securities markets through private litigation brought under the federal securities laws.

The several states also regulate the sale of securities within their borders, much as state insurance commissioners regulate the insurance industry. State statutes require the registration of securities that will be offered for sale within the states, and states also license and monitor the activities of broker-dealers, securities agents, and investment advisers. These state regulatory authorities bodies often combine functions that

---

[13] National Association of Securities Dealers, 'Salomon Smith Barney Fined $5 Million for Issuing Misleading Research Reports on Winstar; Charges Filed Against Jack Grubman and Christine Gochuico', News Release, 23 September 2002, available at http://www.nasdr.com/news/pr2002/release_02_045.html.

might be separated on the federal level; for example, the Wisconsin Department of Financial Institutions is the regulatory authority under both the state banking and securities laws. A second level of regulation at the state level consists of the enforcement initiatives undertaken by state prosecutors enforcing state statutes, and private litigants also have causes of action for violations of state law.

The original focus of futures trading is revealed in the names of the older exchanges, such as the New York Cotton Exchange (1870), the Butter and Cheese Exchange of New York (1872), and the Coffee, Sugar and Cocoa Exchange (1882). Trading in futures contracts for such commodities has been federally regulated since the 1920s, but futures and option contracts are now offered on a range of financial products as well, including foreign currencies, US and foreign government securities, and US and foreign stock indices. Trading in futures and options contracts is regulated by the federal Commodities Futures Trading Commission (CFTC), created in 1974. The CFTC is an independent regulatory commission made up of five commissioners, appointed to staggered five-year terms by the President, with advice and consent of the Senate. The CFTC administers the Commodities Futures Act (CFA), but like the SEC delegates a good deal of regulatory responsibility to private 'self-regulatory organisations,' such as the National Futures Association (NFA) and the individual exchanges on which futures and options are traded. As financial products have increasingly become the basis for futures and options, the CFTC has emerged as an important site of financial market regulation.

IV. Recent developments

All four areas of regulation discussed here are in the process of change, some of which is on-going as this chapter is written. With respect to the CFTC and the regulation of futures and options based on underlying financial products, a number of important developments were contained in the 2000 Commodities Futures Modernization Act (CFMA), which amended the CFA. The CFMA establishes two tiers of regulated markets – designated contract markets (contract markets), and registered derivatives transaction execution facilities (DTEFs). Contract markets operate, and are regulated, most like traditional futures exchanges, while DTEFs are allowed to operate under a more lenient regulatory regime because they must limit access to institutional and other sophisticated users, and trade commodities that are seen as unlikely to be susceptible to manipulation. Commodities appropriate for DTEF trading include contracts based upon interest rates, exchange rates, currency, credit risk or other macroeconomic measures, as well as securities futures, provided the DTEF is a registered national securities exchange. To date, no DTEFs have been registered by the CFCT, and no applications are pending. The CFMA also provides for two markets exempt from regulation – exempt boards of trade (XBOTs) and exempt commercial markets. In recognition of the fact that futures contracts now include futures on securities and securities indices, the CFMA establishes a framework for co-operation between the CFTC and the SEC.

Another important recent milestone was the 1999 passage of the Gramm-Leach-Bliley Financial Services Modernization Act, which, among other things, repealed sections of the 1933 Glass-Steagall Act and modified the 1956 Bank Holding Company Act to allow new financial services holding companies to engage in underwriting and selling insurance and securities, to conduct commercial and merchant banking, to invest in and develop real estate, as well as other 'complementary activities'. Under Gramm-Leach-Bliley the Federal Reserve serves as the umbrella regulator of the new financial services holding companies, and together with the Department of the Treasury determines which activities they may undertake. Regulation of the insurance and securities activities of the new holding companies continues in large part according to the existing regulatory framework.

As discussed above, regulation of the insurance industry has been left largely to the states, with each state having its own insurance authority regulating the sale of insurance products within its borders. Despite their sovereignty over insurance regulation, however, the states have not regulated in isolation from one another, but have instead created bodies such as the National Association of Insurance Commissioners (NAIC) and the National Conference of Insurance Legislators (NCOIL) to facilitate information sharing and coordination on common regulatory issues.

Although in some spheres of governance the fragmented and diverse regulation that results from American federalism arguably benefits the regulated industry by facilitating a deregulatory 'race to the bottom', the accusation being most famously made against Delaware in the context of state corporate law, this appears not to have been the case with insurance regulation. It appears instead that no state has been able to advantage itself over other states by loosening its standards, and that state politicians have probably benefited from positioning themselves as aggressive regulators of insurance industry practices, though doing so risked invoking the ire of the industry at election time. It is not surprising, then, that the insurance industry is actively lobbying for national regulation of insurance products, one of the proposals being for a system of dual federal/state chartering and regulation similar to the dual chartering of banks.[14] This trend has likely been accelerated by the fact that the industry's products are increasingly financial, as opposed to providing traditional insurance, and that other suppliers of financial products are regulated heavily at the federal level. The states, which in 2000 collected approximately $10.5 billion from insurance fees, taxes and fines, have mobilised to oppose federal insurance regulation,[15] instead offering more effective co-ordination and greater uniformity of approach among state regulators via an 'Interstate Insurance Compact'.[16]

This desire for national regulation would seem to be a natural reaction for any nation-wide industry faced with the prospect of regulation by fifty different states, once the states have demonstrated that they are willing and able to regulate the particular field. Thus, although to a regulated industry national regulation is a second-best solution to no regulation at all, in many fields it will be preferable to state-level regulation. Understanding national regulation in this light helps clarify the 'revisionist' critique of the national regulatory state put forth by historians such as Gabriel Kolko. While Kolko's work on the creation of the federal Interstate Commerce Commission (ICC) is cited as evidence that the ICC was actually created at the behest of the railroads it was supposed to regulate, a claim that would parallel the 'public choice' claim that regulation in the public interest is a myth because regulation is in fact 'purchased' by industry, Kolko's work actually shows that the railroads supported the creation of the federal ICC primarily as a defensive reaction to a rising tide of regulatory initiatives by the states. In prior decades, when the states had been satisfied to regulate the railroads on the basis of private litigation and judicially-developed legal doctrine, the railroads had evinced no desire for national regulation. The same dynamic can be seen in the history of futures regulation,

---

[14] Financial Services Roundtable, 'Dual Chartering and Regulation of Insurance,' http://www.fsround.org/dualinsurancetalkingpoints.html (2002).

[15] National Conference of State Legislators, 'Task Force to Streamline and Simplify Insurance Regulation', 2002, available at http://www.ncsl.org/programs/insur/irtfoverview.htm.

[16] National Association of Insurance Commissioners, 'Interstate Insurance Compact', 2002, available at http://www.naic.org/compact/index.htm.

as the industry favoured the 1974 creation of the federal Commodities Futures Trading Commission, and federal preemption of state futures regulation via the Commodities Futures Act, in response to active but patchwork regulation by the states.

Securities regulation has also been affected by Gramm-Leach-Bliley, but by far the most important recent developments have been driven by the collapses of Enron, Arthur Anderson and other giants of the American economy, and the financial scandals that seem to surface daily. The vast number and magnitude of these scandals threatens to numb the senses, so a summary of the facts may be helpful. A recent General Accounting Office study of corporate financial statement 'restatements' found that the number of such restatements rose from 92 in 1997 to 225 in 2001, that the proportion of listed companies on the major exchanges issuing restatements tripled between 1997 and 2001, that increasingly it has been the largest companies that have had to issue restatements, and that an increasing percentage of these restatements have been due to accounting irregularities, especially involving revenue recognition.[17] Many of the regulatory developments described below are as yet incomplete, and in any case are too recent to evaluate in any objective way. Each day's newspaper brings new developments, so the following can only provide a snapshot revealing where things stand at the moment.

The main statutory development to date has been the enactment of the Sarbanes-Oxley Act, signed into law by President Bush on 30 July 2002. Considered the most important federal enactment in the area of corporate governance since the creation of the federal securities laws in 1933 and 1934, Sarbanes-Oxley's eleven titles address a broad range of concerns, including auditor independence, criminal penalties for corporate fraud, analyst conflicts of interest, the structure of the accounting profession, and the funding of the SEC. The magnitude of this regulatory initiative has provoked the predictable criticism that market solutions would have been preferable,[18] but time and experience will be required before one can make this judgment on anything other than

---

[17] General Accounting Office, 'Financial Statement Restatements,' Report to the Chairman, Committee on Banking, Housing, and Urban Affairs, US Senate, GAO-03-138, October 2002, available at http://www.gao.gov/new.items/d03138.pdf.

[18] Larry E. Ribstein, 'Market vs. Regulatory Responses to Corporate Fraud: A Critique of the Sarbanes-Oxley Act of 2002,' *Illinois Law and Economics Working Papers Series, Working Paper no. LE02-008*, University of Illinois College of Law, 2002, available at http://ssrn.com/abstract_id=332681.

ideological grounds. The SEC is now engaged in a massive effort to enact detailed regulations to implement Sarbanes-Oxley, with proposed rules seeming to be released for public comment almost daily. Of particular interest to non-US parties is the fact that Sarbanes-Oxley, as enacted, applies generally to companies filing periodic reports with the SEC.[19] The Act's failure to take into account particular needs or concerns of non-US issuers has drawn considerable criticism, particularly its requirement that executive officers personally certify the accuracy of company financial statements.[20] Given the importance to major foreign companies of maintaining access to US financial markets, this new certification requirement could become a *de facto* international stand-ard, or 'best practice', with little thought being given to how the obliga-tion meshes with non-US rules and practices. It may be, however, that foreign criticism of the rule will lead either to a subsequent relaxation on the US side, or to initiatives on the international level to develop alternatives.

One clear lesson of these scandals has been that US financial markets have been failed by the financial services 'gatekeepers', the 'reputational intermediaries who provide verification and certification services to investors'.[21] These 'gatekeepers' include accountants who serve as inde-pendent auditors, the debt rating services, securities analysts, and others. An important element of Sarbanes-Oxley, designed to improve 'gatekeeper' performance, is its creation of the Public Company Accounting Oversight Board, an odd public–private hybrid established as a non-profit corporation in the District of Columbia. Although the statute places the Board under the supervision of the SEC, and delegates to the Board important public functions with respect to oversight of the accounting profession, the statute provides that 'the Board shall not be an agency or establishment of the United States Government', and that '[n]o member or person employed by, or agent for, the Board shall be deemed to be an officer or employee of or agent for the Federal Government by reason of such service' (section 101(b)). The Board will consist of five members, and although technical accounting

---

[19] John D. Moore, 'US Congress Carries Anti-Fraud Effort Abroad' (2002) 21(9) *International Financial Law Review* 18–23; Ben Maiden, 'Non-US Companies Prepare for Life with Sarbanes-Oxley' (2002) 21(9) *International Financial Law Review* 24–7.

[20] Maiden, 'Non-US Companies', above note 19, at 24.

[21] John C. Coffee Jr., 'Understanding Enron: It's About the Gatekeepers, Stupid', Center for Law and Economic Studies, *Working Paper no. 207*, (Columbia Law School, 2002), p. 5, available at http://ssrn.com/abstract_id=325240.

expertise would seem a logical prerequisite to service on the Board, in an attempt to insulate the Board from 'capture' by the industry it is supposed to regulate, the statute mandates that no more than two Board members may be certified public accountants (Article 101(e)(2)).

As one might expect, staffing the Board has exposed both professional and partisan political interests. The SEC is given authority to appoint the Board, in consultation with the Chairman of the Federal Reserve and the Secretary of the Treasury (Article 101(e)(4)). Given that the *raison d'être* of the Board is to restore investor confidence shattered, in large part, by accounting firm failures and misdeeds, even a hardened political realist might hope that at least the inaugural Board would be chaired by someone with strong reformist credentials. That has not occurred, however, as the early candidacies of Paul Volker, a former Federal Reserve Chairman, and John Biggs, former Chairman and CEO of the giant pension fund TIAA-CREFF, failed to bear fruit. The chairmanship went instead to William Webster, a seventy-eight-year-old former judge, CIA and FBI director, and long-time political insider.

Webster's appointment proved a disaster, widely seen as an example of then-SEC Chairman Harvey Pitt being unable to distance himself from the accounting firms he had so recently represented as a Wall Street lawyer.[22] Though to date Mr Pitt personally has borne the brunt of the disaster, circumstances suggest strongly that blame should be shared with the Bush administration and with some members of Congress. It seems clear that Pitt offered the Board chairmanship informally to Mr Biggs, but that he was forced to withdraw the offer due to private sector opposition to Biggs' expertise and reformist potential. Webster, by contrast, had neither expertise nor reformist credentials, and in fact had been closely associated with two companies with serious legal and financial problems of their own.[23] Pitt knew before nominating him that Webster had headed the audit committee of one of those companies, US Technologies, and that that company was being investigated by the SEC, but failed to inform other SEC members before they voted to appoint Webster. The SEC itself is now investigating Webster's appointment, and although Webster eventually followed Pitt's recent decision to resign, a move that might help restore investor confidence in

---

[22] Diana B. Henriques, 'Wall St. Wants Nonpolitical S. E. C. Chief, and Quickly', *New York Times*, 7 November 2002, p. C1.

[23] Alex Berenson, 'Webster's Public Service Image Not Duplicated in Private Sector', *New York Times*, 5 November 2002, p. C1.

America's financial markets assuming that he is replaced by someone more credible, the larger point is that this debacle is not an anomaly, but is symptomatic of American regulatory culture.

Enron and subsequent scandals have also led to a spate of reforms by the SROs that operate under the SEC. Sarbanes-Oxley mandates that relevant SROs adopt rules to address conflicts of interest affecting securities analysts, and the NASD has submitted proposed rules to the SEC. The NYSE and NASDAQ have also undertaken efforts to restore investor confidence by requiring listed companies to meet higher standards in areas of corporate governance such as board independence, and both exchanges have submitted proposed rule changes to the SEC. Sarbanes-Oxley also seeks to clarify the duties of lawyers who represent corporations, and following US-style notice-and-comment rulemaking, the SEC has released a set of proposed rules for public comment. While these developments suggest that the reform agenda is moving ahead, the teeth can be taken out of any of these initiatives up until the time rule changes become final. With the November 2002 federal elections giving control of both houses of Congress to President Bush's Republican party, it becomes less certain that corporate reform will remain high on the political agenda.[24]

Enron and associated scandals also triggered a wave of important enforcement actions against failed 'gatekeepers' by state regulatory authorities. The best known of these have been undertaken by the New York State Attorney General Eliot Spitzer, whose office has initiated massive investigations against several financial services firms, but such actions are underway in many other states as well.[25] In perhaps the best known of these cases, Merrill Lynch in May 2002 settled with the state of New York for $100 million arising out of charges that its analysts mislead investors in order to boost the firm's investment banking business, the type of conflict of interest that prompted the analyst provisions of Sarbanes-Oxley. As part of its settlement, Merrill Lynch agreed to separate its analysts from its investment banking business, a move that Citigroup has now followed, and that may be adopted industry-wide in the form of an independent, boutique research entity funded by the

---

[24] Stephen Labaton, 'Pitt's Timing Throws S.E.C. Into Reverse', *New York Times*, 7 November 2002, p. C1.
[25] Patrick McGeehan, 'States Talk Tough. Wall Street Sweats', *New York Times*, 20 October 2002, p. C1.

investment banks.[26] Attorney-General Spitzer's office is also investigating Citigroup's Salomon Smith Barney on conflict of interest grounds, based on allegations that the firm touted certain stocks in order to help Citigroup get the investment banking business of the touted firms, and that the firm allocated shares in pending initial public offerings to potential banking customers in order to obtain banking business.[27] Finally, private litigation based on violations of the securities laws has exploded in the wake of America's corporate scandals, with one massive case in federal court reportedly seeking class-action certification to join 300 complaints against 55 investment banks, arising out of 308 initial public offers (IPOs) made between 1998 and 2000.[28]

V. Conclusion

US financial market regulation takes place within a complex patchwork of authorities, state and federal, that can only be understood as a product of our history and political culture. Despite its apparently irrational institutional structure, however, the formal system adapts to cover the necessary jurisdictional terrain. State insurance regulators have traditionally co-ordinated their regulatory efforts, and are now co-ordinating again to resist industry calls for national regulation that have been given added weight by Gramm-Leach-Bliley. Likewise banking regulators, state and federal, have evolved elaborate collaborative mechanisms to overcome the institutional structure within which they have had to work. In substance, too, US financial market regulation appears sensitive to economic forces and interests, and recent developments display the strengths and weaknesses of this sensitivity. Provided that regulation of their various activities remains effective, the new financial services holding companies allowed by Gramm-Leach-Bliley may well represent a step forward. On the other hand, however, Sarbanes-Oxley and the other regulatory reforms underway to try to resurrect confidence in American securities markets demonstrate the problems that can arise when regulators are unable to enact needed reforms over the objections of private interests. Lower-profile and

---

[26] Riva D. Atlas, 'Citigroup Picks a Former Star of Research For a New Unit', *New York Times*, 31 October 2002, p. C1.

[27] *Ibid*.

[28] Tamara Loomis, 'Judge to Weigh Dismissal of IPO Litigation', *New York Law Journal*, 24 October 2002, p. 1.

more targeted reform efforts that were resisted, and ultimately defeated, during the 1990s might well have resulted in more rational improvements than will result from Sarbanes-Oxley. But once the string of scandals brought financial reform within the sphere of popular politics it became much more difficult to maintain a smooth, incremental reform agenda, and the political process instead provided a set of major structural changes that will affect US markets, and thus the world, in ways that are as yet unclear.

PART III

A public international law perspective

5

The regulation of financial services in the European Union

VOLKER RÖBEN

I. Introduction

1. The euro and financial services regulation

The velocity and complexity of securities markets have affected the European Union and its Member States as they have other parts of the world. It is, however, the decision for monetary union, agreed in Maastricht, and in effect since 1 January 1999, in conjunction with the full liberalisation of capital flow within the European Union, that has rendered the regulation of European securities markets particularly urgent. Although Europe's market for corporate bonds still pales beside America's, it is growing quickly. European firms are issuing euro-denominated bonds to refinance bank debt, their traditional source of finance, and to generate capital for takeovers. High growth enterprises depend on the efficiency and transparency of financial markets in order to raise capital. The euro has allowed investors to become much more flexible. European investment funds used to keep a large part of their money for their home market, often because of currency concerns, but are now free to plan by industry rather than geography. The consolidation of the European financial services industry is continuing as financial institutions engage in mergers and acquisitions on a cross-border and cross-sector basis.[1] In equity markets, new trading systems (options

---

[1] Recent developments, notably the Allianz/Dresdner and Nordea/Unibank deals, have produced some of the largest financial groups in the marketplace. The first example of a cross-border European stock exchange – Euronext – is now in place and may lead to further consolidation. The Austrian stock exchange has formed an alliance with Deutsche Börse and created NEWEX, in co-operation with the relevant exchanges for the trading of Central and East European securities. The global dimension of the rationalisation of trading infrastructures was recently heightened by the acquisition by NASDAQ of a majority shareholding in EASDAQ (NASDAQ Europe).

and futures) have made limited progress in attracting liquidity from traditional exchanges. The advent of new technologies, most notably the internet, is a powerful agent of change both at the wholesale and the retail level including cross-border provision of services. However, the fact that new products and technologies are being developed, the range of derivative products is growing, new and increasing numbers of participants are entering the markets, cross-border trading is increasing and that interconnected markets are developing enhances the incentives and opportunities for market manipulation and insider dealing.

2. The European Commission's Financial Services Action Plan, the Lisbon and Stockholm European Councils, and the Lamfalussy report

The European Commission's Financial Services Action Plan (FSAP) sets out the Commission's goal of building by 2006 a fully integrated European financial market to complement the introduction of the euro. Designed to replace and complement a set of first generation Community instruments, the FSAP contains a list of forty-two measures, grouped around three strategic objectives, namely, expanding retail and wholesale markets, improving prudential rules and supervision, and broadening the general conditions for an optimal single financial market such as corporate governance and taxes. The Lisbon European Council endorsed the FSAP in March 2000 and set an implementation deadline of 2005 at the latest, as well as intermediate milestones. The Lisbon conclusions stress that formal regulation is not always the answer. Other alternatives such as co-regulation, self-regulation or agreements between the social partners could sometimes provide more effective solutions.[2] The challenge was to ensure high levels of protection while avoiding over-regulation. The Commission was

---

[2] 'Social partners' encompasses unions, trade organisations etc. This is also a tenet of the White Paper on European Governance (COM(2001) 428 final, Brussels, 25 July 2001). In order to achieve better and faster regulation the Commission proposes to combine policy instruments for better results. The European Union must pay constant attention to improving the quality, effectiveness and simplicity of its regulatory acts. Legislation is often only part of a broader solution combining formal rules with other non-binding tools such as recommendations, guidelines, or even self-regulation within a commonly agreed framework. This highlights the need for a close coherence between the use of different policy instruments and for more thought to be given to their selection. White Paper on European Governance, at, p. 20.

charged with continually monitoring the implementation of the FSAP with half-yearly progress reports to the ECOFIN Council.[3]

The slow pace of implementation of the FSAP had led the European Council to institute a group of independent experts.[4] The ECOFIN Council of Ministers in July 2000 defined the terms of reference for the body of independent experts, the so-called Committee of Wise Men under the chairmanship of Alexandre Lamfalussy,[5] on the Regulation of European Securities Markets.[6] The Nice European Council in December 2000 gave support to the Committee's initial findings[7] and invited the Council of Ministers and the European Commission to report back at the Stockholm European Council.

The core analytic message of the Report is that the basic legislation for an integrated financial market is not in place. It documents the 'Mosaic of European regulatory structures' (A. Lamfalussy) and the different powers and competences. The current regulatory system is considered to be too slow, too rigid and ill-adapted to the needs of modern financial markets. Lack of consistency and clarity are stated to be the cause as much as the little or no effort being made to transpose the agreed texts consistently and to enforce their proper application. This ineffectual system was compounded by other complexities that resulted from fragmented markets, such as inefficient clearing and settlement systems, differences in legal systems and taxation, as well as different cultural approaches. As a remedy, the Committee proposed to concentrate on advancement of regulatory reform. It eschewed a single regulatory authority, which it considered politically not feasible at the time

---

[3] ECOFIN is a configuration of the Council of Ministers of the European Union concerned with economic and financial affairs. See, Presidency Conclusions, Seville, 21 and 22 June 2002, SN 200/1/02 REV 1, at 23.

[4] In its fourth progress report on the Financial Services Action Plan, the European Commission stresses the political challenges, see COM(2001) 286 final.

[5] The following persons served furthermore on the Committee: Cornelius Herkstroeter, Luis Angel Rojo, Bengt Ryden, Luigi Spaventa, Norbert Walter, Nigel Wicks.

[6] It is worth mentioning that the proliferation of committees of independent experts can be seen as symptom of a diminishing role of the Commission in the process of European integration. A committee of independent experts charged by the Member States to elaborate a legislative strategy fulfils, however, precisely these functions and in the process sidelines the Commission. The Commission may be willing to go along with this procedure as long as it has a substantial input in the committee's work and the committee's results reflect the Commission's policy preferences.

[7] Initial Report of the Committee of Wise Men on the Regulation of European Securities Markets (Lamfalussy Committee), 7 November 2000, reproduced as Annex 5 to the Final Report, p. 67, at 87.

given.[8] Rather, the Committee suggested a four-level approach based on the so-called comitology procedure.

The Committee's final report was adopted by the European Council of Stockholm. The Spring 2001 (Stockholm) European Council's key message was that a prosperous EU economy over the next few years depended on the rapid and successful integration of the Union's financial markets. The deadlines set by the heads of state and government to implement the Action Plan by 2005 and to integrate the European securities markets by 2003 were reconfirmed. The Stockholm European Council also confirmed that the regulation of securities markets should be flexible enough to respond to market developments, be transparent and characterised by legal certainty. In detail, the Stockholm European Council priorities are: regulation of distance marketing of financial services; modernisation of investment rules for supplementary pension funds; adoption of international accounting standards; single prospectus for issuers; modernisation of admission to listing; single passport for recognised stock markets; home country control for all wholesale markets and definition of the professional investor.

3. Plan of article

The approach of the European Union[9] to financial services regulation is marked by the objectives that the Union is supposed to pursue according to the treaties: creating a true internal market of financial services while ensuring that appropriate prudential legislation and supervisory structures are in place and that consumers be protected effectively. The plan of this article is as follows: an overview of the basic European approach to legislation and regulation generally will be followed by a presentation of the approach to rule-making and rule-enforcement the Union has taken in delivering the internal market in financial services; finally, the article considers how the Union addresses specific aspects of financial services regulation such as supervision, consumer protection and integrity of the markets.

---

[8] See Initial Report of the Committee.
[9] The term European Union is used here as shorthand to indicate both the European Union and the European Community although it bears repeating that the institutional framework of the Union may act according to the specific powers conferred in either the treaty establishing the European Community or the treaty on European Union.

While the Union's approach to rule-making in this area is compatible with the 'Community method'[10] in many ways it reflects the broader governance issues that the Commission addresses in its recently published White Paper on European Governance.[11] The claim of this paper is that, at least in the European Union's comprehensive, sectoral and cross-sectoral regulatory strategy to financial markets, the regulatory approach must be based on co-operation between the Community and the Member States: The Union's recent approach attempts to combine the effectiveness of a largely expert-driven rule-making process with a sufficient degree of priority setting and oversight by the politically accountable institutions. Expertise drawn from the national regulatory authorities will play the central role under such an approach to governing the segment 'financial services' of the internal market. Transparency and openness need to be ensured at this point upstream of the regulatory process. Otherwise confidence in the quality of the rules will suffer, and rob them of essential self-enforcement.

II. The regulatory-legislative approach of the Union to financial services

1. Treaty framework

The Union acts within an existing treaty framework, which is characterised by fundamental economic freedoms, most notably the free provision of services and the free movement of capital both between Member States and between them and third states, and by monetary

---

[10] The White Paper on European Governance, above note 2, at p. 8 summarises the Community method as follows: 'The European Commission alone makes legislative and policy proposals. Its independence strengthens its ability to execute policy, act as the guardian of the Treaty and represent the Community in international negotiations. Legislative and budgetary acts are adopted by the Council of Ministers (representing Member States) and the European Parliament (representing citizens). The use of qualified majority voting in the Council is an essential element in ensuring the effectiveness of this method. Execution of policy is entrusted to the Commission and national authorities.' The White Paper stresses that the Community method is the guarantor for the constitutional effectiveness of the Union. It ensures fair treatment of all Member States and provides a means to arbitrate between different interests by passing them through two successive filters: the general interest at the level of the Commission, and democratic representation, national and European, at the level of the Council and the European Parliament.

[11] COM(2001) 428 final, Brussels, 25 July 2001.

and economic union. Through this framework, and particularly monetary and economic union, Member States convey the strong presumption that the efficient allocation of financial resources in the Union be left to the market.

(a) The fundamental freedoms

This chapter does not discuss the relevance of the fundamental freedoms for the regulation of financial markets.[12] However, the basic treaty rules on establishment and freedom to provide services do not necessarily mean that a financial service undertaking trading lawfully in one Member State will be able to operate in another Member State without complying with certain of the local rules.[13] Making use of its harmonisation powers under the EC Treaty, the Community has established a set of secondary legislation which is designed to liberalise financial services in specific sectors.

(b) Monetary and economic union

The impact that the public finances have on financial markets is well known in economics. The constraints of monetary and economic union on the budgetary and fiscal policies of states participating are therefore of immediate importance for the financial services market. In principle, even for the participants in monetary union, economic policies remain under national competence. Member States, however, are to regard their economic policies as a matter of common concern and are to co-ordinate them in the Council, EC Treaty, Article 99(1). Under Article 99 of the EC Treaty, each Member State is required to submit to the Council and the Commission information necessary for the purpose of multilateral surveillance on an annual basis in the form of a stability programme. The programme must contain, *inter alia*, the following information: the medium-term objective for the budgetary positions of close to balance or in surplus and a description of budgetary and other economic policy measures to achieve the objectives of the programme. As part of multilateral surveillance in accordance with Article 99(3) of the EC Treaty, the Council is required to monitor the implementation of stability

---

[12] See chapter 6 'The Free Movement of Capital in the European Union' by Till Hafner in this volume.

[13] Cf. John A. Usher, *The Law of Money and Financial Services in the EC* (2nd edn, Oxford, 2000), p. 115.

programmes and the Council identifies significant divergence of the budgetary position from the medium term.[14]

Article 104(1) of the EC Treaty provides for the excessive deficit procedure as a means for co-ordination. According to Article 104(2) the relevant criteria relate to the ratio of the planned or actual government deficit to gross domestic product (GDP). These criteria are further refined in the Protocol on the Excessive Deficit Procedure, according to which government deficit must not exceed 3% of GDP, and government debt must not exceed 60% of GDP. The Stability and Growth Pact consists of a European Council Resolution on the Stability and Growth Pact,[15] together with Council Regulation 1466/97[16] on the strengthening of the surveillance of budgetary positions and the surveillance and co-ordination of economic policies and Council Regulation 1467/97[17] on speeding up and clarifying the implementation of the excessive deficit procedure. The Resolution provides 'firm political guidance to the parties who will implement the Stability and Growth Pact' and sets out 'guidelines' for the Member States, the Commission, and the Council.[18]

2. Home state control: the single passport

The regulatory approach of the Community is based on harmonisation across Member States of essential standards, on mutual recognition by the national supervisory authorities in each Member State of the controls applied in the country in which the head office of a financial services

---

[14] In the summer of 2001 and again in the fall of 2002 certain Member States have proposed to re-interpret the stability pact to refer to spending rather than deficit but have met with resistance from the Commission.

[15] Resolution of the European Council on the Stability and Growth Pact, Amsterdam, 17 June 1997 (97/C 236/01).

[16] Council Regulation 1466/97/EEC (OJ 1997 No. L209/1, 7 July 1997).

[17] Council Regulation 1467/97/EEC (OJ 1997 No. L209/6, 7 July 1997).

[18] The Resolution states, *inter alia*, that the Member States commit themselves to respect the medium-term budgetary objective of positions close to balance or in surplus set out in their stability or convergence programmes and to take the corrective budgetary action they deem necessary to meet the objectives of their stability or convergence programmes, whenever they have information indicating actual or expected significant divergence from those objectives. The Member States are invited to make public, on their own initiative, the Council recommendations made to them in accordance with Art. 99(4) EC.

provider is situated, and on co-ordination of the work of national supervisory authorities in the various countries of operation by the home country.[19] The concept of a 'single passport' encompasses the principle that the financial service provider receives authorisation for all of its operations, regardless of EU location, from its home state authority. The notion of 'home state' indicates the state of incorporation. Continental legal systems such as the German and the French determine the nationality of a corporation according to the *siège social*, i.e. the principal place of management. The compatibility of this doctrine with EC law has been thrown into doubt by the much discussed *Centros* decision of the European Court of Justice.[20]

3. Sectoral legislation

The legislative approach of the Community in this area progresses by sector, with minimum harmonisation prevalent in the opening of the internal market. And it is faced with the familiar problem that host state authorities may not consider home state rules to ensure the public good in the host state.

(a) Banking

The legislation on credit institutions can well be taken as the model for the Community's approach to the completion of the internal market in the area of financial services.[21] The core legislation in place comprises the two 'Banking Directives' of 1977[22] and 1989.[23] The directives provide for authorisation and supervision of credit institutions, supplemented by the directives on the own funds[24] and solvency ratios[25] of such institutions, on their accounts[26] and on their supervision on a

---

[19] The relevant legislation is available, at http://www.europefesco.org/v1/default.asp.

[20] Case, C-212/97 *Centros Ltd.* v. *Erhvervs-og Selskabsstyrelsen*, judgment of 9 March 1999, [1999] ECR I-1459.

[21] Usher, *The Law of Money and Financial Services in the EC*, above note 13, at 115, who points out, however, that Council Directive 85/611/EEC on undertakings for collective investment in transferable securities (OJ 1985 No. L375/3, 20 December 1985) was the first to use the concept of a single passport issued by the authorities in the home state.

[22] Council Directive 77/780/EEC (OJ 1977 No. L322/30, 12 December 1977).

[23] Council Directive 89/646/EEC (OJ 1989 No. L386/1, 15 December 1989).

[24] Council Directive 89/299/EEC (OJ 1989 L124/16, 17 April 1989), amended by Directive 92/16/EEC (OJ 1992 No. L75/48, 16 March 1992).

[25] Council Directive 89/647/EEC (OJ 1989 No. L386/14, 18 December 1989).

[26] Council Directive 89/635/EEC (OJ 1989 No. L386/1, 15 December 1989).

consolidated basis.[27] Under this legislative framework, in principle a credit institution authorised in one Member State may thus open branches or provide services in another Member State.

(b) Transactions in securities

A focus of Community legislation has been on securities markets, primary and secondary, dealing with equities, derivatives,[28] corporate bonds, government bonds, etc. Stock exchange listing, holdings, and investment services are subject to EC legislation. As to the type of market, both regulated markets and alternative trading systems[29] are covered.

Directive 85/611/EEC on undertakings for collective investment in transferable securities (UCITS) establishes a 'single licence' regime for collective undertakings. As a result, collective investment undertakings are now established in all Member States and represent the equivalent of more than 40% of EU GDP. The licence regime, however, applies only to investments in transferable securities (essentially shares and bonds). Moreover, new market practices call for adapted regulation.[30]

The Investment Services Directive 93/22/EEC (ISD)[31] is the cornerstone of EU legislative framework for investment firms and securities markets. In the six years since its entry into force, it has eliminated a first set of legal obstacles to the single market for securities. The single passport conferred on authorised investment firms is widely used. Access to 'regulated markets' and exchanges has been liberalised. Pan-European dealing in nationally-listed securities has been facilitated. Regulated markets are defined in the ISD as markets listed by the Member State where conditions for the operation of the market, conditions for access to the market, and conditions governing admission to listing or dealings on the market are defined by Regulations issued or approved by the competent authorities.[32]

---

[27] Council Directive 92/30/EEC (OJ 1992 No. L110/52, 6 April 1992), replacing Directive 83/350/EEC (OJ 1983 No. L193/18, 18 July 1983).

[28] Including the over-the-counter (OTC) market.

[29] In the United States, alternative trading systems (ATSs) compete head-on with the large exchanges. In Europe, ATSs provide specialised intermediary services for professional participants.

[30] For example, the industry benefits from economies of scale through delegation contracts, by which a management company outsources part of its activities to a third party.

[31] Council Directive 93/22/EEC on investment services in the securities field (OJ No. L141/27, 10 May 1993).

[32] Directive 93/22/EEC, Art. 13(1).

(c) Insurance and supplementary pensions

No EU legal framework, legislative or regulatory, exists yet for pension funds. A proposal for a directive is under preparation so that pension funds can also benefit from the internal market principles of free movement of capital and free provision of services. At the same time, the directive will establish rigorous prudential standards ensuring that pension fund members and beneficiaries are properly protected. By operating freely in capital markets, pension funds can optimise their investment policy and help accelerate EU capital market integration. Increases in pension fund investment returns will benefit employers (decrease in pension contributions) or employees (increase in pension benefits). This needs to be achieved without compromising pension security. In the context of the ageing population, this can help Member States preserve the long-term financial sustainability of existing pension systems and provide risk capital to promote jobs and growth.[33]

(d) Public interest limitations

Under the Banking and the Financial Services Directives, the host state finds itself both empowered to enforce such of its own rules as are justified in the general interest with regard to such institutions, and obliged to enforce certain of the directives' requirements with regard to institutions which operate branches or offer services within its territory.[34] Thus, while Article 21(11) of the 1989 Banking Directive permits credit institutions to advertise in a host state, this right is subject to any national rules governing the form and content of such advertising adopted in the interest of the general good. Local marketing rules of the host state have to be observed.[35] Financial service providers marketing securities face similar hurdles.

---

[33] There are diverging views on three critical contentious points: (i) the scope of the Directive; (ii) the possibility for Member States to apply more detailed, quantitative investment rules; and (iii) the technical provisions. Broadly, the debate is split between those countries that already have 'second pillar' funded pension schemes and which want to avoid imposing rules that would reduce their efficiency and success, and other countries that are concerned that a qualitative approach does not provide an appropriate level of security.

[34] Usher, *The Law of Money and Financial Services in the EC*, above note 13, at 132.

[35] See Anders Björklund, 'The Scope of the General Good Notion in the Second Banking Directive According to Recent Case Law' (1998) 9 *European Business Law Review* 227.

III. The making of rules for a single financial market

At present, the adaptation of EU prudential rules to cope with new sources of instability or to align it with state-of-the-art regulatory/ supervisory practice is slow, as legislative procedure may take three to four years to complete. The Lamfalussy Report, which put the regulatory reform at the centre of its final report, proposes a four-level circulatory approach to making and enforcing the appropriate rules, using both hard and soft law. This proposal is completed by an institutional set-up that draws on Member State expertise and thus corresponds to considerations of quality and compliance. This concern for an expertise-driven legislative process also underlies the capital adequacy policy of the Union.

1. The four-level approach

On the most general level, the Lamfalussy Committee believes that all European financial services and securities legislation should be based around a conceptual framework of overarching principles, which could be enacted in a framework regulation or in amendments to the EC Treaty. The Committee counts among the most important principles: confidence in European securities markets, high levels of prudential supervision, contribution to the efforts of macro and micro prudential supervisors to ensure systematic stability, appropriate levels of consumer protection proportionate to the different degrees of risk involved, respect for the subsidiarity and proportionality principles, and regard for the wider international dimensions of securities markets. On this basis, the level 1 framework legislation should contain the basic political choices that can be translated into broad but sufficiently precise framework norms whereas the more detailed technical measures needed to implement the objectives pursued by legislation would be delegated to level 2. Level 3 measures have the key objective of improving significantly the common and uniform implementation of levels 1 and 2 acts in the Member States. Level 4 refers to the Commission's enforcement of the respective rules adopted. Level 1 framework principles will be laid down in legislative acts, namely directives or regulations, adopted under the co-decision procedure by the Council and the European Parliament on the basis of the EC Treaty. The Council and the Parliament will agree on a case-by-case basis on the nature and extent of technical implementing measures to be decided at level 2 on the basis of Commission proposals. Level 2 implementing measures will be used more frequently to ensure that technical provisions can be kept up to date with market and supervisory developments. They will be adopted in application of the 1999 Council Decision on Comitology, laying down the procedures for the exercise of implementing powers conferred on the Commission.[36] Under this procedure, the Commission submits a draft implementing measure to a Committee consisting of Member States' representatives and chaired by the Commission. In case the Committee votes against it or if no opinion is delivered, the draft measure is submitted to the Council of Ministers as the Commission's proposal. The European Parliament, whose approval is not required, may object that the draft implementing measure exceeds the powers delegated to the Commission. Of course, the question which powers may be delegated to the second level raises important concerns of the democratic legitimacy of the whole process. The European Court of Justice, in a number of judgments, has read Article 202 of the EC Treaty as requiring that the 'essential elements' be included in the empowering piece of legislation.[37]

The Stockholm European Council of 2001 introduced two important innovations with respect to the implementing powers of the Commission. First, it required the Commission extensively to consult on any proposed implementing measure and, second, always to refer an implementing measure to the European Council. This is a guarantee for each Member State that it will not be overruled on an important subject of national interest since the European Council decides by consensus. This feedback procedure corresponds to the growing role of the European Council – and thus of inter-governmentalism – deep in the field of competence of the EC proper.[38]

The Lamfalussy Committee makes important recommendations for flanking measures, *inter alia*: (i) The need for clear mandates and operating methods for the two key level 2 committees; (ii) transparency

---

[36] See Council Decision 1999/468/EC of 28 June 1999, laying down the procedures for the exercise of implementing powers conferred on the Commission, OJ 1999 No. L184/23 (providing for a management procedure, a regulatory procedure and an advisory procedure).

[37] See, e.g., ECJ, Case 25/70, *Einfuhr- und Vorratsstelle für Getreide und Futter mittel* v. *Köster, Berodt & Co.* [1970] ECR 1161, para. 5, judgment of 17 December 1970.

[38] The Commission's White Paper on European Governance, above note 2, points out that the ever growing involvement of the European Council in rather mundane questions of the Union's activity impairs its ability to provide the overall political guidance and impetus that it was designed to deliver.

of the whole process from top to bottom shall be achieved through the necessary procedures both for the Commission and the Regulators; (iii) the legislative process will have to work with fixed deadlines; (iv) the inter-institutional monitoring process is based on regular six-month reports to all the Institutions on the state of affairs. While the Commission has the right of initiative under the Treaty, the Lamfalussy Committee suggests the widest possible consultation before even drawing up a level 1 proposal. In particular the European Parliament should be informed as early as possible, including by more intensive use of the '2005 group', an informal high level group composed of the chairperson of European and Monetary Affairs Committee of the European Parliament, the Presidency of the Council of Ministers, the incoming Presidency, and the Commission. The Lamfalussy Committee felt that it had no 'institutional mandate'. It therefore did finally drop the innovative concept of a *'Parliamentary override'* provision through which the European Parliament could have opposed Commission implementing measures. This is to be regretted. The lack of such a power to intervene at a later stage puts all the weight on the early, level 1 phase of the legislative process. It is also commonplace in some Member State parliamentary systems.

2. Institutional provisions

This four-level regulatory approach proposed by the Lamfalussy Committee is complemented by the establishment of two committees of Member States' representatives that will be active at level 2 of the regulatory process. The two committees are distinguished by competence as evidenced by their composition.

The first, the European Securities Committee (ESC), is composed of representatives of the Member States. It may invite experts and observers to participate in its meetings. The Committee is chaired by the Commission, which will also provide the secretariat. It is to be consulted by the Commission when drafting legislative proposals on securities policy issues. In this respect, it will take on the functions of the existing High Level Securities Supervisors Committee established by the Commission on an informal basis in 1985. Importantly, this Committee may also act as a regulatory committee in the context of implementing powers conferred on the Commission. In its regulatory capacity, it will vote on draft technical implementing measures that develop basic legislation submitted to it by the Commission. The second committee, the Committee of European Securities Regulators (CESR) is composed of high-level representatives of the national public authorities competent in the field of securities. This Committee may invite experts or observers to participate in its meetings. It will set out its own operational arrangements and it will advise the Commission on securities policy issues.

Both Committees will thus advise the Commission on securities policy issues, but their roles will nevertheless be different. When preparing draft implementing measures, the Commission may consult the ESC before mandating the CESR to prepare technical details. The ESC will then act as a regulatory committee and vote on the draft prepared by the Commission and submitted to it. Crucially, the CESR will also play an important role for the transposition of community law in the Member States, the level 3 of the legislative process envisaged by the Lamfalussy Committee. It will enhance consistent and timely day-to-day implementation of the relevant Community law through reinforced co-operation between national regulators, including the setting of standards regarding matters not covered by EU legislation. Such standards could be adopted into Community law through a level 2 procedure. In order to ensure close links between both Committees, the chairperson of the CESR will participate at the meetings of the ESC as an observer. The Commission will chair the ESC and will be represented at all meetings of the CESR, where it will be entitled to participate in debates.

These two Committees may turn out to be the precursor of a European Securities Exchange Commission (i.e. an independent administrative agency competent in the field of securities). The resolution adopted by the Stockholm European Council foresees that in 2004 there will be a full and open review of the institutional side.

The committee structure described above formalises what has been evolving in the practice of the Member States. Member State regulators have long co-operated in FESCO. FESCO is composed of seventeen national statutory securities regulators – one from each of the EU Member States, together with one each from Norway and Iceland.[39]

---

[39] The members of FESCO are: Bundes-Wertpapieraufsicht (Austria); Commission bancaire et financière/Commissie voor het Bank- en Financiewezen/ Kommission für das Bank- und Finanzwesen (Belgium); Finanstilsynet (Denmark); Rahoitustarkastus (Finland); Commission des opérations de bourse (France); Bundesanstalt für Finanzdienstleistungsaufsicht (as of 1 May 2002, previously Bundesaufsichtsamt für den Wertpapierhandel) (Germany); Capital Market Commission (Greece); Financial Supervisory Authority (Iceland); Central Bank of Ireland; Commissione Nazionale per le

FESCO's objectives are: (i) sharing experience and work together to facilitate the fair and efficient realisation of the Single Market for financial services; (ii) uniting efforts in order to develop common regulatory standards in respect of the supervision of financial activities or markets concerning aspects that are not harmonised by existing EU directives and where a common approach is appropriate; (iii) providing the broadest possible mutual assistance and strengthening cross-border co-operation so as to enhance market surveillance and effective enforcement against market abuse.

Following the conclusions of the Lamfalussy Report, the resolutions of the European Parliament[40] and of the European Council,[41] and the recent decision of the European Commission establishing the ESC,[42] the members of FESCO agreed on a draft charter defining the operational arrangements of the CESR. The charter foresees that each Member State will designate a senior representative from the competent authorities in the securities field to participate in the meetings of the CESR. The chair of the CESR will report as requested to the European Parliament. The role of the Committee will be to advise the European Commission on securities policy issues and respond to mandates in respect to the preparation of implementing measures. The Committee will also develop effective mechanisms to promote consistent day-to-day regulatory practices. It will issue guidelines, recommendations and standards. These will be implemented by the Committee members on a voluntary basis but would clearly carry considerable authority. It will conduct peer reviews of administrative regulations and regulatory practices in the Member States to define best practice. Chartering the Committee in this way reflects the political resolution of Member States that the regulators are to carry out all of this work, which is essential to overcome uneven implementation practice. As was requested by the Lamfalussy Report, the Committee will work in an open and transparent manner, in particular the Committee will use the appropriate processes to consult (both ex-ante and ex-post) market participants, consumers and end users which may include, *inter alia*: concept releases, consultative

Società e la Borsa (Italy); Commission de surveillance du secteur financier (Luxembourg); Stichting Toezicht Effectenverkeer (Netherlands); Kredittilsynet (Norway); Comissão do Mercado de Valores Mobiliários (Portugal); Comisión Nacional del Mercado de Valores (Spain); Finansinspektionen (Sweden); Financial Services Authority (United Kingdom).

40 OJ 2001 No. C343/265, 15 March 2001.

41 Presidency Conclusion, European Council of Stockholm, 23 March 2001.

42 Commission Decision of 6 June 2001 establishing the European Securities Committee (OJ 2001 No. L191/46, 13 July 2001).

papers, public hearings and roundtables, written and internet consultations, public disclosure and summary of comments, national and/or European focused consultations.

3. Prudential rules

The prudential legislation for a single financial market must be kept under continuous review. It is here that the need for effective and timely implementation of rules agreed in international fora most strongly arises.

Thus, the recently proposed directive on the prospectus to be published when securities are offered to the public or admitted to trading,[43] which is designed to overhaul the two existing directives,[44] is based on a document published by FESCO in January 2001 entitled: 'A European Passport for Issuers – A Report to the Commission'. The key features of the new system are: introduction of enhanced disclosure standards in line with international standards for the public offer of securities and admission to trading; introduction of the registration document system for issuers whose securities are admitted to trading on regulated markets in order to ensure a yearly update of the key information concerning the issuer; the possibility to offer or admit securities to trading on the basis of a simple notification in the prospectus approved by the home competent authority; concentration of the responsibilities in the home administrative competent authority; and extensive use of the comitology process following the Stockholm European Council's endorsement of the Lamfalussy Report. The proposal indicates which are the non-essential implementing details that should be dealt with by the Commission through the comitology procedure.[45]

---

[43] COM(2001) 280 final.

[44] 80/390/EEC of 17 March 1980 co-ordinating the requirements for the drawing up, scrutiny and distribution of the listing particulars to be published for the admission of securities to official stock exchange listing (OJ 1980 No. L100/1), last amended by European Parliament and Council Directive 94/18/EC (OJ 1994 No. L135/1, 17 March 1980) and 89/298/EEC of 17 April 1989 co-ordinating the requirements for the drawing up, scrutiny and distribution of the prospectus to be published when transferable securities are offered to the public, OJ No. L124/8.

[45] See, e.g., the proposed Directive on prospectuses that sets forth the details of the various instruments provided for in the body of the directive such as the prospectus (Annex I), the registration document (Annex II), the securities note (Annex III), the summary note (Annex IV).

Further, FESCO has published proposals for common European standards for alternative trading systems (ATSs). The paper sets out proposed standards for ATSs in the European Economic Area with a view to providing appropriate regulation under the Investment Services Directive[46] of investment firms operating ATSs. The standards aim is to ensure, in particular, that users of ATSs are adequately protected and the integrity of the market is protected. The need for these additional standards arises because existing conduct of business rules do not fully address the particular risks posed by the specific nature of services provided via ATSs. Intensive consultation on these questions by FESCO[47] reflects both the specific recommendations of the Lamfalussy Committee and the general tendency of the White Paper that favours extensive consultation upstream of Community decision making.

4. International standards

Rule making in the financial services sector can hardly be an autonomous EU exercise and is a process that is inherently open to international standard-setting. The challenge is to ensure that the Union is able effectively and democratically to transpose international standards.

The Commission undertook the review of core elements of the European Union's capital regime for banks in parallel with work in the Basle Committee on Banking Supervision, established as part of the Basle Accord.[48] The EU capital framework, that is, the amount of capital which supervisors require financial institutions to hold in order to cover adequately the risks to which they are exposed, is currently based on the 1988 Basle Accord and its amendments. An international consensus now exists that capital charges for credit risk, which is by far the greatest element in banks' business, need to be revisited. The approach of both the Commission and the Basle Committee is based on minimum capital requirements, a supervisory review process and an emphasis on market discipline. However, this approach has been

---

[46] Investment Services Directive 93/22/EEC (ISD), see text following note 29, above.

[47] Thus, the paper addressed to the Commission was pre-dated by a paper on European Public Offer published in May 2000.

[48] The Basle Accord was agreed by the G10 banking supervisors in the Committee on Banking Supervision of the Bank for International Settlements (known as the Basle Committee). The Committee comprises Belgium, Canada, France, Germany, Italy, Japan, Luxembourg, the Netherlands, Sweden, Switzerland, United Kingdom and United States. The European Commission participates as an observer.

controversial and, corresponding to the Basle Committee's postponement of the implementation of the new Basle Accord on Capital Adequacy to 2005, the Commission decided to undertake a further round of consultations.

IV. Supervision

1. The competent national authority and cross-border co-operation

The Community's approach relies on effective supervision of the institutions of financial services provision by the Member States. For example, the first generation Directive on prospectuses simply requires Member States to identify who are the competent authorities to approve prospectuses.[49] The directives now proposed not only require that each Member State designates the administrative authority competent to carry out the duties provided for in the legislation.[50] The competent authority must also have all the powers necessary for the performance of its functions. For example, the proposed directive on prospectuses spells out in detail what the competent authority shall at a minimum be empowered to do in processing an application to approve a prospectus.

The Community furthermore undertakes to ensure that the competent Member State authorities co-operate. This is a key objective of level 3 of the plan proposed by the Lamfalussy Committee, which is meant to ensure consistent and timely implementation of level 1 and 2 acts by enhanced co-operation and networking among EU securities regulators through the CESR. Beyond that, according to the directives in place or proposed, Member State authorities shall exchange information, and the host Member State authorities shall refer any findings or irregularities to the competent authority of the home Member State. The default powers of the host Member State authorities to take precautionary measures are hedged by, among other things, the provision that the Commission be informed of those measures.[51]

Increased co-operation may render superfluous instituting a European regulator modelled on the USSEC, which has been advocated

---

[49] Council Directive 80/390/EEC.
[50] Proposal for a Directive of the European Parliament and of the Council on the Prospectus to be Published When Securities Are Offered to the Public or Admitted to Trading, COM(2001) 280 Final, 30.05.2001.
[51] See Art. 21(2) of the proposed Directive on prospectuses.

but met with opposition.[52] Cross-sector developments demonstrate the clear need to introduce co-ordination of arrangements between supervisory authorities in each Member State to ensure an efficient and adequate supervision of cross-border financial conglomerates.[53]

2. Financial conglomerates

The marked tendency towards concentration and consolidation in the European finance industry has been behind the emergence of cross-sector groups combining insurance companies, banks and investment firms ('financial conglomerates'). The corresponding central counterparty and settlement systems are also involved in the process of consolidation (clearance and settlement[54]). Some of the biggest financial groups in the Union are financial conglomerate type groups. The birth of such conglomerates has exacerbated both the risks inherent in the business undertaken by each of the regulated entities belonging to the financial conglomerate and the systemic risk for the financial markets. This calls for careful consideration of structures for containing and supervising institutional and systemic risk.

Capital requirements must be adequate and proportionate to meet the risks undertaken in financial groups that straddle traditional sectoral boundaries. The highest standards of prudential regulation for its

---

[52] See Roberta Karmel, 'The Case for a European Securities Commission' (1999) 38 *Columbia Journal of Transnational Law* 9; Benn Steil, 'Equity Trading I: The ISD and the Regulation of European Market Structure', in Benn Steil (ed.), *European Equity Markets, The State of the Union and an Agenda for the Millennium*, London 1996.

[53] The aborted project IX, a merger of the Frankfurt and the London stock exchanges, is a prime example of potential cross-sector developments and indicates the questions that may arise in the future. Under that project, high growth companies were to be listed in Frankfurt, blue chip companies in London. The regulatory questions that this project raised were described as a nightmare. See Amir Licht, 'Stock exchange mobility, unilateral recognition, and the privatization of securities regulation' (2001) 41 *Virginia Journal of International Law* 583 at 595.

[54] Clearing and settlement is the processing of transactions on stock, futures, and options markets after the trade. Clearing confirms the identity and quantity of the financial instrument or contract being bought and sold, the transaction price and date, and the identity of the buyer and seller. It also sometimes includes the netting of trades, or the offsetting of buy orders and sell orders. Settlement is the fulfilment, by the parties to the transaction, of the obligations of the trade; in equities and bond trades, 'settlement' means payment to the seller and delivery of the stock certificate or transferring its ownership to the buyer. Settlement in futures and options takes on different meanings according to the type of contract. Many markets have 'clearinghouses' that handle both the clearing process and some of the settlement process.

financial institutions must be kept up to date with market developments and capital requirements must accurately reflect the risks run by banks, insurance undertakings and securities firms in the Union. The existence of cross-sector financial conglomerates should not impair the objectives of separate supervisors to ensure the capital *adequacy* of the entities for which they have regulatory responsibility.

The Commission has recently put forward a proposal for a directive designed to deal comprehensively with the issue of financial conglomerates.[55] The directive applies to credit institutions, insurance undertakings and investment firms, namely regulated entities, that have their head office in the European Union. Where such entities are part of a financial conglomerate, they are submitted to supplementary prudential supervision to the extent and in the manner prescribed in the directive. The proposal addresses supervisory concerns about intra-group transactions and risk exposures in a financial conglomerate. The aim of the proposed directive is to establish common prudential standards for the supervision of financial conglomerates throughout Europe.

As it is not yet feasible to introduce quantitative limits in this area, an adequate and effective regulatory approach for intra-group transactions and risk exposures should be built on the following three pillars: an internal management policy with effective internal control and management systems; reporting requirements to supervisors; and effective supervisory enforcement powers. The proposal addresses supervisory concerns about intra-group transactions and risk exposures in a financial conglomerate. The aim of the proposed directive is to establish common prudential standards for the supervision of financial conglomerates throughout Europe. In doing so, the Directive will implement the recommendations of the G10 Joint Forum on Financial Conglomerates.

The directive suggests appointing a co-ordinator authority for a financial conglomerate. Otherwise the co-operation between the supervisors involved and information sharing is a precondition for effective supervision.

---

[55] Directive 2000/12/EC relating on the taking up and pursuit of the business of credit institutions, OJ No. L126/1, and Directive 93/6/EEC on the capital adequacy of investment firms and credit institutions, OJ No. L141/1, provide for the consolidation of banking groups, investment firm groups and bank/investment firm groups, whereas Directive 98/78/EC on the supplementary supervision of insurance undertakings in insurance groups, OJ No. L330/1, applies additional group supervision over insurance groups.

V. Consumer protection

1. E-commerce and direct marketing

Technologies of the information age have changed the retail financial services market. Through legislation the Community undertakes to address the related consumer protection issues raised in cross-border provision of financial services.

While the Union's recently adopted e-commerce Directive[56] is not concerned with any specific economic activity, it is designed to ensure that on-line services can be freely provided throughout the Community.[57] It creates a distinct regime in respect of electronic cross-border trade from that using other distance selling modes. Its cornerstone is the 'internal market clause', which enables on-line providers to supply services throughout the Union based on the rules of the Member State where they are established. The e-commerce Directive thus establishes home state control by requiring each Member State to ensure that financial services offered on the internet by a service provider comply with that Member State's relevant national provisions. But the directive also provides for a number of derogations from the internal market clause. A Member State may, on a case-by-case basis, apply restrictions to an information society service from another Member State under the conditions outlined in Article 3(4)–(6) of the e-commerce Directive, which allows Member States to take measures to protect general interest objectives, in particular to protect consumers and investors. This derogation is subject to a Community procedure, which requires, *inter alia*, the notification of the proposed action to the Commission for examination.

The Commission's Communication on e-commerce and financial services is designed to set out the broad policy framework for future work on electronic commerce and financial services.[58] The e-commerce Directive, for its part, will be of great importance for establishing the

---

[56] 2000/31/EC (OJ 2000 No. L178/1, 8 June 2000). See Communication from the Commission to the Council and the European Parliament, E-Commerce and Financial Services, COM(2001) 66 final, 7 February 2001.

[57] Implementation of the Directive had its deadline in January 2002.

[58] The Commission has issued a recommendation on the marketing of home loans together with the communications on e-commerce and financial services and on the prevention of fraud in non-cash payment systems.

market for retail financial services. But, according to the Commission, a number of issues need to be resolved before that can happen: securing coherence between financial services legislation and the e-commerce Directive; securing coherence also between on-line and more traditional provision of financial services; and examining how the Directive's internal market clause will apply in areas where national rules significantly diverge, to avoid exposing consumers and investors to legal regimes that may differ substantially from their own. This does not, however, necessarily require more harmonisation. Rather, a common interpretation of the rules in place may suffice.[59]

The Commission's Communication observes that the existence of significant divergences in national rules applying to on-line financial services fragments the financial services internal market. The Commission plans to develop a new policy framework, covering three policy areas: a programme of convergence covering contractual and non-contractual rules; targeted steps to encourage consumer confidence in cross-border redress and internet payments; and enhanced supervisory co-operation. The Commission will launch a three-part policy to secure increased levels of convergence in respect of consumer and investor protection rules. First, high level harmonisation will be introduced in respect of core marketing rules. Second, steps will be taken towards achieving further convergence in sector-specific or service-specific rules, in particular to standardise the content and presentation of the information consumers receive, to allow easy comparison of prices and conditions between cross-border and domestic services. To pave the way for a country of origin approach to work in practice covering all financial sectors and distance trading modes, this convergence of rules must be at a sufficiently high level. And, thirdly, the 1999 European Council of Tampere requested the Commission to prepare a Communication launching a debate on the possible harmonisation of contract law in order to improve the functioning of the internal market. With the overall objective of providing high quality and comparable information to consumers, convergence will concern primarily core marketing rules. For contractual obligations, legal certainty is the yardstick for offering financial services freely throughout the Community.

---

[59] Thus the ECOFIN Council 'supports the Commission's intention to propose guidance to Member States on the application of Article 3(4)–(6) of the e-commerce Directive in order to promote understanding of the regulatory framework.'

To boost consumer confidence in cross-border trading, a Community-wide network of financial services complaints bodies should provide effective and rapid out of court redress on a cross-border basis. Steps should also be taken to improve security and provide consumers with legislative safety when making payments on line within the Union. Host state authorities are increasingly dependent on the authorities in the country where the provider is established for exercising control effectively. The Commission, together with Member States, will keep the arrangements for the monitoring of cross-border services under continuous review.

An EU-wide complaints network has been established to facilitate consumers' access to out-of-court settlement of cross-border services (Fin-Net).

2. A differentiated approach

A defining characteristic of the Community's recent approach to consumer protection in this field is to achieve a differentiated protection. While the inexperienced consumer should receive full information and have dispute settlement at his or her disposal, sophisticated investors may not need them. A differentiated approach would thus be more effective and – by removing administrative cost – more efficient. A FESCO expert group has worked intensively in this area and, after a comparison of different regimes throughout FESCO members, FESCO adopted in March 2000 a paper on the 'Implementation of article 11 of the ISD: Categorisation of investors for the purpose of conduct of business rules' (00-FESCO-A) following an intense period of consultation. It provides criteria and procedures to implement an appropriate differentiation between categories of investors. These criteria were endorsed by the European Commission in its recent Communication on the interpretation of Article 11 of the ISD.

VI. Integrity of the markets

1. Insider dealing

Market abuse, of which the two main forms are insider dealing and market manipulation, not only increases the cost for companies to finance themselves but also harms the integrity of financial markets and public confidence in securities and derivatives trading. Because such practice dissuades new investors and can have severe consequences, it undermines economic growth and European economic policy. Market abuse may arise in circumstances where investors have been unreasonably disadvantaged, directly or indirectly, by others who have: (a) used information which is not publicly available; (b) distorted the price setting mechanism of financial instruments; or (c) disseminated false or misleading information. The Insider Dealing Directive addresses the problem of market abuse.[60] A new directive proposed by the Commission[61] would take the approach of providing a general definition of what constitutes market abuse which provides legal certainty but is flexible enough to cover new abusive practices which might emerge. The proposed directive's scope would cover not only regulated markets but alternative trading systems as well, and it would address the implementation stage. The directive proposes that Member States should designate a single regulatory and supervisory authority with a common minimum set of responsibilities. Effective co-operation between these national authorities to investigate and prosecute market abuse shall be ensured through mutual information. Since the Community is not competent for harmonisation of criminal law, the proposed directive is limited to setting out the general obligation for Member States to determine and impose sanctions for infringement of measures pursuant to the directive in a way that is sufficient to promote compliance.

The proposed directive is also the first to implement the regulatory approach proposed by the Committee of Wise Men and endorsed by the Stockholm European Council in that it indicates the provisions deemed essential and non-essential. The proposal indicates which are the non-essential technical implementing details to be dealt with by the Commission through the comitology procedure. This procedure will include adaptation and clarification of the definitions and exemptions in order to ensure uniform application and compatibility with technical developments in financial markets. It is in the field of market abuse, in particular, that the regulator needs to be nimble and quick to react; this is evident in the case of practices set forth in Annex B to the Directive.

---

[60] Council Directive 89/592/EEC (OJ 1989 No. L334/30, 13 November 1989).
[61] COM(2001) 281, 30 May 2001.

2. Money laundering

Recent events surrounding global terrorism have heightened awareness for the need to combat the financial underpinnings of global crime. As stated, the Community does not have a criminal law competence but the Union's powers under the provisions on co-operation in police and criminal justice affairs (EC Treaty, Tile VI, Articles 29–42) nonetheless allow for effective action. The Tampere European Council identified the need to combat money laundering as part of its priorities in implementing the 'area of freedom, security and law' envisaged by the Treaty of Amsterdam.

VII. Conclusions

Developments in the financial services sector of the European Union confirm the experience of other sectors of the internal market: Opening up the single internal market requires not so much de-regulation but rather re-regulation. Despite the development of the concept of subsidiarity, non-binding instruments are being replaced by binding directives and regulations affecting the financial services sector. It is within the domain of hard law thus created that the typical soft law instruments of Commission practice will continue to impact the practice. In fact, as indicated above, the Commission relies very much on these instruments to ensure a uniform application of the legislation that is in place, thus combining legal certainty and flexibility.

In the financial services sector, the Commission increasingly relies on the work done in international fora, most notably the G10 and the Basle Committee. This should not come as a surprise since the Commission proceeds in the same way in other areas of Community competence such as the environment. These areas are marked by a high degree of technical complexity and fast changing practices.

The Union's approach to regulating the financial services sector fits into the broader picture of the governance model outlined by the Commission in its White Paper on European Governance. The White Paper sees a correlation between better policies, regulation and delivery of services and refocusing policies and institutions. Realising that the European Union's policies and legislation are growing increasingly complex, the White Paper suggests that the legislative instrument chosen should be limited to essential elements (basic rights and obligations, conditions to implement them), leaving the Commission to fill in the technical details. This is more important in the Commission's view than whether regulations or so-called framework directives are used on the legislative level. The White Paper also recognises that the perceived quality of its legislation depends on the confidence in the expert advice that underlies it. Expertise, however, is usually organised at the national level. This, in turn, is a structural element of the vertical separation of powers specific to a union of constitutional nation states.

6

The free movement of capital in the European Union

TILL HAFNER

I. Economic significance of free capital movements

A sound understanding of some key economic considerations, as well as of the concept of the four basic economic freedoms in the Treaty of Amsterdam and its predecessor treaties are indispensable in order to appreciate fully the freedom of capital movement in Europe and beyond.

The free movement of capital allows for the most efficient allocation of the rare resource of capital in the economic process. It enables capital to circulate freely within an economic area and beyond. In an efficient capital market, capital flows to destinations and into investments where its use is most productive and thus yields the highest rate of return. Such process is referred to in economics as efficient allocation of resources. This need not necessarily be so.[1]

An important consequence of this use of the principal economic freedom of free movement of capital is a significantly heightened competition among market participants seeking capital and attractive funding within an economic area. Such competition, however, does not stop at the door of the individual investor nor a public company seeking to raise capital. National and regional economic systems are being put into global competition for the most attractive funding source. Such competition can be fierce and may in some cases lead to a reduction or even complete loss of macroeconomic sovereignty of entire states. As the global competition debate demonstrates, governments around the globe

---

Dedicated to my wife Leticia in love and gratitude. This article reflects solely the personal opinion of the author. It is not necessarily the opinion of the firm, the author is associated with, nor its partners. It is not intended to constitute legal advice. Under the laws of some jurisdictions, this article may constitute advertisement.

[1] It depends on the capital market theory that is applied. The three main theories are: (i) the efficient capital market theory; (ii) the limited efficient capital market theory; and (iii) the inefficient capital market theory.

have been displeased to see their leeway for policy options shrinking continuously.

While freedom of capital transactions may well lead to stimulation of growth and thereby generate wealth, such liberalisation process is not entirely without downsides. In particular, the perspective of limited policy options as a result of reduced manoeuvring options and the aforementioned reduction of macroeconomic sovereignty has triggered severe concerns, if not strong counter-reactions, among governments and public organisations. Some of the other contributions to this book discuss these and additional risks associated with free movement of capital in greater detail.

The use of high speed information technology plays a key role in today's financial markets since it provides market participants with access to virtually all relevant financial, economical and political data in real time, thereby dramatically accelerating the speed of relevant economic and financial market shifts.

Numerous authors, including some of the contributors to this book, view (temporary/moderate) restrictions on the free movement of capital as preferable, if not desirable, in particular as to the limitation of speculative capital inflows and outflows into emerging markets. Since the peak of the Asian currency crisis, in some part exploited by hedge funds, the idea of limiting international capital flows has attracted growing interest in the political and academic world. The most radical approach of restricting international financial capital flows is the proposed introduction of a transfer tax that would attach every time a cross-border money transfer is being conducted. This tax is usually referred to as Tobin Tax, named after influential Nobel prize winner for economics James Tobin. The loudest, certainly most radical, group of protagonists for the introduction of such tax is the France-based organisation ATTAC. Among the supporters also counts the former German secretary of finance, Oskar Lafontaine.

Respectfully, the author of this chapter rejects the idea of throwing sand into the gearbox of international finance by any means in order to stabilise the world financial system and the economies of both developed and emerging markets. An in-depth analysis of the reasons for the currency crisis of the past decade reveals that the introduction of transfer taxes would have done nothing to prevent such crisis.[2]

---

[2] David F. DeRosa, *In Defense of Free Capital Markets* (Princeton, 2001), pp. 183 et seq.

As mentioned above, free movement of capital does indeed carry some risks. The mixture of free movement of capital and the lack of an efficient banking regulation system is an explosive one that regularly leads sooner or later to some disaster. The solution for such risks, however, does not lie in the introduction of additional taxes or other forms of limitations on cross-border financial flows as advocated by some scholars and politicians but in an effective supervising and monitoring mechanism for the banking and financial services industry and the individuals involved. At the time of the Asian currency crisis, all the economically promising nations in Asia suffered from poor banking supervision and other major gaps in financial regulation. This made the overvalued currencies of several Asian nations a clear candidate for currency devaluation, thus easy prey for currency speculators. The freedom of capital can best unfold its benefits when – in an ideal world – efficient banking regulation and financial services industry supervision are in place. The idea, however, not to liberalise capital transfers fully is not an option since investors can simply avoid investing their capital in countries where restrictions on transfers have been imposed.

II. Free movement of capital as a key element in the concept of the Common Market and European Monetary Union

The concept of European economic integration as evidenced by the European Common Market comprises of the four basic economic freedoms: (i) free movement of goods; (ii) freedom of persons/establishment; (iii) freedom of services; and, finally (iv) free movement of capital. Sometimes, the free movement of payment is added to the list, be it as an integral part of the latter element, be it as the so-called fifth economic freedom of the Common Market.

Fair competition and unrestrained access to the national markets within the European Common Market are key elements of the concept of the Common Market. The legal framework of the market is well designed to safeguard the achievement of the aforementioned goals by ensuring the exercise of the basic economic freedoms and to put into play the necessary and sufficient conditions for fair competition.

A core concept behind the idea of forming a monetary union among the Member States was to reduce if not insulate the exposure of the European economies against the risks resulting from unstable exchange rates, in particular with respect to the US dollar in connection with most

US dollar reserves held in London bank vaults for the Eastern European economies by establishing a currency and economic area large enough to balance the US dollar by the sheer size of the economies that would form such monetary union and back the use of such currency.

In this context – in the hierarchy of reasons – another important motivation for a number of the member states of the European Community, notably France, to hold in check the role of the Bundesbank as the key player in Europe's currency policy, lies second.

The European Monetary Union (EMU), however, is not designed to insulate Europe from the hazards of global competition. The European system of integration itself faces every day the fierce competition of today's rapidly globalising economy from within and without.

III. The relation between US dollar and the euro in the context of EMU

With the introduction of the euro as single currency (sole legal tender) and the completion of the third stage of the EMU, the Member States have unquestionably established the long-intended economic and monetary counterweight against the US dollar dominated landscape. Yet the new currency has not fully developed its role as a second world anchor currency that stands on equal footing with the US dollar. Thus, crude oil, as the most important natural resource which accounts for a huge part of international trading volume, is invoiced almost exclusively on a US dollar basis. In the long run, however, the introduction of the euro does indeed alter the power configuration of the international currency system.[3]

Since the euro overcame the problems typically associated with the introduction of a new currency and the phase of weakness resulting from Europe's poor economic performance over the first two and a half years since it was introduced, the new currency regained value against the US dollar. Still both currencies do not trade at the value when the euro came into life as a book currency on 1 January 1999. Currently, both currencies trade, however, at parity or closely above in favour of the euro.

---

[3] Robert A. Mundell, 'The Euro and the Stability of the International Monetary System' (Paper prepared for the Conference in Luxembourg, 3 December 1998, available at www.columbia.edu/~ram15/lux.html (as at 20 January 2003).

Although the euro is in an upswing movement, the explanation behind this lies probably more in the weak economic condition of the United States in light of the unsettling accounting scandals resulting in a deep-seated loss in investors confidence that took Wall Street by surprise and the events of 11 September 2001 rather than in the strength of Europe's own economic recovery.[4]

Since the completion of EMU, the spotlight of economists has been on the relationship between the two largest currency blocks. As later discussed in this brief overview, the regime for capital movement in the Treaty of Amsterdam provides for the transfers from euro to dollar and vice versa. There can be no doubt that the relation between the US dollar and the euro has emerged as the single most important relation between currencies worldwide.

IV. The current regime as to the free movement of capital

The Treaty of Maastricht was enacted in 1992, stating a European monetary union between the members of the Community as its primary objective, to be achieved by no later than 1 January 1999. The free movement of capital as a necessary prerequisite was enacted in Articles 73a to 73g. Such provisions replaced the former regime of Articles 67 to 73 of the Treaty of Rome. Essentially, the Treaty of Maastricht established the level of liberalisation achieved in Council Directive 88/361[5] on the level of primary EC law in Articles 73a to 73g, but reached further, in particular as to the liberalisation with third (non-member) states.[6]

Article 56 of the Treaty of Amsterdam, which is identical with Article 73b of the Treaty of Maastricht, outlaws in general all restrictions on the free movement of capital except for those that are permitted under the provisions of the Articles 57 to 60 of the Treaty of Amsterdam (previously Articles 73c to 73g of the Treaty of Maastricht).[7] Article 56 makes it clear that restrictions on the movement of capital are the

---

[4] Numerous scholars believe that the Enron and the Worldcom disasters had a stronger negative impact on the US economy than the events of 11 September 2001. This view is shared by CEOs and CFOs of many multinational companies and organisations.

[5] Council Directive 88/361/EEC (OJ 1988 No. L/78/5).

[6] The role of secondary EC law is being described in Volker Röben's contribution in this book (see chapter 5).

[7] The Treaty of Amsterdam merely renumbered the entire provisions of the Treaty of Maastricht. It did not provide any substantive changes to the provisions governing the free movement of capital.

exception. Such exceptions are to be interpreted restrictively, as the European Court of Justice has ruled repeatedly.

Most notably, Article 56 of the Treaty of Amsterdam extends the free movement of capital also to capital transfers between Member States and non-Member States of the European Union. This approach as it relates exclusively to the free movement of capital renders it unique among the four basic economic freedoms. In contrast, the other freedoms granted by the Treaty of Amsterdam provide rights only for citizens of Member States. The freedom of capital reaches further since it attaches to the capital itself rather than to mere citizens and residents of Member States. Thus, the question whether one is a citizen or a resident of a Member State may be considered moot for most considerations, except of course for tax reasons.

In addition, Article 56(2) provides for the freedom of payments both between Member States as well as between Member States and non-Member States. Since payments merely describe the consideration for goods and services exchanged, the focus of the following discussion is rather on the free movement of capital.

Article 56 is the only provision of a basic economic freedom that provides citizens and residents of non-Member States with a subjective public right.[8] As a result, even individuals or companies that reside outside the Community may claim a violation of Article 56 before the organs of the European Community as well as before the organs of Member States, including of course the respective courts. Thus, an investor that resides and operates exclusively from the United States but intends to transfer money from Europe or to Europe may claim a violation of Article 56 of the Treaty of Amsterdam just the same as any European citizen could.

Unlike many provisions in international free trade, the liberalisation with respect to third countries does not depend upon any reciprocity requirement, neither direct nor implied.[9] This unilateral approach of the European Community aims at other countries and trading blocks in order to motivate those to lift their own restrictions on cross-border capital flows so as to establish a worldwide free market

---

[8] Peter-Christian Müller-Graff, 'Europäische Verfassungsrechtspolitik für Wirtschaft und Union' in Peter-Christian Müller-Graff (ed.), *Perspektiven des Rechts in der Europäischen Union* (Heidelberg, 1998), p. 183 at 206, 207.

[9] See Georg Ress and Jörg Ukrow in Eberhard Grabitz and Meinhard Hilf (eds.), *Das Recht der Europäischen Union* (Munich, 2002), loose-leaf collection, Article 56, No. 52 et seq.

for open boundaries. The Community wants to avoid the impression that it is creating a fortress Europe for financial services in order to keep out other countries and organisations as potential competitors. When compared with provisions of capital movements in other free trade agreements, such as those provisions governing financial services in chapters 11 and 14 of the North American Free Trade Agreement (NAFTA), the different approach of the European regime becomes evident. However, Articles 56 to 60 of the Treaty of Amsterdam are considered insufficient to incite the formation of a free world market of finance.

V. Remaining restrictions

Despite the general liberalisation approach, the freedom of capital is neither absolute nor without limitations. This is true for both capital movements within the European Community as well as those between Member States and non-member states. The most significant restrictions with respect to transactions between both Member States and non-Member States are laid out in the key provision of Article 58 of the Treaty of Amsterdam. Such provision enables Member States to leave such tax provisions in effect which distinguish between residents and non-residents with respect to the place where capital is invested. Furthermore, member states are permitted to take appropriate measures to prevent violations of national statutes and administrative provisions, in particular with respect to national tax law and to provisions concerning the supervision of financial institutions. Member States are also permitted to introduce reporting requirements for capital transactions for administrative or statistical purposes and are permitted to take safeguard measures which are justified for public policy or security reasons. However, regulations allowed under Article 58 may not be a means of arbitrary discrimination or disguised restrictions.

VI. Restrictions as to capital movements
with non-Member States

Unsurprisingly, capital transactions with non-Member States are subject to more restrictions than transactions between member states as indicated by the existence of Articles 57, 59 and 60 of the Treaty of Amsterdam.

Article 57 permits the retention of such national restrictions or restrictions adopted under EU law governing capital transactions between Member States and non-Member States, which had been enacted by 31 December 1993. This provision targets transactions involving direct investments, including the acquisition of real property, as well as the establishment and provision of financial services or the access of securities offering to national capital markets. Nevertheless, Article 57 requires unanimity for the introduction of such provisions which are deemed to step behind the current level of liberalisation.

The most far-reaching provision allowing the implementation of restrictions is Article 59, which permits the introduction of restrictions by the European Council for capital transactions from or to non-Member States under unusual circumstances which threaten the functioning of the European EMU. Restrictions may be introduced for a period of six months and may be only implemented if found to be absolutely necessary. The Treaty of Amsterdam does not explicitly address those situations in which restrictions may be introduced. Notwithstanding such uncertainty, it is generally agreed that macroeconomic shocks and extreme volatilities, resulting from capital transactions to and from third states would be a scenario that may justify restrictions under Article 59 (provided, however, such restrictions are absolutely necessary, thus proportional). Restrictions may only be introduced by the European Council and not by Member States in their own discretion. Despite the high volatility in today's financial markets as a result of the rise and fall of technology companies, accounting irregularities and political uncertainty, no situation has risen yet that would call for or justify the implementation of restrictions on capital movements based on Article 59 of the Treaty of Amsterdam. One does not have to be a prophet to predict that short-term capital transfers are most likely to be restricted if ever a fact pattern fulfilling the wording of Article 59 of the Treaty of Amsterdam arises.

It remains interesting as to when and how the European Court of Justice will have to specify the parameters and limitations on the implementation of such restrictions.

Finally, Article 60 of the Treaty of Amsterdam allows the introduction of immediate restrictions of capital movements by both the European Council and Member States for capital transactions in situations of a common political resolution and resolve. This refers in particular to embargo situations, such as to Yugoslavia/Serbia in the early/mid 1990s. It should be noted that the situations in which restrictions based on Article 60 may be introduced are quite narrow.

VII. The free movement of capital in the jurisdiction of the European Court of Justice

Since 1993, the European Court of Justice has had the opportunity on many more occasions to rule on the free movement of capital provisions than in the previous thirty years. In *Bordessa*,[10] the court held that the key provision for the liberalisation in Directive 88/361/EC had direct effect and that Member States may well introduce reporting requirements for cross-border transfers of capital, but that national regulation requiring a permission prior to the transfer itself violates European Community law, even if the permission were to be granted automatically. More recent decisions dealt with the applicability of different tax treatments for residents and non-residents. In *Trummer and Mayer*[11] the court struck down a national requirement whereby mortgages may be recorded exclusively in national currency as violating Article 56 of the Treaty of Amsterdam.

In *Konle*[12] the court upheld an approval requirement for the acquisition of real property by non-residents as an implied restriction on capital movements that is justified by means of zoning law as serving overwhelming public interests.[13] Though the frequency of decisions involving the free movement of capital has increased in the past few years, there is still a great deal of uncertainty as to which indirect/administrative restrictions effecting the free movement of capital may comply with Articles 56 to 60 of the Treaty of Amsterdam.

VIII. Perspectives and outlook

The European Court of Justice made very clear that the current provisions are directly effective, even with respect to non-Member States. This leads the liberalisation debate into a new dimension. Although the Member States did not intend to form a global single market for the free movement of capital, the current capital transaction regime in the Treaty of Amsterdam has a global perspective. Since the liberalisation is non-reciprocal, it should encourage non-Member States to abolish

[10] Joined Cases C-358/93 and 416/93, *Bordessa, Mellado and Maestre* [1995] ECR I-361.
[11] Case C-222/97, *Trummer and Mayer* [1999] ECR I-1661.
[12] Case C-302/97, *Konle v. Austria* [1999] ECR-I 3099.
[13] For a detailed dicussion see Anne Fischer, 'Die Kapitalverkehrsfreiheit in der Rechtsprechung des EuGH', (2000) *Zeitschrift für europarechtliche Studien* 391–415.

their own restrictions as well to allow for a better global allocation of capital. A total liberalisation of capital movement between Member States is a necessary prerequisite for the establishment of a single currency. Consequently, the liberalisation of capital movements developed parallel with the steps of the European monetary integration towards EMU. This is evident by the effective date of Directive 88/361/EC, together with the first step of the Monetary Union, both on 1 January 1990, as well as by the second step of monetary union and the effective date of Articles 73a to 73g of the Treaty of Maastricht.

While it may be fair to say that the free movement of capital has virtually been achieved, the scope of possible limitations remains unclear, in particular with respect to national tax law. A second field of national restrictions that needs clarification as to whether it violates Articles 56 to 60 are implied restrictions. It is fair to anticipate that a considerable degree of uncertainty will remain for quite some time. It may take a decade or so until the European Court of Justice has drawn a more visible line between permitted, non-discriminatory national provisions and such national regulation that allegedly violates the Treaty of Amsterdam.

The European Court of Justice ruled in its Angonese decision in the year 2000 that the provisions of the freedom of establishment have effect not only between citizens and states but also between individuals. It will be interesting to gauge how the Court extends this ruling, most likely in a modified way, to other freedoms, and in particular to the free movement of capital.

The introduction of the euro as a currency and the sole legal tender in the third and final stage of EMU, effective 1 January 2002, did not lead to problems on the global currency, money and capital markets as covered by Article 59 of the Treaty of Amsterdam. Thus, it remains unclear what magnitude of volatility or macroeconomic shock would be necessary until the European Community or Member States call for the introduction of restrictions of capital transfers from and to non-Member States.

A potentially challenging situation might be the joining of the monetary union by the United Kingdom as well as the enlargement of the European Union via admission of the Eastern European countries as resolved recently over the course of the next decade.

The quest for a new global financial architecture that can withstand the pressures of global competition will have to take free movement of capital into consideration as one of the key factors that determine the viability of any such regulatory construction.

7

International regulation of finance: is regionalism a preferred option to multilateralism for East Asia?

QINGJIANG KONG

There are clear signs that in the aftermath of the financial crisis East Asian countries are moving towards regional regulation of finance. Given the fact that the economic volume of the East Asian countries is comparable to that of the United States or the European Union, the question arises whether regionalism is intended to replace the multilateral regulatory regime for international finance. If not, how far will it go?

On this basis, this chapter first summarises the move towards a regional arrangement for the regulation of finance. It further examines the deeply-rooted reasons for such move in East Asia, such as political motivations and economic interdependence. It then explores the legal characteristics of the initiatives for institutionalisation by comparing the emerging arrangement with the European monetary system. It finally assesses regionalism and its impact on existing multilateralism.

I. Introduction

In parallel with the deepening of the globalisation process, regionalism has come to the fore of the international trade and finance regulation. The conclusion of NAFTA established regionalism in North America. The launch of the euro marked the new height of European economic integration. East Asia is no exception. The countries in this region accelerated the pace of regional integration in the fields of trade and finance.

In this respect, it is worth noticing that East Asian regionalism has proceeded much faster in matters of finance than in respect of trade.[1]

---

[1] In the post-war era and particularly in the post-cold war era, there have been a stream of attempts to achieve regional trade arrangements. However, except for the ASEAN Free Trade Area (AFTA) that the ASEAN heads of state and government decided to establish in 1992, most of these schemes were unofficial, privately motivated plans, though a

Table 7.1: *Three-way balance*

	1997, $ bn Output			
	Market exchange rate	Purchasing power parity	Trade with the rest of the world	Official monetary reserve
East Asia*	6,382	9,431	1,380	688
EU	8,093	7,559	1,640	380
United States	7,834	7,665	1,586	71[+]

*ASEAN 10 plus China, Japan and Korea
[+]With gold at official value of $42.42 per ounce; total would be about $140 bn with gold valued at market price

Source: Fred Bergsten (quoted in F. Bergsten, 'Towards a tripartite world', *The Economist*, cover-dated 15–21 July 2000, p. 24.)

East Asian countries are moving towards a regional regulatory regime for finance. It may be a natural response to be more concerned about financial matters that disrupted the regional economy. Given the prevailing market-oriented policies in the region[2] and the economic volume of the East Asian countries (see Table 7.1 for a comparison of East Asian economic volume with that of the United States and the European Union), with huge opportunities for both East Asian and international partners[3] and democracy taking root in many East Asian

certain degree of government involvement was seen from the beginning. See Yoshi Kodama, 'Development of Inter-state Cooperation in the Asia Pacific Region: Considerations for Regional Trade Compacts', (1996) 2 *NAFTA Law and Business Review of the Americas* 70, available via the West Law website. Based on the empirical evidence provided by the European Union, where a regional monetary arrangement began to take shape three decades after the free trade arrangement, one might argue that without free trade arrangement, it is difficult to develop a solid regional financial arrangement. However, as has been pointed out monetary agreements have one advantage over trade arrangements, i.e. while trade arrangements among nations are politically difficult and slow to organise, monetary agreements can proceed without discriminating against outsiders. Of course, the fact that financial issues lay at the heart of the East Asia implosion may also account for East Asian countries' prioritising in the process of regionalism.

[2] Without exception, in all the East Asian countries, traditional government dominance in economic life has given way to market-oriented policy.

[3] The privatisation programmes implemented by the vast majority of East Asian countries illustrate these opportunities.

countries,[4] it is worth paying closer attention to East Asian regionalism in financial regulation.

II. A glance at the current international financial system

1. The International Monetary Fund in expansion

The current international financial system is embedded in the Bretton Woods system, with the IMF as its core.[5]

According to the Articles of Agreement of the International Monetary Fund, the primary responsibilities of the IMF are to maintain the stability of exchange rates and to avoid restrictions on current payments.[6] It is not difficult to observe that of these two purposes, the latter is more important. In fact, maintaining stability of exchange rates is to serve the purpose of free capital movement.

To this end, the framers of the international financial system further devised various mechanisms or added new functions to the existing ones of the IMF that allow the IMF to get increasingly involved in the external and even internal policymaking of its members.

Such involvement is accomplished by two main instruments: surveillance and conditionality. According to IMF, Article IV(3), surveillance shall be limited to members' exchange restrictions, but in practice, surveillance has expanded to cover members' domestic financial policies and hence their trade policies that by nature interact with financial policies.[7]

---

[4] More open elections, enhancement of governance and an increasingly free press in the region, as evidence of democracy, have been taking shape. To name a few, in addition to the well-established democracy in Japan, general elections were held in Taiwan and Thailand; the authoritarian regime in Indonesia was replaced by a more liberal rule; more governance issues have been heatedly debated in Korea, China and the Philippines.

[5] The Articles of Agreement of the IMF were adopted at the UN Monetary and Financial Conference, Bretton Woods, New Hampshire on 22 July 1944 and entered into force on 27 December 1945. Amendment effective 28 July 1969, by the modifications approved by the Board of Governors in Resolution No. 23-5, was adopted 31 May 1968; amendment effective 1 April 1978, by the modifications approved by the Board of Governors in Resolution No. 31-4, was adopted 30 April 1976; and amendment effective 11 November 1992, by the modifications approved by the Board of Governors in Resolution No. 45-3, was adopted 28 June 1990.

[6] See Article I of the Articles of Agreement of the IMF.

[7] The practice has come into existence on the assumption that exchange restrictions have an impact on members' balance of payments and the risk of exchange rate instability. For example, see François Givanviti, 'The Reform of the International Monetary Fund (Conditionality and Surveillance)' (2000) 34 The International Lawyer 1.

Conditionality applies to a member making use of the IMF's general resources to solve a balance of payments problem.[8] In the event of a request of a member for assistance, the IMF shall ensure that the resources are safe while helping the member concerned. Instead of designing contractual mechanisms such as compensation for breach of obligation, the IMF often 'dictates' the requesting member to adopt and implement a specified policy on the basis of a quasi-agreement between the IMF and the member concerned. As a result, the IMF is in a position to annul its commitment to provide assistance on the ground that the requesting member fails to implement the specified policy, which is considered as a breach of obligation on the part of the member concerned in the agreement.

Equipped with the two instruments, the IMF has become an active agent in the formulation of financial and trade policies and even the legal system of its members, with a view to serving the purpose of free movement of capital. As the IMF's role expands substantially – even though it is still open to discussion that such expansion has gone beyond its members' mandate envisaged in the IMF agreement – criticism of its practice has become commonplace.

2. G7 and the decision-making process of the international financial system

The decision-making process of the international financial system has been the subject of acute controversy since its inception. The weighted voting system that is proportionate to each member's financial contribution unduly favours the rich member states of the international financial organisation. As a result of the weighted voting system, the decision-making power of both the IMF and the World Bank actually rests with the rich Western countries, represented by the G7.[9]

---

[8] According to Article V(3)(b) of the Articles of Agreement of the IMF, a member's access to the general resources of the IMF is subject to prescribed limitations.

[9] For example, the G7 as a whole has 984.970 votes in the IMF (45.89%). The United States alone has 371.743 votes in the IMF (17.33%), while the ten ASEAN member states, China, and Korea have only 138.796 votes altogether (6.46%). Given the factor of Japan, ASEAN + 3 have only 272.174 votes (12.68%). The figures are based on the 'IMF Members' Quotas and Voting Power, and IMF Governors', available at http://www.imf.org/external/np/sec/memdir/members.htm.

G7 is an institutionalised forum for the seven most powerful states, aiming at policy co-ordination among them.[10] The G7 Summit gives direction to the international community by setting priorities, defining new issues, and providing guidance to established international organ- isations. At times it arrives at decisions that address pressing problems or shape international order more generally. Summit decisions often create and build international regimes to deal with new international challenges, and catalyse, revitalise and reform existing international institutions. It is no exaggeration to argue that G7 is at the centre of the process of global governance.

The most powerful economic actors often use G7 meetings to discuss global financial issues. Since the decision-making of the IMF is in the hands of these actors, their co-ordinated policy naturally becomes the policy of the IMF. It is not surprising that the G7 has, to some extent, become the quasi decision-making body of the IMF, particularly because the annual G7 Summit is now being held just before the annual Ministerial Meeting of the IMF. Therefore, G7 assumes a major function in respect of the IMF and the IMF in turn becomes the quasi-executive organ of the G7.

According to the classical interpretation, the rule of law, transparency and accountability in member states are the derivative requirements of free market theory. Arguably, the rule of law at the national level should be in tandem with economic democracy at the multilateral level. Ironically, the role of G7 demonstrates how the powerful economically developed countries bully the impoverished developing countries into 'consensus' or, worse, into a simple majority vote.

---

[10] Since 1975, the heads of state or government of the major industrial democracies have been meeting annually to deal with the major economic and political issues facing their domestic societies and the international community as a whole. The six countries at the first Summit, held at Rambouillet, France, in November 1975, were France, the United States, Britain, Germany, Japan, and Italy. They were joined by Canada at the San Juan/ Puerto Rico Summit of 1976, and by the European Community at the London Summit of 1977. Since then membership in the G7 has been fixed, although fifteen developing countries' leaders met with the G7 leaders on the eve of the 1989 Paris Summit, and the USSR, and then Russia, have had a post-Summit dialogue with the G7 since 1991. Starting with the 1994 Naples Summit, the G7 and Russia have met as the P8 ('Political 8'), following each G7 Summit. The Denver Summit of the Eight was a milestone, marking full Russian participation in all but financial and certain economic discussions; and the 1998 Birmingham Summit saw full Russian participation, giving birth to the G8 (although the G7 continues to function along side the formal summits). See the website of the G8 Information Centre: http://www.library.utoronto.ca/g7/what_is_g7.html.

3. An evaluation of the current international financial system

The current international financial system is based on the free market theory. The market is characterised by highly volatile capital or capital accounts being traded in huge volumes in an ever-expanding complex of markets for an evolving portfolio.[11] In face of the need to deal with the complexity of financial markets, the IMF was created to give advice on macroeconomic policy.[12] Such a need also justifies, at least in theory, the IMF's subsequent increase in power. This is in line with the role of the IMF as the presumably best qualified institution to provide such advice. Nevertheless the efforts of the IMF have not always been successful. There is clear evidence that since Bretton Woods the international financial situation has been a record of boom and bust.

It may be difficult and unfair to equate international financial market failure to the international financial system on the basis of such empirical evidence. However, one may ask why, if the IMF design is right, its programmes have worked less well than hoped? Given that governments being supposed to implement the IMF programmes may be accountable for such failures, it is too early to assert the linkage, even though there have already been attempts to portray a picture of IMF failure. However, the recurring financial crises[13] and the general ill-performance of the IMF programmes in the midst of the crisis have intensified speculations about such linkage. In all, the IMF has failed to live up to the hopes including those that paralleled its creation and those expected, such as playing a crucial role in preventing and dealing with financial crises, and naturally all that leaves a prospective target for criticism.

To date, criticism has understandably focused on the increasing expansion of the IMF's mandate and the decision-making process in particular. But, from the present author's point of view, the failure or at least the inefficiency of the IMF results primarily from the imbalanced treatment of the two mandates.

A stable exchange regime means orderly capital movement. However, in the context of current financial markets, stable exchange rates, which

---

[11] John Eatwell, *Global Finance at Risk: The Case for International Regulation* (Cambridge, 2000), p. 5.

[12] The advice is given primarily in the context of the IMF's annual consultations with all its member governments.

[13] Latin America Southern Cone crisis of 1979–80, the developing country debt crisis of 1982, the Mexican crisis of 1994–95, the East Asian crisis of 1997–98, which was followed by the Russian crisis of 1998 and the Brazilian crisis of 1999.

would supposedly defend against risks, would burden the interest of market participants in the free movement of capital. To a certain degree, the movement of enormous amounts of available capital necessitates a free exchange regime as well. Therefore, some caution is needed to keep the balance between the two mandates. However, driven by their respective interests,[14] capital exporting countries place their emphasis on the second mandate: free movement of capital, irrespective of changing conditions. For example, despite that maintaining the stability of the exchange regime proved to be an impossible task in the wake of the fall of the Bretton Woods system in the 1970s, the international financial system has been consistent in sticking to the second purpose. The unbalanced treatment of the two mandates consequently brings about undesirable outcomes.

Apart from its institutional defects, the way that the IMF deals with the needy and poorer member states is another focus of criticism. The IMF is viewed as a major source of technical expertise in the area of finance, and its experience to deal with macroeconomic stabilisation and reform is tremendous. Nevertheless, in the eyes of its critics, its performance is not ideal. First, its expertise is from time to time misguided. For example, in November 1997 when the East Asian financial crisis was obvious to the region's central bankers, the President of the United States was still talking about the crisis as 'a few glitches on the road'. That perception might be reflected in the lack of participation in the Thai support programme in August 1997. Nonetheless, the IMF's technical assistance is often considered to lack flexibility. The global efforts to resolve financial crises should take note of the diverse circumstances and priorities of individual economies at different stages of development. However, nearly all the solutions the IMF has proposed are so inflexibly similar to each other as to accommodate these differences. Second, its practice of packaging its advice and technical assistance with loans and debt relief facilities has gone so far as to impose such expertise. The case of Indonesia is a clear example. When Indonesia turned to the IMF for assistance in the crisis, the IMF demanded that Indonesia should adopt a new bankruptcy code and restructure its judiciary as preconditions for assistance. In relation to the bankruptcy code, the IMF programme

---

[14] For the source country of capital flow, the benefits that derive from free movement of capital are obvious. Just to mention letting the international investors from the West share in the Asian bounty in good times, leaving the disturbed market unturned in bad times.

of 30 April 1998 required the Indonesian government to tighten deadlines, to rationalise the treatment of secured debts, and to appoint ad hoc judges. With respect to restructuring the judiciary, it provided for the establishment of a new commercial chamber in the court system. The programme even specified that the new commercial chamber shall be staffed with judges who are specially trained and receive a considerably higher salary than other judges. It provided that the decisions of the chambers shall be issued in writing and on schedules.[15] Although the Indonesian government accepted the programme as a precondition for the requested IMF assistance, the implementation met considerable opposition from the bureaucracy, from business, and bars.[16] The failure of the IMF in this regard might be attributable to a lack of political will of the major powers, i.e. the G7 regulators.[17] For example, the Contingent Credit Line (CCL) of the IMF, which ought to have played an important role in crisis management, has failed to live up to the hopes that attended its creation. The IMF (and the G7) stuck to what was called 'Washington consensus'[18] and rejected assistance requested at the peak of the East Asian financial crisis. The leading powers of the G7 then either declined to take part in the rescue operations, as the United States did in Thailand, or built the much-ballyhooed 'second lines of defence' so deviously that they could never be used.[19]

The current international financial system with the IMF as its core is focused on how to make global financial markets more efficient. To be fair, this is a critical goal for humankind. But democracy is also about equity, fairness and participation. However, there is a fundamental asymmetry in global financial regulation, between the drive towards total mobility of capital and risk management as well as between the financial powers and the developing world. The IMF has made mistakes in this regard.

[15] Even the IMF admitted 'some structural adjustment programs may have been too detailed, stretching some countries' capacity for implementation'. See Flemming Larsen (Director, Office in Europe of the IMF), 'Globalization, the NGOs, and the IMF: A New Dialogue', Le Monde, 19 September 2000. The English version is available at http://www.imf.org/external/np/vc/2000/091900.HTM.

[16] Quoted Edward S. Knight, 'Legal Infrastructure for New Global Market Place' (2000) 24 The International Lawyer 217.

[17] Gary Hufbauer, The Challenge to G-7 Regulators (submissions to the conference on Crisis and Credit: Restructuring Asia's Financial Sector Asia Society, 1 October 1999, New York City).

[18] The 'Washington consensus' strongly held that deregulation, privatisation, and trade and financial liberalisation were always good.

[19] Quoted from Fred Bergsten, 'Towards a Tripartite World', The Economist, 15 July 2000, p. 24.

Although it is struggling to figure out how to mend the defects, the IMF – for the reasons given later – has not gone so far as to pay enough attention to the vulnerability of the developing world to financial risks and to the involvement of civil society from the developing world in promoting these goals.

It is fair to argue that, since the IMF has the power to bring 'robber baron authoritarian rulers' to heel by the power of conditional loans,[20] there will be an increasing cry for filling in the democratic deficit in this institution also. That may call for changes in issues that are critical to the IMF institution, for example, the-freer-the-better doctrine and even the voting system.

Based on the existing power balance, it is unlikely that the IMF and the G7 will be happy to do so in the end.

III. The East Asian financial crisis

1. The debate on the causes of the crisis

The East Asian crisis 1997/98 can be characterised as a capital flow crisis, the origin of which were large inflows of private capital relative to the underlying current account deficit and of a largely short term nature, followed by a sudden massive reversal of capital flows.[21] The creditor panic that naturally followed the outflow of capital worsened the financial crisis in East Asia.

As to the causes of the financial crisis in East Asian countries, the IMF (as well as the G7 later) and East Asia are clearly divided.

The IMF identified the crisis-stricken countries' internal factors. To be blamed for the crisis were the lack of the rule of law as well as the lack of transparency and accountability, and the accompanying cronyism. The crisis-stricken East Asian countries attributed the crisis to external factors. In the wake of the crisis, their initial analysis was that speculative foreign capital, i.e. hedge funds, was first and foremost among the factors to be blamed.

An impartial appraisal of the factors that contributed to the financial crisis, however, would reveal that the ostensibly contradictory views are not irreconcilable. For example, when the dawn of economic recovery

---

[20] An example is the case of the Suharto regime in Indonesia in 1997.

[21] Asian Development Bank Institute, Asian Policy Forum, *Policy Recommendations for Preventing Another Capital Account Crisis*, p. 2, available at http://www.adbi.org/PDF/ APF/APFpol1.pdf.

was seen in East Asia, US Treasury Secretary Larry Summers, who once had said that 'crony capitalism' was the main reason for East Asia's financial crisis, adjusted his assertion by admitting that excessive capital inflows might have contributed to the crisis.[22] Just as Robert Hormats of Goldman Sachs pointed out, the speculative hedge funds were indeed catalytic factors of the financial crisis.[23] The withdrawal of short-term foreign capital triggered a series of events which finally evolved into a full crisis in East Asian countries. Cheap money available on the East Asian financial market, inefficient use of the money by borrowers in these markets, and an overhang of leverage of corporations, however, are the prima facie causes of the financial crisis.[24] In essence, these factors are closely related to the legal infrastructure in East Asian countries, and can play a role only in this context. A clear example is that the supervision of banks was inadequate by the standards of the Basle Core Principles for Effective Banking Supervision.[25]

2. Reforming financial infrastructure in the post-crisis era

(a) Individual efforts

After the near-death experience, East Asian countries have begun to re-examine what they were told as market wisdom and a new perception of the global economic system has begun to take shape.

East Asia has since retreated from a substantial amount of bad debts, has undertaken a considerable amount of financial restructuring and has upgraded a spectrum of social institutions – extending from politics to higher education, to science and technology.

---

[22] Walden Bello, 'Inviting Another Catastrophe' *Far Eastern Economic Review*, cover-dated 12 August 1999, available at http://www.feer.com/articles/1999/9908_12/p42rethinking.html.

[23] The impact of hedge funds was probably overstated. Take the Indonesia case as an example: more than half of Indonesia's external debt to private creditors at the end of 1997, i.e. approximately $65 billion, represented direct, largely unhedged cross-border borrowings by private non-banking borrowings. Quoted Knight, 'Legal infrastructure' above note 16. For a detailed analysis of the relationship between hedge funds and financial crisis, see Stephen J. Brown, William N. Goetzmann and James M. Park, *Hedge Funds and the Asian Currency Crisis of 1997*, available at http://www.tier.org.tw/apecc/hotnews/Discussion_Papers/98011403.pdf.

[24] Robert Hormats, 'Reflections on the Asian Financial Crisis' (2000) 34 *The International Lawyer* 193–5.

[25] A recent survey by the Basle Committee found that the most acute problem in many emerging markets is the shortage of skilled supervisory staff and that supervisory agencies in many countries are not sufficiently independent to be able to function effectively.

The East Asian countries have realised the necessity of creating the conditions for them to compete internationally with well-prepared economies. With this in mind, many of them have to admit the structural shortcomings of their economies and they have committed themselves to structural and institutional reforms. These reforms aim at promoting the rule of law, streamlining government and the public sector, and encouraging private initiative. They also set the conditions for cheaper and better production in order to enhance competitiveness. In this regard, they were not hesitant to co-operate with the IMF and the World Bank in, for example, the IMF's monitoring compliance as part of its regular Article IV reviews of economies.

Apart from domestic efforts of individual countries in the region, a strong call emerged among the East Asian countries to improve the workings of the international financial system, rather than adopt a hands-off approach.

(b) International response

In the wake of the financial crisis, the G7 put forward a programme of reform for the world's 'financial architecture'.[26] The thrust of the proposal was to urge greater co-ordination in the cross-border regulation of capital flows. It demands a code of conduct for all open economies, requiring rules for the disclosure of financial information and statistics on fiscal and monetary policy, with an agreed approach to corporate governance and a proposal for financial institutions in developed economies to review the practices of peers in developing markets. It designs a new type of credit entitled 'a pre-crisis line of credit'. The G7 statement, whose aim was 'to assist emerging markets in the preparation and process of liberalisation', is in fact an endorsement of the US plans for a new IMF safety net.

The G7 programme is expected to pave the way for a new international system of regulation, designed to prevent future global financial crises and ease the current one. On the institutional side, in line with the G7 response, the IMF, which was under tremendous pressure, reacted with internal restructuring to improve the functioning of the international financial system.[27]

---

[26] Robert Peston and Nancy Dunne, 'G7: Group draws up financial reform scheme', *Financial Times*, 30 October 1998.

[27] The IMF's architecture work programme aimed mainly at strengthening the institution's capacities in three crucial areas: crisis prevention, improving the functioning

It should be noted in this regard that the proposed 'financial architecture' does not touch upon the essence of the financial regulatory regime. It does not specify to what extent the cross-border movement of capital shall be free. A close look at the framing of the new architecture proposal reveals that the new architecture nonetheless aims at a global framework where free movement of resources across borders is secured.

(c) Regional co-operation

In contrast with the reluctant international response, regional members in East Asia responded quickly. As far as funds are concerned, the Thai support package – where the regional contribution was almost three times the size of the IMF's contribution – illustrates the degree of regional co-operation.

It was noted at the outset that in view of regional interdependence, Asian economies must work together to design institutional measures and implement them. The problem facing East Asian countries is whether to submit themselves to the IMF alone or create a regional institution or forum.

3. The East Asian perception for financial infrastructure reform

It may be fair to perceive the common Association of South-East Asian Nations' (ASEAN) position on the reform of the international financial architecture[28] as the East Asian view of such reform.

The ASEAN common position includes the following:

> 'In view of the global nature of today's financial markets, the reform of the international financial architecture must involve the participation of all countries, including the emerging economies.'
>
> 'ASEAN shall adopt a more proactive role at various international and regional fora to ensure that its interests and priorities are given due consideration in any proposal for reform of the international financial architecture.'

of domestic and international financial markets, and the provision of temporary financial assistance, including in times of crisis, in forms that are well adapted to present global realities and diversity of the IMF's membership. See the Statement by the Managing Director to the International Monetary and Financial Committee on Progress in Strengthening the Architecture of the International Financial System and Reform of the IMF, 19 September 2000.

[28] The common position of the ASEAN was adopted at the Special ASEAN Finance Ministers' Meeting in Manila on 30 April 1999, available at http://www.aseansec.org/ 10339.htm.

'Standards of transparency and disclosure must be applied equally to the public and private sectors. In particular, large market participants, such as highly leveraged institutions which have systemic significance, should be subject to regular and timely transparency and disclosure requirements.'

'To complement the ASEAN Surveillance Process, ASEAN shall explore options to strengthen regional support activities.'[29]

East Asian countries emphasise participation of the emerging economies in the reform process and stress their representation. They hold that the balance must be maintained between the two mandates of the IMF. It is particularly noteworthy that the East Asian countries affirm their openness towards regional arrangements. This reflects the doubts East Asian countries have about the current multilateral infrastructure's readiness to address regional concerns.

IV. Forming a regional arrangement or improving the existing multilateral framework?

There is consensus about the need to reform the current international financial architecture.[30] A question that remains unanswered is whether there is a need for a regional financial arrangement in addition to such reform. Given the on-going reform process of international financial institutions the question is whether in future the multilateral infrastructure is capable of preventing such crises as the one in East Asia?

Needless to say, it is too early to predict how the reform process will help to realise this goal. An examination of the reform, however, may be helpful. It must be noted that at the heart of the debate about IMF reform there are moves to expand the mandate of the IMF. The assumption is that expanding the mandate would make the IMF more powerful to deal with the tasks entrusted to it. But, the history of the IMF suggests that the assumption might not hold.

Indeed, in the eyes of proponents of the multilateral financial regulatory regime, the inability of the IMF is, to some extent, a result of its consensus-building mechanisms. The reform that the multilateral

---

[29] *Ibid.*

[30] In this respect, it is noteworthy that there exists a debate on reforming the multilateral financial regulatory regime within the framework of the IMF or replacing the IMF with a new global financial organisation that would be equivalent to the WTO in the trade area. For example, Professor John Eatwell of the University of Cambridge proposed to found a World Financial Authority (WFA).

financial institution should administer is to remedy such inefficient mechanisms. Theoretically, however, biased expansion of its mandate might even be worse than keeping a modest mandate.

In fact, from the viewpoint of the critics, the inadequacy of the current multilateral infrastructure is obvious. The East Asian financial crisis has highlighted the IMF's failure to foretell and prevent crises, let alone secure a sound and healthy international financial situation. This naturally raised doubts about, among other things, the ability of the IMF to prevent and deal with such crises in the future.

On the other hand, proponents of reforming the IMF, rather than establishing regional arrangements, would inevitably argue that it is unfair to expect a multilateral financial regulatory regime to solve all pertinent problems for good. Given the admissibility of the would-be argument, the question may be asked whether the multilateral reform will be resonant with the East Asian reflection of the international financial system.

It is understood that the thrust of the IMF reform is to assist emerging markets in the preparation and process of liberalisation. The major concerns of the framers of the reform programme still centre around the free movement of capital, thus leaving those of emerging market countries on the balance between governments and private interests untouched. Therefore, arguably, no matter how the IMF reform purports 'to increase the IMF's assessments and policy advice',[31] it would not touch the hearts of emerging market countries, particularly where it still remains to be seen whether and how the reform will enhance the relevance of the IMF's technical assistance to its members.

Therefore, it may be argued that, as long as a genuine consensus-building process is not to be instituted by reforming the decision-making process, a reform aiming primarily at expanding the mandate of the IMF would not equip the current multilateral infrastructure with the magic power to prevent a future crisis. Regional arrangements, at least complementary ones, would be an attractive option. As a matter of fact,

---

[31] To this end, the IMF – together with other agencies – has focused on developing codes and standards for financial sector soundness, transparency in macroeconomic and financial policies, provision of data, and corporate governance. The Financial Sector Assessment Program (FSAP), launched jointly by the IMF and the World Bank on a pilot basis in 1999, provides participating countries with comprehensive assessments of their financial systems. The assessment identifies strengths and vulnerabilities; reports on observance and implementation of international standards, codes and good practices; and helps to design policy responses.

self-help is better than seeking help from others, as a Chinese saying indicates (*qiuren buru qiuji*). Inadequacy of the IMF is the catalyst for the emergence of a regional arrangement.

In the context of East Asia, the East Asian perception of globalisation and the advantages of a regional arrangement are additional important factors that contribute to the parallel sprout of regional financial arrangements.

While the East Asian countries see the opportunities offered by globalisation, many of them also recognise the implied risks. Indeed, globalisation brings about increased mobility of capital but also the potential for some countries to run hot one moment and then cold the next – investors rush to inject funds into a region but then withdraw when returns are slow to materialise – which is not good for the sustainable development of these countries. They realise, therefore, that liberalisation of capital accounts must move in tandem with the strengthening of the ability of financial institutions to manage risk.

To some extent, a regional arrangement bases its position on the assumption that common interests are its driving force. Even in a globalised world, geographical proximity, cultural identity, as well as economic interdependence of the East Asian countries, contribute to the commonality of interests of the region, which in turn justifies a regional financial arrangement. On the other hand, given its special expertise and focus, a regional group is often more appropriate to deal with particular problems in the region and consequently regional members may use this better knowledge to improve the decision-making process within multi-lateral agencies (particularly the IMF).[32]

Moreover, a regional arrangement has the great potential for fruitful interaction which will raise understanding, co-operation, co-ordination, and technical standards. In addition, the exclusive dedication of a regional arrangement to regional matters also helps to enhance the efficiency of making the resources from the region available to needy members. In contrast, the IMF lacks the power to provide all the necessary resources to deal with such crises as the one in the East Asian countries.

---

[32] As an Australian central banker pointed out, there can hardly be any doubt that the IMF Indonesian programme would have been quite different if it had had an effective input from the region – the long-term desirability (but low priority) of doing something about the clove monopoly would have been kept in better perspective against the pressingly urgent short-term crisis of massive capital outflow. In macro policy, the overly tight budgets of the IMF's initial prescription might have been avoided.

There is no need to discuss geographical proximity, just to mention shared cultural values and economic interdependence among the East Asian countries. East Asian values – often identified as Confucianism – are at the heart of Asia's position vis-à-vis globalisation and market economy: in favour of market mechanism but against market fundamentalism.

In terms of economic linkage, within ASEAN, economic interdependence has prompted ASEAN member states to forge an ASEAN Free Trade Area (AFTA). Japan has been a traditional major trade partner of the rest of East Asian countries and the primary source of foreign investment: in China, roughly three-quarters of foreign investment comes from Japan, ASEAN member countries and Korea, and two-thirds trade with them.[33] It is arguable that financial crises occurring one after another in the region provide a special example of economic interdependence in the region.

East Asian countries seemed to develop a sense of community in the crisis. They supported their crisis-hit neighbours, and Japan – despite its own financial worries at the time – introduced the Miyazawa Initiative to provide valuable support. China – under pressure in view of the crisis – committed itself not to devalue its currency. The 'Chiang Mai Initiative' of swap and repurchase arrangements among ASEAN members, China, South Korea and Japan (the 'ASEAN + 3'), which will be discussed later, is another example of enhanced regional co-operation.

In all, a regional group can mobilise the strong forces of self-interest and immediate concern that are felt within a small, geographically contiguous group. Regional arrangements can be effective when multilateral agencies are slow or hindered by imperfect assessments of the situation. Just as there are different levels of government (local, national) within a country, not all international issues will be best dealt on a one-world universal basis. Given unique regional interests, it is reasonable to hold that regional financial arrangements might still be important and worth striving for, even in an increasingly globalised world.

With respect to the timing of a prospective regional arrangement in East Asia, it is easy to point towards inadequate representation of East Asia in the IMF (and the World Bank as well) as a catalyst for a regional

---

[33] These figures are based on the statistical data available at the official website of the Ministry of Foreign Trade and Economic Co-operation of the People's Republic of China: http://www.moftec.gov.cn/moftec/official/html/statistics_data.htm.

arrangement.[34] In the face of the crisis, East Asia realised the low degree of its involvement and weak voice in the IMF (and the World Bank as well) and in the overall framework of consultation and decision-making on international monetary affairs and economic policy.

Inadequate representation of East Asian countries in the existing multilateral framework may result in serious problems. For example, the United States will promote the cause of those areas of principal interest to it (principally Latin America) and Europe will promote the interests of its Eastern European neighbours (including Russia), so that the interests of the countries of Asia may be without a potent partner at the multilateral debate.[35] There is a real possibility that countries which get such a seal of approval will be the countries of principal interest to the largest members of the IMF who dominate the Board. It may be difficult to redress this imbalance if the regional voice is not well co-ordinated.

V. Initiatives: towards a regional arrangement of finance in East Asia

1. Mahathir's EAEG

Early in 1990, Mahathir Mohamad, Malaysian Prime Minister, proposed the foundation of an East Asian Economic Group (EAEG),[36] encompassing ASEAN, China, Japan and Korea.

---

[34] Seemingly as a response, membership of BIS has been significantly opened up to non-European members. Moreover, the Board of Governors of the BIS decided to expand the Bank's activities in the Asia–Pacific region by establishing a Regional Treasury dealing room in its Representative Office for Asia and the Pacific. Due to the limited mandate of the BIS, however, the increasing number of East Asian members, in line with other non-European members, in the BIS have contributed few to the voice of East Asia in the multilateral financial system. For example, the main purpose of the new 'Dealing Room' is only to provide central banks with access to BIS banking services during trading hours in the Asian time zone.

At far as the current multilateral framework is concerned, perhaps, a strong regional representation should be prioritised, which would catalyse a better articulation of other aspects of regional interests at the multilateral level. For example, G20 (the lineal successor to G22) now already has the potential to become a premier group for discussing the critical issues of globalisation, with a representative audience no longer dominated by Europeans. The Financial Stability Forum has been formed, again with good representation from the region. What is needed is to hammer out the specifics of financial rules and regulations. Based on the existing power balance, however, it is unlikely that the G7 is fully prepared to do so.

[35] This sort of danger has been foreseen in the Contingent Credit Line programme being devised at the IMF, where countries which receive a prior 'seal of approval' will be able to draw on Fund support more or less automatically in time of need.

[36] It is also reported as bearing the name 'East Asia Economic Caucus (EAEC)'.

Mahathir is an outspoken critic of the West and defender of 'Asian values', which the West deems as a reference to authoritarian rule. His proposal encountered opposition primarily from the United States, which feared for its leading role in Asia.

To make the matter worse, Mahathir's initiative failed to win support from the countries in the region. As a result of US influence, Japan showed unwillingness to support the EAEG initiative. China, having just recovered from the Tiananmen shock, was preoccupied with its domestic economic development. Thus, closer economic co-operation with its Asian neighbours was not its priority. Even ASEAN member states, such as Thailand, Singapore and the Philippines, demonstrated their preference for an alternative initiative, that is, the trans-regional Asia–Pacific Economic Co-operation forum (APEC).[37] Nevertheless, any regional financial arrangement in East Asia potentially embraces the same membership envisaged by Mahathir.

2. Japan: Miyazawa Initiative

Perhaps the most important and striking development in East Asian regionalism in respect of financial regulation is the proposal for an Asian Monetary Fund (AMF) presented by Sakakibara Eisuke, Japanese Vice-Minister of Finance for International Affairs, in 1997.

Japan's proposal was to strengthen its role of political and economic leadership in Asia. However, it inevitably was reminiscent to those countries in the region that suffered from Japan's invasion and occupation in World War II, and China in particular, of the pre-war 'Great East Asia Co-Prosperity Sphere'. Thus, these countries were indifferent towards this proposal.

But the more decisive factor was the US response. The AMF proposal came to a halt after the United States, wanting to maintain its grip on Asian affairs, refused to back it up. Therefore, Japan retreated from the AMF proposal. Instead, in 1998 it came up with the Miyazawa Initiative (so called after Minister of Finance Miyazawa Kiichi). This represents a move to co-operate with other Asian countries facing economic difficulties by using funds from a variety of sources, including the official development assistance programme, the Export–Import Bank

---

[37] This was basically an alternative proposal by the United States. With the support of Japan and Australia and some of the ASEAN members, the initiative finally led to the founding of a trans-regional economic co-operation forum.

of Japan, and the Bank of Japan's foreign reserves. Under this initiative, designed to serve as a supplement to IMF and World Bank assistance, Japan offered to provide bridging loans, low-interest yen loans, and Export–Import Bank loans to support measures to help small businesses and strengthen the social safety net, as well as offering assistance to smooth Asian countries' issuance of bonds and raising foreign capital in international markets.

This diplomatic initiative was launched as one move towards the creation of a new kind of consultative mechanism in Asia for overcoming the kind of difficulties that could arise again and towards the formulation of a system enabling the flexible provision of funds.

3. ASEAN: Chiang Mai Initiative

In the 2000 Finance Ministers' meeting in Chiang Mai, Thailand,[38] ASEAN + 3 formally declared a common position and initiative on a regional financing arrangement to supplement the existing international facilities. The 'Chiang Mai Initiative' proposes an expanded ASEAN Swap Arrangement[39] including all ASEAN countries, and a network of bilateral swap and repurchase agreement facilities among ASEAN countries, China, Japan and the Republic of Korea. As a first step, the 'Chiang Mai Initiative' called for strengthening the existing co-operative framework among monetary authorities.

It leaves open what form a regional arrangement may take by requesting the ASEAN Secretariat to 'lead and co-ordinate a study on other appropriate mechanisms that could enhance our ability to provide

---

[38] The Finance Ministers' meeting followed the 'Joint Statement on East Asian Co-operation' issued by the Leaders of the ASEAN + 3 at their Informal Meeting in Manila on 28 November 1999. The leaders agreed on strengthening the policy dialogue, co-ordination and collaboration on the financial, monetary and fiscal issues of common interest, focusing initially on issues related to macroeconomic risk management, enhancing corporate governance, monitoring regional capital flows, strengthening banking and financial systems, reforming the international financial architecture, and enhancing self-help and support mechanisms in East Asia through the ASEAN + 3 Framework, including the ongoing dialogue and co-operation mechanism of the ASEAN + 3 finance and central bank leaders and officials.

[39] In pursuit of their common objective to promote monetary co-operation among ASEAN member countries, the ASEAN Central Banks and Monetary Authorities on 5 August 1977 established an ASEAN Swap Arrangement ('the Arrangement') for a period of one year, as laid down in the Memorandum of Understanding on ASEAN Swap Arrangement ('the Memorandum'). The Memorandum has been supplemented five times. The latest one was made on 19 September 1992.

sufficient and timely financial support to ensure financial stability in the East Asian region'.[40]

The initiatives for regional arrangements in East Asia, albeit different in terms of institutional structure, have demonstrated that the East Asian countries have recognised that the fiscal and monetary policies of an individual country are of concern to its neighbours, and that subjecting policies to regional scrutiny and, perhaps, discipline is one way to build economic stability internationally.

VI. Institutional characteristics of regional arrangements of finance in Asia: co-ordination or regional regulatory regime?

It seems clear that any future regional arrangement in East Asia will be a purely East Asian arrangement,[41] differing in membership from existing regional institutions, for example, APEC or the Asian Development Bank. Of course, geographical proximity and cultural identity may account for the scenario. But the G7's performance in the East Asian financial crisis – which resulted in questioning their reliability – and its emphasis on the IMF would not justify American leadership and European involvement in the proposed East Asian regional arrangement.

In structure, the ASEAN + 3 is starting to look like the G7. It has become the most active regional grouping outside Europe. It already has a more sophisticated machinery than NAFTA. In matters of finance, however, the East Asian regional arrangement is still at an early stage. With its widely divergent economies, East Asia is not only incomparable to the European Union, but even less ready for monetary union than Latin America.[42] It is easily argued that in the financial area, the new East Asian regionalism takes the form of swaps and sub-regional surveillance.

---

[40] *Ibid.*

[41] Australia, which has shown keen interest in any regional arrangement in Asia, may become a part of such arrangement, although its alleged Asian identity is disputable.

[42] Six Latin American countries, Brazil, Paraguay, Uruguay and Argentina (Mercosur's four key members), along with the two associate members of Mercosur, Chile and Bolivia, signed an agreement committing each country to a set of economic-convergence targets. These were startlingly reminiscent of those agreed by the European Union at Maastricht in 1992 as a precursor to the introduction of the single European currency seven years later. Like Maastricht, the Florianopolis criteria set targets for fiscal and monetary policy, requiring the Mercosur countries to limit their annual inflation rates to no more than 5% between 2002 and 2005, reducing to 4% in 2006 and to 3% thereafter.

Foreign currency swaps could lead to various currency linkages, perhaps ultimately culminating in some form of currency union. For example, there is a fruitful debate underway already as to whether regional currency baskets make sense, and whether Asia seems a suitable case for a currency union. A common currency, which may be modelled on the euro of the European Union, is being discussed.[43] A joint intervention arrangement, with the purpose of replacing the pre-crisis dollar-pegs[44] and the costly free floats imposed by the financial crisis, is also being considered. Nevertheless, an Asian Monetary Fund (AMF) is beginning to form.

One answer could be to resurrect the idea of an Asian monetary fund to act as the regional equivalent of the IMF. The idea was put forward at the height of the regional economic crisis, and rapidly shot down by the United States, which feared the IMF's authority would be weakened in Asia and moral hazard heightened.

Indeed, both the embryonic common currency arrangements among the ASEAN + 3 and the AMF waiting offstage, i.e. the emergence of a financial arrangement in East Asia, clearly signal the sprout of the East Asia regionalism. One may reasonably expect that it will pose a challenge to G7's dominance of the world's financial system, unless East Asia is duly represented in a reformed global financial infrastructure.

Public debt, they stipulate, should be reduced to no more than 40% of the GDP by 2010 and fiscal deficits should not exceed 3% of the GDP from 2002.

[43] The East Asian financial crisis was rooted in those countries' overdependence on the dollar, to which they had effectively linked their own currencies. As an alternative to the dollar peg system, Japanese Minister of Finance Miyazawa Kiichi suggested at the Asia–Europe Meeting (ASEM) in January 2000 that the troubled currencies of Asia be pegged to a basket of the yen, dollar, and euro. The idea gained the approval of the Asian nations present. Some Asian countries, and Japan in particular, have missed two chances to found Asia's own currency. The first came when the Bretton Woods international monetary system crumbled following the 'Nixon shock' – the American president's August 1971 decision to end the dollar's convertibility into gold. The second opportunity came in 1985 with the Plaza accord when Japan had to internationalise the yen, which was aimed at correcting the dollar's overvaluation. See (1999) 26(3) *Japan Echo*, available at http://www.japanecho.co.jp/docs/html/260308.html.

A common Asian currency will be a symbol of Asian autonomy in monetary affairs, and exchange-rate stability within the region. Furthermore, a common currency – an Asian version of the euro – rather than merely promoting the internationalisation of one nation's currency, the yen – will cause less opposition from the other East Asian countries to such a scheme.

[44] Except for China, that adopts a managed floating system, and Japan, that adopts a free float, most of the East Asian countries practice the dollar-pegging system. Hong Kong's exchange rate system is a typical example of this sort.

VII. Obstructions to regional arrangements in East Asia

As Joseph Stiglitz, former chief economist at the World Bank, observed, an Asian monetary fund would be far more attuned to the economic needs of the region than the IMF in distant Washington. An AMF established at a time of relative economic stability would be more adept at crisis prevention, more responsive (should crisis threaten) and far more concerned about encouraging the gentle monetary convergence of Asian economies as a way to build long-term economic strength of the region.

In this regard, it must be borne in mind that even the best regulatory regime, be it regional or multilateral, cannot prevent any possible financial crises, neither can it solve them all. Nevertheless, whether a regional financial arrangement will function effectively depends on the degree to which it eliminates internal disintegrating factors and external obstructions.

Disintegrating factors within East Asia are both political and economic. Competition for leadership, mutual mistrust between China and Japan, the Spratly Islands disputes notably between China and other ASEAN countries, are among the disintegrating political factors. This may prove critical in respect of the crucial issue of leadership in the proposed regional arrangement. In terms of GDP and technological sophistication, the obvious regional leader is Japan. Partly for historical reasons, and partly because of its internal focus, however, Japan has not achieved the sort of leadership which is commensurate with its economic clout. Unless Japan comes to terms with its past, it will have difficulties in playing such a role.[45] In terms of population and potential economic size, in the long run, China might claim the role. China considerably scored in diplomatic terms by delivering an international pledge not to devalue the yuan exchange rate, a commitment that was necessary for China's own purposes.

---

[45] *Japan Echo*, an influential Japanese media, shares this view. It observed that for Japan the '[f]irst and foremost is reflection on the past. That means dispassionate analysis of Japan's history and sincere reflection on past policies to elucidate why one aspect of early modern Japan's development led to the invasion and colonisation of Asian countries. By means of reflection on the past and a correct perception of history, along with apologetic feelings toward the countries and peoples hurt by its invasion and colonial rule, Japan can indirectly demonstrate to the world the driving force behind its present democratic politics and economic development.' *Japan Echo*, above note 43.

However, given its political ideology, China has not yet won the fully-fledged trust from its neighbours. In contrast, ASEAN which in view of its relatively small economic and political clout has been cautious against outside dominance over any regional arrangement in Asia, lacks the ability of leadership. Even the dominant country (Indonesia) within ASEAN, unfortunately, is not in a position, for the moment, to be a vigorous leader of regional arrangements. Thus, the unresolved issue of leadership may hinder progress towards a regional arrangement in East Asia.

In addition, where mutual mistrust exists, submitting confidential information to a regional financial institution may mean providing information which may be used publicly by other members. All this constitutes major political obstruction.

In the economic field, East Asian countries are quite heterogeneous in terms of their economic development, the openness of their capital account, the strength of their banking and corporate sectors, the maturity and strength of regulatory and supervisory institutions, and their political systems. For example, in respect of the degree of liberalisation of financial sectors, they can be classified in two categories: those economies that have substantially liberalised their capital markets and those economies that have not yet substantially done so. This difference poses particular difficulties to an integrated regional monetary arrangement.

Along with internal disintegrating forces, another obstruction to the regional arrangement in East Asia is the external response, particularly from the G7. The answer actually depends on whether a regional financial institution would be acceptable to other major financial jurisdictions outside East Asia. To some extent, this depends on the East Asian countries themselves. At least in two ways they can alleviate the doubts of their major partners in the G7: convincing and reforming.

Although US opposition to the AMF may be due to viewing all this through the IMF prism, no effort should be spared in convincing the G7 to have an open mind, and not to see regional arrangements as rivals but as complementary to multilateral arrangements.[46] A fair degree

---

[46] For example, the APEC welcomed the approval of the new arrangements to borrow (NAB) by the Executive Board of the IMF that enhances the IMF's ability to safeguard the international monetary system. 'We reiterate the importance of the eleventh review of IMF quotas, including adjustments that take into account the relative position of member economies, to ensure that the IMF has sufficient ordinary resources for future operations.' Joint Ministerial Statement of the Fourth APEC Finance Ministers Meeting

of overlap is inevitable. Given that the representational resources are a constraint, one should not be too fretted about the overlap.

It is more important to establish a solid basis for a regional arrangement. In this regard, amid various policy options as to proper regimes for exchange rates, capital flows and debt restructuring, one thread remains fairly constant: the rule of law, the importance of a stable, transparent, and equitably enforced system of norms, and rules for the functioning of local and global markets alike.

VIII. Concluding remarks

The East Asian financial crisis revealed significant weaknesses in the rules governing international capital flows and in the international responses to the crisis. With progress of reform, it is recognised that measures to strengthen the international financial architecture need to include a review of the international financial institutions, as well as the international regulatory bodies, in order to enhance their capacity and capability to contain and resolve crises.

It might be fair to argue that no plausible alternative to the existing financial system has emerged at the multilateral level. But, given the unavailability of a multilateral arrangement that deals with individual regional interests in a manner satisfactory to the region, the regional arrangement becomes an attractive option.

It stirs imagination that the Asian Development Bank (ADB) has played a positive role for development finance for over three decades.[47] A properly structured Asian regional arrangement – whatever its level of institutionalisation might be – could also do much for the international financial system.

In this context, numerous initiatives have emerged. Notably, a real regional arrangement is still at its earlier stage. It should be pointed out that peer surveillance has not taken the major role that it might have, lacking any clear functional model or strong leadership. The current focus on the Chiang Mai swap proposals could be the basis of some important ties, but one should keep in mind that ASEAN has had such swap arrangements in place for quite some time, which did not prove to be much of an advantage in the Asian crisis in 1997. Such arrangements

(Cebu, Philippines, 5–6 April 1997), available at http://www.apecsec.org.sg/virtualib/minismtg/mtgfin97.html.

[47] ADB has been dedicated to reducing poverty in Asia and the Pacific since it was founded in 1966.

are valuable in that they get people together and make them talk about other issues, but it would be a mistake to see them, taken by themselves, as massive breakthroughs in regional co-operation.

In this regard, European integration can provide a positive inspiration for East Asia. It has been observed that deep institutional reform is difficult, and takes many decades to yield results.[48] That observation being true, to establish a functioning institution might involve even lengthier periods of adjustment.[49] The costs in terms of time needed to do so, might become a real hindrance for ambitious East Asian policymakers to risk institutionalising an independent regional financial institution.

Finally, two points should be made clear: first, in order for the proposed regional financial institution to play a positive role, domestic legal infrastructures must be reformed in parallel with the institutionalisation of the regional arrangement. An international regulatory regime can not bring its role into full play if it is not complemented by a facilitating national legal infrastructure no matter how good the design of the international regulatory regime may be. Second, any institutional arrangement regarding international financial regulation must be beneficial to all the members of the region, and should not cause harm to other regions (*jisuobuyu, wushiyuren*). In other words, regional initiatives provide added responsibilities. Countries, particularly in Asia, have to learn the art of speaking frankly to their neighbours when changes in their policies are needed. And countries have to ensure that greater regional integration does not develop at the expense of splitting the world into regional blocs.

---

[48] *Foreign Affairs*, March/April, 1998.
[49] One has reason to believe that an East Asian counterpart to the euro would not take such a long time as the euro to get off the ground, because at the start there was far more scepticism than support among European countries that had so recently been in mortal combat.

8

WTO rules on trade in financial services: a victory of greed over reason?

MICHAEL J. HAHN

The liberalisation of regulations concerning financial services and the pertinent industries do not seem particularly *de rigueur* as of now, i.e. the end of 2002. Most of the OECD members, in particular the countries of the Triad, experience what many people think feels, smells and quacks 'just like' a recession. Although the stock markets reached their climax only in 2000, it seems like a century ago. The rock-star status of the movers and shakers of the financial industry has vanished like the picture of *Dorian Gray*. Liberalisation of international trade in services means, one way or the other, lesser and less infringing government regulations, doesn't it? If you want to win an election these days, be it in America or in Europe, *this* is *not* 'platform material'. Nevertheless, this is exactly what Article XIX of the GATS calls for:

> '(1) ... Members shall enter into successive rounds of negotiations, beginning not later than five years from the date of entry into force of the WTO Agreement and periodically thereafter, with a view to achieving a progressively higher level of liberalization ... (4) The process of progressive liberalization shall be ... directed towards increasing the general level of specific commitments undertaken by Members under this Agreement.'

Indeed, the European Community (very much like the United States and other major trading nations) seems to take that *obligatio de negotiando* seriously:

> '[T]he EC is seeking in the current GATS negotiations to remove significant restrictions on the establishment of companies in the whole financial services sector, to liberalise cross-border trade on certain activities, such as reinsurance and provision of financial information,

and to encourage regulatory frameworks underpinning market access commitments.'[1]

Assuming for the moment that these positions will find their way into the legal documents finalising this first World Trade Organisation (WTO)-round of trade negotiations: would this be an international legal regime impairing governments to provide good governance to their peoples, in particular to protect small investors and provide stringent prudential regulations for savings and pensions? This introductory paper on the WTO rules on financial services will suggest that this does not seem to be the case; to the contrary, liberalisation of trade in financial services and strengthening of domestic and international prudential regimes have historically been inseparable.

I. GATS and financial services

1. Definitions

Despite coming into force just before the closing of the 20th century, on 1 January 1995, the GATS is the *first* non-regional multilateral agreement covering trade and investment in the financial services sector.[2] It is an integral part of the package of agreements which ended the so-called Uruguay-Round of Multilateral Trade Negotiations.[3] They establish the

---

[1] Summary of the EC's Initial Requests to Third Countries in the GATS Negotiations, Brussels, 1 July 2002, to be found at http://europa.eu.int/comm/trade/services/gats_sum.htm (30 August 2005); overviews of the state of play of the Doha Round can be found at http://www.wto.org/english/tratop_e/dda_e/dda_e.htm; relevant US proposals can be found at http://usinfo.state.gov/topical/econ/wto/. See Jeffrey Schott, 'Comment on the Doha Ministerial', (2002) 5 *Journal of International Economic Law* 191 et seq.; Bernard M. Hoekman, 'Strengthening the global trade architecture for development' (2002) 1 *World Trade Review* 23 et seq.; Steven Charnovitz, 'The Legal Status of the Doha Declarations', (2002) 5 *Journal of International Economic Law* 207 et seq.; Terrence P. Stewart, *After Doha* (Ardsley, 2002); Gary Horlick, 'Over the Bump in Doha' (2002) 5 *Journal of International Economic Law* 195 et seq.; see also Dietrich Barth, 'Die GATS 2000-Verhandlungen zur Liberalisierung des internationalen Dienstleistungshandels' (2000) 3 *Zeitschrift für europarechtliche Studien (ZeuS)* 273 et seq.

[2] For an historical introduction cf. Giorgio Sacerdoti (ed.), *Liberalization of Services and Intellectual Property in the Uruguay Round of GATT* (Fribourg, 1990).

[3] Cf. the multi-volume history of the Uruguay-Round negotiations edited by Terence P. Stewart, *The GATT Uruguay-Round – a Negotiating History (1986–1992)* (Deventer, 1993–1999); John Croome, *A History of the Uruguay Round* (Geneva, 1995); Jagdish Bhagwati (ed.), *The Uruguay-Round and Beyond, Festschrift fuer Arthur Dunkel* (Berlin, 1998); interesting related issues of US law are covered in John H. Jackson, 'The Great

World Trade Organisation (WTO) as institutional overhead for a multitude of multilateral (substantive) trade agreements, of which the General Agreement on Tariffs and Trade (GATT), the GATS and the Agreement on Trade–Related Aspects of Intellectual Property Rights (TRIPs Agreement) are the best known. *All* agreements are integral parts of the Marrakesh Agreement establishing the World Trade Organisation (WTO Agreement); participating states had the choice of either accepting the whole package – or to walk away. In the end, all states that had participated in the Uruguay Round took the first option. Thus, the institutional framework of the WTO applies to GATS and its obligations. This includes, in particular, the dispute settlement provisions of the WTO, contained in the Dispute Settlement Understanding (DSU).[4]

What are services, what are financial services? The term 'services' is not defined in the treaty itself.[5] It is understood to cover all commercially 'tradable' services, with the exception of air transport rights and services supplied under government authority. Financial services are defined specifically in the Annex on Financial Services (Annex) which forms an integral part of the GATS.[6] Capital and its (relatively) free cross-border movements are not financial services and will, as such, not be touched upon in this introductory paper. However, the GATS does contain provisions prohibiting restrictions on transboundary payments and transfers which would nullify or impair commitments to market access and national treatment.[7]

Sovereignty Debate: United States Acceptance and Implementation of the Uruguay Round Results' (1997) 36 *Columbia Journal of Transnational Law* 157–88.

[4] An authoritative introduction is provided by David Palmeter and Petros Mavroidis, *Dispute Settlement in the World Trade Organization* (The Hague, 1999) passim; see also Ernst-Ulrich Petersmann, *The GATT/WTO Dispute Settlement System: International Law, International Organizations and Dispute Settlement* (London, 1997).

[5] Proposals included, *inter alia*, a negative definition (activities which do not belong to the primary or secondary sector) and a positive definition (activities resulting in an intangible output). See Friedl Weiss, 'The General Agreement on Trade in Services 1994' (1995) 32 *Common Market Law Review* 1177 at 1189.

[6] Cf. GATS, Art. XXIX. The WTO Secretariat has produced a number of excellent studies on the subject of Financial Services, all to be found under http://www.wto.org; among those the 'Background Note by the Secretariat on Financial Services' (WTO Doc. S/C/W/ 72, 2 December 1998) and the paper by Masamichi Kono, Patrick Low, Mukela Luanga, Aaditya Mattoo, Maika Oshikawa and Ludger Schuknecht, *Opening Markets in Financial Services and the Role of the GATS* (WTO Publ., 1997) stand out.

[7] Cf. GATS, Art. XXI.

According to its Article I(2), GATS covers four modes of trade in services[8]:

Mode 1 – Cross-border supply. An example would be the supply of financial services by an investment banker in the City of London to a client in Switzerland, e.g. by mail, phone or electronic means.

Mode 2 – Supply on the domestic market to a foreign consumer. An example would be a US citizen travelling from the United States to Zurich to deposit funds in a private Swiss bank and having them managed there.

Mode 3 – Supply of services by foreign service supplier by a 'commercial presence' abroad.

'Commercial presence' is defined as 'any type of business or professional establishment, including through the constitution, acquisition or maintenance of a juridical person or the creation or maintenance of a branch or representative office within the territory of a member state for the purpose of supplying a service'.[9] Therefore events prior *and* subsequent to the establishment of a branch are covered, as are both existing and new investment. This, *nota bene*, amounts to the introduction of investment protection into the WTO legal regime; the importance of this (first) step is not diminished by the fact that the level of protection falls short of the standards in some bilateral investment protection agreements.

Mode 4 – Supply through presence of a natural person in the target market, i.e. dependent on cross-border movements of people providing services. An example would be the experienced portfolio manager travelling to her 'high-net-worth' client abroad to provide counsel and advice.

The GATS covers *all measures* of WTO members having an effect on the transboundary trade in services, for example, laws and regulations by the legislative and executive branches of government, including pertinent administrative measures. Article I(3)(a) (i) of GATS reiterates the principle, well established in general public international law, that the obligations of the GATS apply to *all levels of government* of the state party on whose behalf the WTO Agreement was concluded, i.e. to the member's central, regional and local authorities.

---

[8] Cf. Michael Trebilcock and Robert Howse, *The Regulation of International Trade* (2nd edn, London, 1995), p. 281.

[9] Cf. GATS, Art. XXVIII (d).

According to the Annex on Financial Services, *financial* services are services 'of a financial nature' offered by a financial service supplier of a member state. This includes both insurance and insurance-related services, and all banking services.[10] A rather exhaustive list of activities leaves little doubt that the negotiators wanted to comprehensively cover the activities of the financial industry. The Annex on financial services, para. 5 (http://www.wto.org/english/docs_e/legal_e/26-gats.doc, 30 October 2002) reads as follows:

'Financial services include the following activities:
Insurance and insurance-related services

   (i) Direct insurance (including co-insurance):
      (A) life
      (B) non-life
   (ii) Reinsurance and retrocession;
  (iii) Insurance intermediation, such as brokerage and agency;
  (iv) Services auxiliary to insurance, such as consultancy, actuarial, risk assessment and claim settlement services.

Banking and other financial services (excluding insurance)

   (v) Acceptance of deposits and other repayable funds from the public;
  (vi) Lending of all types, including consumer credit, mortgage credit, factoring and financing of commercial transaction;
 (vii) Financial leasing;
(viii) All payment and money transmission services, including credit, charge and debit cards, travellers cheques and bankers drafts;
  (ix) Guarantees and commitments;
   (x) Trading for own account or for account of customers, whether on an exchange, in an over-the-counter market or otherwise, the following:
      (A) money market instruments (including cheques, bills, certificates of deposits);
      (B) foreign exchange;
      (C) derivative products including, but not limited to, futures and options;
      (D) exchange rate and interest rate instruments, including products such as swaps, forward rate agreements;
      (E) transferable securities;
      (F) other negotiable instruments and financial assets, including bullion.

[10] Eric Leroux, 'Trade in Financial Services under the World Trade Organization' (2002) 36 *Journal of World Trade* 413 at 428 emphasises the breadth of coverage.

   (xi) Participation in issues of all kinds of securities, including underwriting and placement as agent (whether publicly or privately) and
provision of services related to such issues;

  (xii) Money broking;

 (xiii) Asset management, such as cash or portfolio management, all
forms of collective investment management, pension fund management, custodial, depository and trust services;

 (xiv) Settlement and clearing services for financial assets, including
securities, derivative products, and other negotiable instruments;

  (xv) Provision and transfer of financial information, and financial data
processing and related software by suppliers of other financial
services;

 (xvi) Advisory, intermediation and other auxiliary financial services on
all the activities listed in subparagraphs (v) through (xv), including
credit reference and analysis, investment and portfolio research
and advice, advice on acquisitions and on corporate restructuring
and strategy.'

It is worth noting that the Annex also gives a very broad definition of
service supplier: it includes not only natural or juridical persons already
in the business of providing a financial service, but also persons who
(just) *wish* to supply it.[11] Thus, other than under general GATS law, not
only those already engaged in the provision of a particular financial
service benefit from the WTO rules on trade in financial services.

2. Structure of GATS

Due to the considerable amount of specialised literature introducing the
new GATS to the students of international economic law, it seems
appropriate to outline just the bare essentials of the regulatory concept
of the GATS, insofar as they have particular importance for the trade in
financial services.[12]

---

[11] Despite the broadness of the definition, it does not include public entities; see GATS
Annex on financial services, para. 5(b), (c). Also, of course, services supplied in the
exercise of governmental authority are not covered by the liberalising rules of GATS and
the Annex; cf. Article I 3(b) of GATS and Annex, para. 1(b)

[12] See, e.g., Friedl Weiss, 'The General Agreement on Trade in Services 1994' (1995)
32 *Common Market Law Review* 1177 et seq.; Harry G. Broadman, 'The Uruguay Round
Accord on International Trade and Investment in Services, (1994) 17 *World Economy*
282 et seq.; Bernard Hoekman, 'Assessing the General Agreement on Trade in Services'

While the drafters of GATS have been inspired by their intimate knowledge of the GATT, they certainly did not transfer the latter's concept lock, stock and barrel to the new regime of the international trade in services. Thus, GATS's regulatory concept differs substantially from the (relatively) straightforward older treaty dealing (only) with goods. Although many obligations of the GATT have, as of today, been re-regulated in depth through 'side agreements' (see, e.g. GATT, Articles VI and XVI on one hand, and its elaboration in the Agreements on the Implementation of Article VI of the GATT 1994 ('Antidumping Code') and the Agreement on Subsidies and Countervailing Measures ('Subsidies Code'), on the other hand), in principle, *all* obligations laid down in the GATT apply *equally* to all contracting state parties to this agreement (unless, of course, an exception applies in a particular case). Most importantly, this includes the obligation to treat goods from other WTO members in a non-discriminatory fashion (most favoured nation principle, GATT, Article I), and to treat all goods, having legally entered the domestic market, not differently from domestic goods (national treatment, GATT, Article III). The legal obligations of any state party to the GATT, with the exception of the level of tariffs,[13] can be derived from the text of the GATT and its side-agreements.

Things are quite different for the members' GATS obligations. While a good number of obligations laid down in GATS do bind the members of the WTO as such, save (as in the GATT) some exceptions apply,[14] many of the most far-reaching obligations are only applicable to the extent that a member state has accepted them *specifically*: This is obviously true for the Specific Commitments of Part III of the GATS, dealing, *inter alia* (and most importantly), with market access and national treatment. These trade privileges, so fundamental for the WTO/GATT-regime of the trade *in goods*, are – with regard to *services* – only granted to the extent a member state has committed itself. Even more remarkably, states have been allowed to maintain (*at least* for the

---

in Will Martin and L. Alan Winters (eds.), *The Uruguay Round and Developing Countries* (Cambridge, 1996), p. 88 et seq.; Pierre Sauvé, 'Assessing the General Agreement on Trade in Services: Half-full or Half-Empty' (1996) 29 *Journal of World Trade* 142 et seq.; Trebilcock and Howse, *The Regulation of International Trade*, above note 8, at 270 et seq.

[13] GATT, Art. II, para. 1(a) obliges each signatory to 'accord to the commerce of the other contracting parties treatment no less favourable than that provided for in ... the appropriate Schedule annexed to this Agreement'. Thus, only by checking those lists of commitments entered one may know what tariffs, say, the EC may charge for bananas or steel products.

[14] E.g. the General Exception of Article XIV or the Security Exception of Article XIV *bis*.

next ten years)[15] measures discriminating between trading partners, provided they listed those discriminatory regulations; thus, as a matter of law, member states have been allowed to retain the *status quo ante* for the time being, and this option has been utilised by a considerable number of members. Sometimes, states were even reluctant to enter commitments matching their domestic *status quo*: in these cases, the wish to retain legal flexibility (i.e. not being bound by *legal* obligations) vis-à-vis their trading partners was stronger than the desire to achieve optimal negotiating results.[16] The ensuing regulatory mess (it is almost impossible to find out, for example, what kind of commitments India, a country with a middle-class almost as numerous as the population of the EU, has made with regard to *asset management*) is a function of conflicting objectives: the wish to establish a regime *à la* GATT for services, on one hand, and the urge, most pronouncedly felt by some developing countries, to limit the extent of legally binding commitments and to preserve economic sovereignty (a doubtful notion, obviously, nevertheless frequently aimed for). Because a number of states were not prepared to grant market access *per se* (thus the paradigm shift to make market access and national treatment contingent on *specific* commitments), more open trading partners insisted on being allowed deviations from the most-favoured-nation (MFN) rule, in order to differentiate between open and closed markets and to prevent 'free riding' of the latter.

3. Financial services as novel subject of multilateral trade law

Why is it, that the GATS is *not* a 'GATT for services'? Why the particular fuss about financial services?

Services in general are a much more regulated area of the national economies than is the case for goods. While typically the import of goods as such has no or little impact on people, a change of the ways

---

[15] See Annex on Article II Exemptions, paras. 5 and 6: 'The exemption of a Member from its obligations under paragraph 1 of Article II of the Agreement with respect to a particular measure terminates on the date provided for in the exemption. ... In principle, such exemptions should not exceed a period of 10 years. In any event, they shall be subject to negotiation in subsequent trade liberalizing rounds.'

[16] Cf. Aaditya Mattoo, *Financial Services and the World Trade Organization. Liberalization Commitments of the Developing and Transition Economies* (World Bank, 1999), available at http://www.worldbank.org/html/dec/Publications/Workpapers/wps2000 series/wps2184/wps2184-abstract.html), p. 5.

health care, education or accounting services are delivered has a clear and visible impact on the very fabric of a nation's society. In particular, the strategic importance and political sensitivity of financial services cannot be overstated: it is not only the largest of all internationally traded services, but also vital for all other economic activity, and is thus a key tool for the control and fine-tuning of national economies.

While for some governments the liberalisation of banking, securities and insurance services were high on their list of priorities for the Uruguay Round negotiations, many developing countries were, at least initially, reluctant to allow increased competition and presence of foreign financial institutions, being afraid that those would undermine their economic autonomy and threaten their national financial institutions, which, if not state-owned, were more often than not close to those in power.[17] But even in many OECD countries, not everybody was a champion of a multilateral approach: bilateral, reciprocal, treaties on market access for foreign financial institutions had proven tremendously successful, for example, between the United States and its European trading partners. The advantages of extending the MFN standard to that sensitive area *and* having the WTO's dispute settlement procedure second-guess decisions did not seem self-evident to all major players.

These conflicting approaches are reflected in GATS's design.[18] On one hand, it allows members to decide which sectors and to what extent they will open to competition by foreign suppliers. The GATS Agreement, and even the GATS-*commitments* of most WTO members do not, as such, create 'open markets'. However, the GATS and the Financial Services Agreement have 'locked in' this important sector, thus subjecting all WTO members not only to some, if few, minimum standards, including supervision through the WTO's dispute settlement system, but also to progress in future negotiation rounds. As of now, more than 110 WTO members have entered commitments with regard to financial services which makes it the sector with the most commitments, before tourism.[19]

---

[17] Brian Hindley, 'Service Sector Protection, Consideration for Developing Countries' (1988) 2 *World Bank Economic Review* 205.

[18] See Geza Feketekuty, 'Assessing and Improving the Architecture of GATS' in Pierre Sauvé and Robert M. Stern (eds.), *GATS 2000: New Directions in Trade Liberalization* (Washington, D.C., 2000), p. 85 et seq.

[19] An excellent overview on the WTO regime on financial services is given by Masamichi Kono, Patrick Low, Mukela Luanga, Aaditya Mattoo, Maika Oshikawa and Ludger Schuknecht, *Opening Markets in Financial Services and the Role of the GATS* (WTO,

The conclusion of the Financial Services Agreement coincided with the financial crisis in Asia.[20] Nevertheless, even the most seriously affected WTO members upheld their commitments to improve access for foreign service providers: obviously, it had become accepted that increased competition and openness would strengthen domestic financial infrastructures rather than weaken them. This view gained support not the least due to the fact that the crisis in Asia was partly caused by aggressive portfolio operations of domestic Asian financial services providers used to somewhat generous supervision. Stronger foreign competition, used to much stricter prudential and (internal) compliance rules might have represented a check on some of these excesses. It helped that the focus of most commitments were on *Mode 3* services, granting foreign service providers the right 'to establish' in the host market: This, of course, entails the influx of fresh capital, an effect which is sought not only in times of crisis.

4. Overview of some particularly important regulations in GATS proper, relating to financial services

(a) MFN, market access and national treatment

As already mentioned, these principles, which are the *'raison d'être'* of the GATT, have, as a matter of law, been structured completely differently from GATT, and from each other, in GATS: the MFN rule, *in principle*, does apply to 'like services and service suppliers'. However, unlike the situation in GATT, members have been allowed to legally carve out countless exceptions to the application of MFN by listing them in the 'Annex on Article II Exemptions', GATS, Article II 2.[21] The term

---

1997); see also Piritta Sorsa, 'The GATS Agreement on Financial Services – A Modest Start to Multilateral Liberalization', *IMF Working Papers* WP/97/66, 1997; Joel Trachtman, 'Trade in financial services under GATS, NAFTA and the EC' (1995) 34 *Columbia Journal of Transnational Law* 37 et seq.; Jeffrey Simser, 'GATS and financial services: redefining borders' (1996) 3 *Buffalo Journal of International Law* 33 et seq.; Philippe Metzger, 'Les services bancaires sous l'accord général sur le commerce des services (GATS)' (1996) 2 *Revue du marché unique européen* 107 et seq.; Welf Werner, 'Liberalisierung von Finanzdienstleistungen' (1996) 51 *Aussenwirtschaft* 327 et seq.; Martin Georges Eckert, *Die Liberalisierung internationaler Finanzdienstleistungen durch das General Agreement on Trade in Services (GATS)* (Hamburg, 1997).

[20] Dilip K. Das, 'Trade in financial services and the role of the GATS – Against the backdrop of the Asian financial crises' (1998) 32 *Journal of World Trade* 79–114.

[21] See Aaditya Mattoo, 'MFN and GATS' in Thomas Cottier and Petros Mavroidis (eds.), *Regulatory Barriers and the Principle of Non-Discrimination in World Trade Law* (World Trade Forum, vol. 2) (Ann Arbor, 2000), p. 51 et seq.

defining the beneficiaries of MFN, i.e. *like services and service suppliers*, has not yet enjoyed the attention its sister provision in GATT has received by panels and, ultimately, the Appellate Body.[22]

Market access and national treatment are only granted if a member commits itself specifically *and* only to the extent it chooses not to take specific reservations (see the text of Articles XVI and XVII). With regard to market access, each WTO member state determines for what, if any, service sectors it wishes to make liberalisation commitments: members are (legally) free to determine the number and nature of the sectors to be included. While many OECD countries have entered commitments 'across the board', a good number of less developed countries (LDCs) have taken advantage of the flexibility the GATS allows and have only liberalised a very limited number of sectors.

Members are not only free to determine the sectors they want to enter 'special commitments' for. Additionally, they enjoy the competence to custom-tailor their sectoral liberalisation commitments through individual restrictions and conditions. This combination of country-specific *positive* schedules of liberalised service sectors with *negative* schedules of qualifications is referred to as 'hybrid liberalisation concept'. As a consequence, the members of GATS do not just cruise *à deux vitesses*; rather (to stay with the picture), every member may determine *both* its flight altitude *and* its speed.[23] It should be kept in mind, however, that the freedom of choice provided by GATS exists only in legal terms. As the delayed conclusion of the Agreement on Financial Services showed, at least the world's biggest producer and consumer of services, the United States, were only prepared to conclude the deal when the price seemed right.

The obligation to provide market access aims at both discriminating and non-discriminating quantitative restrictions; it seems fair to say, though, that with regard to the latter fewer commitments have been entered into. Removing *some* structural impediments has been expressly addressed in certain provisions of the Understanding between

---

[22] So far, the Appellate Body, has not had to explore the concept of likeness according to GATS, Article II. A panel has held that 'to the extent that entities provide these like services, they are like service suppliers'; see Report by the Panel *European Communities – Regime for the Importation. Sale and Distribution of Bananas*, WT/DS/27/R, 22 May 1997, para. 7.336, which was has not so far been modified by the Appellate Body.

[23] See Rudolf Adlung, 'Services Trade Liberalization from Developed and Developing Country Perspectives' in Pierre Sauvé and Robert M. Stern (eds.), *GATS 2000: New Directions in Services Trade Liberalization* (Washington, D.C., 2000), p. 112 et seq.

developed states, discussed in more detail below. Also, the obligations discussed immediately under the sub-headings (b) and (c) below (transparency and certain minimum standards for member states' domestic legal orders) address government behaviour that, at least in theory, is non-discriminatory.[24] The same is true for those government measures listed in GATS, Article XVI(2) which are prohibited once a commitment to allow market access is entered into, *unless* the Member has explicitly reserved the right to use those (*per se* illegal) measures. They include the limiting of the number of service providers through quotas, monopolies or economic needs tests, restrictions on the value or number of service transactions, restrictions on the number of natural persons in a certain service sector, and restrictions on the legal form of foreign subsidiaries or foreign shareholding.

Specific commitments to provide national treatment are, essentially, the (legally binding) promise to provide equal treatment for both domestic and foreign services and providers, both *de iure* and *de facto*. Again, reservations are possible: the hybrid approach set-up by GATS allows an à la carte selection of what WTO members promise to their trading partners.

(b) Transparency

Article III of GATS supposedly does away with legal and administrative surprises for traders, often used to create legal uncertainty and thus stifle market access: traders need legal certainty to properly evaluate the costs of market entry. Members are obliged to publish promptly all legal and administrative documents relevant for the international trade in services. Additionally, all pertinent changes have to be notified to the WTO Council for Trade in Services, established under Article IV(5) of the WTO Agreement. The establishment of one or more inquiry points in each member state, providing, upon request, specific information to other members (GATS Article III(4)), constitutes a very important practical facilitation for traders.

---

[24] Cf. Sidney J. Key, 'Trade Liberalization and Prudential Regulation: The International Framework for Financial Services' (1999) 75 *International Affairs* 61, 66. For the concept of market contestability see, Robert Z. Lawrence, 'Towards globally contestable markets' in OECD (ed.), *Market access after the Uruguay Round: investment, competition and technology perspectives* (Paris, 1996); Edward M. Graham and Robert Z. Lawrence, 'Measuring the international contestability of markets: a conceptual approach' (1996) 30 *Journal of World Trade* 5 et seq.

(c) Minimum standards for domestic legal orders

Articles VI and VII of GATS establish minimum standards for the legal orders of its signatories; remarkably, one finds, besides *substantive* obligations (members agree to 'ensure that all measures of general application affecting trade in services are administered in a reasonable, objective and impartial manner', GATS Article VI(1)), obligations to provide for a fair and impartial *administrative procedure* and even the obligation to make certain *institutional arrangements*. In a nutshell, Article VI(3) and (4) contain the obligation to provide for a modern rule-oriented administrative procedure in which traders are right-holders and not just subjects. Thus, when an authorisation is required for the supply of a service, 'the competent authorities of a Member shall, within a reasonable period of time . . . inform the applicant of the decision'. This has so far not been self-evident in many member states. Article VI(4) of GATS goes a long way to deprive the member states of the possibility to abuse qualification requirements, technical standards and licensing requirements as instruments to keep out or squeeze out foreign service suppliers:

> '[T]he Council for Trade in Services shall . . . develop . . . disciplines [which] shall aim to ensure that [qualification requirements, technical standards and licensing requirements] are, *inter alia*:
>
> (a) based on objective and transparent criteria, such as competence and the ability to supply the service;
> (b) not more burdensome than necessary to ensure the quality of the service;
> (c) in the case of licensing procedures, not in themselves a restriction on the supply of the service.'

However, in the seven years of its existence, only one sector has had the benefit of such guidelines. Nevertheless, for all other sectors, including most financial services, the provision of the following paragraph applies:

> 'Member[s] shall not apply licensing and qualification requirements and technical standards that nullify or impair such specific commitments in a manner which:
>
> (i) does not comply with the criteria outlined [above] . . . and
> (ii) could not reasonably have been expected of that Member at the time the specific commitments in those sectors were made.'

The competent organs of the WTO's dispute settlement system still have to explore this provision: but it seems that the members have, through a provision which seems unspectacular at first glance (GATS, Article VI (5)) accepted the benchmark criteria of GATS, Article VI (4) for their domestic regulations determining market access. This seems quite a far-reaching and remarkable commitment, particularly when considering that these obligations are safeguarded by two modes of (quasi-) judicial review. First, the GATS obliges members *themselves* to maintain or establish:

> 'judicial, arbitral or administrative tribunals or procedures which provide . . . for the prompt review of, and . . . appropriate remedies for, administrative decisions affecting trade in services. Where such procedures are not independent of the agency entrusted with the administrative decision concerned, the Member shall ensure that the procedures in fact provide for an objective and impartial review.'

That the executive branch of government is being bound by the rule of law and subjected to judicial review for its administrative actions, is, so far, not a concept universally embraced by the countries of the world. While at first glance the beneficiaries of these minimum standards will be the Merrill Lynches and Goldman Sachses of the world, one might hope that, once again, these rules and their implementation, will, at the end of the day, have trickled down to 'the real world where people live and work and die'.[25] Internal judicial control of executive branch activities is paralleled by the WTO's own dispute settlement system (see the heading 'Institutional provisions and dispute settlement' below).

Other provisions of significance for the financial services sector, can, due to the restraints imposed on this paper, only be mentioned: Article VII deals with the recognition of education or experience obtained, requirements met, or licences or certifications granted in a particular country.[26] While members are free (even encouraged) to recognise certain foreign qualifications and certifications, they must not use this tool in order to discriminate between members. Article VII (Recognition) reads as follows:

> '1. For the purposes of the fulfilment, in whole or in part, of its standards
>   or criteria for the authorization, licensing or certification of services

---

[25] Cf. *EC – Measures Concerning Meat And Meat Products (Hormones)*, WT/DS26/AB/R, WT/DS48/AB/R, p. 76.

[26] Kalypso Nicolaidis and Joel P. Trachtman, 'From Policed Regulation to Managed Recognition in GATS' in Pierre Sauvé and Robert M. Stern (eds.), *GATS 2000: New Directions in Services Trade Liberalization* (Washington, D. C., 2000) p. 241 et seq.

suppliers, and subject to the requirements of paragraph 3, a Member may recognize the education or experience obtained, requirements met, or licenses or certifications granted in a particular country. Such recognition, which may be achieved through harmonization or otherwise, may be based upon an agreement or arrangement with the country concerned or may be accorded autonomously.

2. A Member that is a party to an agreement or arrangement of the type referred to in paragraph 1, whether existing or future, shall afford adequate opportunity for other interested Members to negotiate their accession to such an agreement or arrangement or to negotiate comparable ones with it. Where a Member accords recognition autonomously, it shall afford adequate opportunity for any other Member to demonstrate that education, experience, licenses, or certifications obtained or requirements met in that other Member's territory should be recognized.

3. A Member shall not accord recognition in a manner which would constitute a means of discrimination between countries in the application of its standards or criteria for the authorization, licensing or certification of services suppliers, or a disguised restriction on trade in services.

4. Each Member shall:
   (a) within 12 months from the date on which the WTO Agreement takes effect for it, inform the Council for Trade in Services of its existing recognition measures and state whether such measures are based on agreements or arrangements of the type referred to in paragraph 1;
   (b) promptly inform the Council for Trade in Services as far in advance as possible of the opening of negotiations on an agreement or arrangement of the type referred to in paragraph 1 in order to provide adequate opportunity to any other Member to indicate their interest in participating in the negotiations before they enter a substantive phase;
   (c) promptly inform the Council for Trade in Services when it adopts new recognition measures or significantly modifies existing ones and state whether the measures are based on an agreement or arrangement of the type referred to in paragraph 1.

5. Wherever appropriate, recognition should be based on multilaterally agreed criteria. In appropriate cases, Members shall work in cooperation with relevant intergovernmental and non-governmental organizations towards the establishment and adoption of common international standards and criteria for recognition and common international standards for the practice of relevant services trades and professions.'

Article VIII obliges members to prevent monopolies and oligopolies to nullify and impair its obligations under GATS and under specific commitments entered into. Article XI, in principle, prohibits the WTO countries from imposing 'restrictions on international transfers and payments for current transactions relating to [their] specific commitments'; this provision is particularly important for the effective protection of direct investments. Specific exceptions are, of course, permitted in the case of 'serious balance of payments and external financial difficulties'.

(d) Exceptions

Just like the GATT, the GATS contains a number of general exceptions, for example, to protect the public order, the life and health of people, animals and plants and to preserve vital security interests. On a proposal by the United States, a rule was introduced permitting taxation measures which discriminate against foreigners if that is the only way to achieve 'equitable or effective' direct taxation.

Unlike Part IV of the GATT 1947, the GATS does not contain a specific chapter on 'special and differential treatment' of developing countries. Instead, it contains a number of provisions on the increasing involvement of developing countries in international trade in services. This includes the negotiation of commitments by the WTO countries on access for developing countries to technologies, to information and to distribution networks, and on market access in sectors of particular export interest for the developing countries. The GATS enables the developing countries to pursue their development priorities through the negotiation of specific liberalisation commitments and explicit permission to liberalise as few sectors or modes of supply as they deem proper, without forcing the developed states' standards upon them.[27]

5. Institutional provisions and dispute settlement

Part V of the GATS contains institutional provisions on the establishment of the GATS Council and sectoral subcommittees, as well as on consultations and dispute settlement. It refers to the WTO's Dispute Settlement Understanding which has proven to be a remarkably effective tool in order to clarify international legal obligations contained in the

---

[27] Cf. Aaditya Mattoo, 'Developing Countries and the New Round of GATS Negotiations: Towards a Pro-active Role' (2000) 23 *World Economy* 471 et seq.

Marrakesh Agreements.[28] In a nutshell, it allows member states affected to have independent panels and, ultimately the Appellate Body rule upon the compliance of a member with its international law obligations. While technically it is up to the member states, assembled in the Dispute Settlement Body to accept or reject the reports of Panels and the Appellate Body, in reality the Appellate Body plays a role very much comparable to an International Court, as only the consensus of *all* member states (including the 'winning' party's) can block the adoption of the pertinent report.[29] Paying tribute to the particular complexity that is a hallmark of trade in financial services, the Annex requires that 'necessary expertise relevant to the specific financial service under dispute' is a prerequisite for panels established according to Articles 6 to 8 of the DSU. Unfortunately (from the point of view of academics and legal services providers), only a few cases dealing with GATS obligations have arisen, none of them dealing with the topic of this paper, financial services.[30]

II. The Financial Services Agreement

Despite the fact that it was primarily the US financial services industry which had convinced the US government, and eventually the rest of the world, to negotiate a 'GATT for services',[31] specific commitments for financial services were not entered into at the conclusion of the Uruguay Round as negotiations on this subject-matter had not yet been successfully concluded. Together with a few other sectors, financial services belonged to the unfinished business of the Uruguay Round, to be dealt with during the first six months after the entry into force of the Marrakesh Agreements. Almost in time an agreement was reached in July 1995, however without the United States 'on board' which considered the specific commitments of several important Asian and South American states as being below acceptable levels of market access. Being

---

[28] See Edwin Vermulst, Petros Mavroidis and Paul Waer, 'The Functioning of the Appellate Body after Four Years – Towards Rule Integrity' (1999) 33 *Journal of World Trade* 1 et seq.

[29] See Friedl Weiss, 'Dispute settlement under the General Agreement on Trade in Services' in James Cameron (ed.), *Dispute Resolution in the World Trade Organisation* (London, 1998), p. 148 et seq.

[30] See Werner Zdouc, 'WTO dispute settlement practice relating to the GATS' (1999) 2 *Journal of International Economic Law* 295 et seq.

[31] See Weiss, 'The General Agreement on Trade in Services 1994', above note 12, at 1179.

not prepared to extend its treatment of, say, European service providers and their products to all WTO members without *some* reciprocity, the US notified MFN exceptions under GATS, Article II and offered no specific commitments. In the history of the World Trading System the lack of US participation had, up to then, meant that a project was moribund. Thus it came as quite a surprise that other members, most notably the European Community, exercised leadership and went ahead, on an interim basis, with this 'second-best' solution. From its entry into force on, this interim agreement on financial services was considered a starting point for future negotiations aimed not only at further liberalisation but even more so at the inclusion of the world's most important economy. Eventually, this led to the successful conclusion of the Financial Services Agreement of 1997, which (initially) prompted some seventy members to enter into specific commitments. Technically it is those specific commitments, attached to the Fifth Protocol to the General Agreement on Trade in Services, which form the Financial Services Agreement.[32] Without wanting to diminish its importance *per se*, there is wide consensus that the importance of the Agreement is not so much an immediate liberalising effect (which it does not have) but the fact that it 'locks in' the financial services sector into the WTO system: according to industry estimates, the Agreement embraces 95% of all exchanges in financial services; the dollar value covered is said to surpass $60 trillion.[33] This impressive economic sector will profit from future liberalisation in trade rounds to come. A second major point is the installation of the Appellate Body as final arbiter also for financial services, which creates the chance that case-by-case a pertinent body of law will evolve, creating stability and predictability.

III. Selective overview of some specific commitments

It is not possible in this paper to even attempt to give an overview over the substantive commitments the state parties of GATS have made. However, it does seem appropriate to provide the reader with a glimpse of what the international *status quo* for the trade in financial services is. Therefore two subgroups of states' commitments will be looked at. First, the rules of the Understanding on Commitments in Financial Services,

---

[32] WTO doc. S/L/45, 3 December 1997.

[33] *Opening Markets for Financial Services – the BI [British Invisibles] Guide to the Financial Services Agreement*, September 1998, p. 7.

concluded by states prepared to move on the *fast lane* of progressive liberalisation will be introduced. Second, the commitments of a very numerous (and heterogeneous) group, the developing countries, will be introduced.

1. The understanding on commitments in financial services

The 'Understanding' is an agreement between state parties to the GATS willing to move further than the majority of the signatories, thus taking 'an alternative approach to that covered by the provisions of Part III of the [GATS]'. These members have, subject to specified conditions and qualifications, included in their schedule of *specific commitments* standards conforming to the ones provided for by the Understanding. Only a very superficial overview shall be provided. By consensus of all parties to GATS the concept underlying the Understanding is compatible with the GATS, if and to the extent that:

> '(i)   it does not conflict with the provisions of the Agreement;
> (ii) it does not prejudice the right of any Member to schedule its specific commitments in accordance with the approach under Part III of the Agreement;
> (iii) resulting specific commitments shall apply on a most-favoured-nation basis;
> (iv) no presumption has been created as to the degree of liberalization to which a Member is committing itself under the Agreement.'

Paying tribute to an old GATT tradition, lastly revived in the Montreal Mid-Term Review of the Uruguay Round, the parties to the Understanding commit themselves to refrain from any *new* (i.e. additional) conditions, limitations and qualifications to existing legislation (in GATT-parlance *stand-still-clause*). Thus the *status quo* is the *plafond* for future changes: existing legislation may only be changed in favour of further liberalisation. This is, it may be added, quite different from the approach many emerging countries and LDCs have taken: for example, both Turkey and Malaysia have chosen to commit themselves to obligations markedly below their actual internal legislation, thus preserving their right to change their domestic laws and regulations.

The bulk of the commitments consolidated in the Understanding aim to facilitate market access for foreign service providers: monopoly rights shall be made transparent (and become obvious subjects of negotiation in future rounds) by listing them; remarkably, WTO members adhering to the Understanding 'shall endeavour to eliminate them or reduce their scope' (best-effort-clause); whilst non-binding, this represents a clear commitment to reduce non-discriminatory structural barriers to international trade, thus laying the groundwork for future harmonisation.

Public entities offering financial services will make sure to treat foreign service providers established in the host state[34] according to MFN-standard and without discriminating them against domestic service suppliers.

Concerning *Mode 1* services, the Understanding restates, by and large, what major trading nations permitted before the conclusion of the Uruguay Round on the basis of bilateral treaties and/or autonomous legislation: only very specialised financial services, offered by a select – and visible – group of service providers, are granted full market access: one example is insurance for 'maritime shipping and commercial aviation and space launching and freight (including satellites)'. It seems that even developed states with strong supervisory and prudential systems in place were held back by a concern that the appearance of many foreign competitors would destabilise host markets and domestic providers, causing unwanted macroeconomic scenarios. With regard to financial services provided for under *Mode 2*, the Understanding is far more generous: each member shall permit its residents to purchase in the territory of any other member the financial services for which parties to the Understanding have entered commitments with regard to *Mode 1* supply plus, by and large, all banking services and other financial services, however, not insurance. Again, this comes at little cost for rich countries, which tend to be Western-type liberal democracies; in these legal orders, it is a matter of course for citizens to be allowed to leave their home country at pleasure. Under these conditions, a prohibition to buy financial services abroad tends to be an exercise in futility. With regard to *Mode 3* supply (commercial presence) parties to the Understanding establish that, unless they enter specific reservations and qualifications in their *specific commitments*, they will essentially grant foreign service providers the right to establish a commercial presence, either by setting up shop or by buying out domestic providers. Also, the parties to the Understanding agree to commit themselves to allow foreign service providers to offer new financial products, thus implicitly prohibiting the stifling of competition through legal petrification of the factual *status quo*. In this context, the obligation to allow

---

[34] Leroux, 'Trade in Financial Services', above note 10, at 434–5 deplores the lack of attention negotiators paid to the definition of the establishment requirement.

temporary entry of certain key personnel[35] should be mentioned; this commitment only refers to foreign service suppliers that are establishing or have established a commercial presence in the territory of the Member. Additional provisions of the Understanding focus on the prevention and elimination of discriminatory treatment.[36] It seems quite evident that *Mode 3*, i.e. the direct investment of foreign service suppliers into some sort of 'establishment' is the area where GATS and the Understanding depart most pronouncedly from the *status quo ante*. This comes as little surprise: for both straightforward economic and political reasons it is to be expected that GATS will (other than GATT) not primarily be a door-opener for foreign financial services *stricto sensu* into host markets. Rather, it is likely that GATS' role will mainly consist in facilitating and guaranteeing direct investments in the service industries of the host countries. Existing commitments and the state of negotiations in the ongoing first round of progressive liberalisation (Doha Round) seem to support this evaluation.

[35] '(i) senior managerial personnel possessing proprietary information essential to the establishment, control and operation of the services of the financial service supplier; and (ii) specialists in the operation of the financial service supplier.' Also, according to para. 9(b) of the Understanding, '[e]ach Member shall permit, subject to the availability of qualified personnel in its territory, temporary entry into its territory of the following personnel associated with a commercial presence of a financial service supplier of any other Member: (i) specialists in computer services, telecommunication services and accounts of the financial service supplier; and (ii) actuarial and legal specialists.'

[36] See para. 10: 'Each Member shall endeavour to remove or to limit any significant adverse effects on financial service suppliers of any other Member of: (a) non-discriminatory measures that prevent financial service suppliers from offering in the Member's territory, in the form determined by the Member, all the financial services permitted by the Member; (b) non-discriminatory measures that limit the expansion of the activities of financial service suppliers into the entire territory of the Member; (c) measures of a Member, when such a Member applies the same measures to the supply of both banking and securities services, and a financial service supplier of any other Member concentrates its activities in the provision of securities services; and (d) other measures that, although respecting the provisions of the Agreement, affect adversely the ability of financial service suppliers of any other Member to operate, compete or enter the Member's market; provided that any action taken under this paragraph would not unfairly discriminate against financial service suppliers of the Member taking such action.

11. With respect to the non-discriminatory measures referred to in subparagraphs 10(a) and (b), a Member shall endeavour not to limit or restrict the present degree of market opportunities nor the benefits already enjoyed by financial service suppliers of all other Members as a class in the territory of the Member, provided that this commitment does not result in unfair discrimination against financial service suppliers of the Member applying such measures.'

Finally, Part C of the Understanding addresses commitments relating to national treatment proper. Foreign financial service suppliers shall be granted access to payment and clearing systems operated by public entities, and to official funding and refinancing facilities available in the normal course of ordinary business. However, this does not entail access to the lender of last resort facilities of the host state. To the extent that membership or participation in self-regulatory bodies or associations of any kind, for example, securities exchanges or clearing agencies, is mandatorily required by the host state as a precondition of doing business, the host state shall oblige those entities to accord national treatment to *all* financial service providers 'resident in the territory of the [pertinent] Member', regardless of their nationality or the nationality of their owners.

2. Commitments of developing countries and countries with economies in transition

Several studies[37] show a correlation between the (relative) wealth and economic importance of developing countries and transition countries and the frequency of entering into binding commitments. Thus, all Eastern European states, almost 70% of all Asian states, more than half of Latin American states and just about a third of the African states (those who did represent 95% of Africa's GDP) entered commitments.[38] According to said studies, the quality of commitments by less developed countries relating to insurance and banking oscillates around 0.5 on a scale from zero (no liberalisation) to one (full liberalisation), compared to 0.7–0.8 for OECD countries. While this does not seem too disappointing, it seems that the differences between developing countries are considerable:[39] some of the least developed countries like Gambia,

---

[37] Aaditya Mattoo, *Financial Services and the World Trade Organization. Liberalization Commitments of the Developing and Transition Economies* (World Bank, 1999), p. 9 et seq.; *Opening Markets for Financial Services – the BI [British Invisibles] Guide to the Financial Services Agreement*, September 1998, p. 14 et seq. gives a country-by-country overview of the *status quo*. Markets covered include the most important industrialised countries, Eastern Europe and Argentina, Brazil, Chile, Columbia, Egypt, Hong Kong, India, Indonesia, Malaysia, Pakistan, Philippines, Singapore, South Africa, Thailand, and Venezuela.

[38] Mattoo, *Financial Services and the World Trade Organization*, above note 37, at 12.

[39] Cf. Mattoo, *Financial Services and the World Trade Organization*, above note 37, at 13, 17.

Malawi and Mozambique have radically opened their markets for financial services, while others have kept theirs closed.[40]

Most commitments made by countries of the former communist bloc and developing countries were only reflecting the domestic *status quo ante*. It is worth noting that the regimes for financial services of many countries concerned were liberalised recently, i.e. during the Uruguay Round and the subsequent negotiations on a financial services agreement which specifically led to three cycles of commitments between 1993 and 1997.[41] The most prominent improvements concern *Mode 3* services: Egypt, El Salvador, Ghana, Hong Kong, Kenya, Kuwait, Mexico, and Singapore are among the very heterogeneous group of countries that either allowed foreign majority participation in domestic institutions or management control. Also, barriers to the establishment of both subsidiaries and branches were noticeably reduced.[42]

Some relatively open markets, for example, the Philippines and South Korea, chose to commit themselves significantly below the level of their present legislation. Two reasons for this perhaps surprising behaviour come to mind: first, some members seem to consider the level of their internal liberalisation to be close to the limit of what is politically feasible. Decision-makers who might have to retreat a bit from the present *status quo* wanted to be able to do so without paying the price of violating a WTO legal obligation. A second reason is due to the unique nature of the negotiations on financial services: while it is a 'trademark' of GATT/WTO-Rounds that every trade issue is connected with every other trade issue, that was not the case for these negotiations. They took place unrelated to other trade issues: as has been mentioned earlier, they were left over from the Uruguay Round and had to be finalised in the first six months after the entry into force of the WTO Agreement. Thus, it seems that some negotiators held back their negotiating chips for future rounds when commitments in financial services might, for example, buy facilitated access for some product group to the markets of industrialised countries.

[40] See Ying Qian, *Financial Services Liberalization and GATS*, 8 February 2000, available at http://www1.worldbank.org/wbiep/trade/manila/financial_services.pdf), para. 14.
[41] Cf. Mattoo, *Financial Services and the World Trade Organization*, above note 37, at 24, note 24 et seq.
[42] Cf. Mattoo, *Financial Services and the World Trade Organization*, above note 37, at 25.

IV. You'll never walk alone: effective prudential and regulatory regimes as corollary for the liberalisation of the trade in financial services

1. Supervision as primary responsibility of member states

In some countries, notably in so-called LDCs or emerging economies, the WTO rules on financial services, and in particular the specific commitments entered into, might lead to noticeable changes in the government's control over financial services and their providers. This may lead to both rapid growth of the pertinent market and increased competition which should increase the risks the domestic banking sector is facing. For mature economies ('mature' *also* meaning 'lessons learned') its seems self-evident that liberal market conditions and strong supervisory systems are the flipsides of a single coin rather than contradictions. Indeed, the financial services sector is one of the most heavily regulated sectors of national economies, due to its real and perceived importance for the well-being of the national economy. However, things being as they are, few LDCs and countries of the former communist bloc have promising track records when it comes to effective regulatory regimes, functioning supervision and adequate implementation. Also, in particular with regard to LDCs, it should be kept in mind that trade liberalisation often entails increased capital flows, which in times of crisis are often abruptly reversed, thus deepening the original difficulties.

In the absence of a global economic government (which does not even exist at a regional level in the Economic Community or in North America) it is up to the WTO members to set up laws and regulations protecting the integrity of their financial markets, their investors and depositors. Indeed, responsible supervisory agencies made clear to their trade negotiators that a General Agreement on Trade in Services would be unacceptable if it would infringe on the states' ability to regulate and supervise financial markets and their professional participants. Thus it is that the Annex on Financial Services pointedly states that members, although always bound to obey the obligation of Article VI to exercise their competences in a fair, proportionate and transparent fashion:

> 'shall not be prevented from taking measures for prudential reasons, including for the protection of investors, depositors, policy holders or persons to whom a fiduciary duty is owed by a financial service supplier, or to ensure the integrity and stability of the financial system. Where such measures do not conform with the provisions of the Agreement, they

shall not be used as a means of avoiding the Member's commitments or
obligations under the Agreement.'

(GATS Annex on Financial Services, 2 (a))

It is difficult to imagine a more comprehensive 'carve-out'. GATS makes
clear that – for the time being – it is not in the standard-setting-business
for prudential purposes. Rather, responsibility for this extremely important matter remains completely within the competence of the member
states. From the point of view of national sovereignty, the only possible 'poisoned pill' could be the second sentence of para. 2(a) (quoted
above), which reminds a bit of the so-called *chapeau* of GATT, Article
XX, which allows members to deviate from certain GATT obligations
provided: 'that such measures are not applied in a manner which would
constitute a means of arbitrary or unjustifiable discrimination between
countries where the same conditions prevail, or a disguised restriction
on international trade'.

The Appellate Body has held that this provision is a custom-tailored
manifestation of the general international law principle of bona fides,
which, of course, is to be defined ultimately by the Appellate Body itself.
Thus, it is conceivable that, one day, this provision would be interpreted
with greater latitude than the simple reading of the text suggests. As of
now, however, not only has the Appellate Body not yet addressed *any*
financial services case, but it also seems evident that a strong consensus
exists that the prudential carve-out should *not* be read narrowly. Rather,
the right of members to establish (non-discriminatory!) pertinent
regimes according to their own priorities seems well-established,
indeed. Thus rules on capital adequacy ratios, limits on risks to be
taken, transparency and disclosure requirements would undoubtedly
be considered to be covered by the prudential carve-out. Of course,
the devil is in the details: there will be areas where it might be disputed
whether a measure serves legitimate prudential interests. If the answer to
the question is negative, they are prohibited if the pertinent sector has
been liberalised and the measure in question has not been scheduled in
its list of restrictions or conditions.

It seems clear that a number of provisions, particularly in the
Understanding might lead to greater harmonisation between national
legislations than is the case today: a provision that essentially condemns
monopolies is, if taken seriously, likely to influence members to ensure
competitive market conditions and thus subscribe to a certain economic
philosophy. Provisions obliging member states to allow the unimpeded

offering of financial services already offered successfully abroad will be influenced by regulatory regimes already dealing with that kind of service. While all this does create pressure to harmonise domestic legal regimes dealing with financial services, the ultimate responsibility of the individual states is unchallenged. More and more this responsibility manifests itself in increased international co-operation in order to match real and perceived dangers resulting from the growth of cross-border trade in services, i.e. to keep track with global service providers and transnational financial services.[43] Collaboration between home and host supervisors and regulators seems to be the obvious *route* to avoid both over-regulation (stifling international trade) and loss of effective control due to the involvement of multiple jurisdictions. Indeed, it is fair to say that the trend towards increasing liberalisation has gone hand-in-hand with international efforts to improve and intensify the cooperation of and coordination between national supervisory and regulatory agencies.

Established by the economically most active states of the world (G7, G8, G10), several international coordinating bodies have adopted pertinent documents with little or no *legal* force but extremely powerful *persuasive* effect on the practice and legislation of participating states. The Annex recognises this trend and allows member states not only to 'recognize prudential measures of any other country in determining how [a] Member's measures relating to financial services shall be applied'. Rather, it specifically recognises that recognition 'may be achieved through harmonisation or otherwise [and] may be based upon an agreement or arrangement with the country concerned'. The Annex also restates that, of course, arrangements between sub-groups of members on prudential matters must not be used as an instrument for covert discrimination. Thus, those agreements must either be open for accession by other states or the state concerned has to be prepared to grant to third states the same substantive treatment.[44]

---

[43] See the impressive list of pertinent international bodies at http://allserv.rug.ac.be/~mcogen/links_financial.html#standard setting agencies (21 November 2002).

[44] cf. *Annex*, para. 3(b): 'A Member that is a party to such an agreement or arrangement referred to in subparagraph (a), whether future or existing, shall afford adequate opportunity for other interested Members to negotiate their accession to such agreements or arrangements, or to negotiate comparable ones with it, under circumstances in which there would be equivalent regulation, oversight, implementation of such regulation, and, if appropriate, procedures concerning the sharing of information between the parties to the agreement or arrangement. Where a Member accords recognition autonomously, it shall afford adequate opportunity for any other Member to demonstrate that such circumstances exist.'

2. Examples of international cooperation

(a) Banking services

The Basle Committee is one of the most visible examples of the close, informal, (legally) non-binding and supremely important collaboration within the central bank 'fraternity'.[45] Established in 1974, it allows central banks and supervisory authorities of the G10 countries to formulate policies on how to manage and supervise transnational banking activities.[46] While the Committee is a legal non-entity (attached to the Bank for International Settlement in Basle, Switzerland) and its 'standards', 'guidelines' or recommended 'best practices' have no legal force whatsoever, its conclusions and recommendations have shaped monetary policy, regulatory regimes and the banking industry itself more than any legally binding text: all major initiatives have resulted in binding national measures implementing the Basle Committee's view of the world. One of the reasons for this remarkable effect has been the Committee's ability to reach out to its peers in non-member countries and to the industry itself. This truly global collaboration has been somewhat institutionalised in International Conference of Banking Supervisors which takes place every two years.

Examples of the Committee's work include the development, since 1988, of a novel approach to capital measurement (Basle Capital Accord).[47] Of course the stability of banks, notably big, transnationally active banks, is of crucial importance to responsible governments in both home and host countries. Even more pertinent to our study is the Committee's work on supervisory coverage of transnational banking services and on internationally active banks. Since its establishment, the Committee has helped fashion international consensus on two basic principles: (1) foreign banking establishments are not to escape

---

[45] Belgium, Canada, France, Germany, Italy, Japan, Luxembourg, the Netherlands, Spain, Sweden, Switzerland, United Kingdom, and United States.

[46] See, as a recent example, Bank for International Settlement – Basle Committee on Banking Supervision (eds.), *Management and Supervision of Cross-Border Electronic Banking Activities* (Basle, October 2002).

[47] It introduced, *inter alia*, a minimum capital of 8% for extended loans, which has been accepted not just in the G10 countries, but has become a global standard. This standard is about to be refined through a three-pronged design: first, minimum capital requirements, secondly, supervisory review of an institution's internal assessment process and capital adequacy, and, finally, the use of disclosure to strengthen market discipline as a complement to supervisory efforts.

supervision; (2) supervision has to be adequate. In order to achieve the implementation of those goals, the Basle Committee has suggested close collaboration between host and home supervisory authorities in order to address transnational banking services and internationally active financial institutions.[48] It was no coincidence that the Committee published 'Core Principles for Effective Banking Supervision' in the year the Financial Services Agreement was concluded. Developed by the supervisory authorities of the G10 and many non-member states, the Core Principles set up a model structure for an effective transnational supervisory system.

While the success of the Basle Committee's work, measured by how many national domestic supervisory systems conform to the Basle Committee's suggestions, is largely due to the economic relevance of the participating states, the quality of its work and the input by many non-G10 institutions, it should also be noted that both the IMF and the World Bank have made adherence to the Basle Committee's blueprint a condition for some of their programmes. Conditions of these two institutions, even when informal, are hard to resist for many states these days.[49]

(b) Other financial services

Inspired by the success of the Basle Committee's work there have been a number of parallel efforts to strengthen the co-operation of financial supervisory authorities.

Thus, almost a decade after the Basle Committee's creation, in 1983, the IOSCO set up shop in Montreal, Canada. Sometimes in close co-operation with the Basle Committee, it has produced several highly influential, legally non-binding documents reflecting a consensus on how to police the transnationally active securities industry. The latest

---

[48] See *Principles for the Supervision of Banks' Foreign Establishments* (May 1983), referred to in state practice and pertinent doctrine as *1983 Concordat*, and its supplements: *Information Flows between Banking Supervisory Authorities* (April 1990), *Minimum Standards for the Supervision of International Banking Groups and their Cross-Border Establishments* (July 1992), *The Supervision of Cross-Border Banking* (October 1996); *Core Principles for Effective Banking Supervision* (September 1997); *Core Principles Methodology* (October 1999); *Essential Elements of a Statement of Co-Operation between Banking Supervisors* (May 2001). All quoted documents can be downloaded from the BIS website.

[49] Cf. Key, 'Trade Liberalization and Prudential Regulation', above note 24, at 61.

pertinent document concerns consultation and co-operation and the exchange of information between the participating authorities.[50]

Just before the GATS entered into force, the International Association of Insurance Commissioners was established in 1994.[51] Following the Basle Committee's example, it has established itself as the premier standard setting body for its field through the establishment of the Principles Applicable to the Supervision of International Insurers and Insurance Groups and their Cross-Border Business Operations (Insurance Concordat) in 1999.[52] These principles aim to improve the supervision of internationally active insurance companies, stating that all insurance establishments should be subject to effective supervision, that authorisation involving cross-border activities should be subject to consultation between the relevant supervisors and that provision should be made for external audits and for information sharing with other supervisors. Together with the Basle Committee and the IOSCO, the IAIS forms the Joint Forum: the blurring of demarcation lines between the different sectors of the financial services industry has led to this *rapprochement* of these three key 'standard-suggesting' bodies.

As indicated earlier, those three institutions are not alone: an impressive group of institutions, both state and industry-sponsored, address the need to establish harmonised regulatory standards which both protect investors and market stability. At the same time, the prospect of vastly harmonised regimes, if not of a one-stop-supervision is a major attraction for the industry, too.

V. Conclusion

The economic benefit of trade liberalisation, while disputed by political activists from the far right and the far left, is a given. It is also given that the so-called free market economies do not sport 'free markets' but highly regulated markets (which keeps the legal profession happy); of

---

[50] International Organization of Securities Commission (ed.), *Multilateral Memorandum of Understanding concerning Consultation and Cooperation and the Exchange of Information* (Montreal, May 2002).

[51] Cf. the extremely informative website http://www.iaisweb.org/.

[52] This document can be obtained at http://www.iaisweb.org; at the same address other pertinent texts can be obtained, *inter alia*, the *Principles on Minimum Requirements for Supervision of Reinsurers* (October 2002); *Principles on Capital Adequacy and Solvency* (January 2002); *Insurance Core Principles* (October 2000); *Insurance Core Principles Methodology* (October 2000); *Principles on the Supervision of Insurance Activities on the Internet* (October 2000); *Principles for Conduct of Insurance Business* (December 1999).

course, there are differences (the US market for guns, say, is less regulated than Germany's, while the United States' food and drug administration regulations still forces cheese *aficionados* to engage in illegal activities).[53] When it comes to services, and in particular to financial services the level of regulation worldwide is extremely high which does, of course, not preclude loopholes or ineffective implementation.

This chapter has outlined the *status quo* of the WTO's rules on trade in financial services: As has been shown, only a most stunning lack of knowledge will prevent a member from fashioning its WTO commitments according to its political preferences and practical possibilities. *If* the liberalisation of the trade in financial services should continue (which is to be supposed), it will continue at a relatively slow pace, allowing members to accommodate to the new international obligations. The danger emanating from international financial institutions escaping supervision through jurisdiction-hopping, has long ago been recognised and dealt with. The question to what extent those international efforts leave room for improvements will have to be answered some other day. For the purposes of this paper it suffices to summarise our bird's view of the issues by stating that effective supervision of financial institutions engaging in transnational business exists. Efforts to bring down existing 'flags of convenience' have increased, particularly after September 11. But this is a different story, too.

The WTO's rules on financial services might indeed represent a victory of big powerful financial institutions allowing them to prepare global diversification, read: expansion. However, this does not seem to be a victory over some legitimate interest: protected (i.e. competition-free) markets for banking and insurance do not serve the poor or the middle classes of the world. They serve the owners of those financial institutions, be they the local billionaire or the government. The WTO approach seems well balanced, reconciling the option for liberalisation (and its economic advantages) with the legitimate interests of states and their peoples to have the prudential regime in place they select.

---

[53] Cf. Burkhard Bilger, 'Raw Faith – The Nun and the Cheese Underground', *The New Yorker*, 19 and 26 August 2002 (The Food Issue), p. 150 et seq.

PART IV

An institutional perspective

9

The European Central Bank as regulator and as institutional actor

THILO MARAUHN

MICHAEL WEISS

I. Introduction: the Treaty basis

During the 1990s European financial institutions experienced far-reaching regulatory reform.[1] In contributing to a stable macroeconomic environment, the EMU adds another building block to strengthen the financial system. With monetary policy at the European level, macroeconomic disturbances can be reduced and the stability of the financial system reinforced.[2]

The European Central Bank (ECB) together with the European System of Central Banks (ESCB) are not only the focal point of the EMU but they are also essential for the functioning of Europe's financial markets. While London has remained and will remain a global and European financial centre,[3] the ECSB and the ECB as well as the EMU have become important for the functioning of this and other centres as part of international financial markets. This was already foreseen immediately after the decision on the EMU as can be illustrated by reference to a speech by Ian Plenderleith, then Executive Director, Bank of England,

---

[1] See, *inter alia*, John A. Usher, *The Law of Money and Financial Services in the European Community* (Oxford, 1994); Mads Andenas, 'The right to provide financial services and the European Commission as legislator,' in Joseph J. Norton (ed.), *The Changing World of International Law in the Twenty-first Century. A Tribute to the late Kenneth R. Simmonds* (The Hague, 1998) 239–58; John F. Mogg, 'Regulating Financial Services in Europe. A New Approach' (2002) 26(1) *Fordham International Law Journal* 58–82.

[2] This is the view taken by the authors of a Working Paper *Prudential Supervision in the Context of EMU*, European Parliament, Directorate-General for Research, Economic Affairs Series, ECON 102 EN rev. 1 (available via EP web-site: http://www.europarl.eu.int/workingpapers/econ/pdf/102_en.pdf), at 39.

[3] Cf. Harold Rose, *London as an International Financial Centre. A Narrative History*, Subject Report, London Business School (London, 1994).

at a conference organised by the International Center for Monetary and Banking Studies in November 1997. Plenderleith argued:

> 'I believe EMU will open up new opportunities for the financial markets. I believe this will be particularly so for the international markets in London. We intend to be ready to take full advantage of these opportunities . . . even though the UK will not participate in EMU at that stage . . . London is the major European financial market, and we think that extending its activity to include financial services in euro is a significant contribution we . . . can make from the outset to the success of the monetary union . . .'[4]

While the ECB and ESCB are not at the heart of international financial markets, they, nevertheless, have an impact on these markets, both as regulators in the European context and, beyond that, as an international actor. This paper will look at the role the ECB and the ESCB play within the European Union and at the international level.

The establishment of ESCB and ECB can best be understood against its historical background.[5] While the idea of an Economic and Monetary Union has been discussed since the early days of the European Communities, it took until the late 1980s that a 'Three Stage Plan' was agreed upon following the Delors Committee Report.[6] Within stage one the objectives were the completion of the internal market, the accession of all Member States to the Exchange Rate Mechanism (ERM), and closer economic convergence. Due to such limited objectives, there was no need to extend the sphere of Community competence by treaty amendment. Focus was on increased co-operation between central banks with regard to monetary policy, removal of obstacles to financial integration, monitoring of national economic policies, and co-ordination of budgetary policy. Within stage two, however, the European Monetary

---

[4] The speech is available at the Bank of England website: http://www.bankofengland.co.uk/ speeches/speech10.htm.

[5] For a general introduction and overview cf. Marcello DeCecco et al. (ed.), *A European Central Bank? Perspectives on Monetary Unification after 10 Years of the EMS* (Cambridge, 1989); Ralph Mehnert-Meland, *Central Bank to the European Union* (London, 1995); René Smits, 'The European Central Bank. Institutional Aspects' (1996) 45(2) *The International and Comparative Law Quarterly* 319–42; Chiara Zilioli and Martin Selmayr, *The Law of the European Central Bank* (Oxford, 2001).

[6] Committee for the Study of Economic and Monetary Union, *Report on Economic and Monetary Union in the European Community* (Luxembourg: Office for Official Publications of the European Communities, 1989), submitted on 12 April 1989, and adopted by the Madrid European Council on 27 June 1989.

Institute (EMI)[7] was established. Stage two was the preparatory stage for the final phase of EMU. It prepared the establishment of the ESCB and included the progressive transfer of monetary policy to European institutions, narrowing the margins of fluctuation within the ERM. Stage three, finally, saw the emergence of the ECB which eventually assumed powers from the EMI.[8] Exchange rates between national currencies were fixed, and national currencies were eventually replaced by a single European currency. Responsibility for monetary policy was to be transferred to the ESCB.

The legal basis for the ECB and the ESCB is twofold, and has its starting point in the Treaty establishing the European Community. Article 8 of the EC Treaty provides that the ESCB and the ECB shall be established in accordance with pertinent Treaty provisions. These stipulate the basic elements of ECB and ESCB, in particular in Art. 105 et seq. Further details are then laid down in the ESCB Statute.[9] The interplay of the relevant provisions is relevant in so far as the ECB and the ECSB have not been established by the Community but by its Member States.[10] While it can convincingly be argued that the Community organs would not have had the power to establish such an

---

[7] It must be noted that the EMI was not originally part of the Delors Report. The Report had proposed to establish the ESCB already within the second stage. This would, however, have created a grey area of Community powers. The establishment of the EMI was a kind of compromise between no institutional changes and the establishment of the ESCB; see Jean-Victor Louis, 'Perspectives of the EMU after Maastricht', in Jules Stuyck (ed.), *Financial and Monetary Integration in the European Economic Community* (Deventer, 1993), p. 1 at 5 and Francis Snyder, 'EMU – Metaphor for European Union?', in Renaud Dehousse (ed.), *Europe after Maastricht. An Ever Closer Union?* (Munich, 1994), pp. 63–99 at 74. The EMI is dealt with by Art. 117 EC.

[8] The EMI was dissolved after the establishment of the ECB on 1 June 1998, according to Art. 123 EC.

[9] Protocol (No. 18) on the Statute of the European System of Central Banks and of the European Central Bank annexed to the Treaty establishing the European Community (OJ 1992 No. C191 68, 29 July 1992), as amended by the Treaty of Amsterdam (OJ 1997 No. C340 1, 10 July 1997), the Treaty of Nice (OJ 2001 No. C80 1, 10 March 2001), Council Decision 2003/223/EC (OJ 2003 No. L83 66, 1 April 2003) and the Act concerning the conditions of Accession of the Czech Republic, the Republic of Estonia, the Republic of Cyprus, the Republic of Latvia, the Republic of Lithuania, the Republic of Hungary, the Republic of Malta, the Republic of Poland, the Republic of Slovenia and the Slovak Republic and the adjustments to the Treaties on which the European Union is founded (OJ 2003 No. L236/33, 23 September 2003).

[10] Cf. Bernhard Kempen, 'Art. 8 EGV' in Rudolf Streinz (ed.), *EUV/EGV. Vertrag über die Europäische Union und Vertrag zur Gründung der Europäischen Gemeinschaft* (Munich, 2003) 306–8 at 307 (margin note 1).

institutional system,[11] we simply note that the institutional structure of the EMU emanates directly from the sovereign will of Member States. This is of major importance with regard to the ECB's position in relation to the European Community.

As far as its tasks and organisation are concerned, the ECB is very much built along the lines of the German Bundesbank. Especially the principle of the German Bundesbank's independence[12] was a model for the creation of the ECB. Its independence from other EU institutions is enshrined in the EC Treaty.[13] Article 108 of the EC Treaty serves to protect the ECB and the ESCB from all kinds of influence coming from the Community organs and from Member States' governments. The ESCB Statute takes up the provisions of Article 108 of the EC Treaty.[14] Geographically, the ECB's independence is underlined by the fact that the bank has its seat in Frankfurt (Germany) and not in Luxembourg or Brussels which caused some debate during the time of its establishment.[15]

---

[11] Koen Lenaerts, 'Regulating the Regulatory Process: "Delegation of Powers" in the European Community', (1993) 18(1) *European Law Review* 23–49 at 42–3.

[12] Under the German Basic Law, Art. 88 provides for the establishment of the Federal Bank (Bundesbank) as a note-issuing and currency bank. The independence of the Federal Bank is guaranteed by statutory law (not explicitly by the Constitution), in particular, s. 12 of the Bundesbank Act (Bundesbankgesetz). In 1992, the Basic Law and the Bundesbank Act were revised in order to meet the requirements of the EMU. Article 88 (2) of the Basic Law now explicitly refers to central bank independence, however, not with regard to the German Bundesbank but in respect of the ECB: 'Within the framework of the European Union, its responsibilities and powers may be transferred to the European Central Bank that is independent and committed to the overriding goal of assuring price stability'. The independence of the German Bundesbank was built along the US Federal Reserve System (which has always given rise to debate; cf. Christoph Buchheim, 'Die Unabhängigkeit der Bundesbank – Folge eines amerikanischen Oktrois?' (2001) 49(1) *Vierteljahreshefte für Zeitgeschichte* 1–30). However, there are more examples around, worldwide, such as De Nederlandsche Bank, the Bank of Canada, the Reserve Bank of New Zealand and, since 1998, the Bank of England.

[13] Art. 108 EC. For a closer analysis and debate see Hugo M. Kaufmann, 'The Importance of Being Independent: Central Bank Independence and the European System of Central Banks' in Carolyn Rhodes et al. (eds.), *Building a European Polity?* (Boulder, Colo., 1995), 267–91; Philip Brentford, 'Constitutional Aspects of the Independence of the European Central Bank' (1998) 47(1) *International and Comparative Law Quarterly* 75–116.

[14] See, in particular, ESCB Statute, Art. 7 – but also numerous other provisions dealing with institutional, personnel (e.g. ESCB Statute, Art. 11), and financial aspects of the ESCB's independence (e.g. ESCB Statute, Arts. 28, 32 and 33).

[15] The decision to establish the seat of the ECB at Frankfurt/Main was part of a package deal on a number of European institutions; contrary to Art. 37 of the ESCB Statute the decision was only adopted after the end of 1992: Decision (of 29 October 1993) taken by

It must be noted, however, that the principle of neutrality even after the entry into force of the Treaty on European Union and the ESCB Statute is not undisputed.[16] Thus, it remains to be seen, in how far the principle of the Central Bank's independence will be touched upon by the Treaty Establishing a Constitution for Europe. Especially, the proposed introduction of an Economic and Financial Committee[17] has given rise to discussions on the maintenance of the ECB's independence. This Committee shall be composed of not more than two members from the Member States, the Commission and the ECB each[18] and shall 'keep under review the economic and financial situation of the Member States and of the Union'. The relevant provisions in Art. III-86 of the Treaty Establishing a Constitution for Europe, however, are broadly worded and it will thus depend on their interpretation – and on their application in practice – whether or not the Central Bank's independence will be encroached upon.

II. The ECB and the ESCB as part of the Union

Since the establishment of the ECB on 26 May 1996[19] there has been a vivid academic debate as to the ECB's position within the European Community. An analysis of the plain text of the EC Treaty shows that the ECB is not meant to be an organ of European Community nor the European Union. Article 7 of the EC Treaty only includes the European Parliament, the Council, the Commission, the Court of Justice, and the Court of Auditors as EC organs. The ECB is referred to in a separate Article (EC Treaty, Article 8), stipulating that a European System of Central Banks and a European Central Bank shall be established. In

---

common agreement between the Representatives of the Governments of the Member States, meeting at Head of State or Government level, on the location of the seats of certain bodies and departments of the European Communities and of Europol; OJ 1993 No. C323 1, 30 November 1993 (Art. 1g).

[16] Criticism is, among others, related to the perceived lack of democratic control and accountability of the ECB and the ESCB; see Robert Elgie, 'Democratic Accountability and Central Bank Independence – Historical and Contemporary, National and European Perspectives' (1998) 21(3) *West European Politics* 53–76.

[17] Cf. Art. III-86 of the Treaty establishing a Constitution for Europe, available at http://europa.eu.int/futurum/constitution/part3/title3/chapter2/section3/index_en.htm.

[18] Art. III-86(2), 2nd sentence, of the Treaty establishing a Constitution for Europe.

[19] The ECB came into operation on 1 June 1998.

parallel to the European Investment Bank,[20] the ECB is granted legal personality by the EC Treaty.[21]

Any attempt by authors to blur the distinction between the legal personality of the Community and that of the ECB,[22] as well as any lack of clarity in this regard[23] runs counter to the intentions of Member States as the founders of the institution. Member States have on purpose distinguished between Article 7 of the EC Treaty – which includes a *numerus clausus* of treaty organs and can thus be perceived as the organisational counterpart of the EC Treaty, Article 5(1)[24] – and Article 8 of the EC Treaty establishing an institution *sui generis*. The starting point of a related analysis must be the question 'Whom is the European Central Bank the Central Bank of?' as identified by Chiara Zilioli and Martin Selmayr,[25] in other words: who founded the ECB, who conferred rights on the ECB, and who enjoys ownership of the ECB's services? As already stipulated, it was the Member States themselves, establishing the ECB. They provided the European Community, the ECB and the European Investment Bank each with legal personality. It would run counter to this construction to consider the ECB as an organ or even a quasi-organ of the European Community.

Nevertheless, it has been argued, that the ECB itself is a kind of 'Community within the Community' or an 'independent specialized

---

[20] See Arts. 9 and 266(1) EC. Cf. European Court of Justice, Case C-370/89 *SGEEM and Etroy* v. *EIB* [1992] ECR I-6211.

[21] Art. 107(2) EC. This provision establishes the legal personality of the ECB (though with functional limitations) under public international law, as can be taken from a comparison with Art. 280 EC. Legal personality according to municipal law follows from Art. 107(2) EC, read together with Art. 9.1 of the ESCB Statute.

[22] Cf. Jim Cloos et al., *Le Traité de Maastricht: Genèse, Analyse, Commentaires* (Brussels, 1994), p. 236.

[23] See Christian Calliess, 'Art. 7 EGV' in Christian Calliess and Matthias Ruffert (eds.), *Kommentar des Vertrages über die Europäische Union und des Vertrages zur Gründung der Europäischen Gemeinschaft* (Neuwied et al. 2nd edn 2002), pp. 423–37 at 425 (margin note 5).

[24] The principle that the Community must act within the limits of its powers (Art. 5(1) EC) does not only apply to substantive legislation and policy-making but also to its procedural and institutional counterpart. The European Court of Justice has developed the principle of institutional balance to this end; cf. European Court of Justice, Case C-70/88 *European Parliament* v. *Council* [1990] ECR I-2041.

[25] Chiara Zilioli and Martin Selmayr, 'The European Central Bank: An Independent Specialized Organization of Community Law' (2000) 37(3) *Common Market Law Review* 591–644, at 599.

organization of community law'.[26] While it is admitted that the ECB is the Central Bank of the European Community, and powers have been transferred to the Community in Articles 105 et seq. of the EC Treaty,[27] the meaning of 'Community' within the EC Treaty, Article 4, setting up the programme for EMU, cannot and should not differ from that in Article 2 where the basic tasks of the Community are formulated.[28] Thus, there is no separate community within the European Community. The ESCB and the ECB form part of the European Union, they fulfil tasks of the European Community and use powers transferred to the Community by the Member States.

The ECB lies at the heart of the ESCB today.[29] Its decision-making bodies (the Governing Council and the Executive Board[30]) also govern the ESCB.[31] The Executive Board is made up of the President, Vice-President and four other members.[32] They are appointed from among persons of recognised standing and professional experience in monetary or banking matters by common accord of the governments of the Member States at the level of heads of state or government. Their term of office lasts for eight years and is not renewable.[33] The Governing Council comprises the members of the Executive Board and the Governors of the National Central Banks of those Member States having adopted the euro as their currency. These states are usually referred to as 'Eurosystem'. Within the ESCB, those two organs are complemented by the General Council.[34] In contrast to the Governing Council it comprises the President and Vice-President of the ECB and the Governors of the National Central Banks of all Member States, including those not having adopted the euro as their currency. The General Council thus serves as an advisory organ linking 'ins and outs of the EMU'.[35]

---

[26] Chiara Zilioli and Martin Selmayr, 'The External Relations of the Euro Area: Legal Aspects' (1999) 36(2) *Common Market Law Review* 273–349, at 285 et seq.; for a critique of this approach see Ramon Torrent, 'Whom is the European Central Bank the Central Bank of? Reaction to Zilioli and Selmayr' (1999) 36(6) *Common Market Law Review* 1229–41.

[27] Wolfgang Weiss, 'Kompetenzverteilung in der Währungspolitik und Aussenvertretung des Euro' (2002) 37(2) *Europarecht* 165–91, at 168.

[28] Weiss, *ibid.*   [29] ESCB Statute, Art. 9(1).

[30] Art. 107(3) EC; ESCB Statute, Arts. 10–13.   [31] ESCB Statute, Art. 8.

[32] ESCB Statute, Art. 11(1).   [33] ESCB Statute, Art. 11(2).

[34] ESCB Statute, Arts. 45–53.

[35] Michael Lloyd, 'EMU: Relations between "Ins" and "Outs"' *Economic Affairs Series, European Parliament, Directorate General for Research, Working Paper* (1998), ECON 106 EN 10/98.

The Treaty Establishing a Constitution for Europe – after some controversies during the negotiations – largely follows the institutional design of the EC Treaty. Thus, Article I-19 of the Treaty defines the institutions of the Union. They include the European Parliament, the European Council, the Council of Ministers, the European Commission and the Court of Justice of the European Union. Similarly to the distinction between Articles 7 and 8 of the EC Treaty, Article I-30 of the Treaty defines the European Central Bank as part of 'the other Union institutions' (Chapter II). Article I-30(3) of the Treaty stipulates that the 'European Central Bank is an institution. It shall have legal personality . . . It shall be independent in the exercise of its powers and in the management of its finances.' It follows from this that the above legal analysis can be largely upheld under the Treaty Establishing a Constitution for Europe.

III. Regulatory powers of the ESCB and the ECB

Basically, the regulatory powers attached to the establishment of the ESCB and the ECB, as their institutional set-up, have a twofold legal basis: the EC Treaty and the ESCB Statute. Article 105(2) of the EC Treaty sets out the core tasks of the ESCB. While the main objective of the ESCB, as laid down in EC Treaty, Article 105(1), is to maintain price stability,[36] it shall also '[w]ithout prejudice to the objective of price stability . . . support the general economic policies in the Community with a view to contributing to the achievement of the objectives of the Community as laid down in Article 2'[37] of the Treaty. Based on these objectives, the main tasks of the ESCB under the EC Treaty are to define and implement the monetary policy of the Community, to conduct foreign exchange operations, to hold and manage the official foreign reserves of the Member States, and to promote the smooth operation of payment systems.[38]

As far as the ECB's regulatory powers are concerned, Article 105(5) of the EC Treaty states that the ESCB shall contribute to the smooth conduct of policies pursued by the competent authorities relating to the prudential supervision of credit institutions and the stability of the financial system.[39] The provision is vaguely worded and, in particular, the question arises, what 'to contribute' is supposed to mean in this context. It can mean a limited role for the ESCB meaning pure support for the authorities mentioned. It can, however, also mean that the ESCB

---

[36] See also ESCB Statute, Art. 2.   [37] ESCB Statute, Art. 2.
[38] Art. 105(2) EC, ESCB Statute, Art. 3(1).   [39] See also Art. 3(3) of the ESCB Statute.

itself shall develop activities and influence, perhaps even guide, the supervision exercised by pertinent authorities.

Before developing an interpretative approach thereto, it is note-worthy that Article 105(6) of the EC Treaty even provides that the Council may 'confer upon the ECB specific tasks concerning policies relating to the prudential supervision of credit institutions and other financial institutions with the exception of insurance undertakings'. This, however, is subject to the assent of the European Parliament and can only be done unanimously on a proposal from the Commission and after consulting the ECB. Furthermore, according to the EC Treaty, Article 105(4), the ECB needs to be consulted on any proposed act of the Community or Member States in its field of competence. The Council has interpreted this as including, amongst others, 'rules applic-able to financial institutions insofar as they materially influence the stability of financial institutions and markets'.[40]

Once the competence of the ECB has been established, the ECB enjoys far-reaching powers, in particular to issue legal acts. According to Article 110 of the EC Treaty,[41] the ECB can make regulations, take decisions, make recommendations, and deliver opinions in order to carry out the tasks entrusted to the ESCB.[42] Furthermore, the ECB is entitled to impose fines or periodic penalty payments on undertakings for failure to comply with obligations stemming from its regulations and decisions.[43] It must be borne in mind that the regulations and deci-sions enacted by the ECB enjoy the status of Community law.[44] While Article 34(1) of the ECSB Statute, in defining the field in which regulatory power can be implemented, also restricts the ECB's regulatory powers, it is important to note that – once the competence has been established – the Bank can adopt directly applicable legal acts.[45] Nevertheless, the ECB generally is confined to rather limited instruments.

1. The ESCB's contribution to prudential supervision

Article 105(5) of the EC Treaty is the outcome of rather controversial debates on the role of the ECB in the supervision of credit institutions in

---

[40] Council Decision 98/415/EC of 29 June 1998, OJ 1998 No. L189/42, 3 July 1998.

[41] See also ESCB Statute, Art. 34.   [42] Cf. ESCB Statute, Art. 34.   [43] Art. 110(3) EC.

[44] See generally Charlotte Schütz, 'Die Legitimation der Europäischen Zentralbank zur Rechtsetzung' (2001) 36(2) *Europarecht* 291–305.

[45] Jean-Victor Louis, 'A Legal and Institutional Approach for Building a Monetary Union' (1998) 35(1) *Common Market Law Review* 33–76 at 58 et seq.

Europe during the negotiations leading up to the Maastricht Treaty. While some favoured a limited role for the ECB, others wanted to preserve national supervisory competence. Eventually, Article 105(5) of the EC Treaty now foresees a limited role for the ESCB. In order to assess the relevance of this provision it is necessary to identify the 'competent authorities' involved, to interpret the term 'to contribute', and to explain the scope of supervisory powers ('credit institutions' and 'the financial system').

At the time of the Maastricht negotiations quite a few central banks were involved in banking supervision at the national level. It was primarily their contribution to financial stability in analysing and preventing systemic risks which was made use of. Since then independent agencies have increasingly been tasked with the supervision of financial services, however, not to the extent that central banks are now excluded from banking supervision. Rather they are closely co-operating with such independent agencies and still heavily involved in supervision. This means that the 'competent authorities' are – at least in part – identical with those contributing to prudential supervision (as part of the ESCB).[46]

The term 'contribution' can best be interpreted in light of the power entrusted to institutions preceding the ECB, in particular the EMI and the Committee of the Governors of the central banks of the Member States. The Committee of Governors[47] and thereafter the EMI were tasked to 'hold consultations concerning issues falling within the competence of the national central banks and affecting the stability of financial institutions and markets'.[48] A contribution is more than mere consultations. While Article 25.1 of the ESCB Statute only refers to 'offer advice to' it can not be excluded that there is a need for the ESCB to coordinate supervisory measures actively. This view finds support in the fact that ESCB Statute, Article 25.1 only deals with the ECB and not with the ESCB as a whole. Thus, its scope is limited in comparison with Article 105(5) of the EC Treaty which foresees a role for national central banks. Although the exact place and role of central

---

[46] Cf. René Smits, 'Artikel 105 EG' in Hans von der Groeben and Jürgen Schwarze (eds.), *Kommentar zum Vertrag über die Europäische Union und zur Gründung der Europäischen Gemeinschaft*, vol. 3 (Baden-Baden 6th edn 2003), 110–37 at 134 (margin notes 70–1).

[47] See Council Decision 63/300/EEC, OJ 1964 No. 77/1206, 21 May 1964, amended by Council Decision 90/142/EEC, OJ 1990 No. L78/25, 24 March 1990.

[48] Art. 117(2) EC.

banks in banking supervision has been the subject of negotiations and legislation political and academic debates have continued,[49] largely limited to national supervisory models – in contrast to the much more comprehensive debate on the regulation of the securities market.[50]

Turning to the scope of Article 105(5) of the EC Treaty, the notion of 'credit institutions' must be addressed. This term can either be interpreted narrowly, i.e. in the same way as it is applied in secondary legislation on banking supervision, and in line with Articles 17–24 of the ESCB Statute, or it can be given a broad meaning. The latter is based on a functional approach, focusing on the protection of creditors and on the stability of the financial system.[51] In practice, such functional interpretation has not gained the support of the institutions which favoured – with good reasons – a coherent interpretation of the Treaty, the Statute and secondary legislation.[52] However, it must be noted that Article 105(5) of the EC Treaty does not limit the role of the ESCB to credit institutions but it entrusts a separate and autonomous task to the ESCB, namely the preservation of the financial system. The ECB is not limited to a purely auxiliary function but enjoys independent operational powers. This is important in the case of systemic crises which may necessitate ECB action protecting financial stability. Its role as a lender of last resort may contribute to this end.[53]

2. Specific supervisory tasks entrusted to the ECB

Article 105(6) of the EC Treaty moves beyond the contributions envisaged for the ESCB in paragraph 5 of the said Article. It foresees specific supervisory tasks conferred upon the ECB by the Council. This provision can be considered as a political compromise resulting from the differences that came up during the Maastricht negotiations on the role

---

[49] See Smits, 'Artikel 105 EG', above note 46, at 134 (margin note 72).

[50] Cf. on the one hand Clive Briault, *The Rationale for a Single National Financial Regulator* (London: FSA, 1999) (FSA Occasional Paper no. 2) and, on the other hand, Gilles Thieffry, 'Towards a European Securities Commission' (1999) *Journal of International Financial Markets – Law and Regulation* 300–7 (the *Journal of International Financial Markets* later merged with the *Journal of International Banking Law* to form the *Journal of International Banking Law and Regulation*).

[51] Cf. Smits, 'Artikel 105 EG', above note 46, at 135 (margin note 73).   [52] *Ibid.*, at 135.

[53] For a discussion of this particular function see the collection of papers from the Financial Markets Group of the London School of Economics Charles A. E. Goodhart (ed.), *Which Lender of Last Resort for Europe?* (London, 2000).

of the ECB in the supervision of financial services. Rather than entrusting the ECB directly with own supervisory powers the Treaty now empowers Community organs to take a political decision on extending the powers of the ECB. In a way thus the decision on whether or not the ECB should enjoy specific powers relating to the prudential supervision of financial institutions was postponed. Member States have delegated it to Community organs.

However, it is not easy to bring such a decision about since there must be a proposal from the Commission, a consultation of the ECB, a positive vote (simple majority) of the European Parliament, and a unanimous decision of the Council. While a Treaty amendment is not necessary, a political agreement within the Community is necessary in order to extend supervisory powers of the ECB. The compromise has another strange feature, namely the exclusion of insurance undertakings from such extension of ECB powers. This does not only mean that in the case that the ECB should enjoy supervisory powers vis-à-vis insurance undertakings a Treaty amendment is indispensable – but also that an involvement of the ECB in unified supervision of financial services within the Community necessitates such amendment.[54] While Article 105(6) of the EC Treaty thus carries some additional potential for the ECB, at the same time it preserves the *status quo* of the distribution of powers in financial services supervision.

This political compromise came up in the second half of 1990 when the Maastricht negotiations were in their final phase.[55] The Dutch authorities obviously feared that central banks could become too powerful in the case of unified supervision. Such fear is all the more surprising since at that time banks and insurance companies increasingly joined their services which raised the question of establishing an adequate supervisory system. Obviously, Member States at that point in time considered it more important to restrain the powers of the ECB and central banks than to pave the way for the ECB and central banks to become part of a single regulator in financial services supervision.

It must be finally noted that so far the powers of the ECB have not been extended on the basis of Article 105(6) of the EC Treaty. Thus, the provision has rather developed a potential to confine than to extend powers of the ECB.

---

[54] Smits, 'Artikel 105 EG', above note 46, at 136–7 (margin note 78–9).
[55] *Ibid.*, at 136 (margin note 78).

IV. Involvement of the ECSB and the ECB
at international level

Finally, a brief look will be taken at the ECB's external competences and its involvement in international financial markets. In the analysis of the external powers in financial matters a distinction has to be drawn between the various entities being potentially capable of representing the Eurosystem: the Community as such, the ECB, Member States or national central banks.[56] The Eurosystem as such, however, has no legal personality and therefore no capacity to act in international fora or conclude treaties.

Cornerstone of external competences in the field of monetary policy is Article 111 of the EC Treaty. It empowers the Council to conclude formal agreements on exchange-rate systems in relation to non-Community currencies, to formulate general orientations for exchange rate policy and to decide on the arrangements for negotiations in monetary or foreign exchange regime matters. The ECB's external powers are accessory to those of the Council.[57] According to Article 111(4) of the EC Treaty the Council can decide to empower the ECB to represent the Community in international institutions and in the conclusion of treaties.[58] Such delegation is excluded in the case of agreements on exchange-rate systems.[59] However, in respect of the other cases a rule was agreed upon in 1998, whereby the Community, in principle, is represented by the Presidency of the Council or – if the Presidency is with a Member State outside the Euro area – by the head of the Eurogroup jointly with the Commission and the ECB.

Membership in the IMF is an example of Article 111(4) of the EC Treaty. According to the IMF Articles of Agreement only States can enjoy membership of the IMF. Thus, the Community is not a party to the Articles of Agreement. Member States participating in the euro face a dilemma: they have to respect IMF standards vis-à-vis IMF

---

[56] For an analysis see Bernd Martenczuk, 'Die Aussenvertretung der Europäischen Gemeinschaft auf dem Gebiet der Währungspolitik' (1999) 59(1) *Zeitschrift für ausländisches öffentliches Recht und Völkerrecht* 92–107.

[57] Art. 111(2) EC is not discussed here.

[58] Cf. Bernhard Kempen, 'Art. 111 EGV' in Rudolf Streinz (ed.), *EUV/EGV. Vertrag über die Europäische Union und Vertrag zur Gründung der Europäischen Gemeinschaft* (Munich, 2003) 1340–6 at 1345 (margin note 14).

[59] This can be taken from Art. 111(4) EC which starts with a safeguard clause in respect of Art. 111(1) EC: "Subject to paragraph 1 . . .".

members while the pertinent powers are no longer in their hands (at least as far as monetary and exchange rate policies are concerned).[60] In 1997, the European Council declared: 'With particular regard to the Community's relations with the International Monetary Fund, they should be predicated upon the provision in that Fund's Articles of Agreement that only countries can be members of that institution. The Member States, in their capacities as members of the IMF, should help to establish pragmatic arrangements which would facilitate the conduct of IMF surveillance and the presentation of Community positions, including the views of the ESCB, in IMF fora.'[61] Meanwhile, a pertinent step has pragmatically been taken within the IMF, granting the ECB observer status within the Board of Directors of the IMF and within the IMF Council.[62] This gives the ECB the power at least to participate in the decision-making process of the IMF by means of information and lobbying. However, this participation is limited to several fields of mutual interest for both the IMF and the ECB.

Another relevant provision to be referred to here is Article 6 of the ESCB Statute which provides that 'in the international field of co-operation involving the tasks entrusted to the ESCB, the ECB shall decide how the ESCB shall be represented'.[63] In addition, the Statute provides that the ECB and, subject to its approval, the national central banks may participate in international monetary institutions.[64] Even though this looks as if the ECB could decide for itself which international monetary institutions to enter into and which politics to promote there, it has to be kept in mind that this power is subject to the Council's control. The ESCB Statute, Article 6(3) provides that the powers set out in paragraphs 1 and 2 of the same Article are without prejudice to the EC Treaty, Article 111(4), which gives the Council the power to decide upon the position the Community represents on the international level and on the question who shall represent the European Community in this context. Therefore, it can be said that, despite its (presumed) strong position within the Community, the ECB's and the ESCB's external powers remain very limited. Especially, they have no comprehensive powers to conclude treaties or other agreements under public international law.

---

[60] Cf. Bernhard Kempen, 'Die Zukunft des Internationalen Währungsfonds' (2000) 3(1) *Zeitschrift für europarechtliche Studien* 13–24.

[61] Conclusions of the European Council of 13 December 1997, no. 10 (OJ 1998 C35/1).

[62] Cf. IMF Press Release no. 98/54 of 22 December 1998, avaliable at http://www.imf.org/external/np/sec/pr/1998/pr9864.htm.

[63] ESCB Statute, Art. 6(1).   [64] ESCB Statute, Art. 6(2).

This power remains with the Council.[65] Thus neither the ESCB nor the ECB can be considered as comprehensive actors on the international level.

As far as the international competences are concerned, reference has finally to be made to Article 23 of the ESCB Statute which confers the power to establish relations to other central banks and financial institutions and to deal with other banks upon the ECB and national central banks. However, this power is rather limited and directed at the conduct of day-to-day business.[66]

V. Perspectives

It has been shown that the ECB has a strong position within the European Union. It is not an organ of the European Community but holds a special position, being independent and enjoying legal personality of its own. Nevertheless, its regulatory powers are fairly limited. While it has a role to play in the supervision of credit institutions, prospects for a more intensive role of the ECB in financial services supervision within the European Union will largely depend upon Treaty amendments. So far, Members States have – for a broad variety of reasons – been reluctant to strengthen the supervisory powers of the ESCB and the ECB. Similarly, at the international level, the ESCB and the ECB enjoy only limited powers. The Council is the key player here and the ECB's powers are only accessory to those of the Council. To promote the position of the euro in international financial markets, it would be helpful to further strengthen the ECB's position both externally and internally. For a strengthened external role the ECB's internal independence will be of vital importance.

---

[65] Art. 111(1), (3) EC.

[66] Smits and Gruber, 'Art. 23 ESCB Statute' in Hans von der Groeben and Jürgen Schwarze (eds), *Vertrag über die Europäische Union und Vertrag zur Gründung der Europäischen Gemeinschaft, Kommentar*, vol. 3, Art. 98–188 EGV, (Baden-Baden, 2003) 473–7 at 475 (margin note 9).

10

The Basle Committee on Banking Supervision – a secretive club of giants?

SUSAN EMMENEGGER

I. Introduction

Since the breakdown of the Bretton Woods system in the early 1970s, the financial landscape has experienced profound and dramatic changes. The progressive elimination of official barriers to capital flows and the advances in communications and information technology encouraged banks and other financial market participants to explore the opportunities offered by the liberalised and computerised business environment. They also raised concerns with regard to the effectiveness of the control systems which were in place: while banking became international, banking regulation remained essentially domestic.

Weaknesses in the prudential oversight system aggravate the risk of bank failures. Because of the increasing international linkages, such failures can easily affect the financial system as a whole. Therefore, the internationalisation of banking made it necessary to upgrade the framework of prudential supervision by adopting international standards rather than keeping a domestic regulatory focus.

A key player in generating international standards of banking supervision is the Basle Committee on Banking Regulations and Supervisory Practices (Basle Committee). The Basle Committee lacks the status of an international organisation. Its Accords, Concordats and Core Principles are not legally binding. Nevertheless, they have become the regulatory standard for virtually all states with international banking activities. Thus, the Basle standards are part of an increasingly important body of international financial regulation which is generated by actors who operate outside the traditional international law categories. This paper examines the circumstances surrounding the establishment of the Basle Committee, its organisational structure, its method of operation, its regulatory programme and its impact on international banking oversight.

In particular, it will highlight the Basle Committee's pivotal role in securing international convergence of prudential banking supervision.

II. The Basle Committee – a secretive club of giants?

International banking regulation is a crisis-driven process: it has consistently been enacted in the wake of a major banking scandal. The experience of the collapse of 'Bankhaus Herstatt' in 1974[1] led the bank governors of the Group of Ten (G10)[2] to form what came to be known as the Basle Committee on Banking Supervision. Its aim was to 'eradicate the worrisome disjunction between the international banking system and the plethora of national banking regulations that have failed to restrain it'.[3] In order to achieve this, the Committee sought to establish an informal forum for consultation and co-operation among the supervisory authorities of the G10 states.

The forum's task is to develop effective supervisory techniques and to promote the convergence of the disparate national supervisory frameworks. It studies and makes recommendations on areas of prudential concern and establishes channels to facilitate the exchange of information among bank supervisors. Rather than attempting to unify the national prudential regimes, the Committee seeks to link them with a view toward ensuring that all banks are supervised according to common principles.[4]

---

[1] The bank had engaged in fraudulent bookkeeping practices. Its failure occurred while it was engaged in a foreign exchange transaction of US $620 million. For an account of the Herstatt and other bank failures see Duncan E. Alford, 'Basle Committee Minimum Standards: International Regulatory Response to the Failure of BCCI' (1992) 26 *George Washington Journal of International Law and Economics* 241 at 246. For a discussion on the effects of banking crisis on international banking supervision see Richard Dale, *The Regulation of International Banking* (Oxford, 1984), pp. 156–67.

[2] The G10 originated in 1962 when ten member countries of the IMF agreed to make resources available to the IMF outside their Fund quotas under the General Agreement to Borrow (GAB). The group was subsequently joined by Switzerland, and, most recently, by Spain, rendering the G10-designation a misnomer. See Bank for International Settlements, About BIS, (September 2001), available at http://www.bis.org/about/profforum.htm (30.11.2002). For a detailed account see Basle Committee on Banking Supervision (BCBS), Compendium of Documents – Volume I: Basic supervisory methods, History of the Basel Committee and its membership, available at http://www.bis.org/publ.bcbsc101.pdf (30.11.2002).

[3] Heath Price Tarbert, 'Rethinking Capital Adequacy: The Basle Accord and the New Framework' (2001) 56 *The Business Lawyer* 767 at 779.

[4] Lawrence L. C. Lee, 'The Basle Accords as Soft Law: Strengthening International Banking Supervision' (1998) 39 *Virginia Journal of International Law* 1 at 31.

Today, the Committee's members come from Belgium, Canada, France, Germany, Italy, Japan, Luxembourg, the Netherlands, Spain, Sweden, Switzerland, the United Kingdom and the United States. Countries are represented by their central bank and also by the authority with formal responsibility for the prudential supervision of the banking business where this is not the central bank. The Committee's twelve-person Secretariat is provided by the BIS. It is mainly staffed by professional supervisors on temporary secondment from member institutions. The Committee itself meets every three months. It operates through a rotating chair and makes its recommendations by consensus. An important motor for its prudential activity are the thirty or so technical working groups and task forces, many of which meet on a regular and frequent basis. The Committee reports to the central bank Governors of the G10 countries and seeks the Governors' endorsement for its major activities.[5]

The Basle Committee is a rather informal type of organisation. It is, quite simply, an agreement between the G10 central bankers. Consequently, it lacks the status of an international organisation.[6] Also, it has no public bylaws. In fact, its existence was first marked, on 12 February 1975, by a press release issued through the BIS.[7] It took five more years before the founding agreement was released to the public.[8] The latter illustrates another characteristic of the Basle Committee: considering its indisputable influence on the world of finance, it is a rather discrete type of organisation.[9] As former Committee Chairman Huib J. Miller has observed: 'We don't like publicity. We prefer, I might say, our hidden secret world of the supervisory continent.'[10]

---

[5] On the Basle Committee's work see generally Joseph J. Norton, *Devising International Bank Supervisory Standards* (Dordrecht, 1995), pp. 171–242.

[6] For the constitutive elements of an international organisation see Ignaz Seidl-Hohenveldern and Gerhard Loibl, *Das Recht der Internationalen Organisationen einschliesslich der Supranationalen Gemeinschaften* (7th edn, Cologne, 2001), pp. 1–14; David Zaring, 'International Law by Other Means: The Twilight Existence of International Financial Regulatory Organisations' (1998) 33 *Texas International Law Review* 282 at 305.

[7] See Norton, *Supervisory Standards*, above note 5, at p. 177 note 19.

[8] Zaring, 'International Law by Other Means', above note 6, at 288 (footnote omitted).

[9] See Norton, *Supervisory Standards*, above note 5, at p. 177: 'Throughout its existence, the Committee has sought to maintain a low profile (informal, and where possible, non-publicised).'

[10] Huib A. Miller, *Address to the 5th International Conference of Bank Supervisors* (1988 May 16), quoted in Tony Porter, *States, Markets and Regimes in Global Finance* (New York, 1993), p. 66. The low-key approach is found at the domestic level of banking supervision as well. Peter Cooke, the former Head of Banking Supervision of the Bank of England, once remarked: '[L]ike prompters in the theatre, banking supervisors carry on

Moreover, most member governments are not directly involved in the activities of the Committee. The Committee members are the central banks and the supervisory agencies. These entities are sub-state actors of a special kind: they normally enjoy a great deal of independence from the legislative and executive branch of their government. Furthermore, the technicality of much of the Basle rule-making has helped to insulate the Committee's activities from the scrutiny of the national law-makers: topics such as capital adequacy or credit risk modelling are brain-teasers for anyone active in the respective field of study; its formulas are unspeakably dull for anyone else.[11]

Lastly, the Committee has chosen to refrain from taking on new members.[12] This accounts for a another characteristic of the Basle Committee: it is not only a rather informal and rather private, but also a rather exclusive circle. Although the Committee has been the driving force behind the harmonisation of banking regulation around the globe, membership is limited to the most industrialised and wealthy. In the words of H. P. Tarbert, 'The Basel Committee is truly a club of giants.'[13]

In recent years, however, the low-key attitude of the Committee has somewhat lessened. First of all, the Committee became a victim of its own success: its 1988 capital adequacy framework (Basle Capital Accord) has become *the* capital adequacy standard worldwide. This also led to a more acute awareness of the Committee's existence. With the revision of the Accord currently in the working, the Basle Committee receives a considerable amount of press coverage. Furthermore, the increasing relations with other bank supervisory groupings[14] or single supervisory agencies has generated additional insights into the Committee's workings, as the non-members are sometimes invited to participate in technical groups and task forces. Lastly, the Basle Committee has become much more accessible and 'public' because of

their work out of the public gaze. They are most effective when they are least noticed.' Peter Cooke, 'Some reflections arising from comparisons between the Swiss and other banking supervisory systems', in Eidgenössische Bankenkommission (ed.), *50 Jahre Bankenaufsicht. Jubiläumsschrift* (Zürich, 1950), pp. 139–50 at 139.

[11] For a discussion of the governmental and judicial non-involment in this area of international law see Raj Bhala, 'Equilibrium Theory, the FICAS Model, and International Banking Law' (1997) 38 *Harvard International Law Journal*, 1 at 23–4.

[12] The notable exception is Spain, which joined the G10, and consequently the Basle Committee, in February 2001.

[13] Tarbert, 'Rethinking Capital Adequacy', above note 3, at 781.

[14] For an account of these activities, see Basle Committee, *History of the Basel Committee, and its Membership* (March 2001), BCBS Compendium of Documents – Volume I: Basic supervisory methods, available at http://www.bis.org/publ/bcbcsc101.pdf (30.11.2002).

the internet. All significant documents are publicly available on the internet site of the BIS.[15] In addition, the Consultative Papers are open to comments by governments, banks, academics, and other interested parties.[16] Thus, this once so secretive engine of regulation is slowly but consistently emerging from its private chambers onto the public arena of rule-making.

III. From procedure to substance – the Committee's regulatory achievements

1. Supervisory procedures – the Basle Concordats, minimum standards and Core Principles

The initial efforts of the Basle Committee focused on the co-ordination of regulatory and supervisory procedure. The first Basle Concordat of 1975 (the Concordat) aimed to close the supervisory gaps that were discovered in connection with Bank Herstatt's international operations. The Concordat's central tenet was (and remains) that no bank should escape supervision. It therefore declared that the supervision of foreign banks should be the *joint responsibility* of the home and the host authorities.[17]

Though an important first step, the shortcomings of the original Concordat became apparent when yet another banking crisis surfaced: the failure of the Banco Ambrosiano in 1982.[18] Spurred by the Banco Ambrosiano scandal, the Basle Committee prepared a revision of the 1975 Concordat. It was completed in June 1983.[19] The revised version

---

[15] See Bank for International Settlements, available at http://www.bis.org (30.11.2002).

[16] Regarding the exclusion of the general public from the Basle process prior to the growth of the Internet see Barbara C. Matthews, 'Capital Adequacy, Netting, and Derivatives' (1995) 2 *Stanford Journal of Law, Business and Finance*, 167 at 189–90.

[17] On the 1975 Concordat see Jarrod Wiener, *Globalisation and the Harmonisation of Law* (London, 1999), pp. 70–90.

[18] Banco Ambrosiano, an Italian bank with a subsidiary in Luxembourg, was left short of US $450 million in its liabilities to its creditors after its subsidiary had made loans of US $1.4 billion to Latin American companies. The incident gave rise to a controversy between Italy and Luxembourg over who should have exercised supervision and who should be the lender of last resort. See Alford, 'Basle Committee Minimum standards', above note 1, at 251–2; Daniel M. Laiffer, 'Putting super back in the supervision of international banking, post BCCI' (1992) 60 *Fordham Law Review*, 470 n. 18.

[19] The official name of the Revised Basle Concordat is 'Principles for the Supervision of Banks' Foreign Establishments (May 1993), see BCBS Compendium of Documents – Volume III: International supervisory issues, available at http://www.bis.org/publ/bcbsc312.pdf (30.11.2002). On the 1983 Concordat, see Peter Cooke, 'The Basle Concordat on the Supervision of Banks' Foreign Establishments' (1984) 39 *Aussenwirtschaft* 151.

incorporated[20] the principle of *consolidated supervision* as one of the core supervisory techniques for international banking groups.[21] The second important principle established by the Revised Concordat was that of *dual key supervision.*[22]

The Revised Concordat of 1983 had corrected some major flaws of the Concordat of 1973. However, the unfolding of another banking scandal revealed that important loopholes remained. The Concordat had abstained from assigning clear supervisory responsibilities for supervising holding companies.[23] This made it possible for BCCI, a holding company headquartered in Luxembourg, to evade supervision by setting up a complex, multinational structure. When, through the co-ordinated efforts of the regulators of eight states, its activities were finally halted, BCCI had accumulated liabilities of US $10.64 billion while retaining assets of only US $1.1 billion.[24]

In response to the BCCI scandal, the Basle Committee reformulated certain principles of the Revised Concordat as *Minimum Standards* in 1992. The first Minimum Standard states that: 'All international banking groups and international banks should be supervised by a home country authority that capably performs consolidated supervision.' Other new requirements include the condition that an international bank must obtain permission from both its home and host country regulators prior to opening a cross-border establishment, and that a host regulator should prevent the establishment of the bank in its

---

[20] The principle itself had been adopted in 1978, see Cooke, 'The Basle Concordat', above note 19, at 153.

[21] Under this principle, the home authority would be responsible for monitoring the overall exposure of the bank, taking into account its worldwide operations, whereas the host authorities were deemed to have primary responsibility for supervising the branches or subsidiaries. See Revised Basle Concordat, above note 19.

[22] See Revised Basle Concordat, above note 19.

[23] Under this approach, parent and host authorities are encouraged to assess the quality of each other's supervision. Where the host authority supervision was deemed inadequate, the parent authority should either extend its supervision or discourage the parent bank to continue to operate the establishment in question. See Revised Basle Concordat, above note 19.

[24] For more details on BCCI's activities see Peter Truell and Gary Gurwin, *BCCI: The Inside Story of the Wold's Most Corrupt Financial Empire* (Boston, 1992); Richard Dale, 'Regulatory Consequences of the BCCI Collapse: US, UK, EC, Basle Committee – Current Issues in Banking Supervision' in Joseph J. Norton, Chia-Jui Cheng and I. Fletcher (eds.), *International Banking Regulation and Supervision: Change and Transformation in the 1990s* (Dordrecht, 1994), pp. 377–97.

jurisdiction if it is not satisfied by the home countries ability to exercise consolidated supervision.[25]

A notable exception to the mainly crisis-prompted regulation was the development of the 'Core principles for Effective Banking Supervision' in 1997. The Principles provide a blueprint for an effective supervisory system. The incentive came from a call of the G7 heads of government that the Committee participate in efforts to improve supervisory standards in the emerging markets. The principles were developed in collaboration with many non-G10 central banks and supervisory authorities.[26]

The continuous discussion and collaboration among the members of the international supervisory community led the Basle Committee to extend its focus beyond the supervision of cross-border banking in the strict sense. To date, the key documents alone fill a three-volume compendium.[27] They address issues ranging from the evaluation of internal control systems to the special risks of electronic banking. Among this myriad of topics, however, stands out one core issue to which most of the Committee's time has been devoted since the mid 1980s: *Capital Adequacy.*

2. Substantive regulation: the Basle Capital Accords

In its founding period, the Basle Committee filled a vacuum concerning transborder regulatory coordination of banking regulations. Consequently, during the first ten years of its existence, it focused on the modalities for international co-operation. Thus, the capital adequacy rules, being substantive in nature, were beyond the initial scope of the Committee's activities. This began to change when, in the early 1980s, there was a

---

[25] Minimum Standards for the Supervision of International Banking Groups and their Cross-Border Establishments (1992). See BCBS Compendium of Documents – vol. III: International supervisory issues, available at http://www.bis.org/publ/bcbsc314.pdf (30.11.2002). For a German translation see Swiss Federal Banking Commission (FBC), 23 FBC-Bulletin (1993), pp. 44–58, available at http://www.ebk.admin.ch/f/publik/bulletin/bull23.pdf (30.11.2002).

[26] See BCBS Compendium of Documents – vol. I: Basic supervisory methods, Core Principles for effective banking supervision (September 1997), available at http://www.bis.org/publ/bcbsc102.pdf (30.11.2002). See also Basle Committee, *History of the Basel Committee*, above note 14. For a German translation see, 33 FBC-Bulletin (1997), pp. 71–137, available at http://www.ebk.admin.ch/f/publik/bulletin/bull23.pdf (30.11.2002).

[27] BCBS Compendium of Documents, available at http://www.bis.org/publ/bcbsc001.htm (30.11.2002).

mounting concern that the capital ratios of the main international banks were deteriorating just at the time that international risks, notably those vis-à-vis heavily indebted countries, were growing. In addition, the globalisation of finance and of financial institutions made increasingly evident that differences in national capital requirements were a source of competitive inequality. Thus, capital adequacy became a main concern for the central bankers who, at the same time, represented their country in the Basle Committee. Their regulatory concerns led to a transition of the Committee from its procedural approach toward the design of substantive prudential rules for capital adequacy.[28] In 1988, a capital measurement system, commonly referred to as the Basle Capital Accord, was approved by the G10 governors.[29]

Even though the 1990s saw several revisions and refinements of the Capital Accord, it remained flawed in several respects, namely with regard its apportionment of all assets in one of four risk categories. In more general terms, its rules proved too simplistic and rigid for the complex world of international banking.[30] Over time, there was an increasing pressure on the regulatory authorities to revise the Accord.[31] In June 1999 and January 2001, the Committee issued its first and second consultative package for a new capital adequacy framework, commonly referred to as 'Basle II' or the 'New Capital Accord'. The New Capital Accord intends to improve the way regulatory capital requirements reflect underlying risks and to better address the financial innovation that has occurred in recent years.[32] The framework itself

---

[28] See Hal S. Scott and Philip A. Wellons, *International Finance: Transactions, Policy and Regulation* (8th edn, New York, 2001), p. 227.

[29] See Basle Committee, International Convergence of Capital Measurement and Capital Standards (Capital Accord), available at www.bis.org.publ/bcbs04 A.pdf (30.11.2002). Whether the main catalyst for the Accord was the debt crises of the developing nations or the domestic concern of the United States concerning the competition issue is controversial, see Bhala, 'Equilibrium Theory', above note 11, 22. For a general history of the Capital Accord of 1988 see Ethan B. Kapstein, *Supervising International Banks: Origins and Implications of the Basle Accord* (Princeton, NJ, 1991). For an overview of its principles see Norton, *Supervisory Standards*, above note 5, at 193–212.

[30] For instance, the Accord flatly fixed banks' capital at 8% of their risk-weighted assets. For an account of the 'seven deadly sins' of the Capital Accord see Tarbert, 'Rethinking Capital Adequacy', above note 3, at 792–802. The Accord is viewed by some as a key catalyst for the 1990s recession and the Asian financial crisis: *ibid.*, 794. See also Scott and Wellons, *International Finance*, above note 28, at 245.

[31] See Bhala, 'Equilibrium Theory', above note 11, at 20.

[32] See BIS, the New Basel Capital Accord: an explanatory note, available at http://www.bis.org/publ/bcbsca01.pdf.

consists of three pillars: (1) minimum capital requirements, which seek to develop and expand on the standardised rules of the 1988 accord; (2) supervisory review of an institution's capital adequacy and internal assessment process; and (3) effective use of market discipline as a lever to strengthen disclosure and encourage safe and sound banking practices.[33] The Committee has finalised the New Capital Accord in June 2004. Implementation is currently planned for the end of 2006.[34]

The new capital adequacy framework has encountered a considerable amount of scepticism among practitioners and scholars.[35] Nevertheless, one should have no doubts about its prospective impact on the world-wide treatment of the capital adequacy question. For this, it is useful to remember the pivotal role of the 1988 Accord: by 1999, over a hundred countries had implemented its standards and requirements.[36] Considering the fact that the 'capital adequacy regime is the single most important set of rules and proposals in both international and domestic banking law',[37] one can say that the near global convergence of this 'multibillion-dollar regulatory scheme'[38] marks a turning point in the international regulation of international banking.

---

[33] For an overview see Peter Nobel, *Swiss Finance Law and International Standards* (Bern, 2002), pp. 317–20; Carlo Lombardini, *Droit bancaire suisse* (Zürich 2002), pp. 64–7; Franz-Christoph Zeitler, 'Internationale Entwicklungslinien der Bankenaufsicht' (2001) 55 *Wertpapiermitteilungen – Zeitschrift für Wirtschafts- und Bankrecht*, 1397 at 1398–400. For a detailed analysis, including a summary of recent literature, see João A. C. Santos, 'Bank Capital Regulation in Contemporary Banking Theory' (2001) 10 *Financial Markets, Institutions and Instruments* 64–70. For a view by a bank supervisor see Daniel Zuberbühler, 'Revision des Capital Accord des Basler Ausschusses für Bankenaufsicht' in Peter Nobel (ed.), *Aktuelle Rechtsprobleme des Finanz- und Börsenplatzes Schweiz* (Bern, 2000), pp. 135–70.

[34] See http://www.bis.org/press/p020710.htm (30.11.2002). The Basle Committee portion of the BIS website contains an extensive documentation of the New Basle Capital Accord, see BIS, Basle Committee, Basle Capital Accord, available at http://www.bis.org/publ/bcbsca.htm (30.11.2002).

[35] See Tarbert, 'Rethinking Capital Adequacy', above note 3, at 802–23 (containing a detailed critical analysis); Rahul Dhumale, 'Levelling the playing field in international financial markets: The Basel Accord Revisited' (2001) 9 *Journal of Financial Regulation and Compliance* 38–41; 'Sweeter Basle', *The Economist*, 18 January 2001, p. 50. For a critical view from the industry see the comments by the Swiss Banker's Association, available at http://www.swissbanking.org/010528_Beilage_zu_New_Basel_Capital_Accord.pdf (30.11.2002).

[36] New Basle Capital Accord, Overview, note 7, available at www.bis.org/publ/bcbsca02.pdf (30.11.2002).

[37] Bhala, 'Equilibrium Theory', above note 11, at 21.

[38] Zaring, 'International Law by Other Means', above note 6, 282.

IV. The Basle rule-making – regulation through co-operation

There is a general agreement that the Basle documents are not legally binding. The Committee itself emphasises the lack of legislative authority:

> 'The Committee does not possess any formal supranational supervisory authority. Its conclusions do not have, and were never intended to have, legal force. Rather, it formulates broad supervisory standards and guidelines and recommends statements of best practice in the expectation that individual authorities will take steps to implement them through detailed arrangements – statutory or otherwise – which are best suited to their own national systems. In this way, the Committee encourages convergence towards common approaches and common standards without attempting detailed harmonisation of member countries' supervisory techniques.'[39]

As an illustration of this principle, the Basle 1988 Capital Accord articulated that the supervisory authorities will introduce and apply these recommendations in light of their different structure and existing supervisory arrangements.[40] Over the years, however, the rhetoric has become more self-assured. The New Accord simply notes that it 'will be applied' to internationally active banks,[41] whereas the explanatory note to the Accord states that it will be implemented by the Committee member countries and that the Committee 'expects that it will also be adopted by supervisors across the world'.[42]

Thus, while not actively involved in law-making, the Basle Committee acts as a generator for the national law-making process. At the heart of this process lies the consensus among its members on the proposal in question. One observer has described the Basle process as 'gentleman's agreement among central bankers'.[43] In more technical terms, the Basle rules constitute international financial 'soft law'.[44] The consensus

---

[39] Basle Committee, *History of the Basel Committee*, above note 14.
[40] Basle Capital Accord, above note 29, at notes 5 and 6.
[41] New Basle Capital Accord, Part 1, para. 1, available at www.bis.org/publ/bcbsca03.pdf.
[42] New Basle Capital Accord, Explanatory Note, Annex 1, available at www.bis/org./publ/bcbsca01.pdf.
[43] Hal Scott, 'The Competitive Implications of the Basle Capital Accord' (1995) 39 *St Louis University Law Journal* 855.
[44] In the international law context, soft law refers to informal duties adopted under formal or informal treaties or multilateral agreements. For a detailed account on the phenomenon of 'soft law' see Hartmut Hilgenberg, 'A Fresh Look at Soft Law' (1999) 10 *European Journal of International Law* 499–515. For an account of the soft law development in international

upon which this rule-making is based assures that the different regulatory backgrounds of its members are taken into account. This, in turn, enhances its chances to be implemented in the domestic context. Whereas the Basle rules are to be considered as soft law, they will, however, often acquire binding force in the process of their implementation within the domestic regime: once the Basle rules are adopted into national laws, they become hard law within that country.[45]

V. Basle's impact – a centrifugal force for international convergence

The original lack of the binding legal force of the Basle documents is in stark contrast to its effective regulatory significance. This is because, as pointed out above, it is regularly integrated into formal domestic law or regulatory practice. One illustration of the growing awareness of the Committee's regulatory impact has been the attempt, by some members, to preempt the Basle process through prior enactment of domestic rules.[46] More generally, the effect of the Committee's various instruments has been that all states with international banks of significant size have reformulated their jurisdictional approaches to prudential supervision. This is particularly true for Basle's most successful 'product', the Capital Accord. Noting that the absence of a legally binding treaty has not prevented capital adequacy laws to be virtually identical throughout the world, H. P. Tarbert has called the Accord a 'peerless breed of internationalised national law'.[47]

One reason for the Committee's ability to act as a catalyst in generating and shaping national rules and practices beyond its exclusive membership circle is the quality of its work. Another is its prestige. An important additional factor is the market power of its members, who happen to be the states with the world's largest banking markets. Their interest in

banking regulation see Lee, 'The Basle Accords as Soft Law', above note 4, at 1. That the Basle documents qualify as 'soft law' is undisputed, see Zeitler, 'Internationale Entwicklungslinien', above note 33, at 1400; Nobel, *Swiss Finance Law*, above note 33, at 311; Lombardini, *Droit bancaire suisse*, above note 33, at 50.

[45]   See Nobel, *Swiss Finance Law*, above note 33, at 311.

[46]   This was the case in 1993, when the European Union promulgated the Capital Adequacy Directive Council Directive 93/6/EEC on capital adequacy of investment firms and credit institutions (OJ 1993 No. L141/1, 15 March 1993), which issued final capital adequacy rules for market risks. For an account of the 'peremptory practices' of the EU Member States see Matthews, 'Capital Adequacy', above note 16, at 187–9.

[47]   Tarbert, 'Rethinking Capital Adequacy', above note 3, at 776.

creating a level playing field for their own banking industry prompts them to 'encourage' non-member supervisory authorities to adopt the Basle standards. For instance, the Basle standards and practices can be made a condition for the foreign bank who wants to do business in a member country. Also, the member country can prevent its banks from opening a subsidiary or branch in a non-member country which is not in compliance with important Basle principles. Another crucial vehicle by which the Committee's influence has been expanded is the IMF. This *de facto* central bank of last resort will, when approving and monitoring its bailout packages, examine the strength of the governmental banking supervision of the recipient country. It does so by referring to the Basle principles.[48] Lastly, the Committee's influence has also been helped by the endorsement of its principles, notably its capital adequacy framework, by another key market player: the rating agencies.[49]

Thus, for a non-member country who refuses to comply with Basle's soft law, the consequences are anything but soft. The fact that non-member countries, especially of less industrialised parts of the world, are forced into the level playing field of the G10 Club of Giants, sheds a somewhat different light on the Basle process. From a more critical perspective, Basle's rules appear as undifferentiated inculcation of domestic law by the rich country bank supervisors. Instead of characterising them as 'soft law', it has been suggested to refer to them as central bankers' 'Club' law.[50]

VI. Conclusion

Modern banking has become internationalised. An effective supervision of the banking industry requires co-ordination among the national supervisors and adherence to international supervisory standards. The centrifugal force in this process has been the Basle Committee on Banking Supervision. The Basle Committee is not a formal international organisation in an international law context. Nonetheless, it has evolved

---

[48] See Lee, 'The Basle Accords as Soft Law', above note 4, at 8, 36.
[49] On the use of the so-called 'Bis-ratio' by the rating agencies see Zuberbühler, 'Revision des Capital Accord', above note 33, at 136.
[50] Christos Hadjiemmanuil, 'Central Bankers' "Club" Law and Transitional Economies: Banking Reform and the Reception of the Basle Standards of Prudential Supervision in Eastern Europe and the Former Soviet Union' in Joseph J. Norton and Mads Andenas (eds.), *Emerging Financial Markets and the Role of International Financial Organisations* (London, 1996), p. 184.

into an unmatched catalyst for the convergence of law-making in the area of international prudential banking regulation. The Basle documents constitute international regulatory soft law. One benefit of Basle's soft law approach is that it offers the possibility of strengthening international banking supervision without the imposition of a new formal legal framework or direct interference with national sovereignty. The voluntary approach built into the formulations of the Basle documents make them flexible enough for implementation in disparate regulatory systems. Furthermore, the exclusivity of its membership assures the efficiency which is needed for a timely regulatory reaction in the rapidly developing field of international banking.

On a more critical note, some scholars have rightly pointed out that the Committee's activities are somewhat outside of the regular constitutional context of law-making. As the Committee lacks the status of an international organisation, it is not only excluded from the prerogatives, but also exempted from the potential discipline of international legal personality.[51] This discipline is not achieved on the domestic level either. In fact, there is a near complete non-involvement of the national law-makers in the Basle process. This has allowed international banking regulation to become a sort of 'club' law, designed and forced upon the world by rich country banking supervisors who act outside the democratic control mechanisms of their home government.[52] So far, however, regulatory alternatives which could achieve Basle's impact while being less of a 'secretive and undemocratic engine of regulation'[53] have yet to be developed. Considering its past accomplishments in the international regulatory convergence process, it can be assumed that the Basle Committee will continue to play a crucial role in international financial regulation.

---

[51] For an account why the Basle Committee does not meet the requirements of an international organisation see Zaring, 'International Law by Other Means', above note 6, at 285.

[52] On the 'democratic deficit' of the Basle Committee see Zeitler, 'Internationale Entwicklungslinien', above note 33, at 1400.

[53] Zaring, 'International Law by Other Means', above note 6, at 327.

11

Strengthening the international financial architecture: contribution by the IMF and World Bank

AXEL PEUKER

I. Introduction

Financial crises have occurred throughout the history of capitalism – from the Dutch tulip mania in 1637–8 and the Indian cotton futures market crash of 1866, over the Great Depression of 1929, to the financial crises of the 1980s and 1990s.

While industrial countries have reduced the incidence and severity of financial crises over the last seventy years, financial crises have become more frequent in developing countries since the 1980s. With every such wave of crises, there are calls for major changes in the governance of financial markets, aimed at improving their efficiency, reducing their vulnerability and increasing their legitimacy. And while sometimes these calls are indeed heeded, in particular when major disruptions occur, many times the appetite for a grand new design diminishes as economies recover. To some extent, this can be said about the latest discussion regarding economic governance of financial markets – which rose to prominence as a quest for a 'new international financial architecture'.[1] Still, with Argentina in severe distress and clouds hanging over Brazil and Turkey, this might be a good time to revisit some of the reforms proposed and enacted in the wake of the 'international financial crises'[2] of the 1990s – the *tequila* crisis in Mexico 1995, East Asia in 1997–98, Russia in 1998, and Brazil in 1998–99. Specifically, this article will look

The author is World Bank staff. However, the views expressed in this essay are those of the author and should not be attributed to the World Bank, to its affiliated organisations, or to members of its Board of Executive Directors or the countries they represent.

[1] Barry Eichengreen, *Toward a New International Financial Architecture: A Practical Post-Asia Agenda* (Washington, DC, 1999).

[2] Larry Summers, 'International Financial Crises: Causes, Preventions, and Cures' (2000) 90(2) *American Economic Review* 1–16.

at the contributions by two global agents, the IMF and the World Bank, to strengthening the international financial architecture in the context of their mandates. Furthermore, a brief report on some ideas which have been floated concerning the governance of these two agents themselves, will be given.

II. The IMF and World Bank mandates[3]

The approach by IMF and World Bank to strengthening the international financial architecture derives, on the one hand, from their respective mandates and comparative advantages, and on the other from their assessment of the nature of the recent crises. As to the mandate, there are important differences between the two institutions. The IMF is charged with the stability and well-functioning of the international monetary and exchange rate regime. At the heart of the Fund's mandate and expertise is its macroeconomic surveillance function. The World Bank's mandate and mission are development and poverty alleviation, and its core functions structural reforms and capacity building. Even though the IMF Articles of Agreement focus on current account transactions, there is little doubt as to the IMF's prime role in addressing financial crises, no matter whether they arise from the current or the capital account side of the balance of payments. For the World Bank, the rationale for its involvement in strengthening the financial architecture is somewhat more indirect, but equally pertinent. Financial crises, even if they are not systemic on a global scale, have enormous economic and social costs, and dramatic impacts on the poor. The costs of currency and banking crises in the 1980s and 1990s have repeatedly exceeded 30% of GDP, and within one year of the East Asian crisis, 30 million people were pushed into poverty (as measured by the US $2 per day benchmark).[4] Hence, the importance of crisis prevention and resolution also for the World Bank agenda.

III. Assessment of the recent crisis and lessons learned

While the exact causes and transmission mechanisms of the international financial crises are still under discussion, there is little doubt

---

[3] For background information on the IMF and World Bank, see www.imf.org and www.worldbank.org.

[4] World Bank, *East Asia: Recovery and Beyond* (Washington, DC, 2000).

that they differ from those of traditional balance of payments problems observed in the past. Traditional crises tended to originate in the current account, whereas international financial crises originate from the capital account, propelled by a loss of investor confidence. The hidden nature of the foreign exchange exposure of the private sector and the balance sheet effects emanating from it are other distinguishing aspects.

The particular dilemma for policy advice has to do with these differences from traditional crises.[5] The remedies for the latter are exchange rate devaluation and tightening of fiscal and monetary policies; but the remedies for today's crises need to take into account the risks to the stability of the financial sector, which would argue for expanding money supply and lowering interest rates. This dilemma poses important challenges for the policy advice dispensed by the international financial institutions – and it can be reasonably argued that the initial response by the IMF did not fully take into account the particulars of these crises. However, the purpose of this article is to highlight the lessons which IMF and World Bank have drawn from the recent crises – lessons embodied in the following approach to strengthening the financial architecture.

1. Continued accent on sound macroeconomic management, but subject to broader surveillance and with more constraints regarding the choice of exchange rate regimes.
2. Increased emphasis on structural and institutional underpinnings of corporate and financial markets.
3. Heightened attention to transparency and accountability in financial markets, *inter alia* to reduce herding behaviour.
4. Improved access to finance for crisis prevention and resolution.
5. Enhanced private sector involvement in crisis prevention and resolution.

Before elaborating how these five lessons have come to be reflected in IMF and World Bank activities, however, it is important to stress that there is another lesson for post-crisis policies which this essay will not be able to touch upon: that is, an increased focus on effective social protection.[6]

---

[5] Anne O. Krueger, 'Conflicting Demands on the International Monetary Fund' (2000) 90(2) *American Economic Review* 38–42.

[6] For an overview, see Asian Pacific Economic Cooperation (APEC), *Social Safety Nets in Response to Crisis: Lessons and Guidelines from Asia and Latin America* (APEC, 2001).

IV. Lesson 1: continued accent on sound macroeconomic management

Sound macroeconomic management remains the *sine qua non* of crisis prevention. Sound fundamentals matter both for economic performance, and for credit ratings and investor perceptions – and thus become doubly relevant in today's setting.[7] However, the post-crisis surveillance of macroeconomic policies goes beyond traditional fiscal and monetary indicators, including for example, much more detailed data on foreign exchange positions. While none of these indicators taken alone are reliable predictors of crises, taken together they can highlight vulnerabilities and help induce corrective actions by the authorities.

Another critical dimension of macroeconomic management is the choice of the appropriate exchange rate regime in light of the 'impossible trinity' of an independent monetary policy, an open capital account and a fixed exchange rate. It is no accident that all of the aforementioned international financial crises have in some way involved a pegged exchange rate regime. In the wake of the crises, there have been calls for 'corner solutions', that is for either fully flexible exchange rates or fully fixed exchange rates, giving up monetary policy independence. It is important to correct the impression that IMF or World Bank have dogmatically embraced this call. As evidenced by Argentina, the economic costs of fully fixing the exchange rate – or even dollarisation – can be tremendous. And there remain 'second-best' considerations which argue against abandoning every attempt at muting exchange rate fluctuations. Nonetheless, the case for policy consistency remains, and more often than not, in a world with increasing capital mobility, this will point in the direction of more exchange rate flexibility to avoid severe currency misalignments which negatively affect economic performance and can give rise to speculative attacks.[8]

V. Lesson 2: increased emphasis on structural underpinnings

In response to the crisis, the IMF and World Bank have stepped up their work on the structural and institutional underpinnings of financial

---

[7] Jeffrey Sachs, Aaron Tornell and Andres Velasco, 'The Collapse of the Mexican Peso: What have we Learned?' (June 1995), *National Bureau for Economic Research*, Working Paper no. 5142.

[8] Stanley Fischer, 'Exchange Rate Regimes: Is the Bipolar View Correct?' (2001) 15(2) *Journal of Economic Perspectives* 3–24.

markets, and of market economies in general. The underlying premise of that work is that *global* financial stability also rests on robust *national* systems and hence requires enhanced measures at both the country and the international level.

The key co-ordinating body for the IMF–World Bank financial sector work is the joint 'Financial Sector Liaison Committee' (FSLC), established in September 1998. It is a unique structure directing work across the two institutions, with a view to enhance operational co-ordination, including more effective use of staff resources. Under the aegis of the FSLC, a new instrument was put at the disposal of the two institutions in May 1999, the FSAP. The country assessments conducted under this programme identify strengths, vulnerabilities and risks of the financial system; ascertain the sector's development and technical assistance needs; assess observance and implementation of relevant international standards and good practices; determine whether key sources of risks and vulnerabilities are being adequately managed; and help design appropriate policy responses. As at the end of June 2002, some fifty assessments were completed, and twenty to twenty-four further assessments are expected to be added each year.

The FSAP has helped to advance 'macroprudential' analysis and indicators, highlighting the two-way linkages between macroeconomic performance and financial sector soundness. Macroprudential indicators comprise both aggregated microprudential indicators of the health of individual financial institutions (e.g., capital adequacy, earnings and solvency), and macroeconomic variables associated with financial system soundness (e.g., volatility in exchange rates and interest rates). Aggregated microprudential indicators have been found to be primarily contemporaneous or lagging indicators of soundness; macroeconomic variables can signal imbalances that affect financial systems, and so tend to be leading indicators.

The FSAP also has included stress tests and scenario analysis, which help in assessing the impact of macroeconomic and other shocks on the profitability and solvency of financial institutions, and provide a useful framework for the identification of vulnerabilities and for discussing these findings with country authorities. The FSAP has further served to assess the observance of international standards – a topic that will be addressed in more detail below, under the heading of 'Heightened attention to transparency and accountability'. Other structural areas which have received heightened attention in recent years particularly in the World Bank, are accounting and auditing, corporate governance, insolvency regimes and debt management practices. Work in these domains has also been boosted by the initiatives to promote international standards, including a much greater emphasis on a systematic approach across countries.

The attention to structural underpinnings of financial markets has also led to a more cautious approach to capital account liberalisation. The basic conceptual case for the benefits of capital account liberalisation – based on increased access to capital and faster productivity growth, risk diversification and consumption smoothing – still holds. Moreover, one should recognise that there is, to some extent, a continuum between current and capital account transactions, which puts into question the very notion of completely closed capital accounts. But there is more recognition today of the downside risks associated with capital account liberalisation, hinging on volatility of capital flows and the potential for reversal (except for foreign direct investment). In fact, there is evidence that capital flows to emerging markets tend to trigger domestic cycles, rather than to accommodate them.[9] Hence, capital account liberalisation should be carefully sequenced, taking into account the development of the financial sector regulatory framework and the capacity of the supervisory bodies.

This raises, of course, the question of the merits of controls on capital flows. Here, in short, a consensus seems to have emerged that Chile-style maturity-based taxation of capital inflows can help in certain circumstances. As a price–based instrument, it presumably should also be preferable to quantitative restrictions embodied in capital adequacy regulation. However, this instrument seems to lose effectiveness over time – one of the reasons why it has been all but eliminated in Chile itself. Finally, there is no consensus on the circumstances justifying controls on capital outflows, nor any support in IMF or World Bank circles for a reversal of capital liberalisation.

VI. Lesson 3: heightened attention to transparency and accountability

Enhancing transparency and accountability in international financial markets was one of the key recommendations of the G22 'Report of the Working Group on International Financial Crises' issued in

---

[9] Mario J. Crucini, 'Country Size and Economic Fluctuations' (1997) 5(2) *Review of International Economics* 204–20.

October 1998. This has deepened the commitment to a large array of standard initiatives – perhaps among the most tangible outcome of the discussion on strengthening the international financial architecture.[10]

The importance attached to international standards has given rise to another joint IMF–World Bank initiative on 'Reports on the Observance of Standards and Codes' (ROSC), launched in early 2000 as an outgrowth of the 1999 IMF work on 'Transparency Reports.' In a world of integrated capital markets, where financial crises in individual countries can imperil international financial stability, a basic global public good argument can be made for minimum international standards – and for a role of multilateral agencies like the IMF and the World Bank.

At the international level, international standards enhance transparency as well as multilateral surveillance. If information on observance of standards is made public, standards assessments can foster market efficiency and discipline by informing investment decisions. At the national level, international standards provide a benchmark that can help identify vulnerabilities and guide policy reform. To best serve these objectives, however, the scope and application of such standards needs to be tailored to individual country circumstances.

Out of over sixty international standards under deliberation,[11] the ROSC exercise is currently covering eleven standards[12] falling under the three broad categories of (a) disclosure and transparency; (b) supervision and regulation; and (c) market infrastructure. Under the first category, the IMF has developed and is assessing standards on: (i) general and special data dissemination; (ii) fiscal transparency; and (iii) transparency in monetary and financial policies. Under the second category, in the context of the aforementioned FSAP, IMF and World Bank are assessing standards on: (iv) banking supervision developed by the Basle Committee; (v) securities market regulation developed by the International Organisation of Securities Commissions; (vi) insurance supervision developed by the International Association of Insurance Supervisors; and (vii) payments and settlements systems developed by the Committee on Payment and Settlement Systems. Under the third category, the World Bank is taking the lead in assessing standards on: (viii) accounting developed by the International Accounting Standards Board; (ix) auditing developed by the International

---

[10] Involving as many actors as described in Annex 1 to this chapter.

[11] For a compendium of standards, see www.fsforum.org/Standards/Home.html.

[12] See Annex 2 to this chapter.

Federation of Accountants; (x) corporate governance based on the 'Principles of Corporate Governance' developed by the OECD; and (xi) insolvency and creditor rights regimes based on the 'Principles and Guidelines for Effective Insolvency and Creditor Rights Regimes' developed by the World Bank in collaboration with other agencies and experts.

More recently, and partly motivated by September 11, attention has focused on the twelfth of the 'key standards' identified by the Financial Stability Forum – the market integrity standards ('40 + 8 Recommendations') issued by the OECD-based Financial Action Task Force to combat money laundering and terrorist finance.

So far, the IMF and World Bank have undertaken standards assessments in over eighty countries. Standards assessment proceed in a modular fashion, with each summary assessment of a standard in a particular country constituting a 'module' for a country ROSC. As of the end of June 2002, some 264 such modules had been prepared – partly as self-standing assessments and partly under the FSAP. This work then feeds into IMF and World Bank country strategies and operations.

In virtually all the standards assessments, as in other areas of importance to IMF and World Bank mandates, there also has been increased emphasis on strategic partnerships – acknowledging that the IMF and the World Bank do not have the resources to systematically conduct these assessments on their own. Thus far, staff from some seventy national and international agencies have participated in financial sector assessment missions. Dissemination of standards work is also done jointly, as for example through the OECD-World Bank country and regional Roundtables on Corporate Governance.

VII. Lesson 4: improved access to finance

Already, following the 1995 Mexican *tequila* crisis, the IMF – and to a lesser extent the World Bank – have introduced new financial instruments to improve access to finance for crisis prevention and resolution.

In 1996, the IMF 'Emergency Financing Mechanism' was created, which allows management to shorten its traditional cycle of approval procedures in response to crisis situations. The 'Supplemental Reserve Facility' (SRF) was introduced in 1997 to provide supplemental short-term financing in access of the regular country quotas. The SRF supports IMF programme countries, and drawings bear a penalty of 300–500 basis points. In 1999, the CCL was implemented, expected to be negotiated well before a crisis arises. It carries both pre-qualifying and post-crisis conditionality. The requirements for entering into a CCL agreement were streamlined in September 2000, to provide greater automaticity in the provision of resources for a country in crisis as result of contagion, and the initial rate of charge on CCL resources was reduced (from 350 basis points to 150, rising over time to a ceiling of 350). In the World Bank, a 'Special Structural Adjustment Loan' was introduced in 1998, to be able to respond in tandem with the IMF SRF, and a contingent credit line ('Deferred Drawdown Option') has recently been added to the World Bank's lending instruments.

These reforms tread carefully a path avoiding two opposing dangers. For the Meltzer Commission[13] and other critics, the financing facilities of the IMF already present a moral hazard issue. For others, the CCL is still a far cry from what they perceive would be a desirable 'lender of last resort' facility.[14] While conceptually valid, there is little empirical support for the claim that IMF facilities pose a significant incentive problem.[15] At the same time, moving further into the direction of a lender of last resort function would not only pose an immense resource challenge. It would also require an extraordinary supervision and resolution capacity and authority – or else indeed invite the abuse which Meltzer and others fear.[16]

VIII. Lesson 5: enhanced private sector involvement

Another dimension of strengthening the international financial architecture is private sector involvement in crisis prevention and resolution, which goes hand in hand with other work by IMF and World Bank to ensure that markets make their investment decisions on a better-informed basis.

As to crisis resolution, the IMF has laid out what it considers the main principles that should guide the international community in the handling of a crisis, including the following: (i) responsibility for negotiations with creditors lies squarely with debtor countries; (ii) action taken in a crisis should not undermine the obligation of debtors to pay their

---

[13] International Financial Institutions Advisory Committee, *Final Report* (Washington, DC, 2000), available at http://www.house.gov/jec/imf/ifiac.htm.

[14] George Soros, 'To Avert the Next Financial Crisis', *Financial Times*, 6 January 1999.

[15] Peter Nunnenkamp, 'Towards a New International Financial Order: Why Reform is so Slow' (2000) 35(1) *Intereconomics* 4–22.

[16] Kenneth Rogoff, 'International Institutions for Reducing Global Financial Instability' (1999) 13(4) *Journal of Economic Perspectives* 21–42.

debt in full and on time; (iii) no one category of private debt should be inherently preferred in resolving a crisis; and (iv) the IMF has a central role in facilitating orderly crisis resolution.

The IMF also sees a certain measure of agreement on the broad operational framework to ensure that the private sector is effectively involved in the resolution of financial crises: if the need for financing is moderate, private sector involvement should be ensured primarily through the IMF's catalytic approach. If the immediate need for financing is large, but prospects for regaining market access on appropriate terms are good, the IMF would still rely primarily on its catalytic approach. If the immediate need for financing is large, and prospects for regaining market access are poor, private sector involvement will have to be ensured through 'concerted techniques', ranging from voluntary agreements with international banks to maintain exposure levels to standstill agreements. If needed to support the viability of adjustment programmes, the IMF and the World Bank are prepared to lend into arrears.

This agreement in principle notwithstanding, there remain differences of opinion among key IMF and World Bank shareholders on important aspects of the agenda for private sector involvement. The previous US administration, in particular, supported a 'case-by-case' approach to private sector involvement – arguing that any pre-established rules for private sector involvement and burden sharing may just accentuate anticipative herding behaviour. By contrast, France and Germany argued for a more clearly spelled out, 'rules-based' framework for crisis resolution.

Today, the debate has shifted, but differences remain. There is now support among all of the G7 countries for a 'contract-based' framework, embodying collective action clauses in bonds which would allow a qualified majority of bond holders to sanction debt restructuring. Ironically, it is the successful emerging market economies who reject such collective action clauses, because they fear that applying such clauses would signal risk of default to financial markets, and hence lead to increased interest payments.

There might be more interest by emerging markets in establishing a 'statutory framework' akin to that applied in domestic bankruptcy. In an efficient insolvency procedure at the firm-level, firms that are insolvent are liquidated and firms that are merely illiquid are preserved, *inter alia*, by invoking a stay on creditors and giving preference to new creditors. The specific proposal under discussion at the country level is a

'Sovereign Debt Restructuring Mechanism' (SDRM), developed by Anne Krueger, former Chief Economist of the World Bank and now Deputy Managing Director of the IMF.[17] However, there are major challenges to implementing the SDRM. To begin with, there is a basic asymmetry compared to firm insolvency procedures: insolvent countries can hardly be liquidated. But even in the case of liquidity problems, important differences remain: for example, creditors can insist on changing firm management. Equally important, even debtor countries might shy away from granting the IMF – often a creditor in its own right – the powers necessary to substitute for the role of a court in a domestic procedure. In conclusion, even though the International Monetary and Financial Committee of the Board of Governors of the IMF (the IMFC) endorsed the SDRM for further consideration at the IMF Spring 2003 meetings, much more work will need to be done to arrive at an operationally feasible and politically acceptable design of the SDRM.

To support the effort at increased private sector involvement, the IMF also created a 'Capital Market Consultative Group' (CMCG). The CMCG has a rotating membership including: (i) commercial banks; (ii) investment banks; (iii) institutional investors; and (iv) insurance groups. To preempt concerns about issues of privileged access and misuse of information, this forum is set up strictly as a consultative group, not as an information exchange, with a mandate to discuss, *inter alia*: (i) measures and practices that could promote a more stable and efficient international financial system; and (ii) ramifications of initiatives of the IMF, and of the official community more generally.

IX. Governance of the IMF and World Bank[18]

As part of the discussion on the reform of the international financial architecture, a number of ideas have been put forward concerning the *governance* of the IMF and World Bank themselves (as opposed to those

---

[17] Anne O. Krueger, *A New Approach to Sovereign Debt Restructuring* (Washington, DC: International Monetary Fund, April 2002).

[18] A more detailed discussion of this topic can be found in Montek S. Ahluwalia, *The IMF and the World Bank in the New Financial Architecture*, International Monetary and Financial Issues for the 1990s (Geneva: UNCTAD, 2001); and in Aziz Ali Mohammad, *The Future Role of the International Monetary Fund*, G-24 Discussion Paper Series (Geneva: UNCTAD, April 2001).

concerning the *mandate* and *role* of these institutions). The backdrop to these proposals has been the important issue of the *voice* of developing countries, in particular emerging markets, in the design of the financial architecture – as key forums, such as the Financial Stability Forum and the Committees created by the G10, have only limited, if any, representation of developing countries.

In contrast, the membership of the IMF and World Bank is universal, and both institutions see it as their role to bring developing country experience and perspectives to the discussions that are underway. Nonetheless, these two institutions are organised as 'co-operatives' with voting power meant to reflect economic weight of the member countries. There is little expectation that the World Bank and IMF would shift to UN-style 'one-country-one vote' representation. Instead, there have been proposals to assign to the Economic and Social Council (ECOSOC) a monitoring role over the Bretton Woods institutions. However, beyond reaffirming the anyhow existing mechanisms for debriefing the ECOSOC, this proposal has not found favour with the key shareholders of the IMF and the World Bank.

Other proposals for reform seek to exploit the scope for improvement of the current governance structure within the parameters of capital-based representation. For one, it can be pointed out that the current distribution of capital does not reflect the increased weight of the Asian economies over the last decades – and a move to re-weighting shares would at the same time increase the importance of emerging market. Also, it has been proposed to review the current grouping of the OECD and developing countries under one chair, as well as the rotation of shared seats in an alphabetical order – for example, from Mexico to Nicaragua, or Malaysia to Myanmar. Finally, it has been argued that the focus of the Executive Boards of Directors could be further shifted to issues of strategic importance, strengthening the deliberative nature of these bodies and perhaps elevating the stature of Board representatives.

X. Concluding remarks

As set out in the introduction, enough time has passed to take stock of the reforms of the international financial architecture. A certain agreement on *broad principles* of reform seems to have taken hold in the official community:

- The critical importance of domestic macroeconomic and structural policies in crisis prevention.
- The case for global collective action in crisis prevention and resolution, notwithstanding the danger of moral hazard, because of market shortcomings, risks of contagion and also because of the impact of crises on the poor.
- The need for private sector involvement, to improve the incentive structure for sound investment practices.
- The need to give adequate voice to emerging markets.
- The continued importance of the IMF – and in different ways that of the World Bank – as global agents in the effort to strengthen the governance of financial markets.

From this brief overview of specific IMF and World Bank initiatives, one can see that, to some degree, these broad principles have been translated into *practical changes* – for example in the area of policy advice, in the launch of the FSAP and the ROSC exercises, and in the creation of new lending instruments. Less tangible, however, have been the efforts to increase private sector involvement, and to give more voice to emerging markets – except, perhaps, for the creation of the G20, which brings together leading industrialised countries and key emerging markets, as well as the IMF and World Bank.

Of course, to those hoping for a more fundamental reordering of the financial architecture, the response and contribution by the IMF and World Bank will appear far too limited. However, the very same political and economic parameters which circumscribe the room for overall reform also determine the space for contributions by global agents such as the IMF and the World Bank. And clearly, for many of the gaps which remain – for example regarding a lender of last resort – the IMF and World Bank not only lack the mandate and capacity, but also the ambition to fill them.

Annex 1: International standards: key global actors

I. Public sector

1. **Consultative fora**
   - Financial Stability Forum (FSF)
2. **Intergovernmental groupings (Ministerial and/or Central Bank):**
   - Asia Pacific Economic Co-operation
   - Commonwealth
   - G7
   - G8
   - G10
   - G20
   - [G22 (ad hoc)]
   - G24
   - [G33 (ad hoc)]
   - G77
3. **International regulatory and supervisory groupings**
   - Basle Committee on Banking Supervision (BCBS)
   - Committee on the Global Financial System (CGFS)
   - Committee on Payment and Settlement Systems (CPSS)
   - Financial Action Task Force (FATF)
   - International Association of Insurance Supervisors (IAIS)
   - International Organisation of Supreme Audit Institutions (INTOSAI)
   - International Organisation of Securities Commissions (IOSCO)
4. **International Agencies and Institutions**
   - Bank for International Settlements (BIS)
   - International Monetary Fund (IMF)
   - Organisation for Co-operation and Development (OECD)
   - regional development banks
   - United Nations agencies
   - World Bank Group

II. Private sector

1. **Consultative fora**
   - G30
2. **Professional associations**
   - International Accounting Standards Board (IASB)
   - International Federation of Accountants (IFAC) through International Auditing Practices Committee (IAPC)
   - International Federation of Insolvency Professionals (INSOL)

Annex 2: Overview over IMF–World Bank standards assessments

Area	Standards/Principles	Methodology/ Templates	Assessment (as of 30 June 2002)
Data dissemination	1. Special Data Dissemination Standard (SDDS) 2. General Data Dissemination System (GDDS)		ROSC
Agency	IMF		IMF
Status	SDDS approved by the IMF Executive Board in March 1996. GDDS approved in December 1997.		50 countries have subscribed to the SDDS 26 ROSC modules completed.
Fiscal transparency	Code of Good Practices on Fiscal Transparency	Manual on Fiscal Transparency	ROSC
Agency	IMF	IMF	IMF
Status	Adopted by the IMF Interim Committee in April 1998	Approved by the IMF Executive Board	41 ROSC modules completed
Monetary & financial policy transparency	Code of Good Practices on Transparency in Monetary and Financial Policies	Supporting document to the Code	FSAP/ROSC
Agency	IMF	IMF	IMF
Status	Endorsed by the IMF Interim Committee in September 1999.	A supporting document to guide members seeking to implement the Code is being developed.	45 ROSC modules completed.
Banking supervision	Core Principles for Effective Banking Supervision	Core Principles methodology	FSAP/ROSC
Agency	BCBS	BCBS	IMF and World Bank
Status	Issued by the BCBS in September 1997	A Core Principles methodology was released in October 1999	47 ROSC modules completed

Annex 2 (cont.)

Area	Standards/Principles	Methodology/ Templates	Assessment (as of 30 June 2002)
Securities market regulation	Objectives and Principles for Securities Regulation	Implementation of the Objectives and Principles for Securities Regulation	FSAP/ROSC
Agency	International Organisation of Securities Commissions (IOSCO)	IOSCO	IMF and World Bank
Status	Issued by IOSCO in September 1998	Self-assessment methodology issued in May 2000	26 ROSC modules completed
Insurance Supervision	Insurance Supervisory Principles	Core Principles Methodology	FSAP/ROSC
Agency	International Association of Insurance Supervisors (IAIS)	IAIS	IMF and World Bank
Status	Issued by IAIS in September 1997.	Developed by IAIS in April 2000	22 ROSC modules completed
Payments and Settlements	Core Principles for Systemically Important Payment Systems (CPSIPS)		FSAP/ROSC
Agency	Committee on Payment and Settlement Systems (CPSS)	CPSS	IMF and World Bank
Status	A consultative document was issued by the CPSS in December 1999.	Work in progress	31 ROSC modules completed
Corporate governance	Principles of Corporate Governance	Corporate Governance Assessment Template	ROSC (FSAP)
Agency	OECD	World Bank	World Bank
Status	Endorsed by the OECD Ministerial Meeting in May 1999	Template published in December 2000	18 ROSC modules completed
Accounting	International Accounting Standards (IAS)	Accounting and Auditing Assessment Template	ROSC (FSAP)

Annex 2 (cont.)

Area	Standards/Principles	Methodology/ Templates	Assessment (as of 30 June 2002)
Agency	International Accounting Standards Board (IASB)	World Bank	World Bank
Status	IASC has promulgated 39 standards	Template published in December 2000	5 ROSC completed
Auditing	International Standards on Auditing (ISA)	Accounting and Auditing Assessment Template	ROSC (FSAP)
Agency	International Federation of Accountants (IFAC)	World Bank	World Bank
Status	ISA issued by IFAC's International Auditing Practices Committee (IAPC)	Template published in December 2000	5 ROSC modules completed
Insolvency and creditor rights	Principles and Guidelines for Effective Insolvency and Creditor Rights Systems	Insolvency Regimes Assessment Template	ROSC (FSAP)
Agency	World Bank	World Bank	World Bank
Status	Principles and Guidelines presented to the Bank Executive Board on 10 April 2001	Template published in December 2000	3 ROSC modules completed.
Debt management	Guidelines for Public Debt Management	Sound Practices in Government Debt Management	Not proposed for FSAP/ROSC
Agency	IMF and World Bank	IMF and World Bank	
Status	Guidelines presented to the Bank Executive Board on 6 March 2001	Under development.	
Anti-money laundering and combating terrorist finance	FATF 40 + 8 recommendations	Questionnaires for self-assessments	Proposed for FSAP/ROSC

Annex 2 (cont.)

Area	Standards/Principles	Methodology/ Templates	Assessment (as of 30 June 2002)
Agency	Financial Action Task Force on Money Laundering (FATF)	FATF	
Status	Issued in 1990, revised in 1996 and expanded in 2001 to include countering the financing of terrorism	No methodology for external assessments yet	Under discussion with FATF

PART V

A policy perspective

12

Liberalisation and regulation of international capital flows: where the opposites meet

PETER NUNNENKAMP

Abstract

The paper discusses the pros and cons of capital account liberalisation. Rather than contrasting liberalisation and regulation of capital flows as irreconcilable antagonisms, we argue that capital account liberalisation requires institutional and regulatory safeguards. Even though the effectiveness of specific capital controls cannot be taken for granted, we reject the view that financial globalisation has deprived national policymakers of the means to protect their economies against crisis. In addition to national safeguards, we assess the chances for crisis prevention and resolution on the regional level and present options to overcome institutional deficits on the global level. We conclude that reforms of the international financial architecture can help prevent illiquidity and ensure a fair burden sharing in the case of insolvency, without aggravating moral hazard behaviour of the parties involved.

I. Economic policy conflicts

The trade-off between financial liberalisation and financial sector stability is well known from the debate on *domestic* financial reforms.[1] Theoretical considerations and empirical findings suggest that liberalised national financial systems promote economic growth in the longer run.[2]

---

[1] John Williamson and Molly Mahar, 'A Survey of Financial Liberalization' in Princeton University, *Essays in International Finance* no. 211 (Princeton, 1998).

[2] For an overview, see Ross Levine, 'Financial Development and Growth: Views and Agenda' (1997) 35 *Journal of Economic Literature* 688–726.

However, financial liberalisation goes hand in hand with a higher exposure to financial crises.[3]

Various financial crises in emerging markets during the last decade point to a similar trade-off when it comes to capital account liberalisation. Domestic financial liberalisation and the removal of capital controls have in common that local financial institutions gain more room for risky transactions. This may not be a major problem if financial markets are functioning perfectly and a welfare-maximising allocation of resources is ensured by intermediaries. This cannot be taken for granted, however, as asymmetric information prevails in financial markets. As a consequence, 'financial markets will ... be affected to some degree by adverse selection, moral hazard, principal-agent problems, and herding behavior'.[4]

Information asymmetries are particularly pronounced in cross-border financial flows.[5] Geographical distance and cultural diversity render it more difficult to collect and correctly assess relevant information. Moreover, contracts are harder to enforce in international capital markets because of the sovereign risk involved. Hence, the benefits of capital account liberalisation have to be balanced carefully against its risks. This is easier said than done: economists have offered policymakers little on which to base their decisions. The economics profession is still struggling with major questions:

- Have countries without capital controls grown faster than countries that maintained controls (section II)?
- Were financial crises caused by capital account liberalisation (section III)?
- How effective is national regulation in containing the risk of financial globalisation (section IV)?
- Does regional co-operation provide a promising means to tie closer safety nets (section V)?
- In which way should the international financial architecture be reformed (section VI)?

[3] Asil Demirgüç-Kunt and Enrica Detragiache, 'Financial Liberalization and Financial Fragility' in IMF, *Working Paper* no. 98/83 (Washington, DC, 1998), p. 2.

[4] Barry Eichengreen, Michael Mussa et al., 'Capital Account Liberalization: Theoretical and Practical Aspects' in IMF, *Occasional Paper* no. 172 (Washington, DC, 1998).

[5] Stephany Griffith-Jones, 'Proposals for a Better International Financial System' (2000) 1(2) *World Economics* 111–33.

The subsequent discussion of these questions reveals the lack of ready-made solutions. Yet, some conclusions may be offered (section VII). First, the chances for a successful capital account liberalisation depend on the *overall* economic policy environment. Second, liberalisation and regulation must not be considered to be irreconcilable antagonisms; capital account liberalisation requires institutional safeguards and regulatory governance. Third, the optimal speed of liberalisation may vary across countries, but recent financial crises provide important lessons on sequencing. Fourth, the threat of further financial crises will remain unless the institutional shortcomings characterising the present international financial architecture are overcome.

II. Why liberalise at all?

With recent financial crises, 'the burden of proof of the gains from free capital flows has shifted to the proponents of open capital markets who are being criticised for having offered more "banner-waving" than hard quantitative evidence on the benefits of financial globalization'.[6] Free international capital flows *may* support economic growth and prosperity, but positive effects cannot be taken for granted.

According to a classical argument, international capital mobility is instrumental in allocating worldwide savings into their most productive use.[7] Capital mobility also renders it easier for a country to smooth short-term income fluctuations. Investment risks can be diversified on an international scale when capital flows are not restricted. Capital importing countries may gain better access to internationally available technologies, and capital inflows may help these countries to develop a sophisticated financial system at home.

All this is underlying the hypothesis that countries without capital controls should grow faster than countries with capital controls. However, the available evidence is in conflict with this hypothesis.

---

[6] Helmut Reisen, 'After the Great Asian Slump: Towards a Coherent Approach to Global Capital Flows' in OECD Development Centre, *Policy Brief* no. 16 (Paris, 1999), p. 7. See also Jagdish Bhagwati, 'The Capital Myth: The Difference between Trade in Widgets and Dollars' (1998) 77(3) *Foreign Affairs* 7–12.

[7] Eichengreen, Mussa et al., 'Capital Account Liberalization', above note 4; Institute for World Economics, *Wohlstandsmehrung durch Freiheit des internationalen Kapitalverkehrs. Gutachten erstellt für die Enquête-Kommission 'Globalisierung der Weltwirtschaft – Herausforderungen und Antworten'* (Kiel, 2000).

Rodrik[8] summarises an empirical study on the link between capital controls and economic growth in about a hundred countries: 'The data provide no evidence that countries without capital controls have grown faster.' Likewise, Grilli and Milesi-Ferretti[9] do not find a correlation between capital controls and growth, once other growth determinants (such as initial income and human capital endowment) are controlled for. Stiglitz concludes: 'The predictions of the advocates of capital market liberalization are clear, but unfortunately historical experience has not been supportive.'[10]

The empirical studies, on which Stiglitz relies, are flawed in several respects. Sample countries are typically grouped into two categories only (with and without capital controls), which ignores the fact that the coverage and strictness of capital controls varies considerably across countries. Quinn[11] addresses this measurement problem by constructing an index reflecting the degree of capital account liberalisation. In contrast to the aforementioned studies, this author finds a positive link between liberalisation and economic growth. The question of causality remains open, however, since Quinn takes no account of the possible endogeneity problem, i.e., capital account liberalisation being the consequence of rising per capita income.

A further critique relates to the missing differentiation between various types of capital inflows.[12] Most economists pin their hopes primarily on inflows of foreign direct investment.[13] Even critics of capital account liberalisation, including Stiglitz,[14] argue in favour of opening up towards direct investment and dismiss the option of complete isolation from international capital markets. In contrast to direct investment, short-term capital flows are regarded as particularly prone to crisis.

---

[8] Dani Rodrik, 'Who Needs Capital-Account Convertibility?' in Stanley Fischer et al., *Should the IMF Pursue Capital-Account Convertibility? Princeton University, Essays in International Finance* no. 207 (Princeton, 1998).

[9] Vittorio Grilli and Gian Maria Milesi-Ferretti, 'Economic Effects and Structural Determinants of Capital Controls' (1995) 42 *IMF Staff Papers* 517–51.

[10] Joseph E. Stiglitz, 'Capital Market Liberalization, Economic Growth, and Instability' (2000) 28(6) *World Development* 1075–86 at 1077.

[11] Dennis Quinn, 'The Correlates of Change in International Financial Regulation' (1997) 91(3) *American Political Science Review* 531–51.

[12] Helmut Reisen and Marcel Soto, 'The Need for Foreign Savings in Post-Crisis Asia', Asian Development Bank and OECD Development Centre, *Sixth International Forum on Asian Perspectives* (Paris, 2000).

[13] Reisen, 'After the Great Asian Slump', above note 6, at 7; Griffith-Jones, 'International Financial System', above note 5, at 111.

[14] Stiglitz, 'Capital Market Liberalization', above note 10, at 1076.

The empirical analysis of the growth effects of different types of capital inflows is still in its infancy. Soto[15] provides evidence supporting the proposition that emerging markets should open up towards equity capital inflows, and should discourage debt-related inflows when domestic financial systems are weak.[16] However, Soto's regression results and his policy conclusions with regard to financial opening are debatable.[17] Hausmann[18] forcefully rejects the idea that emerging markets should favour direct investment over other types of capital inflows. According to Hausmann, a higher stock of direct investment did not induce higher economic growth in the host country. Moreover, in sharp contrast to Soto,[19] he shows the growth effects of direct investment inflows to be weaker than the growth effects of long and short-term credits.[20]

There is further evidence against uniformly positive growth effects of foreign direct investment. According to Borensztein et al.,[21] growth effects are significant only if the recipient countries are relatively well endowed with human capital as a complementary factor of production. Nunnenkamp[22] concludes from correlation analyses: 'FDI must no longer be considered to be a homogenous phenomenon, in order to

---

[15] Marcelo Soto, 'Capital Flows and Growth in Developing Countries: Recent Empirical Evidence' in OECD Development Centre, *Technical Paper* no. 160 (Paris, 2000).

[16] Soto summarises his findings as follows: 'First, foreign direct investment and portfolio equity flows exhibit a robust positive correlation with growth. Second, portfolio bond flows are not significantly linked to economic growth. Finally, in economies with undercapitalised banking systems, bank-related inflows are negatively correlated with the growth rate. This result holds for both short- and long-term bank-related inflows.' (Soto, 'Capital Flows and Growth', above note 15, at 7).

[17] Nunnenkamp points to strange results for controlling variables used in Soto's regressions, Peter Nunnenkamp, 'Ausländische Direktinvestitionen und gesamtwirtschaftliches Wachstum in Entwicklungs- und Schwellenländern' (2000) 2 *Die Weltwirtschaft* 187–206.

[18] Ricardo Hausmann, 'Will the FDI Boom Bring More Growth?' Inter-American Development Bank and OECD Development Centre, *11th International Forum on Latin American Perspectives* (Paris, 2000).

[19] Soto, 'Capital Flows and Growth', above note 15.

[20] For a critical discussion of Hausmann's findings, see Peter Nunnenkamp, Comments on Ricardo Hausmann 'Will the FDI Boom Bring More Growth?' Inter-American Development Bank and OECD Development Centre, *11th International Forum on Latin American Perspectives* (Paris, 2000).

[21] Eduardo Borensztein, José De Gregorio and Jong-wha. Lee, 'How Does Foreign Direct Investment Affect Economic Growth?' (1998) 45 *Journal of International Economics* 115–35.

[22] Nunnenkamp, 'Ausländische Direktinvestitionen und gesamtwirtschaftliches Wachstum', above note 17, at 205.

improve our understanding of the growth impact of FDI . . . It depends on time-varying and location-specific factors whether FDI and growth are positively correlated altogether, and which of these variables leads or lags the other.'

In summary, the evidence on the growth effects of capital account liberalisation is ambiguous. Even the plausible recommendation that emerging markets should rely primarily on less volatile capital imports in the form of direct investment lacks solid empirical foundation.[23] Against this background, theoretical considerations according to which free international capital flows should have positive welfare effects fall short of establishing the case for rash and comprehensive capital account liberalisation. The risks of capital account liberalisation have to be clarified beforehand. Furthermore, the cost-benefit analysis of capital account liberalisation has to consider the effectiveness of national safeguards against risk and the incentive structure embedded in the international financial system.

III. Were crises caused by liberalisation?

As mentioned earlier, information asymmetries are particularly pro-nounced in international financial markets. This invites the question whether recent financial crises followed almost automatically from capital account liberalisation. At first glance, the economics profession seems to be widely apart once again:

Stiglitz[24] relates the increased frequency of crises to capital account liberalisation and claims: 'It is clear that not only there is no compelling empirical case *for* capital market liberalization, there is a compelling case *against* capital market liberalization.'

Dornbusch[25] argues in favour of unrestricted capital flows: 'The capital market offers an important supervisory function over the temp-tations of poor economic policy.'

---

[23] Corsepius et al. had already argued in the late 1980s: 'Neither form of capital inflow [direct investment or credits] can be judged unambiguously superior to the other, and thus recommended for all countries.' (Uwe Corsepius, Peter Nunnenkamp and Rainer Schweickert, 'Debt versus Equity Finance in Developing Countries. An Empirical Analysis of the Agent-Principal Model of International Capital Transfers', *Kiel Studies* no. 229 (Tübingen, 1989)).

[24] Stiglitz, 'Capital Market Liberalization', above note 10, at 1079.

[25] Ruediger Dornbusch, 'Capital Controls: An Idea Whose Time is Gone' (1998) (April) *World Economic Trends* (Trans-National Research Corporation), 23.

Fischer[26] considers it a 'cheering observation', that 'policy-makers in almost all developing countries have no intention of reversing the process of capital account opening ... despite their concerns over the recent crises'.

Analysing the run-up to financial crises systematically, Williamson and Mahar[27] show that financial liberalisation preceded most crises.[28] Furthermore, South Asia may have prevented contagion from the East Asian crisis by maintaining capital controls. However, serious financial crises also occurred in several countries that had not liberalised international capital flows.[29] Some crises in countries with an open capital account had nothing to do with financial openness.[30] Finally, the findings of Williamson and Mahar suggest that 'supervision is a crucial element in avoiding the progression from liberalisation to crisis'.[31]

Hence, liberalisation is not at odds with regulation. Actually, preventive regulatory measures are necessary to ensure the success of liberalisation.[32] Putting apologetics aside, the degree of consensus within the economics profession is more advanced indeed than the quotations at the beginning of this section suggest. Fischer[33] considers China and India to be well advised in pursuing a cautious and gradual approach to capital account liberalisation. Dornbusch,[34] though generally opposing gradual liberalisation, points to some prerequisites to successful liberalisation ('clean-up *followed* by opening'; emphasis added) and observes 'a shocking lack of appropriate supervision'. Stiglitz[35] comes fairly close to the qualifications made by proponents of capital account

---

[26] Stanley Fischer, *Globalization: Valid Concerns?* International Monetary Fund (Washington, DC, 2000), p. 5, available at http://www.imf.org/external/np/speeches/2000/082600.htm.

[27] Williamson and Mahar, 'A Survey of Financial Liberalization', above note 1.

[28] See also Graciela L. Kaminsky and Carmen M. Reinhart, 'The Twin Crises: The Causes of Banking and Balance-of-payments Problems' in Baidyanath N. Gosh (ed.), *Global Financial Crises and Reforms: Cases and Caveats* (London, 2001), pp. 9–47.

[29] Examples are: Argentina (1989), Venezuela (1994) and the Philippines (1981); for details, see Williamson and Mahar, 'A Survey of Financial Liberalization', above note 1, table 8.

[30] For instance, this applies to the Savings and Loan crisis in the United States.

[31] Williamson and Mahar, 'A Survey of Financial Liberalization', above note 1, at 62.

[32] Put differently, the core problem frequently has been the 'inadequacy of prudential supervision and regulation, whose consequences are simply magnified by liberalization' (Eichengreen, Mussa et al., 'Capital Account Liberalization', above note 4, at 21).

[33] Fischer, *Globalization*, above note 26.

[34] Dornbusch, 'Capital Controls', above note 25, at 20 and 23.

[35] Stiglitz, 'Capital Market Liberalization', above note 10, at 1075.

liberalisation when he criticises a rash liberalisation without setting up an effective regulatory framework.[36]

IV. What national policymakers can do

Despite recent crises, hardly any country has abandoned or reversed the process of capital account liberalisation.[37] This surprising observation may be partly because the effectiveness of capital controls has been undermined in a world of highly sophisticated financial markets.[38] Market participants may circumvent controls by referring to innovative financial derivatives. It is therefore arguable whether discretionary controls are instrumental in containing financial volatility and alleviating economic adjustment processes.[39]

Yet emerging markets can protect themselves against the vagaries of international financial markets. National policy options are not restricted to imposing discretionary capital controls, but include shaping the regulatory system and the macroeconomic framework. This section addresses these three issues in reverse order.

1. Macroeconomic policy

When financial globalisation is blamed for having caused recent financial crises, it is frequently ignored that some crises had a fairly conventional character. For instance, Brazil's crisis of 1999 can be attributed to fundamental macroeconomic inconsistencies.[40] It is of course true that the economic costs resulting from inconsistent macro policies can

---

[36] It is interesting to note that Stiglitz considered financial regulation to be fairly advanced in East Asian countries in 1996, i.e., shortly before the financial crisis erupted in these countries: 'What is remarkable is that East Asian governments undertook actions (such as prudential regulation) similar to those taken by more industrial countries, and that they did so at an earlier stage of development. Moreover, these regulatory initiatives succeeded without the abuses that often accompany them elsewhere', Joseph E. Stiglitz and Marilou Uy, Financial Markets, Public Policy, and the East Asian Miracle (1996) 11(2) The World Bank Observer 249–76 at 272.

[37] Fischer, Globalization, above note 26.

[38] Richard N. Cooper, 'Should Capital-Account Convertibility Be a World Objective?' in Stanley Fischer et al., Should the IMF Pursue Capital-Account Convertibility? Princeton University, Essays in International Finance no. 207 (Princeton, 1998).

[39] Institute for World Economics, Wohlstandsmehrung durch Freiheit des internationalen Kapitalverkehrs, above note 7.

[40] Ruediger Dornbusch, Brazil Beyond Tropical Illusions, Massachusetts Institute of Technology (Cambridge, Mass., 1999); Peter Nunnenkamp, Latin America after the

mount tremendously because of the herding behaviour of foreign investors. However, the causes of crises must not be confused with their
effects: under conditions of financial globalisation, macroeconomic
policy has a more important role to play.

The macroeconomic challenge is marked by the impossible trinity of
exchange rate stability, monetary autonomy and free capital flows.[41]
Governments refraining from capital account restrictions have to toler-
ate exchange rate fluctuations or to give up monetary autonomy. The
combination of free capital flows and exchange rate stability requires
the subordination of monetary policy to the exchange rate target. The
combination of free capital flows and monetary autonomy requires
flexible exchange rates, as an exchange rate peg lacking credibility may
be easily attacked by speculators.

Hence, the economic policy implications of rising international capital
mobility reach far beyond specific financial regulations. It is the consistency of macroeconomic policies which matters in the first place if emerging markets want to attract capital inflows on a sustainable basis.[42]

2. Regulatory framework

It is no longer disputed that the efficiency and stability of financial
systems depend on appropriate institutions entrusted with regulation
and supervision. Domestic financial markets have to be sufficiently
developed and strictly supervised before international capital flows
may be liberalised completely.[43] This is not a lesson to be derived only
after the Asian crisis, but rather a forgotten insight of the debate on the
timing and sequencing of liberalisation in the 1980s.[44]

Currency Crash in Brazil: why the Optimists May Be Wrong, Institute for World
Economics, *Kiel Discussion Papers* no. 337 (Kiel, 1999).

[41] Paul Krugman, *The Eternal Triangle: Explaining International Financial Perplexity*,
Massachusetts Institute of Technology (Cambridge, Mass., 1998), available at http://
web.mit.edu/ krugman/www/triangle.html.

[42] For the choice of an appropriate exchange rate regime and recent developments in
exchange rate policy, see IMF, *Exchange Rate Regimes in an Increasingly Integrated
World Economy*, International Monetary Fund, Issues Brief 00/06 (Washington, DC,
2000).

[43] Meanwhile even the IMF concedes: 'Countries need to prepare well for capital-account
liberalization', Stanley Fischer, 'Capital-Account Liberalization and the Role of the IMF'
in Stanley Fischer et al., *Should the IMF Pursue Capital-Account Convertibility? Princeton
University, Essays in International Finance* no. 207 (Princeton, 1998), 2.

[44] For an overview, see Norbert Funke, 'Timing and Sequencing of Reforms: competing
Views and the Role of Credibility' (1993) 46(3) *Kyklos* 337–62.

The Asian crisis confirms that financial intermediaries must bear the risk of financial transactions, in order to ensure an efficient intermediation and reduce the susceptibility to crisis. State interference in lending decisions of banks and the socialisation of financial risk through (explicit or implicit) government guarantees should therefore be avoided. Moreover, Demirgüç-Kunt and Detragiache[45] show that the likelihood of financial crises diminishes if state authorities fight corruption and enforce the rule of law.

In supervising financial intermediaries, national institutions can make use of international best practice with regard to financial safety standards. The enforcement of minimum capital adequacy ratios appears to be particularly important. The Basle Accord of 1988 mandated a capital–asset ratio of 8%. It can be argued that a higher ratio would be appropriate in emerging markets characterised by a riskier environment.[46]

It is more difficult to decide on when to subject local financial intermediaries to competition by foreign banks.[47] On the one hand, free entry of foreign banks to domestic financial markets promises efficiency gains and transfers of management know-how. On the other hand, market opening may trigger a wave of bankruptcies as long as local banks cannot cope with foreign competition.[48]

This dilemma is particularly serious if local banks have accumulated a substantial stock of non-performing loans due to distorted incentives in the past. Frequently, the bad debt problem can only be overcome by creating an independent agency for winding up non-performing loans and by recapitalising the banks. The clean-up of balance sheets, combined with replacing the management of banks, would counteract the temptation of fragile banks to engage in a gamble for resurrection, by pursuing excessively risky financial transactions. However, institutional reforms must ensure that future lending decisions of banks are no longer distorted by bail-out expectations. In other words, the government must credibly present the clean-up of balance sheets as an once-and-for-all operation and bank managers must face effective sanctions in the case of misconduct.

---

[45] Demirgüç-Kunt and Detragiache, 'Financial Liberalization and Financial Fragility', above note 3.

[46] Williamson and Mahar, 'A Survey of Financial Liberalization', above note 1, at 64.

[47] Institute for World Economics, *Wohlstandsmehrung durch Freiheit des internationalen Kapitalverkehrs*, above note 7, at 20 et seq.

[48] Eichengreen, Mussa et al., 'Capital Account Liberalization', above note 4, at 27.

3. Capital controls

Since the Asian crisis, many economists share the view that specific restrictions on capital flows are needed in addition to an appropriate regulatory framework.[49] This applies to controls on capital *inflows* at least. The Asian crisis has led even the IMF to conclude: 'A case can be made that countries with weak financial systems should restrict short-term inflows.'[50] Chile is often presented as a showcase in this context. Capital inflows in the form of loans and portfolio investment were subject to a non-remunerated reserve requirement in Chile in 1991–8. This means that Chilean authorities relied on price-related measures, rather than imposing quantitative inflow restrictions. The aim was to discourage speculative inflows by applying a uniform reserve quota and a uniform deposit period to all maturities. This approach had the effect that the (implicit) tax was higher for short-term capital inflows.

In sharp contrast to Chile, Korea started capital account liberalisation at the short end, and maintained significant restrictions on direct investment inflows until 1998.[51] As a result, the structure of foreign debt was more prone to crisis in Korea than in Chile; short-term obligations accounted for 68% of Korea's foreign debt in 1997, whereas this share was 43% in Chile.

A broad consensus exists that the sequencing of capital account liberalisation in Korea was highly problematic. It is more disputed whether Chile can serve as a model. Dornbusch[52] acknowledges the effectiveness of controls in Chile, but questions whether 'countries with poor governance can effectively manage the situation in the way honest Chile has'. The effectiveness of capital inflow controls is debatable for several reasons.[53] It generally appears that the effectiveness is eroded over time, as market participants increasingly succeed in

---

[49] *The Economist* 12 September 1998, p. 86 argues: 'Indeed the distinction between capital controls and sensible bank regulation can become blurred.'

[50] Fischer, 'Capital-Account Liberalization', above note 43, at 5.

[51] Williamson and Mahar, 'A Survey of Financial Liberalization', above note 1, table 5; Eichengreen, Mussa et al., 'Capital Account Liberalization', above note 4, at 52 et seq.

[52] Dornbusch, 'Capital Controls', above note 25, at 22 et seq.

[53] For a detailed assessment, see Institute for World Economics, *Wohlstandsmehrung durch Freiheit des internationalen Kapitalverkehrs*, above note 7; Eichengreen, Mussa et al., 'Capital Account Liberalization', above note 4, Appendix IV; Claudia M. Buch, Ralph P. Heinrich and Christian Pierdzioch, 'Taxing Short-term Capital Flows – An Option for Transition Economies?' Institute for World Economics, Kiel, *Discussion Papers* no. 321 (Kiel, 1998), and the literature given there.

circumventing controls. The maturity profile of Chile's foreign debt improved only when stricter controls were imposed in the second half of the 1990s. Furthermore, Chile's approach seems to have had limited effects on the volume and volatility of net capital flows, on interest-rate spreads and on the real exchange rate.

Despite these qualifications, precautionary restrictions on short-term capital inflows are widely considered reasonable. By contrast, discretionary controls on capital *outflows*, implemented in Malaysia in September 1998, have gained little support, even though Krugman[54] argued that outflow controls are a better choice for a country whose currency is attacked than steep rises in interest rates or a sharp depreciation of the exchange rate. The government of Malaysia claims to have validated Krugman's view, by pointing to the country's rapid economic recovery from crisis.[55]

It is fair to say that the concern of many economists turned out to be exaggerated, according to which outflow controls would have tremendous costs and would impair Malaysia's access to international capital markets for long. Yet even Krugman[56] concedes that Malaysia's economic recovery 'has not exactly proved the proponents right. For there is a recovery in progress throughout Asia'. Moreover, the controls came into force only when financial panic was subsiding and the ringgit had already fallen by some 40%. Hence, the verdict is still out as concerns the effectiveness and costs of capital outflow controls imposed to fight a speculative attack.

4. Summary

The effectiveness of specific capital controls cannot be taken for granted. Nevertheless, the above discussion contradicts the view that financial globalisation has rendered national economic policy obsolete. It largely depends on the macroeconomic, regulatory and institutional framework in particular countries whether capital imports are used productively and whether financial risks are contained. Capital account liberalisation amounts to 'putting a race car engine into an old car'[57] only if national

---

[54] Paul Krugman, 'Saving Asia: It's Time to Get Radical', *Fortune* (7 September 1998), pp. 74–80.

[55] *The Economist*, 1 May 1999, p. 75.

[56] Paul Krugman, *How Malaysia Got Away with Economic Heresy* (1999), available at http://slate.msn.com/?id=35534.

[57] Stiglitz, 'Capital Market Liberalization', above note 10, at 1075.

policymakers fail to create the preconditions for a successful liberalisation (Stiglitz: 'checking the tires and training the driver').

V. What regional co-operation can achieve

It may be too heroic an assumption that financial crises would be a matter of the past once national policymakers pursue consistent macro policies and tackle regulatory deficits before liberalisation. Still, the failures of global financial markets have to be addressed (see also section VI). The conventional international crisis management has been harshly criticised since the Asian crisis. Especially the critique levelled at the IMF has led Asian governments to consider regional means of crisis prevention and resolution.[58]

First moves towards 'monetary regionalism in East Asia'[59] suggested that East Asia would turn away from the IMF. In the autumn of 1997, Japan proposed setting up an Asian Monetary Fund (AMF), in order for the region to have a larger say in how to prevent and resolve future crises. The idea to design a regional alternative to IMF policy met with stiff opposition, and was soon given up at the request of the United States. Yet Bergsten expects: 'In the medium term, at least, the most important changes to the world's financial architecture are likely to come from the new regional arrangements being fashioned in East Asia by Japan, China, South Korea and the ten members of the Association of South-East Asian Nations (ASEAN).'[60]

Plans of the so-called ASEAN +3 group for mutual financial assistance have taken more definite shape since 2000. A regional system of currency swaps shall enable participating central banks to draw on part of the partners' currency reserves when crisis is looming. In addition to a regional liquidity fund, ASEAN has created a surveillance mechanism, based on early-warning indicators, which shall reveal critical developments and allow for timely policy adjustments. Peer pressure shall help correct economic policy failures in participating countries. Dieter[61]

---

[58] For a more detailed presentation, see Institute for World Economics, *Regulative Folgen der Asienkrise. Gutachten erstellt für die Enquête-Kommission 'Globalisierung der Weltwirtschaft – Herausforderungen und Antworten'* (Kiel, 2001).

[59] Heribert Dieter, 'Ostasien nach der Krise: Interne Reformen, neue Finanzarchitektur und monetärer Regionalismus' (2000) 37/38 *Aus Politik und Zeitgeschichte* 21–8 at 27.

[60] C. Fred Bergsten, 'East Asian Regionalism: towards a Tripartite World', *The Economist*, 15 July 2000, pp. 19–21 at 19.

[61] Dieter, above note 59.

anticipates further steps towards an Asian regionalism on financial issues, for example, by establishing regional institutions in the area of bank regulation.

The IMF has raised no principal objections if IMF activities are complemented, rather than replaced by regional arrangements.[62] A swap mechanism along the lines of the ASEAN +3 model may indeed prove insufficient to fight financial crises. Participating countries may be hit by a *common* shock, which is fairly likely within one particular region. Moreover, it remains to be seen whether economic policy failures are easier to correct through peer pressure of neighbouring countries than through IMF surveillance and conditionality. Scepticism seems justified, especially with regard to Asia where this idea was born:[63] 'How that will work is a mystery: forthright mutual criticism is hardly one of the region's strongpoints'.[64]

VI. How to reform the international financial architecture

The idea of an AMF has won appeal not least because little progress has been achieved in reforming the international financial architecture.[65] The global architecture needs to be overhauled, as recent financial crises have revealed not only policy failure on the national level, but also institutional deficits on the international level.[66] Reform topics cover a broad spectrum:[67]

- Greater transparency and improved data availability shall provide market participants with better information.

---

[62] See Horst Köhler's remarks made at the press conference of the IMF and World Bank meeting in Prague on 9 September 2000, available at http://www.imf.org/external/np/tr/2000/tr000920.htm.

[63] The disenchanting experience of ASEAN and APEC in liberalising current account transactions on a regional level adds to scepticism.

[64] *The Economist*, 13 May 2000, p. 83. Even though Bird and Rajan support the idea of an AMF, these authors, too, question that Asian governments are more inclined to follow policy advice coming from a regional institution than adhering to the IMF's advice, Graham Bird and Raghuram Rajan, 'Is There a Case for an Asian Monetary Fund?' (2000) 45 *World Economics* 135–43.

[65] Bird and Rajan, 'Asian Monetary Fund', above note 64, at 138.

[66] Peter Nunnenkamp, 'Internationales Finanzsystem und die Herausforderung der Liberalisierung der Kapitalmärkte', Konrad-Adenauer-Stiftung, (2000) 16(10) *Auslandsinformationen* 4–22; Institute for World Economics, *Regulative Folgen der Asienkrise*, above note 58.

[67] Various reports on the state of affairs in reforming the international financial architecture are to be found on the IMF's homepage (http://www.ifm.org).

- Financial standards shall take effect on a worldwide scale. Standards laid down in the Basle Accord of 1988 are revised, in order to overcome regulatory distortions revealed by the Asian crisis.[68] It is under discussion to fill regulatory gaps, notably with regard to highly leveraged institutions, in order to stabilise the global financial system.
- The role of the IMF shall be defined more clearly. Both, IMF lending and IMF conditionality are on the agenda in order to help prevent future crises and resolve unavoidable crises more effectively.[69]
- The private sector (i.e., commercial banks and portfolio investors) shall take part in international crisis management. Private sector involvement aims at a fair burden sharing at times of crisis, and may help prevent the deepening of crises caused by co-ordination failure.

The IMF and finance ministers of G7 claim to have made substantial progress in reforming the financial architecture.[70] However, this is true for only some reform issues, including transparency and accountability. Critical issues such as the future role of the IMF remain unresolved, and others such as an obligatory private sector involvement met with the resistance of banks and various governments.[71] Several years after the outbreak of the Asian crisis, it is therefore highly debatable whether the international crisis management is better prepared to deal with financial crises.

Two major challenges remain: the provision of emergency finance to avoid illiquidity in hard currency, and a reasonable burden sharing between debtors and creditors in the case of insolvency. The dilemma is to react quickly and forcefully when crisis is looming, without fuelling moral hazard of debtors, private creditors and governments.

---

[68] Reisen, 'After the Great Asian Slump', above note 6, at 25. The built-in bias in favour of short-term lending is particularly noteworthy in this context.

[69] John Williamson, 'The Role of the IMF: A Guide to the Reports' Institute for International Economics, *International Economics Policy Brief 00–5* (Washington, DC, 2000).

[70] Bundesministerium der Finanzen, *Stärkung der internationalen Finanzarchitektur, Bericht der G7-Finanzminister an die Staats- und Regierungschefs* (Fukuoka, 2000) mimeo. 'Taking stock today I think we can state that the international financial system is more stable thanks to lessons learned and various measures to increase transparency' (Horst Köhler, *The IMF in a Changing World*, IMF, Washington, DC, 2000, 4, available at http://www.imf.org/external/np/speeches/2000/080700.htm).

[71] Peter Nunnenkamp, 'Towards a New International Financial Order: Why Reform Progress Is So Slow' (2000) 35(1) *Intereconomics* 23–30.

Some reform proposals ignore the trade-off between fighting crises effectively and limiting moral hazard, and should therefore be rejected. The demand for putting an end to IMF lending[72] is a case in point. Eradicating IMF-induced moral hazard in this way would come at the cost of more serious contagion in the absence of a financial safety net. The existence of moral hazard under conditions of insufficient information does not establish the case against emergency lending. Rather, safety nets must be designed in a way that moral hazard is contained.

New multilateral institutions could be created in analogy to existing national institutions. National models are underlying proposals to set up an international lender of last resort, an international bankruptcy court and an international financial supervisory agency. However, such an approach may not only involve tremendous administrative costs, but is also likely to be resisted by governments unwilling to see national sovereignty compromised. Furthermore, proposals to create multilateral institutions in analogy to national arrangements tend to ignore that moral hazard is more difficult to contain when various sovereigns are involved.

The intended effects on the functioning of international financial markets may well be achieved without setting up new multilateral institutions.[73] Instead of creating an international lender of last resort, it would be sufficient to extend the toolbox of the IMF in order to stabilise the global financial system when market panic threatens to result in a credit crunch.[74] The combination of a sufficiently funded crisis facility,[75] possible IMF lending into arrears and an obligatory private sector involvement in crisis management could prevent illiquidity and expedite rescheduling. At the same time, moral hazard would be limited if the terms of emergency financing were conditioned on mutually agreed pre-qualification criteria.

---

[72] Deepak Lal, 'Zeit zum Abschied für den Währungsfond', *Frankfurter Allgemeine Zeitung*, 1 October 1998, p. 19.

[73] For an overview on reform measures in the subsequent areas, see IMF, *Report of the Managing Director to the International Monetary and Financial Committee on Progress in Strengthening the Architecture of the International Financial System and Reform of the IMF* (Washington, DC, 2000), available at http://www.imf.org/external/np/omd/2000/02/report.htm.

[74] Fischer has presented a proposal, according to which the IMF would come close to an international lender of last resort, Stanley Fischer, 'On the Need for an International Lender of Last Resort' (1999) 13(4) *Journal of Economic Perspectives* 85–104.

[75] Williamson, 'The Role of the IMF', above note 69, at 16.

Likewise, the aims of an international bankruptcy court could be achieved by more modest means, on which a consensus may be easier to reach. Provisions in international bond and debt contracts, for example, rules on collective representation, sharing clauses and roll-over options, may help overcome co-ordination failure.[76] Such provisions would be conducive to temporary standstills of private investors and creditors; the provisions counteract the incentive of individual market participants to collect their claims at the first sign of trouble, which may transform liquidity problems of debtors into insolvency. Proper application and enforcement of innovative contract provisions could be supervised by a committee of creditors and debtors along the lines of the London Club.

Finally, the development of guidelines for national financial standards provides an alternative to setting up an international agency which would have to supervise all financial institutions operating internationally. Existing multilateral organisations (e.g. BIS, Financial Stability Forum) are working on guidelines, in order to improve transparency and accountability.[77] However, emerging markets should be sufficiently represented in decision processes.[78] Moreover, emerging markets are in need of technical assistance for implementing mutually agreed guidelines.

By defining guidelines multilaterally, institutional competition between national systems of financial regulation would not be eliminated. The non-binding character of guidelines, in combination with the aforementioned provisions in debt and bond contracts, would strengthen the incentive of international investors to carefully assess both, the solvency of a particular debtor and the effectiveness of financial regulation in the country in question.

VII. Summary

There is no panacea in dealing with international capital flows. Yet one can draw some conclusions related to liberalisation and regulation. The relevant question is *how*, rather than *whether* to open the capital account. Even critics eloquently opposing wide-ranging capital account

---

[76] Barry Eichengreen, *Toward a New International Financial Architecture: A Practical Post-Asia Approach*, Insitute for International Economics (Washington, DC, 1999), p. 65 et seq.

[77] It should be noted that Article IV consultations of the IMF include financial supervision in member countries.

[78] Griffith-Jones, 'International Financial System', above note 5.

liberalisation are not arguing in favour of banning all sorts of capital inflows. Hence, it does not make sense to contrast liberalisation and regulation of capital flows as irreconcilable antagonisms. To the contrary, capital account liberalisation requires institutional and regulatory safeguards in order to limit financial risk. It is here where the opposites meet.

The optimal timing of capital account liberalisation may vary from country to country. Emerging markets with weak national financial systems, in particular, are well advised to proceed cautiously with capital account liberalisation. Regulation and supervision are not only required with regard to cross-border capital flows, but also in domestic financial markets.

Financial globalisation has not deprived national policymakers of any means to protect their economies from crisis. Apart from specific financial regulations and institutional safeguards, success or failure of capital account liberalisation depends on the macroeconomic framework. Policy consistency with regard to monetary, fiscal and exchange rate policies is crucially important to fend off speculative capital inflows and a subsequent bust.

The timing and sequencing debate offers some lessons which seem to have escaped the attention of policymakers in some emerging markets. The Korean case, in particular, confirms earlier insights that a country becomes prone to crisis if capital account liberalisation starts at the short end, while long-term capital inflows (notably direct investment) remain restricted. It appears to be reasonable for countries with weak financial systems to limit short-term capital inflows, even though the effectiveness of specific capital controls cannot be taken for granted.

In addition to preventive measures taken on the national level, institutional deficits of the international financial architecture have to be overcome in order to reduce the risk of further crises. Progress in reforming the international financial architecture is still limited. Asian attempts at crisis prevention and resolution by means of regional cooperation in terms of surveillance and emergency financing may complement the international crisis management, but are no substitute for reforms on the global level.

The global challenge is to prevent liquidity crises and to ensure a fair burden sharing in the case of insolvency without aggravating moral hazard of the parties involved. A combination of measures seems to be suited best to escape from this dilemma. The package should include: a sufficiently funded crisis facility, pre-qualification mechanisms for defining conditions of access to financial support, and a closer involvement of private creditors in crisis resolution.

13

Do we need a new international financial architecture?
Many questions and some preliminary policy advice

STEFAN VOIGT

I. Introduction

Ever since the Asian crisis, the issue of a 'new international financial architecture' has been high on the agenda of representatives of international organisations, the global financial community, and academic circles. In the immediate aftermath of the crisis, a consensus that 'something needs to be done' seemed to have emerged. But reaching consensus on a theoretical level on what exactly should be done has almost been as hard to achieve as implementing any reforms, as the postponed implementation of the Basle Accord shows.

No matter what specific economic theory one wants to draw upon, three elements are systematically needed in order to derive feasible or implementable policy advice. The first is a justificatory or legitimating exercise and is thus a normative endeavour. If an international regulation of international financial markets is pleaded for, there must be some procedure justifying not only regulation as such but also regulation on a specific level, here the international one. The second necessary element is positive: we need to have at our disposal knowledge concerning the alternative consequences that a variety of potentially possible rules would cause. Without solid positive knowledge, no serious policy advice is possible. The third element derives policy advice on the basis of this positive knowledge. If it is to be implemented, one needs to take the preferences as well as the restrictions of the relevant actors into account: policy advice which ignores them might become relevant in the long run, but will almost certainly be neglected in the short run.

In the next section, we propose to draw on two economic approaches to formulate some questions that need to be answered in order to say something on the issue concerning the international regulation of financial markets. These approaches are the theory of economic order as mainly developed by Hayek and the new institutional economics. We will assume throughout that all actors, politicians included, are trying to maximise their individual utility. They will thus not be assumed to be interested in benevolently maximising some social welfare function. This constitutes a major departure from traditional welfare economics. In section III of this paper, we will turn from asking questions to presenting some hypotheses. Section IV concludes.

II. Asking questions based on different economic approaches

1. The Hayekian theory of economic order

In the aftermath of the Asian crisis, there was much talk about the necessity of an international financial architecture. Architects – and the engineers co-operating with them – are specialists in creating structures in which all the elements of the structures have a specific function and in which all the elements need to be in a particular position in order to fulfil that function. Over the history of mankind, there has certainly been more than one attempt to structure human societies according to such a notion: consider human beings the elements of such a structure and let them fulfil specific functions according to some master plan. Most of these attempts have, of course, failed miserably: socialism is only the most prominent example.

Hayek[1] is concerned with the order of society. Order is present if a group of actors lives in:

> 'a state of affairs in which a multiplicity of elements of various kinds are so related to each other that we may learn from our acquaintance with some spatial or temporal part of the whole to form correct expectations concerning the rest, or at least expectations which have a good chance of proving correct.'

Hayek[2] distinguishes between two kinds of order: one – which he calls organisation – comes close to the architecture model of society just sketched: there is a specific place for all the participants, a specific function that every participant is to fulfil. The second kind of order is called 'spontaneous order'. In it, the elements are free to use their individual knowledge to pursue their own ends. Now, this might first sound as if only anarchy could result but surely not order. Hayek argues,

[1] Friedrich A. Hayek, *Law, Legislation and Liberty, vol. 1: Rules and Order* (Chicago, 1973), p. 36.
[2] Friedrich A. Hayek, 'Kinds of Order in Society' (1964) 3(2) *New Individualist Review* 3–12.

however, that adequate rules can constrain the participants in such a way that they bring about order in an unplanned, unintended, i.e. spontaneous way. As examples for organisations, he names armies, firms, and government. Examples for spontaneous orders are language, morality, money, and legislation.

In order to be able to evaluate better the crucial difference between the two kinds of orders, let us compare them according to a number of criteria. Spontaneous orders grow unintendedly whereas organisations are purposefully constructed. In spontaneous orders, the participants themselves decide about their concrete positions within the order whereas they are put at a specific place according to some hierarchical imperative in organisations. A spontaneous order can have a multitude of purposes, at the extreme as many as participating elements. Organisations, on the other hand, have one overarching purpose that is determined by the hierarchical top. Interaction between participating elements is co-ordinated by general rules of conduct in spontaneous orders, whereas it is determined by organisation rules in organisations. The last two criteria are of particular significance for our topic: the capacity to incorporate new knowledge and to adjust smoothly to it is quite high in spontaneous orders, since all participants are free to act according to the individually available knowledge. This ensures that such knowledge enters into the order and secures its smooth adjustment to it. In organisations, only knowledge at the disposal of the top hier-archical layer enters into this kind of order. Hayek has shown very early that attempts to implement socialism would not only fail due to incentive problems but also due to information problems. But the huge advantage of spontaneous orders over organisations in terms of knowledge processing capacity comes at a price: modifying the general rules of conduct, one can only influence the general traits of spontaneous orders but not every specific detail. In organisations, on the other hand, the top of the hierarchy can, at least conceptually, determine every specific detail.

Hayek emphasises that many spontaneous orders are indeed enabled by an organisation: the market, as a spontaneous order, depends on the state, an organisation, because the state's monopoly to coerce partici-pants of the spontaneous order market is needed in order to make them behave according to the rules. He also emphasises, however, that there can be spontaneous orders that, in order to be upheld, do not need to be based on an organisation. When discussing the possibilities to increase the quality of the spontaneous international financial order, this should be kept in mind: we cannot simply assume that some international organisation is needed to uphold or improve the international financial order. Instead, this would have to be explicitly proven.

Our capacity to plan and to create welfare-enhancing organisations is severely restricted. Hayek terms the negligence of this fact 'rationalistic constructivism' or 'constructivistic rationalism'. Intentions purposefully to create an international financial *architecture* might therefore be seriously ill-conceived. I therefore prefer to talk about an international financial *order*. Drawing on the two kinds of order just presented, discussions about a modified international financial order should therefore focus on the possibility of establishing the preconditions for a spontaneous international financial order. Such a formulation presupposes that there is no order right now, which is obviously false. We should therefore formulate differently and ask whether there are any possibilities of improving the quality of the international financial order that already exists by modifying the underlying rules of the game.

Before dealing with that issue in a little more detail, we need to make one last preliminary step, namely to clarify the function of (spontaneous) orders: they serve to make expectations of all the individual participants more secure or reliable, i.e. they decrease the uncertainty about what any other participant can or will do in the next instance. Uncertainty reduction can have important economic implications: less uncertainty is generally connected with a longer time horizon. That means that the willingness to make long-term investments will increase as a consequence of reduced uncertainty. It also means that the willingness to enter into a division of labour will increase which will also have welfare-increasing effects. To put it briefly: we expect uncertainty reduction to lead to increased income and wealth.

We are now ready to formulate some questions that would have to be answered were one interested in a reform of the international financial order from a Hayekian point of view. It was said that the general traits of a spontaneous order are determined by the valid rules of conduct. By modifying the rules of conduct, one can therefore change the general traits of the spontaneous order. The first question would thus be:

> Q1. What should the rules look like that are to induce an international financial order?

This is a vast question and the truth of the matter is that we do not know the answer at present. We do, however, have some hints of how to deal rationally with our ignorance. The first deals with the characteristics that rules should have in general, i.e. not only with regard to an international financial order, to make a welfare-enhancing spontaneous order possible. The second deals with a possible procedure to reduce our ignorance. We will deal with both hints in turn.

When developing his concept of two kinds of order, Hayek drew heavily on Kant. Spontaneous orders will only function if the rules that are at their base are what Hayek calls – drawing on Kant – *universalisable*. Simply put, this means that they should (i) be general, i.e. applicable not only to one or a few specific instances but to an unforeseeable multitude of cases; they should furthermore (ii) be abstract, i.e. they should not tell the participants of the order what to do in a specific situation but should be restrained to prohibiting certain modes of behaviour. This ensures that innovation remains possible because actions that those formulating the rules might never have thought of remain legal unless they are explicitly prohibited by a rule. Lastly, rules should (iii) be certain, i.e. formulated in such a way that any interested participant can ascertain with a sufficient degree of certainty whether some possible action falls within the realm of legal action or whether he should expect to be sanctioned subsequent to some such action. It appears safe to argue that the rules at the base of the international financial order should be universalisable and should thus have the three traits just sketched.

The second hint deals with how we can procedurally best cope with our ignorance or uncertainty concerning the 'best' rules with regard to international financial order. If one wants to learn fast, a good way is often to try out a variety of solutions simultaneously. This is thus an argument against an early, possibly even global, harmonisation of rules. If we are uncertain concerning the effects of rules, it makes little sense to harmonise them because that could lead to worse outcomes yet.[3] The idea of abstaining from an *ex ante* harmonisation of rules has been discussed by economists under the heading of 'systems competition', 'competition of institutions' and the like over the last couple of years. This notion directly leads us to our next question:

Q2. In order to generate sought after knowledge, the competition of systems possibly needs to be based on some rule

[3] Non-economists might wonder whether the knowledge we have concerning the functioning of international financial markets is not too much belittled here. Just keep in mind that one of the most dramatic failures in international capital markets was caused by Long Term Capital Management, the company founded and run by a number of noble laureates who are supposed to be some of the best brains around.

framework within which it can take place; what should
this framework look like?

Adherents of the notion of institutional competition should be able to
answer this question in order to make a convincing case out of their
notion. There have been some attempts,[4] but these proposals have often
remained on a very abstract level from which policy advice for the
competition of rules concerned with the regulation of financial markets
are difficult to derive. It can, however, be conjectured that such a
framework would have states as its addressees, and not private citizens.
Within this framework, it would be states that are to regulate interac-
tions undertaken by private parties.

Another question can be based on the observation that over the last
couple of decades, the growth in border crossing trade has almost always
been higher than the growth of the gross world product. This means that
the international trade order has proved to be rather stable. A question
almost suggesting itself thus is:

Q3. What can we learn from the international trade order for
the order of the international financial markets?

Both orders have obvious similarities, the most important of which is
that they are based on border-crossing activities. Given that some of the
preconditions for stable order are analogous, one could learn from the
international trade order given that one can agree on the causes that
brought about the relative stability of the international trade order. It is
impossible to inquire systematically into the causes of the relative
stability of the international trade order here and we just assume that
two major reasons can be named: (i) The establishment of a forum
which allowed the states to communicate on a regular basis. Turning
the GATT into the WTO has improved the capacity of this organisation
to stabilise the international trade order due to the reform of the dispute
mechanism. The establishment of a second pillar next to GATT, namely
the GATS is obviously relevant for the international financial order,
since it deals with border-crossing financial services. (ii) A second
reason for the relative stability of the international trade order has

---

[4] For example,. Wolfgang Kerber, 'Zum Problem einer Wettbewerbsordnung für den
Systemwettbewerb' (1998) 17 *Jahrbuch für Neue Politische Ökonomie* 199–230.

come into the focus of economists over the last years: the new international *lex mercatoria*.[5]

From a theoretical point of view, the order established and maintained by the WTO is a precarious one: the WTO is a forum of conceptually equal contracting parties, it does not establish anything like an international or supranational sovereign which had the capacity to formally sanction its members. Ever since Hobbes, we are used to predicting anarchy and misery in the absence of a sovereign. That the WTO – and its predecessor – have been able to prevent anarchy in the international trade order from materialising, can supposedly teach us something with regard to the international financial order.

Whereas the WTO seeks to restrain government action, the international *lex mercatoria* is a system of rules and conflict solution mechanisms used by the participants in international trade, i.e. primarily private parties.[6] The observation that this is possible in international trade matters leads directly to the next question, namely:

Q4a. What is the potential of privately generated and administered (self-) regulation in international finance?

Q4b. Is there a need to induce such (self-) regulation through (consorted) state action?

Assuming utility-maximising actors, we can expect that the relevant players in the international financial markets bring self-regulation spontaneously about if they can expect to be better off by such action. This statement needs to be qualified in so far as it only holds if we add 'under the relevant restrictions'. If governments are able to change the relevant restrictions accordingly, it might be possible to induce the players in the

---

[5] Bruce Benson, 'The Spontaneous Evolution of Commercial Law' (1988) 55 *Southern Economic Journal* 644–61.

[6] There are estimates that between 80 and 95% of all private contracts that involve actors from more than one jurisdiction contain provisions not to take the case to a state court but to take it to private courts in case of a dispute. The courts that are to settle the disputes are usually not standing courts but its members are selected on an ad hoc basis with the consent of the parties involved. The parties usually accept the dicta of the courts and act accordingly because a refusal to do so would undermine their reputation as business people and would make it difficult for them to find business partners in the future. The whole system thus heavily relies on reputation mechanisms. There are numerous reasons for private parties to resort to this kind of dispute settlement: decisions are less bureaucratic, are usually taken faster, the conflicting parties can often maintain a business relationship albeit the conflict etc. (Stefan Voigt, *Die Welthandelsordnung zwischen Konflikt und Stabilität* (Freiburg, 1992), pp. 175–84 contains a review of private arbitration as used in international business).

international financial markets to generate a lot more self-regulation than can be observed at present.

Maybe an example taken from the national realm can make the implicit hypothesis clearer: in Germany, there is a trend in environmental policy not to rely exclusively on state orders/state regulation but to encourage the private firms who are mainly responsible for pollution to commit themselves to certain reduction aims within a given period of time. As long as government does not credibly communicate its willingness to introduce new state orders, chances that self-regulation will occur are supposedly rather slim. But as soon as government publishes plans on what could be done, the likelihood of self-regulation by specific industries substantially increases. The resulting self-regulation is thus induced by the mere threat of the state to pass some state regulation. We cannot deal with the specific preconditions that must be met for such self-regulation to occur,[7] but there might be possibilities for government also to induce such self-regulation in the area of international financial markets. One could, for example, think of an international equivalent of Interbank Credit Agreements.

Another aspect that deserves some investigation is the weak performance of the international rating agencies in regard to the Asian crisis. This leads to the next question:

> Q5. What possibilities can one think of to make providers of information more reliable?

Over the last couple of years, accountants have been ever more frequently held responsible for incomplete or false information provided by them. This development has a number of consequences for how accountants do their work, for the prices they charge etc. What is relevant for our question is the conjecture that such legal developments will give them incentives to be more careful with the information they provide. One could inquire whether similar developments in regard to rating agencies would improve the quality of the international financial order. To give an example: some parliaments have passed laws according to which accounting firms can only do so many annual balances in a roll in order to have someone to check the books periodically. One could inquire whether similar rules could improve the quality of the information provided by the rating agencies.

---

[7] But see Stefan Voigt, 'Freiwilligkeit durch Zwangsandrohung – eine institutionenökonomische Analyse von Selbstverpflichtungserklärungen in der Umweltpolitik' (2000) *Zeitschrift für Umweltpolitik und Umweltrecht* 393–407.

In the introduction, three necessary elements for giving policy advice were named. Until now, we have not yet dealt with basic normative issues. It might appear awkward to deal with the positive issues first and only then turn to the normative ones. Yet, as has already been pointed out in the introduction, policy advice can only be generated if we can draw on some positive knowledge. The handful of questions just identified are a clear indicator that our positive knowledge is very unsatisfactory at present. Therefore, we deal with the normative issues only on a very abstract and almost hypothetical level.

The nation-state is a relatively young concept; it has only been around for a little more than 200 years. It is thus by no means the only feasible way to organise collective action. To draw such a conclusion based on the observation that today almost all societies are organised on the basis of the nation-state would furthermore be equivalent to committing the naturalistic fallacy. But the nation-state is the *status quo*. Any proposal arguing for reducing its sovereignty and (partially) shifting it to some supranational body needs to justify the proposed change. As Buchanan[8] would have it: 'Any proposal for change involves the status quo as the necessary starting point. "We start from here," and not from some place else.'

Within the framework of normative constitutional economics mainly proposed by Buchanan and his various co-authors, institutional change would be justified if one could show that rational individuals could expect to be better off if some of the competences now on the nation-state level would be transferred to some international organisation. Ideally, every single individual would have to consent to proposed rule changes in order to justify them. But often, some individuals will be adversely affected by a proposed new allocation of consequences and would thus have incentives to veto the proposed re-allocation. Two devices have been proposed to deal with this problem: Buchanan and Tullock[9] stress the notion of uncertainty: let people decide today for a measure to be implemented only x years from now. Rawls[10] asks the (hypothetical) rule choosers to walk through a veil of ignorance that takes their knowledge concerning their own living circumstances (such

---

[8] James M. Buchanan, *The Limits of Liberty – Between Anarchy and Leviathan* (Chicago, 1975), p. 78.

[9] James M. Buchanan and Gordon Tullock, *The Calculus of Consent – Logical Foundations of Constitutional Democracy* (Ann Arbor, 1962), p. 78.

[10] John Rawls, *A Theory of Justice* (Cambridge, 1971).

as capacities, age, sex, religion, resource endowments etc.) away from
them. These two notions are thus attempts to get away from the *status
quo*, at least conceptually and to lay the basis for deriving rules that could
be unanimously consented to by rational individuals. Like always, God
is in the details: depending on how one defines 'rationality', quite
diverse sets of rules can be thought of as hypothetically consensuable
by unanimous consent.[11]

2. The new institutional economics

Shortly before the Asian crisis, a well-known economist[12] published a
paper dealing with the Washington consensus, the consensus of the
Washington-based international organisations concerning the necessary
ingredients of successful policy reforms in less developed countries that
includes both macroeconomic and microeconomic components. He
compared the performance of countries that had undergone policy
reforms in Latin America and in Asia and noted that although Latin
American countries had taken microeconomic reforms much more
serious than their Asian counterparts, they had not systematically
fared better than the latter. He thus seemed to argue that microeconomic reform might not be that crucial after all. In the meantime, there
does not only seem to be a consensus emerging that microeconomic
reform is just as important as macroeconomic reform but also that
institutions deserve special attention: countries that have adopted essentially identical policy reform packages have performed very differently.
The current wisdom of the international financial organisations points
at differences in the underlying institutions as the central factor in
explaining these differences.[13]

Institutions can be defined as commonly known rules that are to
structure repetitive interaction situations that are endowed with an
enforcement mechanism ensuring that non-compliance with the rule-
component gets sanctioned. Institutions thus consist of two components, namely the rule component on the one hand and the sanctioning

---

[11] A more systematic treatment of the weaknesses of this approach can be found in: Stefan
Voigt, *Explaining Constitutional Change – A Positive Economics Approach* (Cheltenham,
1999), ch. 2.

[12] Dani Rodrik, 'Understanding Economic Policy Reform' (1996) 34 *Journal of Economic
Literature* 9–41.

[13] World Bank, *Dividends and Disappointments: Learning from the Success and Failure of
Foreign Aid*, Discussion Draft, 24 July 1998.

component on the other. Various taxonomies concerning institutions have been proposed. For our purposes, it is sufficient to stress that institutions need not necessarily be enforced by the state. There are a number of institutions whose non-compliance gets sanctioned within the private realm: think of conventions (where no participant is able to increase his utility by deviating from the convention), of ethical norms (where participants try to bind themselves), of customs (that are kept in an informal manner by other participants who sanction custom-deviating behaviour), and of organised private enforcement (e.g. by merchant courts administering the above-mentioned international *lex mercatoria*). The state enforces none of these groups or classes of institutions. It is an important insight of the new institutional economics that upholding an institution does not necessarily depend on the force attributed to the state. As the groups or classes of institutions just mentioned should show, there are a host of institutions that structure human interaction without being explicitly backed by any state.

Closely connected to Hayekian thinking introduced above, it has been argued for a long time that institutions securing the so-called 'rule of law' are amenable to economic growth. The most important trait of the rule of law is that the law is to be applied equally to all persons (*isonomia*), government leaders included. It is therefore also called government under the law. No power used by government is arbitrary, all power is limited. Drawing on Immanuel Kant,[14] laws should fulfil the criteria of universalisability as already introduced above.

There are a number of institutional provisions regularly used in order to maintain the rule of law. Amongst the most important ones are the separation of powers and the closely connected judicial review, the prohibition of retroactive legislation, the prohibition of expropriation without just compensation, *habeas corpus*, trial by jury, and other procedural devices such as protection of confidence, the principle of the least possible intervention, the principle of proportionality and the like. Empirically, a 'perfect' or 'complete' rule of law has probably never been realised: men and women have been treated differently just as members of different races have been. Logically, a rule of law-constitution does not imply that the political system be democratic.

The stability of orders is, *inter alia*, dependent on the degree to which rules are factually enforced, i.e. on the degree to which non-rule-abiding

---

[14] Immanuel Kant, *The Metaphysics of Morals – Introduction, translation, and notes by Mary Gregor* (Cambridge, 1797/1995).

behaviour is sanctioned. Sanctioning threats incorporated in national laws will not have the intended deterrence effect if they are not carried out. The stability of orders thus also depends on the congruence of *de iure* and *de facto* law. It has been shown that many national governments have problems in making their promises – and their threats – credible. Take the example of a no bail-out rule: A national government might have a general law stipulating that in case a financial organisation operating within its jurisdiction is threatened by bankruptcy, it will not jump in in order to save the troubled company. If such a pledge is credible, private investors will be scrutinising the companies they invest in much more carefully than if they expect the state to jump in in case of financial problems. A more stable financial order will result. The problem with this story is that as soon as a financial organisation is in trouble, many governments can make themselves better off by not sticking to their pledge: often, at least important parts of the public will demand some state action to save the threatened jobs. Situations in which optimal *ex ante* behaviour differs from optimal *ex post* behaviour are analysed by economists under the name of 'time inconsistency problems'.[15]

The implications of such problems are easy to identify: if potential investors anticipate that the government will not stick to its promise *ex post*, they will be less careful in their investment behaviour, thereby increasing the risk of financial turmoil and thus the instability of the financial order. Institutional economists would now ask for possibilities to make government promises credible. The logic behind possible solutions to the time inconsistency-problem is always identical: look for ways to make it costly for the government not to stick to its promises. If it can be made costly to lie, then people will lie less. If it is costly to deviate from one's promises, people will stick to them. Often, there are no adequate solutions to this problem on the national level. Conceptually, the separation of powers can be interpreted as such an attempt, because the independent judiciary can stop the executive from violating the law. In reality, the possibilities of the judiciary to stop the executive are often less than perfect.[16] Searching for credible

---

[15] Finn W. Kydland and Edward C. Prescott, 'Rules Rather than Discretion: The Inconsistency of the Optimal Plans' (1977) 85 *Journal of Political Economy* 473–91.

[16] Lars Feld and Stefan Voigt, 'Economic Growth and Judicial Independence: Cross Country Evidence Using a New Set of Indicators', mimeo (2002); Universities of Marburg and Kassel.

commitment mechanisms, one could thus turn to the international level for solutions.[17] The question then is:

Q6. Can international (financial) organisations be used in order to reduce the credibility problems of national governments?

Rational governments could anticipate that *ex post*, they will have incentives not to stick to their *ex ante* promises. If they are interested in the stability of financial markets, they could thus try to devise mechanisms which make it costly for them to behave differently from the behaviour announced *ex ante*. Such behaviour could be termed the 'Ulysses-procedure'. Governments could thus agree on a set of rules that constrains their own behaviour. In order to make such an agreement credible, sanctions for rule-deviating behaviour need to be passed. Simply passing such rules on the international level will, however, not be sufficient to make them credible. Suppose that sanctioning a rule-deviating government is costly. Then all rule-abiding governments are interested that the rule-deviating government be sanctioned. But for all rule-abiding governments, it would, of course, be the best solution, if 'someone else' did the sanctioning job because it is costly. In other words, sanctioning rule-deviating behaviour is a public good which will only be supplied in sub-optimal quantities, if at all. But suppose this problem could be solved by an adequate allocation of the (sanctioning) costs, then it is possible that the existence of an international organisation can make rules on the national level more credible. It could thus improve the stability of the international financial order.

So much for the theory. Getting a little closer to the Asian crisis, we are confronted with a puzzle: here, the promises made by national governments seem to have been more credible than the promises iterated by the international financial organisations: many decisions to invest into Asian companies were based on the assumption that the Asian currencies would be closely bound to the dollar, a promise made by many of the Asian governments. This induced investment because

---

[17] To make the possible solutions to this problem more complete, informal or internal institutions need to be mentioned: if there are values or norms that enable citizens to produce the public good opposition spontaneously when needed and politicians anticipate this correctly, then these internal norms can effectively constrain the behaviour of politicians, see: Stefan Voigt, 'Breaking with the Notion of Social Contract: Constitutions as Based on Spontaneously Arisen Institutions' (1999) 10(3) *Constitutional Political Economy* 283–300.

one of the risks of investment in other currencies, the currency risk, seemed to have been taken care of by the government. On the other hand, we have the Washington-based financial organisations who promised not to bail out countries should they be subject to financial crises. The imprudent investment behaviour of many foreign investors seems to be a clue that this pledge was not credible.

This seems to be an empirical example where the credibility of commitments pronounced on the national level seems to have been quite high. There are other such instances: it has been argued that low inflation rates can be induced by independent central banks. Monetary policy is an area where time inconsistency problems loom large: government has incentives to announce a policy of tight money. If wages are negotiated on such expectations, the government can induce additional economic growth by so-called 'surprise inflation'. The problem is, of course, that rational individuals will anticipate exactly this and the government is not able to surprise its citizens any more. Instead, this will induce an inflationary bias, i.e. an inflation rate that is higher than it could be and that only has economic costs. An independent central bank that is not subject to this type of time inconsistency problems can be a solution. It has been argued that, at least in the OECD countries, variances in the inflation rates can be explained by differences in the degree of independence of the various central banks.[18] The literature on the effects of independent central banks could lead to the following question:

Q7. Is it possible to draw analogies from the independence of central banks with regard to the supervisory bodies of private banks?

The conjecture behind this question is that supervisory bodies that are part of, say, the ministry of finance have an incentive not to enforce regulatory measures if that amounts to closing some of the banks. This could be the case because closing down banks is unpopular and governments that want to be re-elected need to remain popular. Rational bank owners anticipate this and have thus incentives not to play by the rules if that is costly. Therefore the question whether one can think up an incentive structure of a independent supervisory body that is sufficiently

---

[18] For a recent survey of this literature see: Helge Berger, Jakob de Haan and Silvester Eijffinger, 'Central Bank Independence: An Update of Theory and Evidence' (2001) *Journal of Economic Surveys* 3–40.

different from the structure of a government-dependent body just sketched.

We have hopefully been able to show that drawing on Hayekian thinking as well as on the new institutional economics, a host of interesting questions can be generated. For improving the co-ordination quality of the international financial order, being able to answer them with a certain degree of confidence is crucial. Since Socrates, being aware of one's limited knowledge has been a noble trait of academics. In the next section of the chapter, we nevertheless dare to come up with some preliminary policy advice which will, hopefully, also be somewhat provocative.

III. Some preliminary policy advice

Rodrik asks: 'Has globalization gone too far?'[19] For many observers, the Asian crisis seems to be clear evidence that the question should be answered in the affirmative. Some of the countries most severely hit by the crisis had followed the advice of the Washington based financial organisations and had liberalised their capital markets. Some of the observers now claim that these countries were punished for liberalisation. Even worse, the crisis also negatively affected some of the neighbouring countries that had been more cautious in their own liberalisation policies. In other words: they claim that there were spillover-effects or, as economists would put it, that the liberalisation policies had negative externalities on the more cautious countries. From this evaluation of the course of events, it is only a small step to demand controls in capital flows, for example by way of the much discussed Tobin tax. In this section, it will be argued that such policy advice is not well founded on positive knowledge. Before giving such policy advice, one needs to look at the course of events more closely and then draw the appropriate conclusions.

Often, two issues seem to get neglected: the relevance of exchange rate pegs and the issue of moral hazard. We will deal with both these issues in turn.

A currency whose exchange rate is pegged to another currency seems – at least prima facie – to involve fewer risks than freely floating currencies. Many of the Asian currencies were pegged to the US dollar. This led foreign investors to believe that there were no exchange rate

[19] Dani Rodrik, *Has Globalization Gone Too Far?* (Washington, DC, 1997).

risks involved in investment in these countries. The expected yield was higher than if investors had taken the exchange rate risk explicitly into account. But there are limits to the promise of governments to peg their own currencies to foreign currencies. If the actors in the financial markets do not believe the promise to be credible any more, this can lead to a fast reduction of foreign reserves of the national bank. The limit of pegging one's currency to another one is reached as soon as foreign reserves are gone. But suppose that foreign investors expect the peg to be upheld. This means that more capital than warranted will flow into the respective country.

Most of the countries severely hit by financial crises recently have been countries with somehow pegged currencies.[20] Such regimes can thus come at very high cost. In order to give advice on more preferable regimes, one would have to compare benefits and costs of pegged currency regimes with those of fixed and floating ones. This cannot be carried out here, however.[21]

Credibility has a lot to do with past performance. If promises have been kept in the past, observers will expect that they also be kept in the future. In other words, consistently sticking to one's promises can lead to a corresponding reputation. The Washington-based financial

---

[20] Fischer names Thailand, Korea, Indonesia, Russia and Brazil, Stanley Fischer, 'On the Need for an International Lender of Last Resort' (1999) 13(4) *Journal of Economic Perspectives*, 85–104.

[21] It might, however, be useful to point to a specific kind of fixed exchange rate regime that would seem to deserve some attention, namely currency boards; in such a regime, the domestic currency is fixed to an 'anchor currency.' Holders of the domestic currency have the right to change their assets against the pegged currency at a fixed rate at any time. Monetary supply is not determined by a central bank any more but depends on the quantity of reserve assets (usually the peg currency and other foreign currencies as well as gold). Monetary supply thus directly hinges upon the balance of payments. The establishment of a currency board is almost equivalent to the abdication of a domestic monetary policy. Thus, monetary policy decisions are delegated externally and taken by an organisation beyond the immediate reach of domestic actors, namely those (foreign) central banks that serve as the anchor of the domestic currency.

Ghosh et al. show that inflation under currency board arrangements is about four percentage points lower than under other pegged exchange regimes. The authors note that this better performance cannot only be attributed to what they call the *discipline* effect, namely the restrictions in monetary growth, but mostly to what they call the *confidence* effect, i.e. the expectation that a currency board will perform better. They also note that the differences in performance cannot be explained by the fact that countries with a lower proclivity to inflation being more likely to adopt a currency board. Indeed, the results remain significant even after controlling for regime choice endogeneity, Atish Ghosh, Anne-Marie Gulde and Holger Wolf, 'Currency Boards: The Ultimate Fix?' *IMF Working Paper* no. 98/8.

organisations have often insisted on not being ready to bail out countries in case they were subject to a serious financial crisis. But when Mexico was in trouble in 1994, the US government as well as the IMF were eager to support the Mexicans. Given that track record, investors built up the expectation that these organisations would behave similarly in future cases. The expectation that the financial organisations served as a sort of insurance against the greatest risks induced them to take more risks than they would otherwise have been ready to accept. This is what economists call moral hazard.

If this observation is correct, then the IMF could be considered as causing some of the troubles rather than as solving them. In order to prevent this from happening again in the future, the question of how the IMF-member states can credibly commit themselves not to bail out entire countries in the future must be convincingly answered.[22] Partial answers could consist in reducing the possibility to increase the amount of special drawing rights (the IMF currency) available, of reducing the current amount of special drawing rights, or even in an outright abolition of the IMF.[23] Such a proposal can be complemented by the demand to broaden and/or to strengthen the WTO and especially the GATS, i.e. the pillar most relevant for financial markets.

The experience with the Asian crisis could lead to a number of additional recommendations: those countries with strong sets of rules concerning financial markets have been hit substantially less than countries with a loose set of rules.[24] This means that contagion did not take place in an unpredictable manner. Schwartz even talks about the 'myth

[22] This is not to deny that there might be justifiable bail-outs, such as those occurring after a natural catastrophe, that destroy important amounts of exported crops or substantial parts of a country's infrastructure. Such natural disasters can, of course, deteriorate a country's position substantially. But, even in such cases, the danger of moral hazard looms large: if people expect to be bailed out in the aftermath of such crises, then they might not adequately insure against such risks in the first place.

[23] This policy proposal has not only been advanced by critiques of globalisation but also by those who argue that the need for such an organisation has ceased with the disappearance of a fixed currency regime in the 1970s. Sally describes the GATT/WTO as having a clear mandate, a small budget and an efficient secretariat whereas the Washington-based organisations are seen as having a diffuse mandate, as acting intransparently, and as being inefficient, Razeen Sally, 'Looking Askance at Global Governance' in John Kirton, Joseph Daniels and Andreas Freytag (eds.), *Guiding Global Order* (Aldershot, 2001), pp. 55–76.

[24] Fischer, above note 20; Mishkin names Singapore, Hong Kong and Taiwan as examples, Frederic Mishkin, 'Global Financial Instability: Framework, Events, Issues' (1999) 13(4) *Journal of Economic Perspectives* 3–20.

of contagion'.[25] It could also be interpreted as an argument against the need of regulatory rules implemented on the international level. And it is, of course, an argument of establishing clear-cut regulatory rules domestically.

A second observation during the crisis was that countries with a high amount of currency reserves were substantially less affected than countries with few reserves.[26] Currency reserves do serve a purpose and the policy advice to build them up almost seems to suggest itself. But if central banks have a reputation of not truthfully revealing the amount of foreign currency held, creating a currency board might be an adequate alternative.[27]

In some of the Asian countries, loose regulations of the banking sector are combined with high protectionist barriers to entry for foreign banks.[28] From a politico-economic point of view, this set-up can be easily explained: banks protected from international competition can secure supernormal profits and the bankers will be grateful for the politicians enabling them to make these profits. In some countries, attractive banking jobs are given to the friends and family of government members.[29] If these countries opened up their markets for foreign banks, this would not only improve their services and lower their prices, but it would also lead to a dissipation of the risks involved with banking on more shoulders. The corresponding policy advice thus is to get rid of protectionist barriers in the financial sector.

IV. Summary

The first part of the paper served to show that our knowledge concerning the adequate rules of conduct of the international financial order is very limited. A number of questions were proposed that need to be answered before solid policy advice can be given. In the third part of the chapter, we focused on some experiences made during the Asian and

---

[25] Anna Schwartz, 'International Financial Crises: Myths and Realities' (1998) 17(3) *Cato Journal* 251–6.

[26] Kenneth Rogoff, 'International Institutions for Reducing Global Financial Instability' (1999) 13(4) *Journal of Economic Perspectives* 21–42.

[27] The Thai Central Bank deceived markets by overstating the amount of foreign currency held. Once this became known, it led to capital flight, James Dorn, 'Money in the New Millennium: The Global Financial Architecture' (1999) 18(3) *Cato Journal* 311–20 at 317.

[28] Rogoff, above note 26.

[29] Gerard Caprio and Patrick Honohan, 'Restoring Banking Stability: Beyond Supervised Capital Requirements' (1999) 13(4) *Journal of Economic Perspectives* 43–64.

other recent financial crises and asked whether it was possible to learn from these crises in order to prevent them from happening again. For most of the policy proposals discussed, international co-ordination or even a supranational body are not necessary. Regulatory improvements, adequate currency regimes and opening up domestic financial markets to the forces of international competition can all be established unilaterally. It is thus still the nation-state governments that are key to the further development of the international financial order.

14

Proposing built-in stabilisers for the international financial system

KUNIBERT RAFFER

The lack of stabilising factors within the present international financial system was forcefully demonstrated by the Asian crash and the immediately following crises in Russia and Brazil. These shocks led to calls for an International Financial Architecture, and to activities of high level working groups.[1] However, once this shock was overcome, the need for change was also seen as less pressing, even though the underlying problems continue to exist, strongly suggesting better not to wait for the next big crisis to resume discussions on how to avoid it.

This contribution presents four proposals to make the international financial system more stable, to improve the regulatory environment of capital flows, and to abolish destabilising market distortions. While not pretending to be a full fledged new architecture, these reforms would already bring about substantial improvements.

Speed bumps decelerating international capital flows

Measures to deal with excess volatility and speed of capital flows are needed. Unfortunately, measures so far increased speed and volatility. The risk weight given by the Basle Committee to short run flows to banks outside the OECD region, or regulatory changes necessary to allow institutional investors to invest in Mexican *tesobonos* before 1994–5 illustrate this trend. By contrast proposals to decelerate capital flows have been shunned so far. The IMF has forced member countries in need of resources to liberalise further, even though rather far-reaching capital controls are membership rights under its own Articles

---

[1] Cf. OECD (ed.), *Reports on the International Financial Architecture: Report of the Working Group on International Financial Crises* (1988), available at http://www.oecd.org/subject/fin_architecture.

of Agreement. In contrast to the *ex post* socialisation of wholly private debts governments were forced to accept in East Asia, thus bailing out private speculators, capital controls would not have been at the cost of taxpayers, but would have bailed in these short term investors.

Speed bumps can be of different kinds. Using the measures allowed by the IMF's Articles of Agreements would be one. Basically establishing a liberal regime for trade – the precise term is 'current transactions' including more than purely trading activities – they allow an array of capital controls, as Malaysia illustrated recently. Transactions that should be generally exempt from controls are not defined without restrictions pursuant to Article XXX(d)(3), which only subsumes 'payments of *moderate* amount of amortisation of loans or for depreciation of direct investments', or Article XXX(d)(4) subsuming '*moderate* remittances for family living expenses'[2] under 'current transactions'. Article VI(1)(a) stipulates that members are not allowed to use the Fund's general resources to meet a large and sustained outflow of capital. The Fund may even 'request a member to exercise controls to prevent such use of the general resources of the Fund. If, after receiving such a request, a member fails to exercise appropriate controls, the Fund may declare the member ineligible to use the general resources of the Fund.' Members are only entitled to make reserve tranche purchases to meet capital transfer. Reality, however, has been different.

In open violation of its own statutes the IMF has forced crisis countries not to exercise their rights. Bringing the rule of law to the IMF by making it respect its own statutes and the use of membership rights during crises would allow sensible measures to defuse crises cheaply and fairly. Additionally, they would bring market risk to bear, thus substantially reducing the present moral hazard situation where speculators and investors have reason to expect being bailed out. Naturally, if countries applied capital controls it would be better and also fairer to investors to apply restrictions to inflows rather than outflows.

The second way to decelerate flows is increasing the costs of short-term transactions, either by interest free deposits or via taxing foreign exchange transactions. The former is usually connected with Chile, although other countries did use this mechanism as well, as, for example, the German *Bardepot* illustrates. The best known example for the latter is Tobin's proposal to tax foreign exchange transactions. Until the main discussant promoting the Tobin tax in the 1990s was silenced by

---

[2] Emphasis added.

US legislators[3] a vivid discussion had taken place. As a rule proposals by great economists do not trigger laws against discussing them in Western democracies. Tobin's idea is the famous exception said to confirm the rule.

For reasons of space this discussion cannot be reproduced here. Interested readers are referred to Raffer,[4] who surveyed and summarised it, showing that no valid technical argument against Tobin's proposal exists. Suffice it to illustrate the paucity of counter-arguments by mentioning that even the assertion was used that transactions would not be known and could therefore not be taxed. If true, banks would not be able to declare their income properly, nor – one has to fear – collect their fees. The argument was also used that monetary and fiscal authorities cannot co-operate sufficiently well, and would be unable to function properly. Stotsky,[5] for example, doubts that 'monetary authorities would have the ability and independence to administer such a tax wisely'. It is unclear whether she means Tobin's original or Spahn's[6] two-tier version. Logically this would raise the question what simple task monetary authorities can fulfil sensibly at all. Such arguments highlight the apparent lack of convincing counter-arguments. If they were taken seriously one would have to argue against the principle of taxation as such, and against any activity by governments or monetary authorities.

Compared with deposits a Tobin or any currency transaction tax (CTT) is more market-friendly. The Tobin tax is a good means to prevent short-term interest rate arbitrage. It would have been a strong disincentive to 'carry trade' in Asia that boomed prior to the crash, and thus a stabilising factor. Creating larger margins by which interest rates can differ between two currencies it re-establishes some freedom of manoeuvring for central banks. But it cannot serve as a disincentive to large-scale speculation against a currency, as illustrated by the example of speculators against the European ERM, who sought and got returns in excess of what any likely Tobin tax could counteract. However, one cannot expect one measure to correct everything – reality does not know

---

[3] For details see Kunibert Raffer and H. W. Singer, *The Economic North South Divide: Six Decades of Unequal Development* (Cheltenham, 2001; paperback, 2002), p. 239 et seq.

[4] Kunibert Raffer, 'The Tobin-Tax: Reviving a Discussion' (1998) 26(3) *World Development* 529 et seq.

[5] Janet G. Stotsky, 'Why a Two-Tier Tobin Tax Won't Work' (1996) 33(2) *Finance and Development* 28 et seq.

[6] Paul Bernd Spahn, 'The Tobin Tax and Exchange Rate Stability' (1996) 33(2) *Finance and Development*, 24 et seq.

panaceas. The Tobin tax would reduce interest arbitrage, the attractiveness of small exchange rate changes, and produce revenue. It might have prevented the Asian crisis. In 1994–5 a transaction tax would have raised funds from foreign investors and should, *ceteris paribus*, have reduced their exposure in Mexico unless all investors behaved cost-inelastic. Reduced exposure would mean lower bail-out sums in the case of a bail-out. Speculators would pay a percentage of the bail-out themselves. It would thus be an economically efficient way of bailing-in private investors, even though sums actually collected by a Tobin tax would be relatively small. As capital is definitely undertaxed worldwide nowadays, fairness would demand a shift towards capital taxation as well. This would also reduce the economically harmful bias against real investments that are taxed more heavily, which in turn further encourages investment in financial instruments.

Looking into the matter of the Tobin tax for the IMF, Spahn elaborated Tobin's idea further, advocating a two-tier tax, following Keynes' idea of differentiating transaction costs within pre-set rules according to national policy choices. A low underlying transaction tax should combine with an exchange surcharge severely taxing excessive volatility. The possibility of increasing the tax quickly and substantially if needed could be a powerful instrument against speculative attacks on currencies such as in the case of the pound in the early 1990s. This stabilising device against speculation would provide official income in contrast to regular bail-outs: 'Instead of depleting public assets it would generate revenues.'[7] It would bail in speculators much more strongly than Tobin's original. Like Tobin's own Spahn's variant is a possibility to decelerate capital flows. However, the low rate during 'normal' times should not be too low to generate resources. Furthermore, capital controls during and because of crises may still be needed.

Meanwhile an international capital transaction tax is even proposed by an IMF *Working Paper*.[8] Although a disclaimer states that the views expressed are not necessarily the IMF's, a *Working Paper* is 'published to elicit comments and further debate'. By publishing it the IMF has taken a step to renew the debate and seems to have changed its position on this issue considerably. Zee[9] qualifies the 'argument that volatile capital

---

[7] *Ibid.*, 27.
[8] Howell H. Zee, 'Retarding Short-Term Capital Inflows Through Withholding Tax', *IMF Working Paper* WP/00/40 (March 2000).
[9] *Ibid.*, p. 10.

movements could have a destabilising impact on the domestic economy of a country' as 'uncontroversial'. Therefore he recommends a withholding tax on all private capital inflows with a credit and refund provision operating within the administrative framework of the existing domestic tax system. The tax would be refunded on export receipts and the sale of assets abroad, credited against income tax in the case of any income (interest, dividends, repatriated profits). Thus only 'financial inflows of a capital nature'[10] would have to bear the tax or taxpayers deciding not to declare income from abroad. It might be difficult to tell sales of assets from speculative capital movements, but this problem is not tackled. Recalling that Malaysia's capital controls also exempted dividends, interest earned or rental income, one might wonder whether this relatively successful practical example influenced research within the IMF. The recommended rate of 'rarely' more than 1% is higher than the rates usually proposed by advocates of the Tobin tax at present. Zee sees his tax as the better alternative to non-remunerated reserve requirements. Although a national measure this comes very close to Tobin's proposal if many countries introduce it with the same rate. Its economic effects would then be equivalent.

Zee[11] argues that while the Tobin Tax 'is aimed at reducing global destabilising speculative movements' his own goal is 'more modest', namely 'to merely moderate the impact of volatile world capital flows on a country's domestic economy'. This distinction is not logically convincing because Zee[12] rightly points out that his variant would be 'equivalent to a prohibitive income tax rate' on short term movements. How rates can be prohibitive without reducing volumes goes unexplained.

Like some Tobin tax critics Zee takes up the point whether governments would remain virtuous with large revenues generated by such a tax. He sees huge problems about their disposal by governments, recommending that 'part or all' of the revenues should go to the financial institutions charged with withholding the tax. Very much along neoliberal lines a tax would thus be transformed into a banking fee. The effect on non-banks would be the same, but apparently the idea that governments might raise money by new taxes *and* use it – for instance to finance social expenditures – is still anathema within the Fund.

Zee rightly points out that his tax could be implemented easily, as administrative structures exist and financial institutions are well

---

[10] *Ibid.*, at 7.   [11] *Ibid.*, at 4.   [12] *Ibid.*, at 7.

equipped technically to collect the tax. This is not a distinctive feature vis-à-vis the Tobin tax, as Zee claims. Collecting the Tobin tax by those national governments that have introduced it, was proposed as the simplest way to levy it by many authors, including Tobin.[13] Zee is right pointing out that his withholding mechanism makes collecting easy – but there is no reason not collect the Tobin tax this way. All in all Zee seems somewhat too eager to highlight differences. He repeats arguments against the Tobin variant that have already been proved wrong, such as the need to apply it universally, which is refuted by the securities transaction tax in the United Kingdom, also known as 'stamp duty'. Griffith-Jones[14] describes this precedent for taxing international capital transactions in detail, showing that capital flight to places where the tax is not levied is extremely limited indeed. The stamp duty creates substantial revenue in one of the most sophisticated markets in the world – whose market players are most likely to find mechanisms of evasion, as she rightly observes. Nevertheless Zee's publication is much less inimical towards taxing transactions than the Fund used to be, and one may hope that it actually elicits further discussion. Strong opposition against any CTT continues to exist, but there are also signs of a slow re-orientation. Also, within the United Nations' *Financing for Development* Initiative NGOs are strongly lobbying for it.

Without a CTT other methods to increase transaction costs are used, for example compulsory deposit requirements, which do not create government revenue but cost investor's money. Generating income *ceteris paribus* as well is a superior solution.

Reforming loan loss provisioning

In their attempts to make the banking system more stable the Basle Committee focused on risk weighted capital adequacy, somewhat disregarding the stabilising potential of proper provisioning rules. One reason might be that differences in provisioning were considered too problematic to tackle. The basic idea, to give lower weights to less risky claims, is correct. In practice, however, those risky short-term flows were encouraged and that brought about the Asian crash of 1997. The

---

[13] Cf. Raffer, 'The Tobin-Tax', above note 4.

[14] Stephany Griffith-Jones, 'Institutional Arrangements for a Tax on International Currency Transactions' in Mahbub ul Haq, Inge Kaul and Isabelle Grunberg (eds.), *The Tobin Tax, Coping with Financial Volatility* (Oxford, 1996), p. 146 et seq.

Basle system accorded a low risk weight of 20% to claims vis-à-vis private banks in non-OECD countries with maturities up to, and a weight of, 100% if maturities exceed one year. This problematic decision may be seen a micro–macro problem, as Andrew Crockett did at a hearing at the German *Bundestag* on 14 March 2001.[15] For any individual loan a shorter maturity means *ceteris paribus* less risk than a longer one. But if 'all loans to Thailand are with three-months maturity' there is a problem, their effect becomes highly destabilising. This is a correct observation. But as rules and norms are made for all lenders rather than for single individual loans, this macro-effect should have been foreseen. Correcting this wrong incentive is an urgent issue for the new Basle II.

Unfortunately, though, the stabilising function of loan loss provisioning has not received due attention, possibly so because of fundamental differences in tax deductibility among G7 countries. The continental European system of tax deductibility stabilises credit markets substantially.[16] Theoretically, reserves correct gaps between nominal and real, impaired values of claims, which may but need not be reflected in secondary markets. Whenever reserves equal losses of value, non-deductibility actually means taxing illusory income. Deductibility recognises economic facts correctly, fairly, and in line with basic principles of taxation. Encouraging higher provisions tax-deductibility is a built-in stabiliser and economically not less sound than weighted capital requirements.

The often heard allegation that tax deductibility of loan loss reserves is at taxpayers' expense is economically wrong. Costs to taxpayers, and hence benefits to banks (or creditors at large), have always been strongly exaggerated. Thus a closer look at actual effects of tax deductibility seems advised. Tax authorities in countries restricting tax deductibility are at least implicitly of the opinion that losses occur when the respective entry correcting a loan's nominal value is made in the creditor's books. According to this perception a loan would be granted by the Treasury over the period between the year in which reserves are established and

---

[15] In *Öffentliche Anhörung zur Entwicklung der internationlen Finanzmärkte, zur Verschuldungsfrage und zu einem internationalen Insolvenzrecht* (Public Hearing on the Development of International Financial Markets, on the Question of Indebtedness and on International Insolvency Law) on Wednesday, 14 March 2001, Deutscher Bundestag (German Parliament), 14th Legislative Period, Finance Committee, 7th Committee, Protocol No. 90 (chair: MP Christine Scheel), p. 66.

[16] Cf. Kunibert Raffer, 'Tax-Deductible Loan Loss Reserves and International Banking: An Economist's Unbiased Analysis', *Working Papers in Commerce* WPC 91/19, Birmingham University, Department of Commerce, Birmingham Business School. Its main arguments are summarised here.

the year in which the loan is finally written down or off, or reserves are finally dissolved and taxed. Tax deductible provisions only shift losses (or taxes) over time. Assuming reserves of £100, a tax rate t, and an interest rate i_g at which the government itself can borrow, the annual costs to taxpayers are

$$£100ti_g \qquad (1)$$

These costs are the additional amount which would have been paid as tax if no provisions had been made or these provisions would have been fully subjected to taxation multiplied by the interest rate the government pays as a borrower. In continental Europe this loan carries no interest – not only in the case of banks, but of all enterprises. At a tax rate of 50%, and an interest rate of 6% at which the government itself borrows, reserves of £100 cost taxpayers £3 annually. Clearly, ti_g is the upper limit for any estimate of costs. If one sees tax deductibility this way one conclusion logically follows: the longer it takes to solve a crisis (= to realise losses) the higher will costs to taxpayers become. Delaying a solution to the debt crisis – as our governments have done – has negative financial effects on taxpayers according to this view. These effects are increased if irrecoupable debts have grown further beyond what they would have been if a quick and efficient solution had been applied early on, as they usually do.

The assumption of the time lag between the years in which reserves are set aside and when they are used is not unassailable. Loans still kept at 100% in the books will have lower factual or real values once the creditworthiness and economic standing of debtors have become doubtful, as the existence of secondary markets proves. From an economic and factual point of view money is actually lost before nominal claims are finally adjusted downwards in the books. Recognising diminished values of claims is just another way of stating that the sum of net assets, and thus the tax base, have declined.

To the extent that provisions reflect actual losses in the values of loans already suffered but not yet booked, they do not economically constitute taxable income. This would be the case if loan loss reserves set aside during one year are equivalent to the change in factual values during that year. Increasing reserves continuously in line with declining factual values would thus not really cost taxpayers a single penny. Should the economic outlook of the debtor improve these reserves would, of course, have to be reduced accordingly to keep provisions in line with actual values. Tax regimes without tax deductibility of reserves thus tax illusory profits, which only exist due to accounting practices. Looking at the matter this way, it might be argued that banks grant interest free loans to the Treasury by shifting losses to the future.

Because the real world is not an economist's comfortable blackboard, uncertainty will not allow a precise estimate of probabilities (and thus factual values) in practice, and one might discuss whether reserves actually match losses already suffered. If reserves are larger than these losses banks get a loan by tax authorities equivalent to this difference between reserves and changes in the values of loans; if reserves are smaller the difference is taxed as illusory income. In contrast to the first example above the costs of the tax-loan are not £100ti$_g$ for reserves of £100, but only ti$_g$ times this difference if reserves are greater than actual losses. Or, more formally,

$$£[100(1 - p) - \text{reserves}]ti_g \qquad (2)$$

where p is the probability of repayment, and 100p hence the expected value. The first term in square brackets expresses actual losses. If set aside reserves are smaller than actual losses the term in square brackets is illusory income taxed. Assuming that supervisory authorities keep reserves roughly in line with the decline in value of dubious loans, one can say that both costs to taxpayers and taxation of illusory profits will be very low or negligible. A substantial stabilising effect can be obtained at no or minimal real costs to taxpayers. Economically, provisions have the important function of spreading losses over some years, which might ruin a creditor if they had to be absorbed within one year. The theoretical alternative of actually writing claims down to their factual values is rather impractical, not least because of its moral hazard effects on debtors, who might be encouraged not to honour obligations already written off. It can be argued that under the assumption of a sufficiently well functioning regulatory framework – authorities abler than, for example, Stotsky assumes them to be – only no or negligibly small costs to the budget are possible. The latter might be outweighed by greater stability, as loan loss reserves perform an important stabilising function in financial markets.

By contrast, increases in assets not already realised in liquid form should not be taxed for the very same reason: stabilisation. If one applied the reasoning above symmetrically to tax, say, on increases in the value of land as measured by changes in market values, that would drive many perfectly viable firms into bankruptcy because they lack adequate liquidity to pay taxes calculated this way. Real estate bubbles such as in Japan should drive this point home. While the stabilising function of provisioning strongly suggests tax deductibility of reserves, the destabilising effects of taxing unrealised profits prohibit such taxes.

Whether to have a tax system that encourages more prudential provisioning this way is a also political question, which should not be decided without considering the alternatives. Continental Illinois or the US Savings and Loans institutions may suffice to show that extremely limited tax deductibility does not necessarily mean no costs to taxpayers.

International Chapter 9 insolvency for states

Such procedures are a necessary part of any meaningful international financial architecture as a means to solve the problem of debt overhangs in an economically efficient and fair way. Additionally, they would provide a disincentive to misallocations of funds as those occurring during the 1970s when lenders assumed that 'sovereign risk' was actually no risk because countries would always eventually repay.

In connection with the Asian crisis proper insolvency procedures for firms are seen as essential for avoiding future crises. The Reports on the International Financial Architecture published by the OECD recommend it strongly, but avoid the I-word when it comes to sovereign debtors. Nevertheless the Working Group on International Financial Crises proposed an insolvency procedure in all but name, demanding the international community to provide: 'in exceptional and extreme circumstances . . . a sovereign debtor with legal "breathing space" so as to facilitate an orderly, co-operative and negotiated restructuring'.[17] The High-Level Regional Consultative Meeting on Financing for Development of Asia and the Pacific called for an international bankruptcy procedure,[18] adding that there is a need to ensure that private debt does not become government debt – quite possibly a lesson from the Asian crisis.

Emulating insolvency features, such as debt reduction by qualified creditor majority or 'Collective Action Clauses' for sovereign bond contracts, was recommended as a critical contribution to 'creating the institutional structure needed to encourage orderly workouts',[19]

---

[17] OECD (ed.), *Reports*, above note 1, at 37.
[18] Cf. http://www.unescap.org/drpad/fin_dev/reportses1.htm.
[19] OECD (ed.), *Reports*, above note 1, at 21.

because a 'binding insolvency regime for sovereign debtors is unlikely'.[20] The Report even admits that 'a purely voluntary approach' might not be feasible because 'the government may not have the bargaining power to obtain sustainable terms',[21] for example if creditors demand destabilisingly high interest rates. It remains to be asked why one shied away from the obvious conclusion – the need of an independent entity empowered to decide in such cases – and why all the advantages praised by the Working Group in the case of firms should not be equally advantageous in the case of sovereign debtors. Obviously, no convincing technical or economic arguments against it were identified by the Working Group. Why then emulate features of insolvency instead of simply using the existing model, which can be adapted so easily?

Crashes such as Mexico 1994–5 or Asia 1997 briefly shocked some decision-makers – such as Alan Greenspan or Rep. Jim Leach of Iowa, then Chairman of the House Banking and Financial Services Committee – into considering sovereign insolvency. It was even informally discussed before the G7-Summit at Halifax in 1995.[22] But once the shock was overcome stern opposition to this economically indicated work-out has resumed, even though traditional debt management by creditors has proved unable to solve the problem. Meanwhile many NGOs have taken up the proposal of an international insolvency modelled after the basic ideas of the US Chapter 9, a special procedure for debtors with governmental powers. Quite often they prefer the formulation Fair and Transparent Process of Arbitration to avoid 'insolvency', in particular NGOs from the South.

Already Adam Smith recommended state insolvency as the 'the measure which is both least dishonourable to the debtor, and least hurtful to the creditor'.[23] Immediately after 1982 a British banker recommended to apply corporate insolvency to countries (US Chapter 11 insolvency). This proposal was taken up and discussed widely. Economically it is perfectly sound. Private creditors applied Egyptian insolvency laws to solve the Egyptian debt crisis of 1876. After a surprisingly short time this concept (which also applied debtor protection in favour of the population) was economically successful for creditors and debtor

---

[20] Ibid., at 19.   [21] Ibid., at 30.

[22] Cf. Kunibert Raffer and H. W. Singer, The Foreign Aid Business: Economic Assistance and Development Co-operation (Cheltenham, 1996; paperback, 1997), p. 203 et seq.

[23] Adam Smith, An Inquiry into the Nature and Causes of the Wealth of Nations, vol. II, Glasgow edition by R. H. Campell, A. S. Skinner and W. B. Todd, (Oxford, 1979; originally published in 1776), p. 930.

alike[24] – a vivid contrast to present policies of official creditors. There is, however, a legal killer argument: as reorganisations of firms do not by definition take sovereignty into account this proposal is not legally viable. But the little known US Chapter 9 insolvency is. Designed and used for decades in the United States as a solution to the problems of debtors vested with governmental powers – so-called municipalities – its basic principles can be applied immediately to sovereign lending. Like all good insolvency laws it combines the need for a general framework with the flexibility necessary to deal fairly with individual cases.

As this idea, initially proposed in 1987, was elaborated in detail elsewhere[25] the essential elements of this solution with a human face are presented briefly. It deals with debtors having governmental powers, and protects those affected by the composition plan, giving them a right to be heard. Section 904 titled 'Limitation on Jurisdiction and Powers of Court' is the crux, making it clear that the court's jurisdiction depends on the municipality's volition, beyond which it cannot be extended, similar to the jurisdiction of international arbitrators. The concept of sovereignty does not contain anything more than what is protected by section 904 in the case of a municipality. A municipality cannot go into receivership. Elected officials cannot be removed from office by the court – but, of course, by voters at the next elections. All this makes Chapter 9 especially suited as *the* solution of sovereign over-indebtedness. The transparency and participation established by the right to be heard are an additional bonus.

During the Great Depression Chapter 9 procedures were introduced precisely to avoid prolonged and inefficient negotiations and reschedulings in the case of overindebted US municipalities, that kind of 'debt management' practised internationally for decades. A first draft by municipalities themselves that did not bar interventions into the governmental sphere was rejected by lawmakers as unconstitutional.[26] Creditor interventions such as those usual in developing countries

---

[24] Cf. Edouard Dommen, 'Comment un noble étranger libéra le khédive de sa dette – un conte oriental', (1999) (September) *Choisir* 26 et seq.

[25] Kunibert Raffer, 'Applying Chapter 9 Insolvency to International Debts: An Economically Efficient Solution with a Human Face' (1990) 18(2) *World Development* 301 et seq. is the usually quoted source. More recent publications – including critical comments on the IMF's new proposal of sovereign insolvency – are available at http://mailbox.univie.ac.at/~rafferk5. See also Anne Krueger's speech of 26 November 2001, available at http://www.imf.org/external/np/speeches/2001/112601.HTM.

[26] James E. Spiotto, 'Municipal Bankruptcy' (1993) 14 *Municipal Finance Journal* 1 et seq.

nowadays were considered unacceptable. A new version containing section 904 was enacted. Technically, Chapter 9 thus offers the legal possibility to implement an economically sensible solution for sovereign debtors, finally heeding Adam Smith's advice.

Internationally, one minor change of its basis framework is necessary: a neutral court of arbitration – a traditional mechanism of international law – instead of national courts to avoid decisions influenced by national interests of creditors or debtors. Clearly, the arbitration panel could sit anywhere, including the debtor or its neighbouring countries. It was never demanded that the panel 'be headquartered in a neutral country that is neither an active international lender nor borrower', as Eichengreen[27] erroneously characterised my proposal. One may suppose this error to stem from the passage: 'The reason why no court, whether located in a creditor or debtor country, should chair the procedures is self-evident: its impartiality is not guaranteed',[28] which refers to courts, not courts of arbitration. Language apart, the illustrating example – the US Court of Appeal for the Second Circuit of New York, definitely no court of arbitration – proves this beyond doubt. Although other authors – for example, Rogoff[29] – do not make this remark, Eichengreen's error nevertheless suggests the use of 'panel' whenever discussing arbitration. This might also be helpful to differentiate the proposed ad hoc panels from a permanent court of arbitration. Technically, a permanent entity could handle such cases as well. But ad hoc panels can be established much more quickly, and too much time has already been wasted because of creditors. Furthermore it is to be hoped that – once the backlog of cases is resolved – this kind of arbitration will not be needed frequently. Finally, ad hoc panels might have the advantage of being custom made for each case.

The interests of the population affected by the plan could be defended by trade unions, entrepreneurs' associations, grassroots organisations, religious or non-religious NGOs, or international organisations such as UNICEF. The right to be heard in fair and equitable proceedings and the possibility of describing the expected effects on the poor in public would certainly have mitigating effects, contributing to an adjustment with a

---

[27] Barry Eichengreen, *Toward a New International Financial Architecture, A Practical Post-Asia Agenda* (Washington DC: Institute for International Economics, 1999), p. 126.

[28] Raffer, 'Applying Chapter 9', above note 25, p. 304 et seq.

[29] Kenneth Rogoff, 'International Institutions for Reducing Global Financial Instability' (1999) 13(4) *Journal of Economic Perspectives* 21 et seq.

human face. Besides, the arbitrators would have to take particular care to ensure that a minimum of human dignity of the poor in the debtor country is safeguarded – exactly as the court would do in a US Chapter 9 insolvency case. This procedure differs fundamentally from present debt management where creditors are judge, jury, experts and bailiff all in one, sometimes even the debtor's lawyers.

International Financial Institutions (IFIs), such as the Bretton Woods twins, cannot be arbitrators. They are party, controlled by majorities of creditor states and creditors in their own right. Thus proposing the IMF to fulfil the role of the panel is absurd. Barring IFIs from being arbitrators is but fair to other – particularly to private – creditors, as IFIs have not been unbiased when making decisions affecting their own claims as well as those of other creditors. The publication *Emerging Markets this Week* of the German Commerzbank expresses this concern clearly: the Bretton Woods Institutions 'will be concerned *with protecting their own balance sheets* rather than with fair "burden sharing"'. Therefore the 'IMF and World Bank are not suited either as arbitrators or as objective regulators of sovereign insolvency procedures'.[30] Familiar with insolvency as an appropriate means to solve debt problems in other cases, people from the banking community usually see the proposal in a more professional way than official creditors once it becomes clear that this mechanism must be fair to all sides – it would rightly not be generally accepted if it were not.

Insolvency relief is not an act of mercy but of justice and economic reason. Substantial shares of present debts exist only because of prolonged, unsuccessful debt management by official creditors refusing necessary debt relief over years. This increased debt burden is creditor caused damage, a damage done by delay, as even the International Bank for Reconstruction and Development (IBRD)[31] concedes. Insolvency procedures established themselves because they are the best solution of a debt overhang. The question is thus simply whether they can be adapted to the specific case of sovereign debtors. Chapter 9, successfully applied within the United States over decades, proves that there is no reason why this should be impossible in the case of sovereign debtors.

The basic function of any insolvency procedure is the resolution of a conflict between two fundamental legal principles. In a situation of over-indebtedness the right of creditors to interest and repayments

[30] (1999) 26 (October 15) *Emerging Markets this Week* (stress in original).
[31] IBRD, *World Debt Tables 1992–93*, vol. I, (Washington, DC: IBRD, 1992), p. 10 et seq.

collides with the principle recognised generally (not only in the case of loans) by all civilised legal systems that no one must be forced to fulfil contracts if that leads to inhumane distress, endangers one's life or health, or violates human dignity. Briefly put, debtors cannot be forced to starve themselves or their children to be able to pay. Although their claims are recognised as legitimate, insolvency exempts resources from being seized by bona fide creditors. Human rights and human dignity of debtors are given priority over unconditional repayment. It is important to emphasise that insolvency only deals with claims based on solid and proper legal foundations. In the case of odious debts, for example, no insolvency is needed, as these are null and void. Demands for cancelling apartheid debts are therefore based on the odious debts doctrine.

In analogy to the protection granted to the population of indebted municipalities by US Chapter 9 the money to service a country's debts must not be raised by destroying basic social services. The principle of debtor protection demands exempting resources necessary to finance humane minimum standards of basic health services, primary education etc. for the poor, and funds necessary for sustainable economic recovery. This can only be justified if that money is demonstrably used for its declared purpose. Not without reason creditors as well as NGOs are concerned that this might not be the case.

The solution is quite simple – a transparently managed fund financed by the debtor in domestic currency. In a discussion with public servants of the G7 and representatives of the IMF and the IBRD Ann Pettifor[32] proposed a poverty action fund as a means to guarantee that the money is actually used for the poor and for expenditures necessary for a fresh start of the debtor economy. The management of such a fund could be monitored by an international board or advisory council with members from the debtor as well as from creditor countries. They could be nominated by NGOs and by governments (including the debtor government). As this fund is a legal entity of its own, checks and discussions of its projects would not concern the government's budget, which is an important part of a country's sovereignty. Counterpart funds have worked quite successfully so far.

Debtor protection is one of the two essential features of insolvency. The other is the most fundamental principle of the rule of law: one must not be judge in one's own cause. Civilised insolvency laws applicable to

---

[32] Ann Pettifor, *Concordats for debt cancellation, a contribution to the debate*, Jubilee 2000 Coalition UK (18 March 1999) mimeo.

all debtors except developing countries demand a neutral institution assuring fair settlements, creditors must not decide on their own claims. Even at the time of debt prisons creditors were not allowed to do so – in contrast to present international practice violating this very minimum required by the rule of law most flagrantly. Unrestricted creditor domination is not only an open breach of the rule of law, a principle presently preached to developing countries by OECD governments, but also inefficient from a purely economical perspective. Creditors tend to grant too small reductions too late, thus prolonging the crisis rather than solving it.

The introduction of Chapter 9 insolvency would provide an incentive to lenders to make loans basically if repayments can be expected from proceeds. Debts which have to be serviced out of the budget should remain the exception, particularly so in very poor countries. Being sure to lose their money eventually, commercial lenders would stop lending if previous loans were not put to efficient use. Thus, if international insolvency had existed in the 1970s the debt burden would be much lower, maybe there would not even be any debt crisis.

Financial accountability of multilateral institutions

The increased role of IFIs in international capital markets since 1982 contrasts sharply with a total lack of financial accountability. Enjoying *de facto* 'preferred creditor status' IFIs may and often do gain institutionally and financially from crises, as well as from their own errors and failures, even if they cause damages by grave negligence. This is a severe moral hazard problem and an economically totally perverted incentive system.

While private creditors are supposed to grant debt reductions, feeling the sting of the market mechanism, IFIs increase their exposure, knowing that they will be protected. Meanwhile, they have started the absurdity of giving loans for debt reduction. The history of Ecuador's Brady deal, on which Ecuador defaulted, illustrates that point well. Commercial banks granted 45% debt reduction, but the time series of Ecuadorian debt shows no more than a small blip. If all creditors had reduced their claims by 30% the country would in all probability have been economically afloat again, while commercial banks would have saved fifteen percentage points.

There might even be some awareness that crises are in the institutional self-interest of IFIs. During the Asian crisis the IMF's First Deputy Managing Director still argued – using Thailand and Mexico as supporting evidence – that the prospect of larger crises caused by capital account liberalisation would call for more resources for the IMF to cope with the very crises the IMF's proposal would create in the future.[33] This is easily explained by the present lack of financial accountability, which is at severe odds with any market friendly incentive system. From the narrow point of view of institutional self-interest it makes more sense than using contractual rights to capital controls, an option that would not require increased IMF resources.

To increase IFI-efficiency and to improve their role in capital markets, market incentives must be brought to bear. The international public sector must become financially accountable for their own errors in the same way that consultants are liable to pay damage compensation if/when negligence on their part causes damage or as OECD governments are if they create damages by negligence or violating laws. By contrast, the IMF has been allowed to violate its own statutes with impunity. Finally, the present privileged position of international public creditors discriminates unfairly against private creditors suffering avoidable losses because of IFI privileges when countries are unable to service their debts. This urgently calls for mechanisms to correct present inefficiencies.

Discussing financial accountability, one needs to differentiate between programmes and projects. As it is practically impossible to determine the fair share of one or more IFIs in failed programmes, Chapter 9 provides a clear and simple solution, finally 'bailing-in' the public sector. All official creditors including IFIs should lose the same percentage of their claims as private creditors. This would automatically introduce an element of financial accountability of IFIs. Accumulated bad projects financed by loans or a string of unsuccessful programmes would eventually lead to insolvency reducing all official creditors' claims. As IFIs – like donors – control the use of loans, this would be highly positive. While the importance of decisions by official creditors may vary it has always been particularly strong in the poorest countries. Lack of local expertise to participate appropriately in decision-making as well as high dependence on aid are the reasons. Svendsen[34] calls debts

---

[33] Stanley Fischer, 'Capital Account Liberalization and the Role of the IMF', IMF Seminar *Asia and the IMF*, Hong Kong, 19 September 1997, available at http://www.imf.org/external/np/apd/asia/fischer.htm.

[34] Knud Erik Svendsen, 'The Failure of the International Debt Strategy', *CDR-Report n. 13*, (Copenhagen: Centre for Development Research, 1987), p. 27.

accumulated by such countries 'creditor-determined', (mainly) the result of creditors' decisions. This is a fundamental difference to private creditors usually limiting themselves to lending without any additional consulting activities. The present practice of letting 'recipients' pay for failures, errors or negligent work of their creditors-cum-consultants is particularly unjustified for countries with high IFI involvement, which have been forced to orient their policies according to IFI 'advice' for quite some time. As the shares of multilateral debts are relatively higher in the poorest countries, protecting IFIs from losses is done at the expense of particularly poor clients, often highly dependent on solutions elaborated by IFI staff.

It must be recalled that the IBRD's Articles of Agreement recognise default as a fact of life. Article IV(7) titled 'Methods of Meeting Liabilities of the Bank in Case of Defaults' describes in detail what the Bank has to do if one of its sovereign clients defaults.[35] Unaware of any preferred creditor status, a legal concept which cannot be found in its Articles of Agreement and does not formally apply to the IBRD,[36] the Bank's founders wanted it subject to some market discipline rather than totally exempt from it. Mechanisms allowing the Bank to shoulder risks appropriately were designed. Thwarting its founders' intentions the IBRD has refused to apply them when indicated, wrongly claiming this would make development finance inoperational. The IBRD's very statute proves that financial accountability is necessary and possible.

Although an improvement, symmetrical treatment is not yet a satisfactory solution. In the case of projects financial accountability must go further. As errors can often be isolated and proved with less difficulty IFIs should be liable for damage done by them in the same way private consulting firms are liable to their clients. The present practice of 'IFI-flops securing IFI-jobs',[37] to some extent also valid for donors, must stop.

If a project goes wrong the need would arise to determine financial consequences. In the simplest case borrower and lender agree on a fair

---

[35] This point is presented in detail by Kunibert Raffer, 'Introducing Financial Accountability at the IBRD: An Overdue and Necessary Reform', paper presented at the conference *Reinventing the World Bank*, (Northwestern University, Evanston, Ill., May 1999), available at http://www.worldbank.nwu.edu or via http://mailbox.univie. ac.at/~rafferk5.

[36] Catherine Caufield, *Masters of Illusion, The World Bank and the Poverty of Nations* (London, 1998), p. 323.

[37] Kunibert Raffer, 'International Financial Institutions and Accountability: The Need for Drastic Change' in S. Mansoob Murshed and Kunibert Raffer (eds.), *Trade, Transfers and Development, Problems and Prospects for the Twenty First Century* (Aldershot, 1993), p. 158.

sharing of costs. If they do not the solution used between business partners or transnational firms and countries in cases of disagreement could be applied: arbitration. This concept is well introduced in the field of international investments. If disagreements between transnational firms and host countries can be solved that way, or the International Chamber of Commerce offers such service, there is no reason why disputes between IFIs (or donors) and borrowing countries could not be solved by this mechanism as well. Ironically, the IBRD's own *General Conditions* (section 10.04) foresee arbitration to settle disagreements with borrowers, be they members or not, *inter alia* for 'any claim by either party against the other' not settled by agreement.[38] The procedural provisions how to establish the panel are, by the way, nearly identical to my Chapter 9 proposal.

A permanent international court of arbitration – different from ad hoc insolvency arbitration mentioned above – would be ideal. If necessary this court might consist of more than one panel. It decides on the percentage of loans to be waived to cover damages for which IFIs are responsible. The right to file complaints should be conferred on individuals, NGOs, firms, governments and international organisations. As NGOs are less under pressure from IFIs or member governments their right to represent affected people is particularly important. The court of arbitrators would of course have the right and duty to refuse to hear apparently ill-founded cases. The need to prepare a case meticulously would deter abuse. The possibility of being held financially accountable would act as an incentive for donors and IFIs to perform better and protect the poor from damages done by ill-conceived projects.

Last, but not least, it would force donors and IFIs to respect human rights when financing projects, enabling victims of aid to receive damage compensation. Quite often people living on land wanted for development projects are expropriated without proper, if any, compensation. Forced resettlements occur to make room for dams, highways, harbours, even an IFI conference.[39] While IFIs and donors keenly preach human rights or respect of private (especially foreigners') property they have not seen great problems in financing projects violating these values, particularly so when the victims were indigenous people. The right of victims to make donors accountable for what they facilitate would also improve the lot of the poor, whose human rights, sometimes even lives,

---

[38] Cf. Raffer, 'Introducing Financial Accountability at the IBRD', above note 35.
[39] Cf. Raffer and Singer, *The Foreign Aid Business*, above note 22, at 20, 52, 208 et seq.

are too often considered unworthy of respect by their governments as well as their governments' public financiers.

Financial accountability would be economically beneficial to IFIs themselves. It would give their staff good arguments against pouring money into regions just because of lending targets, political interference by important politicians or shareholders, including demands for bail-outs. There would be less institutional interest, if any, in crises as these would mean losses to anyone. Projects and programmes financed under accountability would have much better success rates and development impacts. The root of the problem, non-accountability and the systemic failures it causes, would be eliminated. Bilateral donors have already acknowledged the necessity of debt relief for quite some time by reducing official debts. IFIs, by contrast, are still allowed preferential treatment. Naturally it would cost IFI shareholders something to clean up the failures of the past but there is no more reason to spare IFI owners than any other shareholders. Big bail-outs cost money as well, though the money of different people, on top of destabilising the financial system. If IFIs cannot survive financial accountability, dissolving them would be economically indicated, because no project or programme at all is preferable to a costly flop – at least for those having to pay for it. As IFI activities in former communist countries illustrate, the problem of efficiency and accountability has even gained importance. If subject to economic scrutiny and damage compensation claims the amount of IFI activities will strongly decrease, but those financed will become economically much more viable.

Conclusion

Correcting wrong incentives and increasing stability, the measures proposed by this paper would allow capital markets to function better and more efficiently. As built-in stabilisers weakening or abolishing wrong signals, such as moral hazard, they improve market incentives. It is not intended to restrict market activities unduly. Thus capital controls are suggested for special situations, comparable to emergency brakes, not used most of the time, but critically useful if and when needed. Similarly, sovereign insolvency is a way out of a hopeless debt overhang. Its mere existence is an incentive for a better allocation of resources, making its own practical application less likely and needed. These few stabilisers might not change capital markets as dramatically as a New Architecture, but they would improve the functioning of these markets considerably.

Conclusions and agenda for further research

RAINER GROTE AND THILO MARAUHN

1. There seems to be a widespread consensus today that some form of regulation of international finance is needed in order to take full advantage of the potentially huge benefits of open markets for capital while at the same limiting the risk of serious economic breakdown resulting from the inherently volatile character of those markets. It is generally recognised that the dismantling of exchange controls which started in the 1970s together with the development of modern computer and telecommunications technology over the last two decades have created unprecedented opportunities for global investment and international trade in capital: time and space have become virtually irrelevant in global financial markets. On the other hand, experience has shown that the sound operation of financial markets is threatened by instabilities which are far greater than those involved in the trade of goods and services. Financial collapses have a unique capacity for projecting their effects right across the domestic economy, and in the worst cases far beyond that, across the region and even across the world. The root causes for the instability of financial markets lie in the insufficient screening of investments risks by the providers of foreign capital and the local financial intermediaries alike, as well as in the huge potential for speculation created by the liberalisation of foreign exchange markets which can give rise to extreme fluctuations in short-term capital movements.

2. The need for regulating international financial markets can therefore hardly be questioned in principle. It is far more difficult to determine, however, to whom the responsibility for the regulation of financial markets should be assigned and what kind of regulation would be needed in order to achieve the objective of open but stable capital markets. Outside the European Union, the regulation of

316

financial markets has so far been the exclusive prerogative of national governments and of the regulatory agencies operating under their control. Binding international agreements which would effectively limit the regulatory powers of individual states in this field are virtually non-existent. Although there exists a surprising number of standard setting bodies at the international level, their formal powers are limited to the adoption of mere policy recommendations. The standards which they formulate become legally binding only once they have been transformed into domestic law. Moreover, states participating in the work of the standard-setting bodies are reluctant to enter into any formal commitment that the standards will indeed be transformed into formal legal rules.

From an international law perspective, this leaves states with an almost unfettered discretion in the formulation of their regulatory policies with regard to financial markets. In practical terms, however, the exercise of their regulatory powers must take into account the considerable pressures resulting from the stiff international competition for capital in the era of globalisation. Due to the existence of open markets and the benefits of advanced communications technology, investors today are in a position to take full advantage of profitable investment opportunities by shifting large amounts of money almost instantaneously from one point of the globe to another. As they choose their markets, they choose the laws and regulations applicable in such markets. This unprecedented regulatory arbitrage enjoyed by investors means that regulatory competition is no longer confined to competing claims of jurisdiction in cases of cross-border financial transactions. It also affects the substance of domestic regulation by limiting the range of regulatory choices open to national authorities even with regard to persons and actions which are nominally entirely within their jurisdiction.

3.   This finding raises the question whether the desirable stabilisation of international financial markets cannot be achieved more efficiently through a process of permanent institutional innovation fuelled by the ongoing competition between different national regulatory models than by introducing a new, and potentially costly, layer of regulation at the international level. According to this argument, which is also developed in greater detail in this book (chapter 13 by Stefan Voigt), institutions can best be understood as fallible hypotheses about a way of organising human co-existence that must pass permanent tests. As no agent is in possession of perfect knowledge in most areas of social life,

nobody can say what the best regulatory regime is. In such a situation, a variety of institutions or regulatory models is a prerequisite for finding the solution which serves the desired purposes at the lowest costs. The potential and probability for the development of new and better institutional arrangements is much greater in a competitive than in a non-competitive environment, such as that found under a harmonised legal regime.

Apart from stimulating institutional and regulatory innovation, regulatory diversity may also be said to offer additional benefits in terms of democratic legitimacy. Legal heterogeneity pays respect to national preferences in regulatory policy that take into account local differences in risk tolerance, income, and other factors. Moreover, at least in those countries which are governed by elected institutions accountable to their national constituencies, the regulatory policy adopted by the national authorities tends to reflect the basic needs and preferences of the population more faithfully than any harmonised legislation would be able to do.

Even if one is inclined in principle to acknowledge the potential benefits of regulatory competition, however, this does necessarily weaken the case for an international regulatory framework for financial markets. For one thing, the benefits of regulatory competition in practice are rarely as evident as they appear in theory. It is far from certain that in a competition between different national regulatory systems that system will 'win' which achieves the desired purposes most efficiently. The success of a specific regulatory model may depend less on its inherent qualities than on the regional or even global importance of the market for which it was designed. If, for example, a *de facto* harmonisation of securities regulation will take place along the lines of the US securities law, as some observers predict, this development may be attributed more convincingly to the gravity of the US capital market than to a perceived superior quality of US securities regulation. Besides, the efficiency of a given regulation can only be measured in relation to the purposes which it pursues. These purposes may, however, differ from country to country. In some countries regulators may have a preference for a 'light' regulatory regime which pays little attention to proper risk management standards of financial institutions in order to attract huge inflows of capital, while in others the authorities may be more willing to restrict the opportunities for risky financial transactions through detailed prudential regulation in the interest of stable economic development. This diversity would not be a major cause for concern if it were possible to limit the risks of wrong policy choices made by national authorities to the jurisdiction to which they apply. In a world of increasingly integrated financial markets, however, this is not the case. It is precisely the contagious nature of financial collapses, which more often than not transcend national boundaries and produce dire consequences across whole regions, which creates a legitimate interest of third countries and the international community as a whole in the proper regulation of the financial markets, not only in developed countries, but also in a growing number of emerging market economies.

Moreover, the decision for some form of international regulation of financial markets does not automatically forfeit the benefits of regulatory competition. As is well known, legal harmonisation comes in different forms and aims at different targets. Below the level of formal legal harmonisation, the central players and institutions in the markets may try to develop shared international standards in specific sectors of the banking, securities and insurance sectors. This is what is actually done in the various committes hosted by the BIS and other similar groups. More ambitiously, some kind of formal legal framework may be established, although one which is limited to basic principles and concentrates on some key regulatory issues. As has been shown in the chapter on financial regulation in the European Union, this form of minimum harmonisation is the approach prevailing in the regulation of the EU capital market. Only the third form of harmonisation which results in detailed and uniform legislation being imposed on all participating legal systems would seem to leave no room at all for competition between different national regulatory standards. As things now stand, however, there exist no plans for such a comprehensive regulation within the framework of supranational organisations or international standard setting bodies. Most calls for international regulation being made in the current discussion aim at the establishment of a body of certain core regulatory standards which would have to be implemented by all participating states but would not exclude the adoption of additional and more stringent rules at the national level.

4. It has been suggested, however, that the necessary mechanisms for the creation of formal legal rules which would go beyond the currently existing non-binding standards, but still be sufficiently flexible to adapt to the rapidly changing market structures, simply do not exist at the international level. According to this argument, the traditional law-making through treaty is too cumbersome, takes too long and does not provide any guarantee that all relevant markets will finally accept the

agreed principles, as no country can be forced to sign and ratify an international treaty. Moreover, the formal revision and amendment of an international treaty can be almost as time-consuming as its conclusion. This creates seemingly insurmountable obstacles with regard to the continuous adaptation of the negotiated standards which would be necessary to keep track of the rapid evolution of the relevant markets.

While this criticism points to serious shortcomings of the established concept of rule-making in international law, they do not properly take into account the alternatives to the traditional conventional law-making developed by modern international practice. These changes include modifications of the existing treaty-making techniques as well as the use of new non-conventional forms of law-making. In some areas of international law, like environmental law and arms control, new techniques for the elaboration and amendment of negotiated instruments have been introduced which could also be used in the field of regulation of international financial markets. In particular, this concerns the technique to include only the most fundamental regulatory principles in the treaty text and to leave the elaboration of more detailed rules to expert committes or bodies. These 'secondary' rules are not included in the treaty itself, but in special schedules or protocols which can be amended in a simplified procedure.

The so-called directives used in the European Union provide another model for flexible regulation at the international level. The directives, which are based on the EC Treaty, are legally binding upon the Member States only with regard to the objectives to be achieved, but leave to the national authorities the choice of the means which are required for their effective implementation within the relevant national jurisdictions. As has been analysed in detail in the chapter on financial market regulation in the European Union, the European Union is currently discussing an even more sophisticated approach to rule-making in the context of the EU capital market. This concept is based on the recognition of four different levels of rule-making and rule-enforcement, using both hard and soft law. The main regulatory choices are made at the first and the second level: the first level concerns the basic principles for financial services regulation whereas the more technical measures needed to implement the key objectives contained in the framework legislation are delegated to the second level.

These few examples show that regulatory flexibility and diversity are also possible at the international level. A lot of additional research is needed in order to analyse the respective qualities of the different law-making techniques used in contemporary international law and to assess their suitability with regard to the particularly complex and anarchic character of international financial markets. What seems to be clear, however, is that the resources of international law are far greater and more diverse than is often thought, and that the establishment of a legally binding international framework for financial regulation does not depend on the vicissitudes of the traditional treaty-making process.

5.   An important issue which will have to be addressed in this context concerns the role of the existing international standard-setting bodies in the creation of a legally binding framework for international finance. One of the striking features of the current situation is the variety of institutions and groupings involved in international standard-setting and the diversity of their respective membership. The chapters contained in this volume have highlighted the contribution of some of the most important organisations and bodies which take part, in some way or another, in the establishment and surveillance of regulatory standards for international financial markets, including the IMF and the World Bank, the Basle Committee on Banking Supervision and the parallel bodies in the securities and insurance sectors, the WTO and – at a regional level – the ECB. While these institutions undoubtedly have been successful, although to a varying degree, in shaping international financial standards, their influence has largely been exercised informally. Moreover, given the great number and variety of standard-setting bodies, the diversity of those bodies' composition and the complexity of their reporting lines, areas of overlap and duplication are hard to avoid. The move towards a more rigid, legally binding framework for international financial markets will therefore involve a far-reaching transformation of the existing institutional structure of governance in international financial markets, with a view to streamlining the processes in which norms aimed at the regulation of those markets are generated and implemented. The establishment of the Financial Stability Forum marks an important step forward in this direction. The role of the Forum, however, remains limited by the logic of informal co-operation: it has been created to improve co-ordination and the exchange of information between the various authorities responsible for financial stability but does not have the mandate or the power to adopt and implement a regulatory policy of its own.

The creation of a binding normative framework for international financial markets would require further changes in the institutional structure of regulatory authorities. In particular, it would be necessary to determine which institution or set of institutions should be assigned primary responsibility for regulating the new international financial order. If they are to be effective, the development of the relevant regulatory policies and principles must follow closely the rapidly changing structure of the international financial markets. In practical terms, this means that the competent body must possess comprehensive expertise and experience in dealing with the regulatory issues arising in a financial services industry that transcends territorial boundaries and appears as a 'seamless web' in which the traditional distinctions between the activities of banks, securities firms and insurance companies are no longer relevant. These criteria would seem to favour the extension of the regulatory functions of bodies like the Basle Committee on Banking Supervision, the International Organisation of Securities Commissions and the International Association of Insurance Supervisors which can draw on the experience and expertise of national regulators and enjoy the confidence of governments and the international community. Conversely, a greater regulatory role for institutions like the IMF and the World Bank seems less promising. With regard to the IMF, a strong case can be made for a clear separation between the roles of regulator and of international lender in times of crisis. From a functional perspective the task of dealing with normal risk over the entire financial services industry is quite different from dealing with a liquidity crisis generated by abnormal risk. Moreover, while the IMF is well acquainted with regulatory problems arising in the financial services industry of emerging economies, it has little, if any, experience in developing and enforcing regulatory standards for prosperous developed countries.

However, the standard-setting by informal bodies and groupings like the Basle Committee suffers from a number of shortcoming in terms of legitimacy which would have to be addressed convincingly if those bodies were to be given a prominent role in the adoption and implementation of a binding regulatory framework for global financial markets. Their success in the development of common standards so far has largely been due to the principles of informality and consensus which govern the discussions between the national experts drawn from a limited number of – mostly developed – countries. If they were to acquire more formal powers for the purpose of elaborating generally binding principles and rules of international finance, their membership would have to be broadened considerably in order to allow for a more adequate geographical representation and to avoid the impression that the work of these bodies is nothing more than a technical device to impose the financial

standards favoured by the developed countries on the weaker economies. On the other hand, the move towards fairer geographical representation would almost certainly destroy the homogenity of views which
has prevailed in the standard-setting bodies in the past and thus make
the adoption of common standards by consensus much more difficult.
This in turn raises the spectre of majority decisions in international
financial regulation and of a corresponding transfer of sovereign legislative rights from individual states to the international financial authority, a development which is bound to meet with resistance from many
countries.

The second concern relates to the transparency and democratic
legitimacy of the rule-making processes involved. The establishment of
international financial standards is a complex task of a highly technical
nature. This creates the danger that the elaboration of the relevant rules
is largely left to specialist experts and that the views of the broader public
are only insufficiently represented in the law-making process, or are not
effectively represented at all. The widespread fear of a 'rule by techno-
crats' establishing rules in a relatively closed environment, outside
democratic control and accountability, is well known from the discussion which has been taking place for some time within the European
Union on the so-called 'democratic deficit' of the European institutions.
In the context of international financial regulation, the necessary balance between efficiency and legitimacy might be even more difficult to
achieve. It would seem that only a multi-level approach, which leaves
room for the input of smaller expert groups as well as for a broad
consultation process in which a wide variety of interests is represented,
can create a proper base for legitimate rule-making in the field of
international finance. However, much more thought needs to be given
to the parameters of democratic legitimacy involved and the way in
which they can be integrated into a coherent institutional framework for
international financial regulation.

6.   As has already been indicated, one of the most difficult questions
connected with the establishment of an effective regulatory regime for
global financial markets concerns the structure of international regulation. The single most important characteristic of international financial
markets is their extraordinary dynamism. Since the 1970s the transformation of market structures has been taking place at a breathtaking
speed. Over the past thirty years, national regulators have developed new
regulatory approaches and techniques to respond to the ever increasing
pace of market innovation produced by liberalisation, some of which

have been discussed in this book. A few lessons may be derived from these national experiences. The most important is that regulatory standards have to be developed in close contact with the markets if they are to be effective. This suggests that policy development will be an important function of any international regulator – a function which transcends traditional rule-making and standard setting and has important consequences for the requirements of transparency and legitimacy which the international authority would have to satisfy. On the other hand, any international regulation will have to provide the national authorities with sufficiently precise and detailed guidelines if the objective of the regulation, to create a reliable and effective global framework for international finance, is not to be missed. One way to achieve the necessary balance between flexibility and stability would be to include only the fundamental regulatory principles in the basic convention itself, while the elaboration of the technical details could be left to some form of 'secondary law'. This 'secondary law' could either take the form of schedules or protocols to the original treaty or be embodied in model or uniform laws which would be established by the competent international law-making agencies for specific areas of regulation and then be presented to the member states of the original treaty and/or to other interested parties for ratification.

A most challenging task in this context consists in the definition of the fundamental principles of regulation to be included in the constituent treaty. In order to determine the scope and the content of the guiding principles of international financial regulation, it is necessary to identify its basic purposes more clearly than has been done so far. In most discussions, the stability of financial markets figures as the primary and most important goal to be achieved by means of international regulation. In this perspective, properly functioning financial markets constitute a common good since they create the indispensable conditions for the growth and stable development of modern economies. Thus financial regulation is regulation in the public interest, at home as well as at the global level.

While this interpretation undoubtely reflects an important aspect of regulatory activities in the field of financial markets, such activities are not necessarily limited to the protection of public interests. A global regulatory framework for international finance may be also be considered desirable in the interests of the market participants themselves. While legally binding rules may contribute to curtailing their freedom of action in the international context, they can also expect considerable benefits from global financial regulation. First of all, the establishment of legally binding uniform standards throughout the world constitutes an important step towards 'a levelling of the playing field' and greater transparency in markets which increasingly ignore territorial boundaries. Moreover, the transformation of standards which have hitherto been part of informal or soft law arrangements into hard law marks a significant increase in legal certainty with regard to the existence and the contents of the rules concerned, a certainty from which international investors and the providers of cross-border financial services stand to gain most: the legal remedies available for the enforcement of laws usually are far more effective than those existing with regard to the implementation of informal arrangements. This latter observation hints at a possible shift of emphasis in international regulation with potentially far-reaching consequences. Unlike informal financial standards, legally binding rules can confer specific legally enforceable rights on the individuals and firms which operate in the markets concerned. Such a shift of emphasis from the protection of markets to the protection of individual expectations concerning the proper functioning of those markets would by no means be inconsistent with the broader individualising trend discernible in contemporary international law. Quite on the contrary, it would confirm and even strengthen the developing tendency in regional and economic law to recognise certain fundamental freedoms of the individual with regard to his/her commercial activities as and to take them as basis for economic regulation.

7. Among economists and lawyers who concede the need for a binding regulatory framework of international financial markets, it is generally recognised that certain prudential rules and principles should be part of that regime. In this volume it is even argued that liberalisation of trade in financial services and strengthening of international prudential regimes have historically been inseparable (see chapter 8 by Michael J. Hahn). Prudential regulations are those which take care of potential or actual imperfections in the design of financial markets and thus have a 'positive', market supporting function. Target areas for prudential regulation which have been identified so far include comprehensive accounting and disclosure requirements for financial data and book keeping standards, common rules for the licensing of financial service providers, guiding principles for the effective surveillance and implementation of regulatory standards and, if all other means fail, provisions for the restructuring and the eventual closure of delinquent or failing

institutions. Such rules have become, in one way or another, part of the regulatory regimes introduced in the developed economies during the last two decades (see the articles on the regulatory systems of Britain, Germany and the United States in this volume).

One difficult issue which has arisen in this context has been to which extent, if any, the market participants themselves should be responsible for regulating the markets in which they operate. After all, they are closest to the market and should know more about what is happening there than the authorities. It is still not clear, however, whether self-regulation provides an adequate mechanism for fairly balancing the different private interests affected by the regulation in question. Moreover, market participants will almost always underestimate the costs which their market activities impose on society as a whole. The definition of the public interest in the long-term stable development of financial markets, which is of crucial importance in defining the prudential standards to be observed by the market players, is a matter for the democratically accountable public authorities and cannot be left to the players themselves. While there should be a role for the market participants in the elaboration of financial regulation, they cannot replace the public authorities, national and international, in their decision-making capacity. How that supportive role of market players and institutions can be structured properly is a topic for further discussion.

In any case, the tremendous difficulties which any attempt to establish certain common principles of prudential regulation will face should not be underestimated. This can be demonstrated by using two key components of such regulation, accounting standards and capital adequacy requirements, as examples. Reliable and comprehensive information on the financial conditions of borrowers as well as lenders is essential for the proper operation of financial markets. A single set of accounting standards would help enormously in providing accurate information and early warning of the kind of financial crisis that hit Japan, East Asia and Latin America in the recent past. Nevertheless, progress so far toward anything more than the common lowest denominator in international accounting standards has been painfully slow. Asset valuation often meets with enormous difficulties, a problem that is compounded by the tendency of the market to invent ever more complex financial products and by macroeconomic factors, like large swings in exchange and interest rates.

Capital adequacy requirements, which have become the regulatory focus of the Basle accords, have not fared much better. The original Basle accord, which was based on a two-tier definition of capital and a method of weighting risks so that loans and other assets could be measured against the capital of the bank in a meaningful way, did not work well. Criticism focused on the credit risk weights which used very broad categories of assets, thus producing judgments far out of line with the market's finer-grained risk assessments. Basle II has responded to this criticism by giving ratings produced by private rating agencies a role in calculating the new credit risk weights, and by providing banks with the opportunity to use their own risk modelling to determine the capital required for credit risk purposes. But even this new, improved accord has come under heavy fire from financial economists. They fear that banks will design assets to fit particular categories of risk, bending whatever connection there might have been between a rating applied after the fact and the level of risk. More fundamentally, they challenge the underlying rationale of the whole regulatory approach as such by pointing out that capital requirements are inevitably based on some readily quantifiable aspect of a firm's portfolio, whereas it typically is inattention to the less quantifiable risks which leads to failure.

At the heart of those controversies lies the difficulty of identifying objective criteria for the assessment of financial risks. Further research on the basic elements of prudential regulation in international financial markets would therefore have to address the question whether valid criteria for the objective assessment of risks can indeed be found, or who, in the absence of such criteria, should bear the consequences of wrong risk assessment. For that purpose a comparative analysis of risk assessment, risk management and risk distribution principles and techniques which have been developed in other areas of law, namely in technology and in environmental law, could be helpful.

8.   Whereas a basic consensus seems to exist on the desirability of prudential (or microeconomic) rules for international financial markets, the need for interventionist (or macroeconomic) regulation is far more controversial. Interventionist regulatory policies aim to restrict the volume of international financial transactions by imposing controls on external capital movements. Regulatory schemes of this type can pursue different purposes. They can be used as an instrument to promote the stability of global capital markets in the interests of the international community as a whole. The Tobin tax which provides for a small levy on all foreign exchange transactions by national financial actors would fall into this category. As has been shown in this book (in chapter 14 by Kunibert Raffer), the tax acts as an effective

disincentive to destabilising capital movements by cutting profit margins on short-term trading. But macroeconomic regulation can also be used as a means to protect specifically those national economies which are particularly vulnerable to short-term capital movements. This type of interventionist regulation introduces an additional aspect in the debate on international financial regulation, i.e. the divergent needs of developed countries on the one hand and of emerging market economies on the other. Regulatory devices like the interest free deposit requirements imposed by Chile on short-term foreign investments reflect the needs of those countries which are particularly exposed to the risks connected with the massive inflow of short-term capital, i.e. the economies in transition to a fully developed market economy (whereas the main concern of the poorest countries is to attract any foreign capital at all).

The principal question concerning interventionist regulation is whether it makes economic sense or not. This question has been discussed extensively in the chapter on the policy perspective of international financial regulation (see chapter 12 by Peter Nunnenkamp, and chapter 14 by Kunibert Raffer). From a legal perspective, the issues raised by macroeconomic regulation depend on the level at which the relevant measures are conceived and applied. If capital controls were to be imposed within a multilateral framework, few legal questions would arise. The participating countries would have to amend existing treaty arrangements providing for the abolition of capital controls to which they are a party or – less likely – to apply for a (temporary or even permanent) waiver of the relevant provisions. If the capital control were to be imposed in the form of a levy on cross-border transactions, they would also have to negotiate the purpose for which the tax revenues could be used. Given the huge discrepancies between financial markets in developed and developing economies, and the resulting need for differentiated levels of protection, it would seem to be much more appropriate, however, to recognise capital controls as a national regulatory device which could in principle be imposed unilaterally. In this alternative, international regulation would have to define the formal and may be even some broad substantive requirements for the proper exercise of the national power to impose capital controls. In view of the potentially huge negative effects of an unco-ordinated recourse to capital controls on the development of highly integrated financial markets, at least the most disruptive forms of capital control would have to be subject to international regulation and surveillance.

9.   Some of the most complex issues related to international financial regulation concern the implementation, enforcement and surveillance of international financial standards. In this context it is useful to
distinguish between enforcement as a legal concept, referring to the
legislative and executive measures which have to be taken to give full
effect to legally binding rules, and implementation as a broader factual
concept, which is not limited to enforcement measures in the legal sense,
but does include all measures, legal or not, which are aimed at achieving
the result prescribed by the relevant rule. In the present international
environment, enforcement powers almost exclusively rest with the
competent national authorities – legislatures, administrative authorities
and courts. Even within the European Union, the enforcement of community rules is primarily a matter for national governments and courts.
The move to legally binding rules in the international regulation of
capital markets does not necessarily require the establishment of an
international authority with enforcement powers of its own. Nor would
the creation of supranational enforcement powers in the field of financial market regulation be desirable. The successful enforcement of those
rules depends even more than their drafting on a day-to-day dialogue of
regulators with the market players they are supervising; an international
authority would never be able to perform this function effectively, for
sheer lack of supervisory capacities.

The primary responsibility of national authorities in the enforcement
of international financial regulation does by no means preclude, however, a role for international bodies in the implementation of those rules.
The IMF already takes into account, when approving and monitoring its
bail-out packages, the extent of the member country's adherence to
relevant internationally accepted standards, and in particular to the
Basle principles of banking supervision. This idea has been taken one
step further by the Meltzer Report which proposed to make immediate
access to IMF financial assistance dependent on the recipient country's
compliance with certain minimum prudential standards. If those standards were to be included into a formally binding international treaty
document, the case for some form of 'linkage' between adherence to
those standards and access to IMF funds, at least in the case of states
which are parties to the treaty, would even be stronger. Another tool for
promoting implementation of generally accepted standards through the
application of international pressure would be the eligibility for more
favourable risk weighting in connection with capital requirements for
bank. Under this scheme, capital adequacy requirements would be less

stringent for claims on banks and securities firms whose home countries have implemented or at least endorsed the relevant international regulatory standards than for claims on financial institutions whose principal place of business is in countries which have not done so. At a more general level, the regular publication of 'progress reports' by competent international institutions about the efforts of individual countries in implementing international financial regulations could be a vital source of information for international lenders and investors and thus add to the pressure on the countries concerned to move towards greater compliance with the standards in question.

This last point raises the question whether the establishment of a binding legal framework for international finance should be complemented by the creation of a central supervisory authority at the international level. There are good reasons to believe that such a central authority is indeed desirable. In a decentralised system of law enforcement there is always the risk that major inconsistencies with regard to the application of the uniform rules will arise due to diverging national approaches to their interpretation. Without a credible international mechanism to reconcile the diverging viewpoints this development could produce serious disruptive effects for the functioning of the global capital market, effects which the adoption of common regulatory principles and rules was meant to avoid in the first place. The functions of such an international supervisory authority would include the collection of data on the national enforcement policies and, on the basis of these data, the assessment whether a country's regulatory policies are consistent with the prudential and other binding international standards to which it has subscribed. This assessment would also be binding for other international institutions with a role in the implementation of international financial standards, for example the IMF. Moreover, the supervisory authority would be competent to negotiate with the country concerned the measures necessary to remedy its non-compliance. The supervisory authority might even be given the right to intervene in cases of complex cross-border transactions in which the applicable law is not easy to determine on the basis of the traditional conflict of law rules. It would almost inevitably assume a major role in preventing the occurrence of such conflicts, by working towards the global acceptance of the principle of mutual recognition of national supervision. The harmonisation of the substantive law of financial regulation would pave the way for the introduction of the principle of mutual recognition, as the European Union has already done.

Finally, a globally centralised supervisory authority would be indispensable with regard to sovereign borrowers. States do not only play an important role in their capacity as policy-makers and legislators; they are also directly influencing the performance of the markets through their lending and borrowing activities. In this as well as in their regulatory capacity they are subject to the surveillance by the IMF. However, in the past the surveillance powers of the IMF have often been insufficient to prevent the default of sovereign borrowers on their foreign debts and the resulting negative effects this produced upon the stability of the financial markets. Nor does the IMF statute provide for a credible mechanism which could be used to address the problem of excessive foreign debt of sovereign borrowers successfully and to restore the confidence of the markets in the solvency of the countries concerned. The creation of such a mechanism transcends the object of the present study, however, since it concerns the role of international institutions in the management of international financial crises, and not the role of international regulation in the prevention of those very crises.

INDEX